THE SOCIAL AND ECONOMIC CONSEQUENCES OF DEREGULATION

Recent Titles from Quorum Books

THE SOCIAL AND ECONOMIC CONSEQUENCES OF DEREGULATION

The Transportation Industry in Transition

Paul Stephen Dempsey

Quorum Books

New York • Westport, Connecticut • London

Library of Congress Cataloging-in-Publication Data

Dempsey, Paul Stephen.
  The social and economic consequences of deregulation : the
transportation industry in transition / Paul Stephen Dempsey.
      p.   cm.
  Bibliography: p.
  Includes index.
  ISBN 0–89930–380–3 (lib. bdg. : alk. paper)
  1. Transportation—United States—Deregulation.   2. Transportation
and state—United States.   I. Title.
HE206.2.D46   1989
380.5'9—dc19   89–3168

British Library Cataloguing in Publication Data is available.

Library of Congress Catalog Card Number: 89–3168
ISBN: 0–89930–380–3

First published in 1989 by Quorum Books

Greenwood Press, Inc.
88 Post Road West, Westport, Connecticut   06881

Printed in the United States of America

The paper used in this book complies with the
Permanent Paper Standard issued by the National
Information Standards Organization (Z39.48–1984).

10 9 8 7 6 5 4 3 2 1

Copyright Acknowledgments

The author and publisher gratefully acknowledge permission to reprint portions of the following articles by Paul Stephen Dempsey:

"The Empirical Results of Deregulation: A Decade Later, and the Band Played On," 17 *Transportation Law Journal* 31–100 (1988).

"Antitrust Law & Policy in Transportation: Monopoly I$ the Name of the Game," 21 *Georgia Law Review* 505–99 (1987).

"The Dark Side of Deregulation: Its Impact on Small Communities," 39 *Administrative Law Review* 445–65 (1987).

"The Deregulation of Intrastate Transportation: The Texas Debate," 39 *Baylor Law Review* 1–28 (1987).

"The Interstate Commerce Commission: Disintegration of An American Legal Institution," 34 *American University Law Review* 1–51 (1984).

"Transportation Deregulation—on a Collision Course?" 13 TRANSPORTATION LAW JOURNAL 329–92 (1984).

"Rate Regulation and Antitrust Immunity in Transportation: The Genesis and Evolution of this Endangered Species," 32 *American University Law Review* 335–75 (1983).

"Congressional Intent and Agency Discretion—Never the Twain Shall Meet: The Motor Carrier Act of 1980," 58 *Chicago Kent Law Review* 1–58 (1982).

"The Experience of Deregulation: Erosion of the Common Carrier System," 13 *Transportation Law Institute* 121–76 (1980).

"Erosion of the Regulatory Process in Transportation—the Winds of Change," 47 *ICC Practitioners' Journal* 303–20 (1980).

"The Rise and Fall of the Civil Aeronautics Board—Opening Wide the Floodgates of Entry," 11 *Transportation Law Journal* 91–185 (1979).

This book is dedicated
to the memory of
THOMAS COOLEY
and
JOSEPH EASTMAN
men whose dedicated service
to American government
made the United States a better nation.

CONTENTS

The Parable of the Great Fish

And it came to pass that God looked down upon the Great Fish and inquired, "You are a wise old fish. Tell me, what is this thing, water, in which ye swim?"

And the fish thought for a moment, and replied, "I can neither taste, nor smell, nor see it. I know not what water is, Oh Lord."

And many months passed.

And lo, one day black clouds rolled across the sky and blotted out the Sun, and there came a great squall, and a tempest, and a storm which washed the Great Fish onto the land.

The Great Fish struggled mightily, but the waves grew calm and the tide receded and left him landward.

And as the clouds parted, and the Sun's rays began, first to warm, and then to bake his scales, the Great Fish looked skyward and said, "Dear God, I know now what is 'water.'"

PREFACE

Much has been written about the contemporary political and economic phenomenon of deregulation. Most of the literature, particularly that authored by economists, applauds deregulation as a masterpiece of enlightened public policy change. If one read only that, one would be compelled to conclude that more of the same would be better still, and that utopia could be found in the land of laissez faire.

Despite the fact that deregulation has not been without adverse consequences, much of the literature skirts over many of the significant problems emerging under deregulation. This book attempts to fill that void in the literature.

The generation that grew up in the Great Depression and World War II saw government as a friend—a mechanism for achieving greater social good for society. But the generation which grew up during the 1960s and 1970s grew up cynical, perceiving government as a malignant sore. Those on the left abhorred Watergate and the war in Vietnam. Those on the right were offended by the Great Society and high taxes. Both converged on a path that viewed government with some hostility.

Hence, in the 1970s and early 1980s, deregulation became a bipartisan movement, one which swept America profoundly and provided a new order of radically less government intervention in the market. Under Presidents Carter and Reagan, we had significant deregulation of major industries—broadcasting, banking, telecommunications, oil and gas, electric power production, airlines, bus companies, trucking companies, and railroads. That was coupled with partial deregulation in areas such as the environment, antitrust, safety, and health.

Curiously, the more we have it, the more dissatisfied various constituencies become with deregulation. Slowly, but increasingly, there is a growing recognition that government has a proper role to play in protecting the public interest, and that we had best get on with identifying what that role should be.

That is a dramatic shift indeed. And a positive one as well, for responsible government oversight is a desirable companion to a free market, not only to keep the market free, but to achieve social benefits that are ignored in a regime of laissez faire.

This book focuses on one of the largest industries in America, transportation. Transportation was the first industry to be regulated, and the first to be significantly deregulated. But strong parallels exist between the results here and those of other industries subjected to deregulation. With deregulation sweeping transportation more comprehensively than most other industries, the impact of deregulation here should serve as a barometer as to what we may expect should the crusade of deregulation sweep other industries more profoundly than it already has.

Unlike most of the literature, which pretends to provide a balanced assessment of the costs and benefits of deregulation, this book simply offers a fair appraisal of that which deregulation's proponents choose to ignore. By reading this book in addition to the others on the subject, one will, at last, have a balanced presentation of the costs, benefits, strengths, and weaknesses of regulation and deregulation.

Finally, the author would like to thank Dean Ed Dauer of the University of Denver and the Hughes Research Foundation for their support in making this book possible.

1

INTRODUCTION

Deregulation is among America's most important contemporary legal and political issues, for it has profound social and economic implications. It has dominated the domestic policy of recent presidents, and its implementation has been more comprehensive than anyone would have dared dream at its inception.

For the past decade, America has basked in the sunshine of deregulation—deregulation of telecommunications, banking, oil and gas, and transportation. Transportation was the nation's first industry to be regulated by government, and a century later, the first to enjoy significant deregulation. We have now had a decade to evaluate the social and economic impacts of that experiment. This book examines where the great American transportation experiment has been, where it is, and where it appears to be going.

One can only observe with fascination that the transportation industry has come full circle from its genesis in an unrestrained laissez-faire economic environment, through almost a century of comprehensive governmental regulation of entry, rates, and other corporate activities, and now back again to the unconstrained free market. The excesses of the market preceded regulation, and those excesses have reappeared under deregulation.

Market failure gave birth to economic regulation. In the late 19th century, pricing discrimination and destructive competition in the transportation industry prompted Congress to establish our nation's first independent regulatory agency, the Interstate Commerce Commission, in 1887.[1]

Beginning in the late 1970s, regulatory failure became the catalyst for deregulation. Various forms of *de jure* and *de facto* interstate deregulation resulted both from legislation passed by Congress in the mid–1970s and early 1980s and from the appointment by Presidents Carter and Reagan of individuals fervently dedicated to deregulation to the federal regulatory commissions. The federal statutes partially deregulating various aspects of the transportation industry include the following:

The Railroad Revitalization and Regulatory Reform Act of 1976
The Air Cargo Act of 1977
The Airline Deregulation Act of 1978
The International Air Transportation Competition Act of 1979
The Motor Carrier Act of 1980
The Staggers Rail Act of 1980
The Household Goods Transportation Act of 1980
The Bus Regulatory Reform Act of 1982
The Shipping Act of 1984
The Civil Aeronautics Board Sunset Act of 1984
The Freight Forwarder Deregulation Act of 1986

During the 1980s, deregulation swept not only through transportation, but through the other infrastructure industries as well—telecommunications, oil and gas, and, to a lesser extent, electric utilities. The high-water mark of deregulation as a blossoming political movement seems to be behind us, having peaked late in the Carter and early in the Reagan administrations. As the American people have had more experience with the grand experiment in deregulation, they have become less enamored with it. Congress has not passed a major deregulation bill in recent years and is now considering various reregulation proposals for those transport modes that have experienced the most comprehensive deregulation—airlines and railroads. And while a few states jumped on the bandwagon and adopted intrastate trucking deregulation in the early 1980s, that momentum seems to have died too, for no state has opted for intrastate deregulation since 1984. Today, the overwhelming majority of states continue to regulate intrastate motor carriage.

This book will examine the experience of transportation deregulation and the likely impact that additional deregulation would have. We will begin with an analysis of the events which led our nation to establish a regime of economic regulation over the transportation industry. We will then examine the metamorphosis toward deregulation and focus on several of the areas in which deregulation has had a significant adverse impact, including economic efficiency, pricing, service, and safety. In addition, the question of federal preemption of intrastate transportation and the experience of intrastate deregulation in the few states which have followed the federal lead will be explored. We will also examine the issue of whether more deregulation is in the public interest and, if economic regulation is to be retained, what form it should take. We will conclude with an analysis of the public interest in transportation—the policy objectives essential to accomplish social and economic goals beyond allocative efficiency.

We will examine the empirical evidence surrounding deregulation of all the major domestic transport modes—airlines, railroads, and bus and trucking companies. While these industries have somewhat different economic characteristics, they are strikingly similar as well, and in many markets compete for the same traffic. Moreover, their experience is particularly interesting in that airlines, railroads, and bus companies have undergone far more comprehensive deregulation at both the interstate and (by virtue of federal preemption) intrastate levels than have trucking companies.[2] Hence, they serve in some ways as a barometer for what the public can expect from additional motor carrier deregulation. And because the economic rationales and regulatory structure created for regulation of the other infrastructure industries (i.e., telecommunications and energy) have so many parallels with those for transportation, the empirical experience with deregulation in this industry should provide insights into the impact of additional deregulation in telecommunications, oil and gas, and electric power.

Today, transportation is among the nation's most important industries. In 1987, the total cost of moving the nation's goods and people totaled $792 billion, or 17.6% of the gross national product.[3] Hence, the role government plays has major economic and social consequences.

Federal deregulation has had more than a decade to prove its superiority to the system it replaced. The time has come to evaluate the empirical evidence and determine whether the policy achieves desirable social and economic ends.

NOTES

1. P. DEMPSEY, LAW & ECONOMIC REGULATION IN TRANSPORTATION 7–17 (1986).

2. A decade ago, America deregulated its airline industry. With the promulgation of the Airline Deregulation Act of 1978, Congress liberalized, and after a transition period, deregulated entry and pricing, preempted the states, and (effective December 31, 1984) abolished the Civil Aeronautics Board. For more than a decade, airlines have been subjected to a more intensive and comprehensive scheme of deregulation, and over a longer period, than any other formerly regulated industry.

Alfred Kahn, the Godfather of this revolution in American public policy, assured us that deregulation would result in more competition (not less), a healthier airline industry (not one chronically ill), and that neither safety nor service to small communities would suffer. A decade later, we see how wrong he was:

• The industry has become a national oligopoly and, in many markets, a monopoly.
• The industry has suffered the worse economic losses in its history.
• Pricing is highly discriminatory.
• Small communities pay more for poorer service.

- Labor-management relations have deteriorated.
- Airline service has declined.
- The margin of safety has been squeezed.

Promises Didn't Pan Out, Critic Claims, USA TODAY, Oct. 5, 1988, at 14A.
   3. *Gridlock!*, TIME (Sept. 12, 1988) at 52, 55.

2

A CONCISE HISTORY

The progress of civilization is reflected in our accomplishments in transportation: the invention of the wheel; the voyages of Leif Ericson and Christopher Columbus; the explorations of Cook, Drake, and Magellan; Charlemagne's construction of the canal system of Europe; the driving of the golden spike into the tracks at Promontory Point, Utah, linking the American east and west; the construction of the Suez and Panama Canals; the Wright brothers' flight at Kitty Hawk; the assembly lines of Henry Ford; the transatlantic flight of Charles Lindbergh; the construction of the German Autobahn and the American Interstate Highway System; and Neil Armstrong's "giant leap for mankind" onto the surface of the moon.[1]

Transportation has been a fundamental element in the growth of civilization and industrial development, and has had a profound effect on collective economic growth. Most of the major cities of the world owe their rise and fall to their proximity to trade routes. For example, Brugges, Belgium, was an important and prosperous member of the Hanseatic League during the Middle Ages that ceased to thrive and became frozen in time when its canal linking it to the North Sea became clogged with silt and impassible. Rothenburg-ob-der-Tauber is today the only German city encircled by its original medieval walls, It, too, was frozen in time when trade routes shifted east, to Nürnberg.

Transportation is a fundamental component of economic growth. It is the infrastructure foundation upon which the rest of the economy is built. Any region which loses access to the transportation system, and thereby the means to participate in the broader market for the exchange of goods and services, will wither on the vine.[2]

ORIGINS OF COMMON CARRIER REGULATION

Throughout civilization, transportation has been perceived as an industry imbued with a particular public interest. The Roman Empire codified laws of liability for common carriers around 200 B.C. Bills of lading from that era are remarkably similar to those which exist today. Roman commercial law was passed on to the legal systems of every Western European nation and serves as the foundation for modern rules of liability in the area of bailments and common carrier loss and damage.[3]

During the Middle Ages, business occupations which affected the public interest, including transportation firms, were subjected to regulation. The obligation of common carriers to serve all without discrimination continued as a responsibility enforced by the Anglo-American common law courts until the late 19th century, when the judicial system was replaced with a regulatory one.[4]

BIRTH OF A NEW CONTINENT: GOVERNMENT PROMOTION OF HIGHWAYS, CANALS, AND RAILROADS

With the European conquest of North America, towns and villages sprang up first along the Atlantic and Gulf coasts, at bays and rivers deep enough for navigation. Settlers gradually moved inland, and towns began to spring up along rivers.

Away from the rivers, most roads were Indian trails, which could be traversed only by pack horses or mules. A few private toll roads were constructed during the 18th century, some with governmental assistance.

It became increasingly apparent that transportation was essential to link the remote and sparsely settled nation together—to facilitate communications, trade, economic growth, and defense. Public sentiment for increased governmental support for infrastructure construction began to grow.

The first federal highway, the Cumberland Road, stretching from Cumberland, Maryland, to Vandalia, Illinois, was built between 1806 and 1838. It became important in settling the midwest.

Despite road improvements and the development of the steamboat in 1807, transportation costs remained high. To link the nation's waterways, canal construction began during the early 19th century. The first major canal was the Erie Canal, begun in 1817 and completed in 1825, stretching 360 miles from the Hudson River at Albany to Lake Erie at Buffalo, New York. It so significantly reduced shipping time and costs between New York City and the west as to make New York the largest city on the east coast, surpassing Philadelphia and Baltimore. Pennsylvania responded by building a canal linking Philadelphia and Pittsburgh. Another canal was built linking the Potomac and Ohio rivers.[5] Most canals were financed by the states, hoping to enhance their economic development. Soon, however, the canals were operating in the shadow of the railroads.

The first common carrier railroad in the nation, the Baltimore and Ohio, was chartered just two years after the Erie Canal was opened. By 1834, the B&O linked Baltimore with Harpers Ferry, West Virginia, and by 1852, the Ohio River at Wheeling, West Virginia. The Rock Island Railroad crossed the Mississippi River in 1854.

Compared to canals, railroad construction was not so seriously barred by topography. Moreover, many canals were frozen and inoperable during winter months. The railroads were soon found to be a more economical, reliable, and expeditious means of transport, and many canals soon fell into disuse.[6]

Everywhere, railroads were causing towns and cities to be built. Before two railroads crossed tracks where a city now called Atlanta (named after the Atlantic and Western Railroad) is located, there was only a pine forest.

In the relatively densely populated eastern United States, railroads had little difficulty securing private capital for construction, although a few were built by the states. But private investment shied away from the sparsely settled midwest, particularly west of Chicago. It soon became apparent that if America's hinterland was to be settled and developed, railroad construction would have to be subsidized from public treasuries.

Midwestern state and local governments soon became promoters of railroad development. They provided construction incentives in the form of tax exemptions, stock subscriptions, loans, loan guarantees, and outright capital donations.[7] They also participated in the land grant system, as did the federal government. In the decade preceding the Civil War, the states granted 32 million acres of land to the railroads. Between 1862 and 1871, the states granted 17 million acres of land to the railroads and the federal government granted 130 million acres.[8] These grants made it possible for the railroads to extend their lines into the sparsely settled prairies and mountains of the west. The federal government also encouraged rail expansion with loans and remissions on the duty on imported iron.[9]

In a race for land, the Union Pacific Railroad laid track west from Omaha, and the Central Pacific built east from Sacramento. In 1869, the nation was linked from coast to coast by a transcontinental rail system with the driving of a golden spike into a tie at Promontory Point, Utah.

Rail expansion continued robustly. In the 1880s, some 70,000 miles of track were laid. More than any other single factor, the rail network unified the nation. But the impact of enormous overexpansion was to haunt the rail industry for decades.

CONSOLIDATION OF THE RAIL NETWORK

Cornelius Vanderbilt began the string of consolidations that led to intensive competition among the railroads. He noted that in 1860, 30,000 miles of rail were carrying 70% of the freight, but that they were segmented among scores of small firms. A passenger wishing to travel from New York to Chicago would have to change trains 17 times, from one small line to another. Although steamboats had made Vanderbilt the richest man in the nation, between 1857 and 1862 he sold his steamboat interests and began buying railroads. By 1868 he had consolidated a number of smaller railroads into the New York Central Railroad, allowing a passenger to go from New York to Chicago without changing trains, and reducing transit time from 50 hours to 24.

Others followed Vanderbilt's lead, and three additional railroads soon competed between New York and Chicago—the Pennsylvania, the Baltimore and Ohio, and the Erie. Without sufficient traffic to support multiple lines—a situation created by a combination of excessive expansion and a rash of consolidations—competition became intense and was intensified further by the Panic of 1873 and the depression which followed.[10] Large shippers served by more than a single railroad enjoyed special low rates, underbilling, and, in some instances, rebates, sometimes even on the shipment of competitors' traffic.[11] (This was, indeed, one of the means by which John D. Rockefeller managed to take over the refineries in Cleveland which competed with Standard Oil, and eventually, establish a national petroleum monopoly.)[12]

One example of the rate wars was that between the New York Central and Erie railroads. After a series of price wars which brought the price of moving cattle from Chicago to New York down to $1.00 a car, Jim Fisk, president of the Erie, bought all the cattle available and shipped them aboard the New York Central.[13]

Rate wars in competitive markets drove down profits, leading carriers to raise prices to shippers without alternative means of transport. Often, a farmer located along an intermediate point served by only a single railroad would find the price he was charged to get his grain to market was higher than that shipped by another, even though the other farmer's grain would be moved a longer distance over the same line. Hence, pricing became highly discriminatory. Prices were generally low, but unstable, between points served by competing railroads, or having access to navigable waterways, and generally high at points between which shippers had no alternative means of transport.[14] Pricing began to reflect the level of competition in market rather than the cost of providing service.

All of this occurred in an era prior to the existence of the antitrust laws. Ruinous rate wars, often of a predatory nature, designed to drive competitors out of business, were interspersed with price fixing and pooling agreements, whereby carriers in competitive markets would agree to raise prices and pool revenue and freight, whereupon rates soared. Hence, there was tremendous rate instability, even in larger markets.

POLITICAL CORRUPTION AND FINANCIAL PIRACY

The enormous concentrations of wealth and power stemming from rail-roading led to political corruption, as railroad entrepreneurs bribed legis-lators and judges, sold them stock at less than fair market value, and gave them free passes in order to avoid taxation and regulation.[15]

Many carriers also issued watered stock, manipulating its price up or down to make quick profits. One example involved Cornelius Vanderbilt's attempt to take over the Erie Railroad, which competed with Vanderbilt's New York Central. The Erie was owned by Jim Fisk, Daniel Drew, and Jay Gould, who got wind of the attempted takeover and began issuing watered stock. Said Fisk, "If this printing press don't break down, I'll give the old hog all he wants of Erie." Although Vanderbilt himself had issued watered stock from time to time, he was taken. In the ensuing battle over the Erie, both sides bribed New York legislators and judges. As a result of such stock manipulation the Erie was unable to pay dividends for half a century.[16] Jay Gould subsequently gained control of the Union Pacific and led it to purchase the inflated stock of other rail carriers he controlled. These actions injured both investors and the shipping public, for the carriers found it necessary to maintain rates in order to pay dividends on these inflated stock issues.[17]

The Panic of 1873 gave fuel to the fire of wildly fluctuating rates. The Panic was precipitated by the financial failure of James J. Hill, the financier of the Northern Pacific. By the end of the year, nearly one fifth of the nation's railroad mileage was in bankruptcy.[18] A long depression followed. During the decade of the 1870s, rail revenues fell by approximately one third.[19]

The environment left nearly everyone dissatisfied. The rate wars, rebates to favored shippers, and low rates rendered the railroads' returns on in-vestment inadequate. Farmers felt that their rates were excessively high and wanted protection against discriminatory rate practices. Shippers in com-petitive markets desired greater rate stability and wanted some assurance that they would not be placed at a competitive disadvantage vis-à-vis ship-ping a like product.[20]

CREATION OF THE INTERSTATE COMMERCE COMMISSION

The Granger Movement

After America's young men returned to the farm following the Civil War, the production of cereal crops increased and prices fell. Moreover, rate discrimination and financial piracy became widespread. The Patrons of Hus-bandry, more commonly known as the Grangers, led the political charge for regulation.

As noted above, the desire for economic growth led both the federal and many state and local governments to provide economic incentives to railroads to build westward. The railroad promoters also turned to individuals located along the rights-of-way for investment capital. Many mortgaged their farms, starry-eyed with the prospect of lucrative dividends and reasonably priced access to eastern markets. They were disappointed on both counts. Dividends were poor or nonexistent. Many railroads went through bankruptcy and reorganization and the value of their stock was wiped out. Some had issued watered stock in order to raise money fraudulently. Many farmers were left with a mortgage, worthless stock, and expensive transportation or none at all. In the meantime, their taxes were increased to cover the parallel investment made by their state and local governments. This led to a blind antagonism toward the railroads. The result was a political movement calling for regulation.[21] The first political victories were enjoyed at the state level in the mid 19th century.[22]

The State Commissions

As early as 1836, the Massachusetts legislature reserved to itself the authority to regulate rail rates. But soon it became apparent that legislatures had neither the time, talent, nor expertise to regulate so complex an industry as transportation, and they established regulatory commissions to perform the task.

The first commissions were those having only advisory powers, such as those established in eastern states like Rhode Island (1836), New Hampshire (1844), Connecticut (1853), New York and Vermont (1855), Maine (1858), and Ohio (1867). These early commissions appraised the value of property committed to rail development under eminent domain powers and enforced rail safety standards, but lacked ratemaking power.

The modern regulatory movement began with the creation of the advisory Massachusetts Board of Railroad Commissioners in 1869, with broader powers than the earlier commission.[23] That same year, the Illinois legislature passed the first statute requiring the railroads to offer just, reasonable, and uniform rates.[24] In 1871, Minnesota enacted a law that regulated maximum rates and prohibited unjust discrimination. During the ensuing 15 years, Iowa, Wisconsin, California, Nebraska, Kansas, Oregon, and several southern states passed similar legislation.[25]

U.S. Supreme Court Decisions

The Constitution vests in Congress the "power to regulate commerce with foreign nations, and among the several States, and with the Indian tribes."[26] Three 19th-century decisions by the U.S. Supreme Court were instrumental in defining congressional power over interstate commerce and gave impetus to federal economic regulation.

Gibbons v. Ogden addressed the question of whether the state of New York could grant a monopoly franchise to operators of steamboats in New York waters and prohibit others from entering the trade.[27] Aaron Ogden, who had been assigned the monopoly franchise (earlier granted to Robert Livingston and Robert Fulton), argued that the constitutional term "commerce" referred only to the purchase and sale of goods and did not comprehend navigation. The court disagreed, concluding that commerce included "every species of commercial intercourse" between states or between the United States and foreign nations, including navigation, and that such commerce was subject to the exclusive regulatory province of Congress.

Munn v. Illinois addressed the fundamental issue of whether private property was under the exclusive control of its owners, or whether certain enterprises were of such character as to become quasi-public institutions in which the people had an interest.[28] The case involved the question of whether Illinois could properly regulate the rates of grain storage elevators within the state. The U.S. Supreme Court held that private property used in a manner affecting the general community becomes "clothed with a public interest" and subject to control "by the public for the public good."[29] Said the court:

It has ... been customary in England from time immemorial, and in this country from its first colonization, to regulate ferries, [and] common carriers ... and, in so doing, fix a maximum charge to be made for the services rendered. ... [W]hen private property is "affected with a public interest, it ceases to be *juris privati* only." ... Property does become clothed with a public interest when used in a manner to make it of public consequence, and affect the community at large. ... [Common carriers stand] in the very "gateway of commerce," and, take a toll from all who pass. Their business most certainly "tends to a common charge, and is becoming a thing of public interest and use."[30]

Hence, a state government could regulate private property dedicated to a public use.

But the real catalyst for federal legislation establishing economic regulation over common carriers was the decision in *Wabash, St. Louis and Pacific Railway v. Illinois*, issued in 1886.[31] In *Wabash*, the U.S. Supreme Court, striking down as unconstitutional an Illinois law regulating interstate rail rates, held that even in the absence of federal regulation the states could not regulate the interstate rates of the railroad: "the right of continuous transportation from one end of the country to the other is essential in modern times to that freedom of commerce from the restraints which the State might choose to impose upon it."[32] Because nearly three fourths of the commodities shipped at the time were transported in interstate commerce and were rendered immune from state control, the *Wabash* decision became a powerful stimulus for federal legislation.

The Movement toward Federal Regulation

The pressure for regulation of the railroads was not just targeted at the states. The Granger movement also had an impact in Washington, D.C.

In 1872, President Grant requested a congressional investigation of the industry. Two years later, the Windom Committee issued its report. It found that the principal complaint against the railroads involved allegations of unreasonably high rates by the farmers. The committee recommended more competition as a solution to the problem, including construction of new canals and track, and federal or state railways in competition with the private railways.[33] (This was, incidentally, the approach subsequently adopted by Canada to deal with the problem of monopoly railroads.)

Pressure mounted for rail regulation. Complaints expanded beyond rate levels to discrimination in pricing and service against persons, places, and commodities, the loose financial practices characterizing railroad capitalization and construction, and the monopoly nature of the industry, including both the size of the railroads and their extensive pooling arrangements to suppress rate wars.

In 1886 the Cullom Committee Report was issued, which recommended federal legislation prohibiting unreasonably high rates, discriminatory rates, and rebates. It also called for the creation of an impartial tribunal to adjudicate complaints against the railroads.[34] The *Wabash* decision was issued that same year, and the stage was now set for Congress to act.

Creation of the Interstate Commerce Commission

In 1887, Congress promulgated the Act to Regulate Commerce,[35] which established the nation's first independent regulatory agency—the Interstate Commerce Commission (ICC). The Act succinctly established a comprehensive regulatory regime over the rail industry. It granted the ICC the authority to regulate the interstate rates charged by railroads, thereby ensuring that the rates would be just and reasonable. Under the Act, rail carriers could no longer discriminate in rates or services between persons, localities, or traffic. Furthermore, they could no longer charge a higher rate for a shorter distance that was included within a longer haul over the same line in the same direction. Nor could the rail carriers pool freight or revenues. Most important, railroads were required to make their rates public, file them with the newly formed commission, and adhere to the published tariffs.[36]

Although all but one of the rail industry witnesses favored regulation, the Act was still rather effective consumer legislation. While it included provisions the industry favored (i.e., requirements that rates be just and reasonable and that unjust discrimination, preference, and prejudice be abolished), it also included provisions against which the railroads had lobbied (i.e., the prohibition against pooling and charging more for a short haul than a longer haul over the same line in the same direction).[37]

Never before had Congress established an independent regulatory commission to exercise the commerce power conferred under Article I Section 8 of the Constitution. President Grover Cleveland appointed the distinguished jurist Thomas Cooley to the Interstate Commerce Commission and Cooley was elected its first chairman.

Cooley, a former chief justice of the Michigan Supreme Court, a law professor, and an author of treatises on constitutional law, torts, and tax, was among the most prolific and gifted lawyers in the nation. Shortly after his appointment to the Interstate Commerce Commission, Cooley recommended creation of an association for state utility regulatory commissioners. It was he who was the father of NARUC, established on March 5, 1889. The NARUC (National Association of Railroad Utility Commissioners, subsequently named the National Association of Regulatory Utility Commissioners) held its first convention in Washington, D.C., on that date, the day after the inauguration of Benjamin Harrison as 23rd president of the United States.

The Significance of the Creation of the Interstate Commerce Commission and the Birth of the Modern Regulatory Movement

Perhaps it was inevitable that government would come to play a role in protecting the public and the transportation industry from the ravages of economic instability and exploitation. As a contemporary observer of the era in which economic regulation emerged recently remarked, "the genesis of the public policy [in favor of economic regulation] lay in the significance of railroad transportation to the fastest growing nation in world history. The railroad dominated this country's economy and society in the 19th century. The domination existed from every standpoint, capitalization, employment, community impact or entrepreneurial opportunity. There was no force, industrial or religious, which matched the societal impact of the railroad after the first third of the 19th century."[38] As another contemporary commentator has noted, "the ICC is one of the earliest instances we can point to where the federal government intervened directly in the economy to protect the economically weak from the economically strong."[39]

Still another observes that, "from our own perspective, a century later, the greatest significance of the 1887 Act to Regulate Interstate Commerce lies in its creation of the prototypical federal regulatory agency."[40] Indeed, during the ensuing decades the ICC became the model for economic regulation of a host of infrastructure industries and the numerous federal and state agencies which have emerged to perform the regulatory function.

JUDICIAL EROSION AND CONGRESSIONAL RESTORATION OF ICC JURISDICTION

During the ensuing years, the U.S. Supreme Court issued several decisions which significantly reduced the ability of the nascent commission to regulate rates effectively.[41] Congress restored and augmented the ICC's power with legislation promulgated in 1903, 1906, and 1910.[42] During the period from 1889 to World War I, not only was the power of the Interstate Commerce Commission enhanced, but strong regulatory commissions were also established in a substantial majority of the states.

WORLD WAR I AND NATIONALIZATION OF THE RAIL SYSTEM

American involvement in World War I required the movement of a flood of commodities to eastern ports. The ensuing chaos of congestion as rail cars clogged the system led Congress to take over the national rail industry and run it as a single system. It created the United States Railway Administration (USRA) to perform this task, and the USRA ran the system from December 28, 1917, until March 1, 1920.[43] During the war, rolling stock was maintained in good condition, but the roadbed was allowed to deteriorate. By the end of the war it was apparent that the industry would need assistance in regenerating itself. This led Congress to promulgate the Transportation Act of 1920, also known as the Esch-Cummins Act.

The new legislation was preoccupied with the financial health of the industry. The ICC was given jurisdiction over minimum rates (to supplement its existing authority over maximum rates), power to regulate entry and exit from markets (by issuing certificates of public convenience and necessity), authority to regulate intercorporate relationships, mergers, and the issuance of securities (to ensure a sound financial structure), and a mandate to draft a plan for consolidating the multiple parallel rail companies into a more efficient and fewer number of larger firms.[44] The effort to consolidate the rail system died stillborn for lack of support from the industry.

EMERGENCE OF THE MOTOR CARRIER INDUSTRY

The early 20th century saw the emergence of a new form of competition, the motor carrier. In 1904, there were but 700 trucks operating in the United States, most powered by steam or electrical engines. The following year, the first scheduled bus service began in New York City. The technological development of the gasoline engine and the pneumatic tire made this mode increasingly competitive for freight and passenger traffic. Nonetheless, growth of this important means of transport was hampered by poor roads and the economic dominance of the railroad industry.

Congress recognized the potential importance of motor carriage and began to promote its growth with federal matching grants for highway construction, beginning with the Federal-Aid Road Act of 1916 and then the Federal Highway Act of 1921. Soon dirt horse and wagon trails were extended, straightened, and paved.

World War I demonstrated the potential for motor transport. Thousands of motor vehicles were produced for the army. On the fields of battle, they quickly proved their superiority in transporting men and material to the front. After the Great War, thousands of surplus army trucks became the vehicles for growth of the commercial motor transport industry.

By 1918, the nation had more than 600,000 trucks. With the development of a national system of highways in the 1920s, motor carriers became an increasingly viable competitor to railroads. The combination of the pneumatic tire, hard-surface roads, and assembly-line production brought sensational growth to the industry.

Soon, the nation had an extraordinary distribution system which vigorously stimulated national economic growth. Manufacturers of apparel, appliances, hardware, and a thousand other items soon found that their markets were no longer limited to large cities. The new distribution system of trucks taking merchandise to the farthest corners of the nation meant that they could now sell their goods on Main Street of the thousands of small towns and hamlets sprinkled across the continent.

And the complexion of Main Street itself changed. No longer would general stores, which carried everything from fertilizer to soap, dominate the market. Specialized shops sprang up. Consumer choices multiplied. A lady on the plains of Kansas could now buy the same fashions on Main Street that were available on Park Avenue. The distribution system of the trucking industry made possible this tremendous growth in production and sales, and thus served as a catalyst for one of the most significant periods of economic growth in the nation's history.

ORIGINS OF ECONOMIC REGULATION OF MOTOR CARRIERS

But not all was well. The trucking industry was plagued by its own growth. A down payment on a truck and a driver's license were all it took to get into the industry. Many entrepreneurs were unsophisticated, had little idea what their costs were, and took freight for nonremunerative prices. Sometimes they were victimized by shippers with monopsony power dictating excessively low rates. Wages were poor. Many firms dropped into bankruptcy, but their trucks were simply recycled by used truck dealers and the capacity problems persisted. Industry overcapacity drove trucking rates down to a level that made it impossible for many truckers to maintain their equipment, and highway safety suffered.

All of this led many states to regulate motor carriers, limiting entry and requiring that rates be reasonable. By the mid–1920s, 33 states regulated motor freight transport and 43 regulated bus companies. But the U.S. Supreme Court in 1925 handed down a decision which stripped the states of their ability to regulate interstate movements.[45]

After that, uncontrolled rate wars broke out among interstate carriers. Bankruptcies proliferated. Safety problems were again exacerbated. Unscrupulous truckers sometimes stole the freight that had been entrusted to them. Unscrupulous bus companies and brokers sometimes stole the ticket revenues of unwary passengers.

The Wall Street stock market crash of 1929 made things even worse. It set in motion the most prolonged and severe economic depression in modern history. It had a profound impact upon economic and political policy in the United States. It shook to the very core American faith in laissez faire. The prevailing view soon became that the market had failed to serve our society's needs, and failed badly. Only enhanced government involvement in the national economy could restore the stability required for economic growth. With 3.5 million trucks on the highway, and with thousands of factories shutting down, there was less freight to fill empty trucks. The economic condition of the industry spiraled downward.

Congress first attempted to restore stability by promulgating the National Industrial Recovery Act, allowing industries to establish "Codes of Fair Competition" to diminish the heated level of competition between them. Such codes were adopted by many industries, including motor carriers. But in 1935 the U.S. Supreme Court struck down the legislation on constitutional grounds.[46] Recall that it had earlier prohibited the states from regulating interstate motor carrier operations, so the net result was that such activities were once again unregulated.

In 1933, President Franklin Roosevelt appointed the distinguished ICC commissioner Joseph Eastman to the position of Federal Coordinator of Transportation, with the responsibility to recommend legislation "improving transportation conditions throughout the country." The National Association of Railroad and Utility Commissioners had sponsored a bill (the "Rayburn Bill") calling for economic regulation of the trucking industry. This position was quickly endorsed by Eastman and the Interstate Commerce Commission.[47]

During the Great Depression, the motor carrier industry was plagued with an oversupply of transportation facilities. Intensive competition among truckers depressed freight rates excessively and caused hundreds of bankruptcies. Entry into the industry was easy. The ranks of the unemployed provided an endless pool of drivers; with a drivers license and a used truck they could haul goods for hire. Not knowing what their costs were, or victimized by shippers with greater market power, they frequently took traffic at below-cost rates. They drove for gas money, or to cover their monthly payments on the truck, and kept rolling until needed repairs brought the truck to a halt.[48] Soon they were bankrupt, while their truck was patched up and sold to yet another entrant and the cycle repeated itself.[49] All the while, efficient and productive trucking companies and railroads were also hemorrhaging dollars.

It was feared that a continuation of such unrestrained market forces might lead to a loss of service or higher prices for small shippers and small communities, leaving the surviving carriers to concentrate on high-revenue traffic. Thus, as Joseph Eastman said, "the most important thing, I think, is the prevention of an oversupply of transportation; in other words, an oversupply which will sap and weaken the transportation system rather than strengthen it."[50] The destructive potential of excessive competition was everywhere apparent. The Senate report that accompanied the new legislation had this to say:

Motor carriers for hire penetrate everywhere and are engaged in intensive competition with each other and with railroads and water carriers. This competition has been carried to such an extreme which tends to undermine the financial stability of the carriers and jeopardizes the maintenance of transportation facilities and service appropriate to the needs of commerce and required in the public interest. The present chaotic transportation conditions are not satisfactory to investors, labor, shippers or the carriers themselves.[51]

Congress was also motivated by the need to achieve equality in the regulatory scheme (railroads were regulated, while their trucking competitors were not), protect wages and working conditions (which were severely depressed), provide stable service and reasonable rates for shippers, and ensure that carriers operated safely and were financially responsible.[52]

Bus operations were also of significant concern. "Wildcatters" were cutting rates below compensatory levels and victimizing customers. Shippers were also subjected to the unscrupulous practices of trucking companies.[53]

The need for legislative relief was manifest. With the support of the ICC, most of the state public utility commissions (PUCs), the truck, bus, and rail industries, and many shippers, Congress promulgated the Motor Carrier Act of 1935, adding bus and trucking companies to the jurisdiction of the Interstate Commerce Commission.[54] It gave the ICC authority over entry and rates of motor carriers of passengers and commodities. Safety was also a principal concern. The new legislation gave the ICC power to establish requirements for the qualifications of drivers, maximum hours of service, and standards of equipment.

As Representative Sadowski, a principal sponsor, noted, "the purpose of the bill is to provide for regulation that will foster and develop sound economic conditions in the industry."[55] Economic stability and enhanced safety were its major purposes.

Under economic regulation, the industry grew and prospered. Motor carriers became responsible, reliable, and safe enterprises. Competition became healthy, with modest government oversight of rate levels and entry. Efficient and well-managed carriers earned a reasonable return on investment. The stability of the motor carrier industry provided a foundation for national economic recovery.

AIRLINE REGULATION

During the Great Depression, Congress also held hearings on the state of the infant airline industry. It concluded that its economic condition was unstable and that a continuation of its anemic condition could imperil its tremendous potential to satisfy national needs for growth and development. In order to avoid the deleterious impact of "cutthroat," wasteful, destructive, excessive, unrestrained competition and the economic "chaos" which had so plagued the rail and motor carrier industries, Congress sought to establish a regulatory structure similar to that which had been devised for the other industries that had been perceived to be "public utility" types of enterprises—the railroads and motor carriers.[56]

Three years after motor carriers were brought under the regulatory umbrella, Congress added airlines to the regulatory scheme, promulgating the Civil Aeronautics Act of 1938. In so doing, Congress created a new regulatory body to regulate this industry, the Civil Aeronautics Board (CAB).[57] Like so many agencies created to engage in economic regulation, the CAB was modeled after its older sibling, the Interstate Commerce Commission.

WORLD WAR II AND ANTITRUST IMMUNITY

World War II again saw the rail, motor carrier, and airline industries mobilized to supply the logistical needs of the nation. After the war, the nation had some 7 million trucks and a healthy transportation industry.

Rate bureaus emerged as efficient mechanisms for rate coordination among carriers and stability of pricing. But a U.S. Supreme Court decision struck down such activities on antitrust grounds.[58] Congress, believing that the rate bureaus performed an important public function augmenting the federal regulatory mechanism, responded by passing the Reed-Bulwinkle Act of 1948, over President Harry Truman's veto. The legislation shielded the rate bureaus from the application of the antitrust laws when the ICC had approved carrier ratemaking agreements. The Senate report described the act as "harmonizing and reconciling the policy of the antitrust laws, as applicable to common carriers, with the national transportation policy in such a manner as to protect the public interest."[59]

THE EMERGENCE OF INTERSTATE HIGHWAYS AND THE DECLINE OF THE PASSENGER RAILROADS

During the 1950s, it was President Dwight Eisenhower who saw the need to build a national system of interstate highways to link the country for, among other things, purposes of national defense. It was during his administration that a 17-year construction period was begun. The market share of freight transported by trucking companies began to enjoy a corresponding growth. Today, Americans share 42,500 miles of high-speed interstate highways with regulated motor carriers.

During the first half of the 20th century, railroads were the dominant means of intercity transport for passengers. In 1929, there were 20,000 passenger trains. But after World War II, demand for rail service began to decline as passengers chose alternative means to get them to their destinations—the bus, the airplane, or the automobile. In 1958, Congress passed legislation which allowed railroads to discontinue passenger trains with ICC approval. Under the ICC's auspices the number of passenger trains fell 60%, until by 1970 only 360 trains were left. Congress filled the void by passing the Rail Passenger Services Act of 1970, which established Amtrak.[60] Today, Amtrak serves more American cities than all the airlines combined.

The growth of interstate highways led to a shift of traffic from rail to the motor carrier industry. That, coupled with the move of industry out of the northeastern "rust belt" into the southeastern and western "sun belt," led to a decline of railroad profitability. Conrail was formed in 1973 with the merger of the bankrupt Penn Central (formerly the Pennsylvania and New York Central railroads) and five smaller railroads.[61]

By the mid–1970s, the political mood in Washington had shifted against economic regulation. The bankruptcy of the Penn Central, Rock Island, and, later, Milwaukee railroads made Congress fearful that it would end up owning and operating the nation's rail system. Regulatory failure took much of the blame for the anemic state of the rail industry. In order to restore the health of the rail industry, Congress passed the 3R Act of 1973, the 4R Act of 1976, and the Staggers Rail Act of 1980. Collectively, the legislation removed rail ratemaking from the jurisdiction of the ICC, except where the traffic in question was "market dominant." Rail exit from unprofitable markets became easier. The legislation also partially preempted state jurisdiction over rail rates and operations.

The political movement in favor of a reduced governmental presence found support at both ends of the political spectrum. It was a mass psychology of antagonism toward government that was stimulated on the right by the Great Society and the growth of government and taxation, and on the left by Watergate and the war in Vietnam. For once, both sides viewed government as an enemy rather than as a friend.

AIRLINE DEREGULATION

In the 1960s and early 1970s, a number of economists published articles critical of economic regulation. Principal among their criticisms was that pricing and entry restrictions gave consumers excessive service and insufficient pricing competition, inflated airline costs, and made the industry's profits unsatisfactory. Senator Edward Kennedy chaired subcommittee hearings which served as the political genesis of congressional reform. The Kennedy report concluded that airline deregulation would allow pricing flexibility that would stimulate new innovative service offerings, increase industry health, allow passengers the range of price and service options dictated by consumer demand, enhance carrier productivity and efficiency, and result in a superior allocation of society's resources.[62]

With the inauguration of Jimmy Carter as president in 1976, the movement had a disciple in the White House. Carter appointed Cornell economics professor Alfred Kahn as chairman of the Civil Aeronautics Board. Kahn criticized traditional CAB regulation as having "(a) caused air fares to be considerably higher than they otherwise would be; (b) resulted in a serious misallocation of resources; (c) encouraged carrier inefficiency; (d) denied consumers the range of price/service options they would prefer; and (e) created a chronic tendency toward excess capacity in the industry."[63] As CAB chairman, Kahn implemented a number of revolutionary deregulatory initiatives which liberalized entry and pricing. The immediate results were overwhelmingly successful, with carriers in the late 1970s stimulating new demand by offering low fares, filling capacity, and enjoying robust profits.

Working with the White House, Kahn put his charismatic personality solidly behind the legislative effort for reform. Working in favor of deregulation was Federal Express and United Airlines, the latter the largest airline in the free world. Congress responded by promulgating the Air Cargo Deregulation Act of 1977 and the Airline Deregulation Act of 1978. The legislation received overwhelming bipartisan support, which was surprising in that the bills were advanced from the top down; they had no widespread grass-roots support among the people.

The predictions as to what deregulation would bring were quite optimistic, in spite of strong misgivings among most industry analysts. CAB chairman Alfred Kahn characterized the opposition as follows: "The most general fear about [deregulation] is that when the CAB withdraws its protective hand from the doorknob, the door will open to destructive competition—to wasteful entry and cut-throat pricing—that will depress profits, render the industry unable to raise capital, and so cause a deterioration in the service it provides—on the whole, it must be admitted good service."[64]

Kahn saw the fear as unrealistic. What about the fear that the industry might gel into a national oligopoly, or in many markets, a monopoly? According to Kahn, "almost all of this industry's markets can support only a single carrier or a few: their natural structure, therefore, is monopolistic or oligopolistic. This kind of structure could still be conducive to highly effective competition if only the government would get out of the way; the ease of potential entry into those individual markets, and the constant threat of its materializing, could well suffice to prevent monopolistic exploitation."[65] Kahn saw few economies of scale in the industry; hence entry, or the threat of potential entry, would keep monopolists from extracting monopoly profits.[66] This was the theory of contestable markets, upon which deregulation was largely premised.

Kahn was optimistic that the benefits of deregulation would be universally shared: "I am confident that . . . consumers will benefit; that the communities throughout the nation—large and small—which depend upon air transportation for their economic well-being will benefit, and that the people most closely connected with the airlines—their employees, their stockholders, their creditors—will benefit as well."[67] In the ensuing chapters, we will evaluate the accuracy of these predictions.

In the late 1970s, the immediate results of deregulation were quite positive and created a general euphoria in Washington and in the media that we were on the right path. As a young CAB attorney, this author was also swept up in the movement. In 1978, this author published a law review article praising the benefits of deregulation:

The objective of [deregulation] has been to provide the consumer . . . with improved service at reduced fares. In general, the theory has been that increased competition among air carriers will lead to improved quality and an increase variety of services available to the public at competitive costs reasonably related thereto, and that the price elasticity of the passenger market will ensure increased utilization of capacity for the carriers and, consequently, increased revenues. Enhanced reliance upon competitive market forces has tended to lower air fares and stimulate innovative price/quality options. It has also tended to fill empty seats and thereby increase carrier revenues. The policies appear to have had an affirmative impact upon both consumers and the regulated industry that serves them.[68]

The Airline Deregulation Act was intended to provide a gradual transition to deregulated entry and rates, although the CAB quickly dropped any notion of "gradual" deregulation under Chairman Marvin Cohen. Implementation of the new policy was immediate and comprehensive, and as the 1970s came to a close, the industry became unhealthy again.[69] The Airline Deregulation Act also called for the "sunset" elimination of the CAB in 1985, when its remaining responsibilities were transferred to the U.S. Department of Transportation.

MOTOR CARRIER REGULATORY REFORM

In 1980, Congress passed both the Motor Carrier Act and the Household Goods Transportation Act to liberalize entry and rates of trucking companies. Although not intended to create deregulation, it was so interpreted by a highly politicized and ideological Interstate Commerce Commission under the chairmanship of economist Darius Gaskins. However, this is one area in which Congress did not preempt state jurisdiction over transportation. The state public utility commissions continue to hold extensive authority over the intrastate operations of trucking companies.

In 1982, Congress passed the Bus Regulatory Reform Act, creating pricing, entry, and exit flexibility and partially preempting state jurisdiction over bus companies.

THE CONTEMPORARY STRUCTURE OF THE TRANSPORTATION INDUSTRY

A century of economic regulation facilitated the growth and evolution of the transportation infrastructure and the complex markets it serves. America's transportation industry became the most sophisticated and efficient system in the world, satisfying the needs of a robust global economy. There are approximately 300 railroad companies operating in the United States. More than 1,500 bus companies operate over 21,000 buses traveling over a billion miles and carrying almost 375,000,000 passengers annually. Today, the trucking industry employs more individuals than any other private industry in the United States, some 9,000,000 people, of whom 2,000,000 are drivers. It hauls approximately 75% of the nation's industrial products. The nation spends $110 billion a year to transport commodities by truck. Trucking companies serve some 60,000 communities across the United States. Tens of thousands of them have no alternative means of transport. They have come to rely on this industry to satisfy the needs of commerce.

Technology has made trucks bigger and longer, and therefore more efficient and economical to operate. Fuel efficiencies have improved, as has labor productivity. Sophisticated computers now trace shipments from origin to destination. The speed and efficiency with which the trucking network is able to dispatch orders has reduced the requirement for local or regional warehousing. Today's commodities can be shipped expeditiously and economically from the manufacturer to the retailer without the necessity to maintain costly inventory. The growth of intermodal transportation has made possible the expeditious and efficient movement of commodities in a global economy.

The distribution system created by the transportation industry enables producers of millions of products to reach millions of consumers in every corner of our nation, efficiently and at a fair price. Today, transportation is among the nation's largest and most important industries.

NOTES

1. Dempsey, *Rate Regulation and Antitrust Immunity in Transportation: The Genesis and Evolution of This Endangered Species*, 32 AM. U.L. REV. 335 (1983).

2. Dempsey, *The Dark Side of Deregulation: Its Impact on Small Communities*, 39 ADMIN. L. REV. 445 (1987).

3. P. DEMPSEY & W. THOMS, LAW & ECONOMIC REGULATION IN TRANSPORTATION 255 (1986).

4. M. FAIR & J. GUANDOLO, TRANSPORTATION REGULATION (8th ed., 1979).

5. P. DEMPSEY & W. THOMS, *supra* note 3, at 4.

6. *Id.* at 4–5.

7. Dempsey, *supra* note 1, at 337.

8. *Id.* at 338–39.

9. C. RAPER, RAILWAY TRANSPORTATION 197–202 (1912).

10. *Id.* at 205–06.

11. Brewer, *Regulation—The Balance Point*, 1 PEPPERDINE L. REV. 355, 366 (1974).

12. H. BRAGDON & S. McCUTCHEN, HISTORY OF A FREE PEOPLE 391–92 (1967).

13. Dempsey, *Transportation Deregulation—On a Collision Course?* 13 TRANSP. L. J. 329, 334 (1984).

14. DEP'T OF TRANSPORTATION, A PROSPECTUS FOR CHANGE IN THE FREIGHT RAILROAD INDUSTRY 118 (1978) [hereinafter PROSPECTUS FOR CHANGE].

15. S. MORRISON, THE OXFORD HISTORY OF THE AMERICAN PEOPLE 730–31, 763–64 (1965).

16. N. PLATT & M. DRUMMOND, OUR NATION FROM ITS CREATION 444–45 (1964).

17. H. BRAGDON & S. McCUTCHEN, HISTORY OF A FREE PEOPLE 427 (1967).

18. Chandler, *The Interstate Commerce Commission—The First Twenty-Five Years*, 16 TRANSP. L. J. 53 (1987).

19. *Id.* at 54.

20. PROSPECTUS FOR CHANGE, *supra* note 14, at 118.

21. P. DEMPSEY & W. THOMS, *supra* note 3, at 8.

22. Chandler, *supra* note 18, at 53.

23. W. JONES, REGULATED INDUSTRIES 31–33 (2d ed., 1975).

24. *Id.* at 37.

25. Dempsey, *supra* note 1, at 339.

26. U.S. CONST., Art I, sec. 8.

27. 9 Wheat. 1, 6 L.Ed. 23 (1824).

28. 94 U.S. 113 (1876).

29. *Id.* at 119.

30. *Id.* at 113, 126. Although Munn dealt with grain elevators, the principle announced therein was subsequently extended to railroads. See C B & Q R Co. v. Iowa, 94 U.S. 155 (1876), Ruggles v. Illinois, 108 U.S. 526 (1883), and Illinois Central v. Illinois, 108 U.S. 541 (1883).

31. 118 U.S. 557 (1886).

32. *Id.* at 572–73.

33. W. JONES, *supra* note 23, at 44.

34. *Id.* at 44–45.

35. Interstate Commerce Act, ch. 104, 24 Stat. 379 (1887) [codified as amended at 49 U.S.C. sec. 10101–11917 (Supp. IV 1980)].

36. Dempsey, *supra* note 1, at 341.

37. Chandler, *supra* note 18, at 55.

38. Auerbach, *The Expansion of ICC Administrative Law Activities*, 16 TRANSP. L. J. 92 (1987).

39. Miller, *Keynote Address to ICC Centennial Celebration*, 16 TRANSP. L. J. 40–41 (1987).

40. T. McCRAW, PROPHETS OF REGULATION (Boston: Belknap Press, 1984).

41. *See* e.g., ICC v. Cincinnati, N. O. & T. P. R. Co., 167 U.S. 479 (1897), and Interstate Commerce Commission v. Alabama Midland Railway, 168 U.S. 144 (1897).

42. In 1903, Congress enacted the Elkins Act, which granted the ICC authority to impose civil and criminal penalties for intentional acts of discrimination and intentional violations of published tariffs. Three years later Congress passed the Hepburn act, which gave the ICC jurisdiction over express, sleeping car, and steamship companies, as well as fuel pipelines. This act also conferred jurisdiction to determine and prescribe maximum rates for the future in those situations in which existing rates were deemed unlawful. Additionally, it gave the ICC the power to establish through routes and joint rates among noncompeting carriers and to prescribe their divisions. And in 1910, Congress passed the Mann-Elkins Act, which revitalized the long- and short-haul provisions and established new rate procedures. Under this act the ICC could, on its own motion, suspend tariffs pending an investigation on their lawfulness.

43. Calhoun, *The Interstate Commerce Commission, 1912–1937*, 16 TRANSP. L. J. 59, 61 (1987).

44. P. DEMPSEY & W. THOMS, *supra* note 3, at 12–13.

45. *See* Buck v. Kuykendall, 267 U.S. 307 (1925).

46. *See* A.L.A. Schechter Poultry Corp. v. United States, 295 U.S. 495 (1935).

47. W. JONES, REGULATED INDUSTRIES 494 (2d ed., 1976).

48. Thoms, *Rollin' On...To a Free Market: Motor Carrier Regulation 1935–1980*, 13 TRANSP. L. J. 43, 48 (1983).

49. W. JONES, *supra* note 23, at 499–500.

50. Thoms, *supra* note 47, at 48.

51. S. Rep. No. 482, 74th Cong., 1st Sess. 2 (1935).

52. Dempsey, *supra* note 1, at 335, 344.

53. Thoms, *supra* note 47, at 49.

54. Baker & Greene, Jr., *Commercial Zones and Terminal Areas: History, Development, Expansion, Deregulation*, 10 TRANSP. L. J. 171, 176 (1978).

55. *Id.* at 178.

56. Dempsey, *The Rise and Fall of the Civil Aeronautics Board—Opening Wide the Floodgates of Entry*, 11 TRANSP. L. J. 91, 95 (1979).

57. The agency was initially named the Civil Aeronautics Authority.

58. Georgia v. Pennsylvania Railroad, 324 U.S. 439 (1945).

59. *See* Dempsey, *supra* note 1, at 358.

60. Dempsey, *supra* note 2, at 450–52.

61. Dempsey, *Antitrust Law & Policy in Transportation—Concentration I$ the Name of the Game*, 21 GA. L. REV. 505, 547 (1987).

62. Dempsey, *supra* note 55, at 114–18.

63. Quoted in P. DEMPSEY, LAW & FOREIGN POLICY IN INTERNATIONAL AVIATION 24 (1987).

64. A. Kahn, Talk to the New York Society of Security Analysts, 14 (Feb. 2, 1978).

65. *Id.* at 24.

66. *See id.* at 26.

67. Statement of Alfred E. Kahn before the Aviation Subcommittee of the House Public Works and Transportation Committee on H. R. 11145, 8 (Mar. 6, 1978).

68. Dempsey, *The International Rate and Route Revolution in North Atlantic Passenger Transportation*, 17 COLUM. J. TRANSNAT'L L. 393, 441 (1978).

69. *See* Dempsey, *supra* note 1.

3

DEREGULATION: THE EARLY RESULTS

In 1977 and 1978, Congress promulgated legislation deregulating the air cargo and air passenger industries, respectively. In 1980, Congress followed suit with regulatory reform legislation for the rail and motor carrier industries. These legislative efforts were accompanied by the presidential appointment of fervent free-market ideologues to head the Civil Aeronautics Board, the Interstate Commerce Commission, and the U.S. Department of Transportation. The net result was the expeditious (some would say hasty) and comprehensive implementation of deregulation to a level that exceeded the more conservative legislative mandate.

Much of this political momentum was stimulated by the initial successes of airline deregulation in the late 1970s. By lowering prices, passenger demand (which is inherently elastic) was stimulated, thereby filling seats which otherwise would have flown empty. By increasing capacity levels, exiting thin markets, and reducing the "frills" of exorbitant service, the airline industry earned the highest profits in its history. It looked like a win-win situation. Consumers enjoyed lower prices and carriers earned generous profits.

But the euphoria was to be short-lived. By the fourth quarter of 1978, well before the economic recession of the 1980s began, airline profitability began to plummet. Service levels, particularly to small towns, and labor-management relations began to deteriorate. Mergers began to grow. By the early 1980s, the airline industry suffered its worst losses in the history of domestic aviation. And problems began to arise in surface transportation as well.

This chapter explores those early empirical results. It provides two Polaroid snapshots of the industry—the first in 1980 and the second in 1983. As the ensuing chapters reveal, many of the problems which surfaced early on are still with us.

This author also made several predictions in 1980 as to what America might expect from this grand experiment in transportation deregulation. Those are reproduced in this chapter as well. So let us look at the industry and its various modes as it appeared in the early 1980s, through the glass darkly.

DEREGULATION AS IT APPEARED IN 1980, AND PREDICTIONS AS TO THE FUTURE

Service to Small Communities

Although Congress was assured by Secretary of Transportation Neil Gold-schmidt that deregulation of motor carriage would not adversely affect service to small communities, and by Senator Kennedy that deregulation would actually improve such services,[1] it is clear that Congress was unsure of the precise effect its new legislation would have upon such service. Thus, it proceeded to require the ICC to prepare a report on the impact of reg-ulatory reform upon small communities, emphasizing communities with a population of 5,000 or less.[2] If, indeed, the impact of such legislation was adverse, the economic effects could be tragic, for 65% of the communities in the United States are completely dependent upon motor carriage for their freight transportation.[3] Studies of small communities universally reveal that under regulation they received a satisfactory level of transportation service.[4] One wonders whether such service will remain adequate in an open entry environment. The minority report of the Senate Commerce Committee con-cluded that:

Evidence before the Committee showed convincingly there is no practical or feasible way the motor common carrier can be expected to carry out any semblance of common carrier obligations if the industry it faced with an avalanche of unrestricted competition that will assume no responsibility nor recognize any obligation.... [Small community service] frequently consisting of small shipments to off-line points, are not always the most profitable. In many cases, the traffic is marginal. But the carrier is able to maintain this service, and carry out the full obligations of his authority, because he can balance the less desirable operations with the more prof-itable traffic moving between major traffic centers. The latter traffic would be natural prey for the thousands of new operations that would be unleashed by elimination or extreme weakening, of entry controls. In order to retain this traffic under the rate war that inevitably would ensue, the existing carriers would either have to charge much higher rates for less truckload traffic and for small shipments, or abandon these services altogether.[5]

Although the ICC never revoked a carrier's certificate for failing to provide service to a remote community or a shipper, it held up pending operating authority applications and suspended authority of various carriers for failure to meet their consumer carrier obligations.[6] It was believed that the failure of the commission to police such service may well lead to a deterioration in small community less-than-truckload service and/or a discriminatory increase in the price of such transportation to small shippers and remote communities:

The rates per unit of service are lower now than they would be if universal competition prevailed, because unrestrained price competition would drive rates down in lower cost traffic lanes and would drive rates up in higher cost markets. Since traffic density is a major cost element, the rates on movements to the relatively sparsely settled rural areas would rise or else the level of service would drop.[7]

Concern over the potential loss of air service to small communities led Congress to expand the system to direct federal subsidization in the Airline Deregulation Act of 1978. Essentially, the new provisions prohibit the termination of "essential air service" to "eligible points" unless the Civil Aeronautics Board first secures a replacement carrier, even if it must offer a subsidy to cover operational losses and provide a reasonable profit.[8]

Curiously, there is not an analogous provision in the Motor Carrier Act of 1980 to insure the provision of adequate surface transportation, despite the fact that one would imagine that the movement of freight is far more essential to the economy of a small community than the movement of passengers, at least in markets whose economies are not based on tourism.

If the experience of airline deregulation is any indication, small communities will suffer a loss both in the quantity and quality of service they receive.[9] For example, 34 hub and 281 non-hub airports received less service on February 1, 1979, than they had enjoyed a year earlier.[10] Between July 1978 and July 1979, departures declined at 37% of 663 cities surveyed. All scheduled service had been terminated at 49 cities, representing a total of 974 weekly departures. And 44% of the 663 cities experienced a loss of available seats.[11] Thus, even where the CAB was able to secure a replacement carrier to provide "essential service" at an "eligible point" (at taxpayer expense), many of these communities suffered a loss in the quality and quantity of service which they had previously enjoyed. Moreover, most replacement carriers are commuter carriers, which have a 300% poorer safety record than scheduled airlines.[12]

Safety

The legislative history of the Motor Carrier Act of 1980 reveals congressional concern over the potential for deterioration in motor carrier safety that regulatory reform may bring. Thus, the House Public Works Committee acknowledge that "increased entry will open the highways to truckers who may have little concern for the safe operation and maintenance of their vehicles, thereby posing a threat to those who share the highways with them."[13] The minority report of the Senate Commerce Committee expressed even greater concern over the potential for a loss of carrier safety:

We believe one of the most persuasive arguments against deregulation is that compliance with safety standards will likely suffer. The Bureau of Motor Carrier Safety of the Department of Transportation has found that regulated carriers have a lower accident rate than exempt carriers.

Accidents involving exempt carriers are also more severe than those involving regulated motor carriers, according to BMCS data. The severity of property damage for exempt truckers is $15,000 per accident, nearly twice the property damage per accident for regulated motor carriers.

The study by Dr. D. Darryl Wyckoff [of Harvard University] certainly shows a definite correlation between regulation and safety. Wyckoff found that company drivers in the regulated sector of the trucking industry have a safety and compliance record which is substantially and consistently superior to the exempt carrier. Wyckoff's survey of thousands of drivers found that company drivers in the common carrier sector compared to exempt owner-operators have:

A lower average cruising speed;
Lesser incidence of keeping multiple log books;
Lesser incidence of regularly exceeding the driving hours' limits;
Fewer moving violations per 100,000 miles; and
Fewer reportable accidents per 100,000 miles.

In addition, Wyckoff found that exempt for-hire carrier drivers were found to be involved in more than three (3) times as many accidents per hundred thousand miles of travel as drivers for regulated motor carriers.[14]

By 1980 safety had become a matter of serious concern in the motor carrier industry. Accidents increased from 25,666 in 1976 to more than 34,000 in 1978, while truck driver fatalities increased from 717 to 962 during the same period. Between 1977 and 1980 more than 10,000 highway deaths have resulted from accidents involving medium and heavy commercial vehicles. Such accident fatalities grew at double the rate of increased truck miles traveled.[15]

Although the thought may be heretical to suggest, could it be that there is any correlation between these figures and the liberalization of entry by the ICC during this same period? The grant rate for motor carrier operating authority applications grew progressively from 80% in 1976 to over 98% in 1979.[16]

As has been indicated, Professor Wyckoff noted a definite correlation between absence of safety and unregulated sectors of the industry.[17] This would tend to confirm the view held by many that the expansion of the commercial zone has made our cities dumping grounds for unsafe equipment, and that haulers of exempt unprocessed agricultural commodities are not the best-trained and do not operate the safest trucks. The Department of Transportation, which holds primary jurisdiction over motor carrier safety, has no practical means of locating exempt carriers in order to evaluate their compliance with safety standards.[18]

The ICC's principal means to insure carrier safety rests with its power in operating authority proceedings to evaluate the fitness, willingness, and ability of carriers to perform proposed operations and conform to the provisions of the Interstate Commerce Act and the commission's rules and regulations promulgated thereunder.[19] The Department of Transportation (DOT) failed to participate in these proceedings to a satisfactory extent.[20]

Nevertheless, in promulgating the Motor Carrier Act of 1980, Congress again left to DOT the responsibility to insure that motor carriers perform safe operations. The legislation confers upon DOT the authority to establish minimum financial responsibility for bodily injury and property damage for interstate motor carriers.[21]

According to the proponents of deregulation, the immediate impact of regulatory reform will be significantly increased competition.[22] Such an increase was immediately felt by the airline industry shortly after the promulgation of the Airline Deregulation Act of 1978. In fact, competition reached such an extreme that net losses for the last quarter of 1979 and first quarter of 1980 totaled $500 million—the worst in the history of U.S. aviation.[23]

One of the dangers of poor or nonexistent profits for an industry such as transportation is the natural tendency of management to curtail costs; and among those which can be significantly diminished are maintenance costs, including mechanics' wages, spare or replacement parts, and idle vehicle time during inspection and maintenance. This was already the case in the railroad industry where, because of a chronic period of unsatisfactory profits,[24] deferred maintenance became a serious concern.[25]

The problem of deferred maintenance now seems to have afflicted the airline industry as well. In 1979, the Federal Aviation Administration recovered or attempted to recover $1,500,000 in maintenance fines from Braniff, $385,000 from PSA, $166,000 from Prinair, $500,000 from American, and $100,000 from Continental.[26] The fact is, airline economics are such that it is difficult to keep a jet on the ground because a $50 replacement part is unavailable, when that jet in the air could realize $50,000 in gross revenue, the danger to life notwithstanding.[27] Further, the Civil Aeronautics Board, in its haste to deregulate the airline industry, has exacerbated the safety problem by so diluting the fitness criteria as to make them effectively meaningless.[28]

What will this mean for motor carriage? ICC chairman Darius Gaskins, a form CAB employee, may well pursue an analogous course and dilute the fitness criteria so that they pose neither a significant barrier to entry nor any realistic means of protecting the public against unsafe operators. Further, dramatically increased competition may well cause carriers to cut costs and, as in the rail and aviation industries, defer maintenance. In essence, lives may be lost unnecessarily as a result of these efforts.

Industry Economics

Among the principal justifications for regulatory reform in transportation has been that competition in the industry should be increased so that service costs will be lowered. The results of lower transport costs, it is argued, will be passed on to consumers in the form of diminished inflation. Exaggerated claims that such reform would save the nation some $5 billion were repeatedly made by Edward Kennedy, Alfred Kahn, and Barry Bosworth.[29] Some contended that unnecessary government regulation of transportation was costing the public $16 billion annually.[30]

Indeed, the immediate effect of regulatory reform may well be increased competition, at least for the short term. Many entrepreneurs will invest in a truck and enter the motor carrier business, fighting for traffic at lower and lower rates, rates which may or may not cover marginal operating costs. Trucking is inherently an intensely competitive industry. But in such a hostile economic environment, many small and marginal operators will not survive and bankruptcies will continue to rise. The greatest irony of all may be that small businesses, now free from any meaningful governmental constraints on entry, will be able to enter the trucking business only to find themselves in bankruptcy some 18 months later, with creditors fighting over their real and personal property. Already, with the liberal entry policies established by the ICC and court decisions such as *Liberty*[31] and *P. C. White*,[32] carrier bankruptcies are increasing. As has been indicated, diminished profits may well make it difficult for motor carriers to provide service to small communities or to insure that their operations are reasonably safe.

Among the immediate financial impacts to the industry have been the loss in the value of certificates of public convenience and necessity and the concomitant diminution in the value of carrier securities on the major stock exchanges. In 1980 the industry carried some $4 billion worth of ICC certificates on its balance sheets—representing operating authority that had only a fraction of that value.[33]

For example, although operating authority between Baltimore and Washington sold for $200,000 only three years ago, the asking price was $20,000 in 1980.[34] Many of the major carriers have significant balance sheet problems as a result of regulatory reform:

Consolidated Freightways holds about $36 million worth of operating authorities equal to $2.77 a share out of book value of $26.36 a share. Roadway Express has more than $24 million in operating authorities—$1.20 a share out of $15.52 in book value. McLean Trucking holds $12 million for $2.13 a share vs. $19.36 book value. Overnite Transportation holds $6.6. million, or $2.05 a share vs. $27.24

book. Transcon Lines holds $16 million, or $5.14 a share vs. $14.62 book. U.S. Truck Lines holds more than $6 million or $1.41 a share vs. $17.33 book. Yellow Freight System holds $34 million, or $2.37 a share vs. $15.24 book.[35]

These figures may explain why Standard and Poor's trucking stock index plummeted almost 50% from its 1976 level.[36] Unless Congress responds with some means of direct or indirect compensation for the loss in value of operating authority resulting from its new policies (either through direct payment or some means of tax credit), the financial posture of many carriers will be uncertain, at best.[37]

Although the short-term benefit of regulatory reform is likely to be increased competition, it may also cause many carrier mergers and bankruptcies, thereby increasing concentration in the industry over the long term. As ATA (American Trucking Associations) chairman Bennett Whitlock has noted:

There are 16,000 ICC-regulated motor carriers. Of these, 12,453 gross $500,000 or less. Deregulation would promote concentration not competition. In the regulated motor carrier industry, the top four carriers account for 10 percent of the total revenue; the top eight, 14 percent. Compare this with other American industries, industries which are "regulated" by the general antitrust laws which deregulationists advocate as better regulators of the trucking industry than the Interstate Commerce Act.

In the motor vehicle manufacturing industry, the four largest companies account for 91 percent of the volume, and the eight largest for 97 percent. In the steel business, the four largest account for 47 percent of the business; the eight largest, 65 percent. In the cigarette industry, the four largest have 84 percent of the total; the eight largest, virtually 100 percent.

Only two major industries have less concentration than does the motor carrier industry—miscellaneous machinery and feminine wearing apparel.[38]

The experience of deregulation in both Australia and Great Britain was that following a limited period of intensive competition and carrier bankruptcies, the less-than-truckload sectors of the motor carrier industry became oligopolistic in character.[39] In Australia, the industry is controlled by no more than four companies.[40]

The airline industry is another example. Shortly after promulgation of the Airline Deregulation Act, mergers were attempted or consummated by Seaboard/Tiger, Continental/Western, Pan Am/National, Southern/North Central, and Republic/Hughes Airwest.[41] Because of the dismal financial condition of many airlines (which are frantically reducing service and laying off employees in order to reduce expenses) we may well see some major carrier bankruptcies in the near future.[42]

The railroad industry is another in which unsatisfactory profits[43] have led to bankruptcies, mergers, and acquisitions[44] to such an extent that we are nearing the point where only a handful of rail carriers will be serving the entire nation.

A major cause of the economic problems of the rail industry has been the increased loss of traffic to motor carriage. Although rail transported 77% of intercity tonnage in 1929, its share of the market fell to only 36% in 1977.[45] As the list of exempt commodities for motor carriage is expanded and price competition in the motor carrier industry is increased, this trend will become more pronounced and the rail industry may continue to suffer.[46]

Fuel Consumption

Rail is the most energy-efficient mode of transportation. The tragedy of regulatory reform in motor carriage, from a national energy perspective, is that it may exacerbate the shift of traffic from rail to motor carriage, a significantly less energy-efficient mode. The relative energy efficiencies are as follows:[47]

Pipeline	420	BTU's per Ton-Mile
Rail	675	BTU's per Ton-Mile
Waterways	750	BTU's per Ton-Mile
Truck	3,440	BTU's per Ton-Mile
Air	37,500	BTU's per Ton-Mile

The deregulation of the transportation of commodities by air, under the Air Cargo Deregulation Act of 1977, led to some shift of traffic from the surface modes to air carriage, the least energy-efficient means of transportation. Major manufacturers and distributors of apparel, for example, were known to have closed regional warehouses from which stocks had traditionally been shipped via motor carriage, in favor of a single national distribution point from which deliveries could be made by air freight. Although the cost of maintaining regional warehouses may be significantly greater than the cost of air freight, such business decisions increase fuel consumption dramatically. Additionally, the deregulation of the airline industry brought about a significant growth in aircraft purchases and increased flight frequencies in the most heavily traveled corridors, dramatically increasing both fuel consumption and environmental pollution.[48]

The Motor Carrier Act of 1980 seeks to permit "carriers to expand their service while eliminating inefficient and fuel wasteful restrictions. Two of these restrictions marked for elimination are gateway and circuitous route restrictions which now prevent carriers from traveling the most direct routes."[49] Typical among arguments by proponents of regulatory reform was this statement by Senator Schmitt:

Existing regulation . . . causes many carriers to operate less efficiently than they could, which raises their costs and wastes fuel. Empty backhauls, partial loads, and circuitous routes often result. DOT and ICC data show that more than 16 percent of general purpose ICC-regulated vehicles travel empty. An even larger percentage of exempt vehicles travel empty. For example, under the current system, any exempt agricultural carrier may carry fresh, unprocessed produce to the canning plant but may not transport processed commodities on the return trip without entering into a leasing arrangement with a regulated carrier.[50]

As will be indicated below, it may not be possible to eliminate all empty backhauls because of traffic imbalances due to the inherent market characteristics of certain regions. Thus Florida, with an economy based principally on tourism, imports manufactured goods and exports little, other than citrus products.[51]

Insofar as energy consumption by motor carriers is concerned, the existing regulatory regime has been defended as follows:

Energy—A charge has been raised that the statutory requirement of an operating certificate in order to handle freight is creating empty backhauls and thereby wasting fuel. It is helpful here to first look at the available facts concerning empty backhauls in order to view the impact of the certification requirement in context. The following are the results of an actual statistical study made of empty intercity mileage covering the entire year 1976:

Comparison of empty truck miles, van type equipment, year 1976

Type of carrier:	Percent Empty
ICC authorized	12.2
Exempt	27.4
Private	26.7

Several conclusions are apparent from those figures. First, the ICC-regulated carriers are producing much better-balanced two way hauls and lesser mileage than the unregulated sector—by a margin of over two to one. Second, the amount of empty backhauling by the regulated carriers approaches the optimum, when it is appreciated that there is a certain amount of directional imbalance of freight due to certain cities and regions being primarily producing regions and others are primarily consuming regions.

From these facts it appears that, since deregulating freight is neither going to produce more freight nor change the directional nature of shipments, the primary result of deregulation on the energy picture would be to produce greater empty mileage. As an unlimited number of carriers would be introduced into a relatively limited freight market, fronthauls grabbed by one carrier would frequently be the backhauls otherwise available to presently existing carriers.[52]

Liberalized entry may only put more trucks on the highway than is demanded by market or fuel efficiency. Such increased capacity, while stimulating price competition among carriers in a vigorous contest for what little traffic there is, will nevertheless cause economic injury to the industry and exacerbate our national energy crisis.

Perhaps the contemporary policies of the ICC that do cause severe, unnecessary fuel consumption are the new liberal entry policies enunciated in *P. C. White* and *Liberty*, which (with the objective of increased competition) seem to permit the certification of a number of carriers greater than that which the market can efficiently and economically support. Because the commodities transport market is virtually price inelastic, such policies would seem to force existing carriers to travel emptier and emptier, thus exacerbating our national energy problem.

True, there is some price elasticity between modes or carriers. For example, in a market which can economically and efficiently support a single carrier, that carrier may be able to provide truckload movements on a regular basis. Inherently, this is an optimum transportation-shipper relationship from the standpoint of fuel efficiency. Recently, the ICC has been vigorously certificating new entrants as if the commodities market were infinite. The aggregate effects of these thousands of Lilliputian decisions, coupled with the commission's efforts to encourage price competition, may cause aggregate fuel consumption to rise dramatically. For example, three carriers might compete for traffic that one handled before. By lowering their prices, each might be able to acquire approximately a third of the market; and if they provide service comparable to the level previously performed by the incumbent, they may each be able to have their trucks one-third full, at least until one or all drop out of the market or go bankrupt. In the meantime, fuel consumption has risen by 300%.

Nevertheless, price competition may be able to attract traffic from competing modes. But to the extent traffic leaves rail and enters trucks, fuel efficiency is sacrificed and the financial posture of rail carriage is made more hopeless.

Predictions

In 1980, this author had the temerity to make the following predictions as to the three stages through which the deregulation metamorphosis would proceed:

"Deregulation of transportation will proceed in three stages. In the first, price and service competition are increased, carriers become innovative and imaginative in the types of price and service combinations they offer, and consumers thereby enjoy lower priced transportation. Carriers are free to maximize their profits by leaving unprofitable markets and investing in more lucrative ones. In the airline industry, lower prices initially generated increased passenger traffic, thereby enabling air carriers to fill seats which might have otherwise flown empty.[53] As has been indicated, air carriers left many of the small, remote, isolated communities of our nation and transferred their aircraft to the more heavily traveled markets. Passengers in these dense markets enjoyed intense pricing and service competition. Airlines generally enjoyed higher profits, at least during stage one.

"As a result of the *de facto* deregulation of entry by the ICC, with a massive increase in both the percentage of applications granted and in the number of applications filed,[54] the motor carrier industry also finds itself in stage one of deregulation. New entrepreneurs are entering the industry, freight prices are being reduced drastically, and less-than-truckload carriers are beginning to lose truckload "cream" traffic to expanded contract carriers and new operators.[55] The larger carriers are likely to respond with their own competitive prices and to reduce service in the less lucrative markets. In any event, the consumer of transportation services is likely to enjoy reduced rates, at least during the first stage. The first stage is the one to which deregulators point to demonstrate the attributes of deregulation.

"The second stage is an embarrassment to deregulators. This is the stage in which the airline industry now finds itself. Because of excess capacity and unrestrained price and service competition, air carrier profits have plummeted; indeed, the industry is experiencing the worst losses in the history of domestic aviation. In order to retrieve some of their operational losses, carriers have begun to raise prices drastically in all but the dense, highly competitive markets in which they may wish to preserve their market shares. Thus, airline fares rose 34% from June of 1979 to March of 1980, an increase which far exceeds the increase in the price of fuel as well as other operational cost increases.[56] One economist has succinctly summarized the market effects of deregulation upon the airline industry:

In the short run, deregulation does indeed seem to be the promised land. Prices rise more slowly, productivity increases, service expands, and everyone is happy. However, after the initial euphoria, it turns out that profits are not really increasing after all.

As a result, rationalization of the route structure begins, which turns out to mean price-cutting on primary routes, coupled with higher prices and less service on secondary routes.

When this happens, the gain in productivity slows or even reverses, thereby negating much of the benefits of deregulation. We end up with no improvement, or even higher prices and lower productivity in that industry.... [In situations where] natural monopolies exist—*i.e.*, where duplication of service leads to a decline rather than an increase in productivity—total deregulation is not the answer either. For that leads to two untoward sets of events: use of more fuel, and less efficient and productive methods of manufacturing and retailing. While these costs are not apparent for several years, in the long run they represent a significant additional burden on the economy.[57]

"The continued inability of many carriers to balance their sheets due to the intensive competition they are forced to endure under deregulation will force many carriers to float 'belly up' in bankruptcy. This will occur with greater frequency in both the airline industry and the motor carrier industry. During the second stage, prices will continue to be set at reasonable levels in highly competitive markets, and will continue to grow at unreasonable rates in monopolistic or oligopolistic markets. Service will begin to deteriorate in both.

"Stage three of deregulation will constitute the ultimate transportation system with which the nation is left under deregulation. The carriers which have suffered most during stages one and two will, by this point, have gone bankrupt, leaving many markets with very little competition. A monopolistic or oligopolistic market structure will result in high prices, poor service, and little innovation or efficiency. Potential entrants, having witnessed the economic calamity of destructive competition, may be unwilling to enter so cutthroat an industry. Because the economic barriers to entry are greatest in the rail, air and less-than-truckload motor carrier industries, concentration will be greatest here. Small communities will receive poorer service and/or higher rates than larger communities. Much of the industry, particularly small carriers, may be unhealthy, leading to some question as to stability of service. In the end, the industry structure as created by the free market may be much less desirable than that which was established by federal economic regulation. Former ICC chairman A. Daniel O'Neal has said:

The existing regulatory system provides for the allocation of resources in the motor carrier industry, not only on the basis of market forces, but also in an attempt to secure certain social objectives. The marketplace allocates resources based on dollar votes cast by consumers in the marketplace. A regulatory system will allocate resources in part based on real votes cast by consumers in the legislative and political process. The marketplace will, theoretically, produce the most efficient economic system. But economic benefits are not necessarily the same as social benefits . . . [Economic] regulation provides a basis for determining and assuring "minimum levels" of service to all parts of the country at a "reasonable rate," even if the demand for trucking service in small towns or inner city areas would justify the same level of service at the same level of rates. By so doing, regulation promotes the economic development of less populated areas. Regulation, by preventing "unjust discrimination," can prevent large shippers and large carriers from exercising their market power to compel preferential treatment, where that treatment is not justified by lower costs. A regulatory role adds a measure of stability to the industry by providing a forum for the discussion of changes by all affected parties. It can operate to reduce concentration in the industry, by affording a measure of protection to smaller carriers.

Those are significant virtues, and they can be realized only if the government plays a role in allocating economic resources through the regulatory process.[58]

"Let us hope that two things occur. First, let us hope that Congress will continue to monitor the impact of deregulation on the transportation industry. Second, let us pray that this pessimistic portrait the author has painted of deregulation turns out to be inaccurate, for if the effects of deregulation are less than desirable, can all the king's horses and all the king's men ever put it back together again?"[59]

DEREGULATION AS IT APPEARED IN 1983

Economic Decline

Since airline deregulation preceded motor carrier deregulation, let us first examine the airline industry. By 1980, as deregulation began to run its course, airlines broke new economic loss barriers. That year, the airline industry suffered record losses of $280 million.[60] In 1981, the 12 largest air carriers alone surpassed this threshold by threefold, losing $641 million.[61] Worldwide losses for all of commercial aviation, domestic and foreign for 1982 were $900 million,[62] despite the fact that the industry carried 7 million more passengers than it did the preceding year.[63] Losses for the first half of 1983 exceeded half a billion dollars.[64] If you add that to the burden of expenditures in interest payments on debt, the airline industry's revenues fell more than $2 billion short of breakeven during 1982. In fact, 1982's airline revenues represented the first year-to-year decline in the industry's history. For more than three years, the industry suffered operating losses of more than a million dollars a day, or nearly $2 billion overall.[65] By 1983, the industry's debt had ballooned to 70% of invested capital.[66]

Air New England, Braniff, Continental, El Al, Laker, and 16 other air carriers entered various stages of bankruptcy after the promulgation of the Airline Deregulation Act of 1978.[67] Carriers such as Air Florida, Eastern, Pan Am, Republic, Western, and World were placed on the "endangered species" list.[68] During 1982, Pan Am sustained operating losses of $700,000 a day.[69] Even a traditionally healthy carrier like Delta was feeling the crunch, posting its first operating losses since 1947.[70] A number of the nation's large air carriers would be thrown into bankruptcy if the financial institutions holding their long-term debt (estimated to be $10.1 billion for the 16 largest airlines) demanded timely payment.[71] Prudent bankers, quite simply, are not interested in entering the used aircraft business; and certainly, calling in the outstanding loans would only result in the acquisition of large fleets of jets which, in this depressed economic environment, would be worth little.[72] These losses have had a ripple effect on aircraft manufacturers such as Boeing, whose earnings have plunged 42%,[73] and Lockheed, which has recently been forced to virtually abandon commercial aviation.[74]

One source predicts that "the number of major airlines will probably be reduced to five or six within the next five years as one or two more go into bankruptcy or merge operations with other air carriers."[75] Another adds that the "airline industry under deregulation is on a course where competition is being wrung out by the creation of an oligopoly of a few remaining large airlines; the public is not being served by this process."[76] Unemployed workers of Braniff and 12 other airlines have applied for economic relief under the special provisions of the Airline Deregulation Act of 1978, alleging that airline deregulation is the cause of widespread industry unemployment.[77] The CAB reports that since December of 1979 more than 40,000 full-time airline employees have lost their jobs.[78] At least one commentator has described the promulgation of the Airline Deregulation Act of 1978 as perhaps "the worst disaster in history for the U.S. airline industry."[79] Another suggests that "some common-sense approach should be figured out that would prevent deregulation from becoming, in effect, a hunting license that enables established companies to pick off the competition. . . . [A]n untrammeled free market is not necessarily synonymous with the public interest."[80]

Since the enactment of the Motor Carrier Act of 1980, several hundred motor carriers have gone bankrupt, out of business, or have otherwise discontinued operations.[81] Dun and Bradstreet reported that almost 400 motor carriers declared bankruptcy during 1980 alone, more than twice the number of the preceding year.[82] These figures represent only a small percentage of trucking companies which have actually gone out of business, for many have closed their doors without declaring formal bankruptcy.[83] Carriers which have gone "belly up" accounted for more than $3.2 billion in annual revenues and 65,000 jobs.[84] Among the established top 100 carriers which have "bitten the dust" of insolvency are Cooper-Jarrett, Eazor Express, Gordon Transport, Hemingway Transport, Johnson Motor Lines, Jones Motor Co., Motor Freight Express, Spector-Red Ball, T.I.M.E.-D.C., and Wilson Freight Co.[85]

De facto deregulation of the motor carrier industry began with the liberalized approach of the Interstate Commerce Commission in 1977 and 1978, when the ICC began issuing operating authority more broadly defined, from a commodity and territorial perspective, than ever before. The nation's economic recession did not begin until 1979, yet every leading economic indicator shows that the industry has progressively suffered virtually every year since 1977. For example, return on equity for motor carriers was cut in half from 15.27% in 1977 to 7.51% in 1981. For the first nine months of 1982, it was merely 3.88%.

In contrast, the return on equity for all manufacturers was 14.5% in 1977, rose to 16.45% in 1978, and fell to 13.54% in 1981—a much less steep dive than that experienced by the motor carrier industry.[86] The motor carrier industry today enjoys the lowest profit margin of all major American industries, with the exception of iron and steel.[87] The operating ratio of motor carriers (defined as total carrier operating expenses divided by gross freight revenues) grew from 94.76% in 1977 to 98.29% in 1982.[88] Carrier debt has risen significantly during this period. The debt to equity ratio rose steadily until 1981, from 55% in 1977 to 77% in 1980.[89] Interest payments as a percentage of carrier income grew from 15% in 1977 to 70% for the first nine months of 1982.[90] Curiously, these trends parallel the issuance of operating authority by the ICC. In 1977, 16,606 common carriers held certificates of public convenience and necessity; by 1982, 24,037 carriers had been issued operating authority.[91] The year 1982 has been described as the

worst year in history for the I.C.C. regulated motor carriers. The previous low point was in 1960 when the industry achieved an operating ratio of 97.48—approximately one point *better* than at present—and a profit margin of 0.83 percent—60% better than at present.[92]

The ICC reported that during 1982, net income for the nation's top 100 motor carriers fell to $64.3 million, and the rate of return on shareholder's equity fell to a paltry 2.9%.[93]

By 1982 net carrier income had fallen 42% since the promulgation of the Motor Carrier Act of 1980.[94] The *Atlanta Constitution* noted that the nation's "$48 billion regulated trucking industry is in the midst of a major shakeout, the dimensions of which are unprecedented, and thus, unpredictable."[95] The *Wall Street Journal* reported that "a bankruptcy epidemic is sweeping American business, and there is no letup in sight. . . . Transportation deregulation is contributing mightily to the failure rate."[96] *Forbes* characterized the contemporary economic demise in transportation as a "cruel restructuring."[97]

As was noted in *Dun's Business Review*:

After nearly two years of deregulation under the 1980 Motor Carrier Act, the trucking industry is in turmoil. Following the pattern set by the airlines, competition among truckers has intensified to an unprecedented degree, new carriers have been entering the business at a record rate, and fierce price wars have erupted. Heavy losses have already forced a number of trucking firms into bankruptcy—the beginning of what is expected to be a severe industry shakeout.[98]

Why is the industry unhealthy? Proponents of deregulation point to poor management, rising fuel prices, and the recession, arguing that deregulation did not contribute appreciably to the industry crisis.[99] Melvin Brenner, a former vice-president for TWA and American Airlines, has responded to these allegations as follows:

1. The slide of airline earnings started at the very time that deregulation became a fact (*i.e.*, 4th quarter of 1978), and that preceded by many months the jump in fuel prices and the recession.
2. This industry previously experienced the impact of a steep jump in fuel prices plus a recession in the mid–1970's, following the Arab oil embargo. But there was

not then the special element of deregulation, and the airlines came through with only a brief, limited financial setback.

3. Granting that Braniff's problem can partly be blamed on its own intemperate over-expansion, the same charge cannot be leveled at the many other airlines which are also in deep financial trouble.

Airline economics have much in common with the traditional "public utility," for which it has long been recognized that the public is best served with some containment of normal marketplace forces. That is why regulation was adopted in the first place. That is why every other country in the world still regulates its air transport system.[100]

If indeed, high fuel prices and the recession were principal causes of the industry's woes, then certainly the economic upswing and the degeneration of OPEC of the mid–1980s would save the day.[101] A 10% reduction in the price of aviation fuel saves the industry a hefty $1 billion.[102] But one suspects that this is only part of the story.

The industry's principal problem is excessive rate wars.[103] Deregulation of entry brought a host of new entrants to many heretofore healthy markets.[104] Between 1980 and 1983, 49,726 new certificates for motor carrier operating authority had been granted by the ICC; this included certification of 13,806 new carriers.[105] Similarly, more than 30 new air carriers have entered the airline industry.[106] Since transportation is an industry inherently vulnerable to overcapacity (for an empty seat or a partially filled trailer is an instantly perishable commodity), unconstrained entry must necessarily lead to distress-sale pricing in those markets in which competition is excessive.[107] Thus, motor carriers filed more than 115,000 independent rate actions with the ICC during 1981, and more than 180,000 during 1982.[108] The proliferation of discount airline fares has undoubtedly driven many travel agents to seek psychiatric assistance.

Declining Safety

Serious questions arise as to whether an unhealthy industry can be a safe industry.[109] One of the dangers of poor or nonexistent profits for an industry such as transportation is the natural tendency of management to curtail costs; among those which can be significantly diminished are maintenance costs, including mechanic's wages, spare or replacement parts, and idle vehicle time lost during inspection and maintenance.[110] Unsatisfactory profits in the rail industry led it to defer maintenance on equipment and trackage, leading in turn to a repeated series of derailments, often causing loss of human life.[111] One of the nation's major air carriers was repeatedly cited by the Federal Aviation Administration (FAA) for its safety violations prior to its bankruptcy.[112]

Twenty-six percent of the nation's airline fleet is already obsolete, and there will be a major need to reequip.[113] The cost of a moderate-size jet is

$20 million.[114] Without investor confidence, the airlines cannot finance the aircraft they need.[115] Although many existing aircraft are obsolete and should be replaced, since the enactment of the Airline Deregulation Act of 1978, cancellations for newly ordered aircraft have grown more than 300%.[116] Professor Frederick Thayer of the University of Pittsburgh reminds us that "safety always has suffered when airlines were largely unregulated."[117] Indeed, he notes that "deregulation is both inefficient and dangerous."[118] It "threatens to give us the worst of all worlds, a combination of many exorbitant fares (to cover empty seats) and a decline in safety."[119]

Pricing Discrimination

Prior to deregulation, there was some measure of cross-subsidization within the transportation industry. While carriers were allowed to serve specified lucrative routes, they were also required to serve geographically related, less lucrative or marginal markets as well. Carriers were expected to internally cross-subsidize losses or meager profits in their small community service with their healthier earnings in lucrative markets, and to provide just and reasonable rates to both. Deregulation was designed to end such cross-subsidization.

Actually, cross-subsidization seems merely to have been reversed in direction, rather than eliminated. Today, carriers extract higher rates from small communities to cross-subsidize the losses they are suffering as a result of the intense competitive battles they are waging for market dominance between larger communities.[120] Radically intensified entry, coupled with effectively deregulated ratemaking have made it possible for carriers to charge predatory rates in competitive markets (or to large shippers) and cross-subsidize such losses with excessive, discriminatory rates in oligopoly markets (or to small shippers).

While prices have become lower for large shippers or in densely traveled corridors, prices have risen substantially in less competitive markets.[121] As an example, in 1982 transcontinental air fares fell to $99, one way.[122] You may remember that World Airways begged the Civil Aeronautics Board to put an end to predatory pricing in that market.[123] World argued that its $142 fare was not compensatory, even though it was among the most cost-effective carriers in the industry.[124] To World's pleas, the CAB turned a deaf ear.

Although a one-way transcontinental air passenger ticket cost $99 in 1982, a flight between Washington and Omaha cost $287. Flights between Seattle and Orlando cost $326 round-trip while round-trip transportation between Seattle and Phoenix cost $437.[125] US Air charged its passengers $24 more between Buffalo and Albany than if they remained on the same plane and flew the 100 additional miles to Boston; the carrier was free to impose a premium rate between Buffalo and Albany because it had no competition in that market.[126]

In 1982, it cost $77 to fly between New York and Miami, but $168 to fly 500 fewer miles, between New York and Myrtle Beach, South Carolina.[127] TWA charged $201, or 29¢ a mile, between Peoria and Wichita; American charged $255, or 23¢ a mile, between Lubbock and Dayton. Compare these rates with those charged in competitive markets, such as the $90 charged by American, or 10¢ a mile, between Chicago and Dallas, or the TWA rates of $129, or 6¢ a mile, between Chicago and San Francisco.[128] After deregulation, air passenger fares between points in California doubled, on average, by 1983.[129] Air fares had increased 116.6% in small and medium sized communities by 1983, while average U.S. fares increased only 48% during the same period.[130] This "twilight world of airline economics" is beginning to be described by consumers as "outrageous," "unfair," "chaotic," and "nightmarish."[131]

In the absence of regulation, less competition almost always means higher fares. When Sir Freddie Laker's airline went bankrupt, transatlantic fares were increased sharply by the surviving carriers.[132] When Braniff went bankrupt, American and Delta raised fares dramatically in markets radiating from Dallas (Braniff's former hub). When Continental abandoned and TWA reduced service in the Chicago-Los Angeles market, United and American raised fares sharply.[133] Hence, whatever benefit some communities now enjoy in terms of air fare bargains may "disappear once competition is extinguished."[134]

The business traveler pays several times the rate of the vacation traveler seated next to him, and both enjoy less leg room.[135] Flights are cancelled or chronically overbooked, schedules are changed, and routes are obliterated without notice.[136]

Motor carrier competition for the traffic of large shippers or densely traveled markets has created a phenomenon which *Distribution* magazine labels "the Great Trucking Wars."[137] Regional discounting and large shipper discounting has become very pronounced in the trucking industry.[138]

Service Deterioration

Service to small communities has deteriorated significantly. During the first year of deregulation, 260 cities lost air service.[139] During the first two years of deregulation, 40% of our nation's airports lost service.[140] Two hundred communities lost 50% or more of the seats they previously enjoyed.[141] Over 100 communities lost all their scheduled service in just the first two years of deregulation; it had taken 10 years for a comparable number of communities to lose such service prior to deregulation.[142] Service in less-populated states has eroded demonstrably since deregulation.[143] Much of the air service which remains for small communities is provided at taxpayer expense;[144] the federal government paid $113 million in air passenger subsidies during fiscal year 1981.[145] Curiously, no such subsidies will be paid to ensure that small communities receive a reasonable level of motor carrier service at nondiscriminatory rates, even though 65% of America's communities are completely dependent upon motor carriage for freight transportation.[146] Further, scheduled air carriers have frequently been replaced by commuter carriers. Recent statistics indicate that a passenger stands a 300% greater chance of losing his life on a commuter carrier.[147]

A similar result is occurring in the motor carrier industry. The *Wall Street Journal* reported that intrastate deregulation in Florida cost many small communities their scheduled bus service.[148] Since November 1982, one of the nation's largest bus companies has petitioned 43 states for permission to eliminate service to more than 1,300 points;[149] one of its senior executives acknowledged that deregulation had enabled it "to cut out 90–95% of our small towns."[150]

Erosion of Carrier Liability

After deregulation was inaugurated, many air carriers sharply limited their liability for loss and damage. Such unilaterally imposed limitations have been quite imaginative. Prior to airline deregulation, shippers uniformly had nine months and nine days to file a loss or damage claim. By 1983, the industry had imposed at least four different time limits, some as short as 120 days, depending upon the carrier employed. Moreover, two air carriers even insisted on the filing of a "notice of intent" to file a claim, one within 15 days and the other within 30. Before deregulation was inaugurated, shippers had two years in which to file a suit; two air carriers have now cut this "statute of limitations" in half. Prior to deregulation, shippers had two years in which to file overcharge claims; today there are at least five different time limits, one as short as 180 days.[151] Similarly, the time limits for bringing suit on an overcharge claim have been reduced by some carriers to as little as 180 days, in contrast to the pre-deregulation rule of two years and six months from disallowance.[152]

One year before deregulation the CAB concluded an exhaustive investigation in which it determined that liability limits on domestic air transportation were unconscionable and archaic, and should therefore be raised from 50¢ per pound to the standard established by the Warsaw Convention of $9.07 per pound.[153] But with the promulgation of the Air Cargo Deregulation Act of 1977, air carriers were freed from these requirements. Eleven carriers soon reduced their liability limits to 50¢ per pound for the entire shipment. Fourteen took a step further by limiting the 50¢ to the weight of the package lost or damaged.[154] Prior to airline deregulation, excess value charges were limited to 10–15¢ per $100 of excess value declared; since deregulation, 29 carriers have increased these charges to 40¢

per $100. If you combine the new 50¢ per pound ceiling on liability with the increase of excess valuation to 40¢ per $100, the aggregate net result is a 3,900% increase.[155] Unsophisticated shippers are ordinarily unaware that such provisions have been unilaterally inserted by carriers in their bills of lading until they are faced with a lost or damaged shipment. They tend instead to select a carrier on the basis of price and service, at least until they are faced with a catastrophic loss.

The Railroading of America

Widespread marketplace abuses by the railroads served as the initial catalyst for the introduction of economic regulation of transportation in the United States in the late 19th century.[156] Up to now, this chapter has been somewhat silent as to the deleterious impacts of deregulation with respect to the railroad industry and the shippers it serves. Because the experience of rail carriers has been significantly different than those of air and motor carriers, the author has chosen to treat them separately.

Of course, all modes of transportation share a common economic characteristic—they involve the movement of passengers and commodities between designated points. But of the several modes discussed, rail transportation more closely satisfies the definition of a natural monopoly, at least for certain types of commodities and geographic regions.[157] Certainly, there is some competition between the motor and rail modes with respect to truckload, boxcar, and trailer-on-flatcar long-haul service. And, where time is a factor, some competition exists between air and motor carriage for less-than-truckload traffic. But for large shipments of bulk commodities, rail carriers enjoy a virtual monopoly.

Thus, the price of rail transportation would have to be exceptionally high before Wyoming coal shippers would find it feasible to replace 100-car coal trains with a convoy of trucks having an equal capacity, not to mention the associated fuel consumption and highway repair costs. Similarly, the cost of rail carriage would have to be enormously high before Nebraska grain shippers would find it feasible to airlift their grain to market. And the price of rail movements would have to grow to astronomical proportions before such shippers would find it feasible to lay their own tracks and build their own railroads to compete with carriers determined to exact monopoly profits. Long before any of these things happened, consumers of coal (i.e., public utilities) would find it feasible to import coal from abroad (as some now do) and grain shippers would find the world market for their exports declining (as it may well be). Both impacts would further exacerbate our nation's balance of payments deficit.

Although deregulation has significantly increased air and motor carrier competition by flooding markets with new entrants and greatly increasing the territories they may serve and the commodities they may haul, it has had no such effect on railroads. Indeed, there is significantly more abandonment and merger activity than entry in rail transportation, further reducing the number of actors in the nation's rail oligopoly.[158] Professor William Thoms notes that "[r]egulatory freedom for railroads meant freedom to merge, freedom to abandon trackage, and freedom to change (usually raise) rates."[159]

After more than a decade of serious and comprehensive merger activity, by 1981 the nation was left with but seven major rail carriers, which together were responsible for 85% of revenue ton miles.[160] In the northeast, Conrail is the only major carrier, itself the result of a 1973 merger between the Penn Central and five smaller railroads.[161] (The Penn Central was the product of the 1968 merger between the Pennsylvania and New York Central.)[162] South of Conrail there are but two large remaining railroads—the CSX and the Norfolk Southern. The CSX is the product of the 1980 merger between the Chessie and the Family Lines.[163] (The Chessie resulted from the 1963 merger of the Chesapeake and Ohio, the B&O, and the Western Maryland; the Family Lines resulted from the 1971 merger of the L&N and the Seaboard Coast Line—the latter a product of the 1967 merger between the Seaboard Air Line and the Atlantic Coast Line.)[164] The CSX enjoyed net income of $367.7 million during 1981 on revenues of $5.4 billion.[165] The Norfolk Southern is the result of a 1981 merger between the Norfolk & Western and the Southern, whose combined earnings that year totaled $500 million on revenues of $3.59 billion.[166]

In the west, there are four large railroads, the Burlington Northern, the Tri-Pac (or PacRail), the Southern Pacific, and the Atchison, Topeka and Santa Fe. The Burlington Northern resulted from a 1980 merger between the BN and Frisco (the BN resulted from a 1970 merger between the Great Northern, the Northern Pacific, the Chicago, Burlington & Quincy, and the Spokane, Portland and Seattle).[167] Its 1981 earnings were $223 million on revenues of $3.9 billion. Today, it serves 25 states and two Canadian Provinces, from the Pacific Northwest to the Florida panhandle and from the prairies to the Gulf coast.[168] The Tri-Pac merger of 1982 brought together an even larger system with the merger of the Union Pacific, Western Pacific, and Missouri Pacific.[169] The Santa Fe and Southern Pacific also announced plans to merge to form the nation's third largest railroad. The merged holding companies will have combined assets exceeding $10 billion.[170]

As has been indicated, deregulation for railroads has in many instances enhanced the ability of rail carriers to raise their rates. However, Congress recognized that not all freight is competitive; in promulgating the Staggers Rail Act of 1980, it did not intend to subject captive shippers to the rigors of the marketplace.[171] Hence, jurisdiction over reasonableness of rates was left in the ICC under circumstances where market dominance is deemed to exist.[172] However, the ICC has significantly diluted its jurisdiction over market-dominant traffic by promulgating broad exemptions over TOFC/

COFC service,[173] boxcar service,[174] and export coal,[175] as well as by its philosophical flirtation with Ramsey Pricing.[176] Shippers of market-dominant traffic have become increasingly dissatisfied with the rail-rate decisions of the ICC. One group which appears to have been adversely affected by rate increases and jurisdiction limitation decisions are shippers of coal.[177] Specifically, coal shippers have alleged the following deleterious impacts of rail deregulation:

- Rapid increases in rates for hauling coal, including increases of nearly 15 percent in 1980 and 1981, increases that are far more than necessary to account for inflation.

- U.S.-produced coal is less competitive with other fuels in domestic markets, slowing the conversions from foreign oil to domestic coal.

- U.S.-produced coal is less competitive in international markets because of high rail rates, with foreign customers increasingly turning to other nations for their supplies.

- Many U.S. coal mines have been closed and there is high unemployment among coal miners. Nationally, 32 percent of miners were unemployed during the first quarter of 1982. Unemployment has ranged as high as 60 percent in southern West Virginia and western Pennsylvania, a situation due to a large extent to a general down turn in business, but also affected negatively by ICC rulings.

- Major coal-hauling railroads have become highly profitable and have been increasingly diverting their capital into other industries, such as real estate, other forms of transportation, and natural resources, a matter which indicates that railroad revenues are significantly in excess of amounts required to recover costs of providing railroad services, including a reasonable rate of return from captive traffic.[178]

At the risk of overgeneralizing, the net effect of railroad deregulation seems to be a more desirable economic environment from the perspective of most rail carriers, and a less desirable environment from the perspective of most captive rail shippers. Professor Friedlaender noted that this might well be a result of deregulation in her 1969 treatise on the subject:

To the extent that regulation prevents railroads from exploiting their potential monopoly position with respect to noncompetitive bulk commodities, deregulation should lead to increased rates and concomitant reductions in the incomes of the producers of these commodities. This would particularly affect the western farming and mining interests. Furthermore, insofar as rate competition would end the existing discriminatory pricing policies on which many past locational decisions have been based, additional producers would probably be hurt. The millers and small coal producers are especially vulnerable in this respect. Since the present blanket rate structure tends to discriminate in favor of rural and suburban areas, deregulation might also lead to rate increases in these areas.[179]

THE EARLY RESULTS OF DEREGULATION: A SUMMARY

The benefits of responsible economic regulation of transportation included the provision of an adequate level of service at a reasonable price to all communities and shippers, no matter how large or small. The industry enjoyed healthy competition without industry concentration.

Excessive entry coupled with the abdication of governmental oversight over predatory ratemaking and other unlawful practices (and the recession as well) created an economic environment in which a series of cutthroat rate wars was inevitable. *Newsweek* summarized the intense problems faced by the airline industry as follows:

Since the Carter Administration began to ease Federal restrictions on the troubled U.S. airline industry in 1977, numerous unprofitable routes have been abandoned. Service has deteriorated, and the airlines are frantically manipulating fares up and down to attract business and to satisfy shareholders nervous about their mounting financial losses. The desperation tactics make air travel more complicated and, since they defy reason, they have brought some big carriers dangerously near financial collapse.[180]

Thomas G. Plaskett, vice-president of American Airlines, described the 1981 economic environment in these terms: "Deregulation has encouraged the concentration of services on major, dense routes, and this has led to excessive, destructive competition and over-capacity.... We find it difficult to reconcile such destructive competition with the overall public interest."[181] Richard Ferris, chairman of the board of United Airlines, admitted that "restructuring an industry as large as ours means shakeouts, fallouts, irrational behavior, and a topsy-turvey marketplace."[182] His counterpart in Western Airlines, Neil Bergt, noted that "airlines are out there cutting each other's throats and bleeding to death."[183] Similarly, Eli Timoner, chairman of Air Florida, remarked that "it's like lemmings throwing themselves off a cliff. There's no logic to it at this point. It's unbusinesslike."[184] James Worsham, president of Douglas Aircraft Co., said "the airlines are on a kamikaze path."[185] He suggested that a blue-ribbon panel of airline executives be established to work closely with Congress to solve the industry's problems. One major daily newspaper summarized the problems of the deregulated airline industry as follows:

Airlines have less room for differentiation [than do department or grocery stores]. ... They tend to match each other in convenient departures. That leaves little to fight about except ticket prices, and so far they've been pricing themselves to destruction.

That has lowered many fares. But it has created a bewildering world where some passengers pay twice as much as a seatmate, and more for short haul routes than transcontinental flights. Service to many smaller cities is vanishing. The public has cause to join airline employees in hoping order returns to the chaotic skies.[186]

Although initial airline price competition generated additional price-sensitive travelers, lower rates for freight will not have the corresponding effect for carriers of commodities, for the freight transportation industry is relatively price inelastic.[187] Nor is an unhealthy transportation industry likely to be a safe industry, leading to unnecessary loss of equipment, commodities, and, unfortunately, human life. Furthermore, such intense competition is limited to high-density markets, creating inevitable price discrimination against small shippers and small communities. In oligopoly or monopoly transportation markets, rates have risen substantially. Undoubtedly, the incentives for locating industry in rural America will be diminished, while the incentives for locating in urban locations will be correspondingly increased. Urban America seems to be turning its back on the "outback."[188] Moreover, the ripple effect of discriminatory rates upon the American economy will constitute an additional contribution to the economies of scale that large industries already enjoy, thereby exacerbating an environment in which most American industries ultimately become highly concentrated, while smaller competitors struggle, fail, or are absorbed into the conglomerate giants. Thus, smaller industries will pay higher prices for transportation services while their larger competitors enjoy relatively lower shipping costs; consumer costs will likely reflect such discrimination.

The prolongation of contemporary rate wars will force even more carriers into bankruptcy or merger, ultimately leading to an economic environment in which there will likely be few effective competitors, particularly in those sectors of the industry (e.g., less-than-truckload transportation) where entry costs are relatively high.[189] Hence, the structure of the transportation industry will come to more closely resemble every other major, mature American industry. *Forbes* magazine predicted that, in the short term:

deregulation will bring a rash of new competition into the trucking business: competitors who will price-cut their way into the market and set off a wave of mergers that will transform trucking into a far more concentrated business than it is now. The short haul and regional truckers may well be squeezed out and the big national companies—outfits like Yellow Freight, Roadway Express, [and] Consolidated Freightways...will come to dominate the industry.... [L]ong-term deregulation of trucks and rails...[will] only lessen competition in trucking, encourage prices to rise and could further weaken the railroad industry.... If the aim of deregulation is to bring freight rates down, the result may be...to reduce rather than enhance competition.[190]

In the words of *Dun's Business Review*, we are witnessing a "severe industry shakeout." During the shakeout, many Americans employed by carriers, and many stockholders of or lenders to transportation businesses, will be expected to pay the price of the grand experiment in deregulation.[191] Many U.S. air and motor carriers will not survive the transition. The experience of deregulation in both Australia and Great Britain was that following a limited period of intensive competition and carrier bankruptcies, the less-than-truckload sectors of the motor carrier industry became oligopolistic in character.[192] Professor Garland Chow's study reveals that deregulation in Australia created an economic environment in which only four major motor carriers survived.[193] Many industry experts predict that the ultimate result of transportation deregulation in the United States will be sharply increased industry concentration (the *Washington Post* predicted that rail mergers will reduce the number of our nation's railroads to as few as three).[194] Horizontal integration may well result in the creation of enormous multimodal carriers. Pointing out that carriers such as CSX Corporation (itself the product of the 1980 merger between the Chessie and Seaboard Coast Line Railroads) have begun buying trucking companies, purchased natural gas pipelines, and expanded aircraft services operations, the *Wall Street Journal* predicted that "[o]ver the next few years, a handful of giant companies are expected to evolve, each offering global door-to-door service.[195] It went on to point out some of the dangers of such accentuated concentration:

Some observers fear that if a handful of multimodal companies come to dominate the transportation industry, a lack of competition would inflate freight rates.... [T]he newly powerful rail industry has shown that it is capable of running roughshod over potential competition, a circumstance that has some shippers and elected officials demanding that railroads, power be curbed. Ultimately, with fewer competitors, the United States will likely enjoy higher rates and poorer service than that which existed prior to deregulation.[196]

The airline industry, too, is likely to become more concentrated as deregulation progresses. "Experts say the shakeout may continue for another five or 10 years, with only three big carriers ultimately serving domestic routes and just one U.S. line carrying international travelers."[197]

Many are beginning to argue for the reintroduction of some moderate form of responsible economic regulation.[198] The president of one of our nation's largest air freight forwarding companies conceded "with great reluctance...that the task (of restoring the air transportation industry to economic balance) can best be accomplished through the reintroduction of moderate government regulation of route entry.... We can, by judicious reapplication of regulation, correct excesses that not debilitate us all so extensively."[199] Not only carriers are criticizing the grand experiment in deregulation. The executive director of the Shippers' National Freight Claims Council, describing deregulation as a "dismal failure," urges the reintroduction of responsible regulation, saying:

The obvious solution is to start anew with a sound regulatory policy, carefully administered by transportation-oriented experts instead of economists, and to reinstate air transportation as a public service requiring reasonable prices and service for all citizens and communities on a non-discriminatory basis.[200]

An airline labor leader asserted that "judging from the destructive impact on airline profits, the declining level of passenger safety and convenience, and the overwhelming burdens placed on airline employees, I can only conclude that deregulation has been a disaster."[201] Academicians are also beginning to join the ranks of those calling for responsible regulation of transportation.[202] Professor Jerold Muskin notes that:

Transportation, as a principal part of the community's physical distribution infrastructure is too important to leave to the uncertain (at best), or perverse (at worst), performance of the free market.... The argument that the unconstrained marketplace necessarily functions to produce improved results for our nation is simply wrong. It is a doctrinaire shibboleth. One need not look far for examples of market failures that must be cured by government intervention. Highway common carriers stripped of rules, responsibilities and rights, it is submitted, fit into this category.[203]

Similarly, Professor Frederick Thayer argues:

Free market mythology is so entrenched in the U.S. that neither liberals nor conservatives are yet disposed to admit that it is time to begin again. If ever there was a need for a national commission to develop a sensible regulatory system, and to link together the domestic, international, and even military aspects of air transportation, the need is now.[204]

The time has come to reexamine the grand experiment in the economic theory of deregulation, for it seems not to have fulfilled the promises of its proponents. The time has come to compare marketplace performance since deregulation with the strong parallels which existed prior to regulation, lest we repeat an unfortunate history—a history from which our forefathers learned that responsible economic regulation of transportation was and is essential in order to protect the public interest.

NOTES

1. *Economic Regulation of the Trucking Industry: Hearings before the Senate Comm. on Commerce, Science and Transportation*, 96th Cong., 1st Sess. 380 (statement of Sen. Edward Kennedy) [hereinafter *Senate Hearings*].

2. MOTOR CARRIER ACT OF 1980: REPORT OF THE HOUSE COMM. ON PUBLIC WORKS AND TRANSPORTATION, H.R. REP. NO. 96–1069, 96th Cong., 2d Sess. 5 (1980) [hereinafter HOUSE REPORT].

3. MOTOR CARRIER REFORM ACT OF 1980: REPORT OF THE SENATE

COMM. ON COMMERCE, SCIENCE AND TRANSPORTATION, S. REP. NO. 96–641, 96th Cong., 2d Sess. 85 (1980) [hereinafter SENATE REPORT]. The deregulation philosophy has been summarized as follows:

Let the small shipper, the small town, or the small consumer of goods—sink or swim . . . If the factory, city, town, community, part, or region, "can't hack it" in a society free of the government beast, that's only the way things should be—let it and them go under. Let the social and development consequences be what they may!

Id. at 80.

4. *Id.* at 94.

5. *Id.* at 96.

6. *Senate Hearings, supra* note 1, at 35 (testimony of A. Daniel O'Neal).

7. *Id.* at 46 (statement of A. Daniel O'Neal).

8. 49 U.S.C. § 1389 (1979).

9. *Deregulation Route Shifts Accelerate,* AV. WEEK & SPACE TECH. (Feb. 5, 1979) at 29.

10. *CIVIL AERONAUTICS BOARD, REPORT ON AIRLINE SERVICE: STATUS ON FEBRUARY 1, 1979* 43–50 (1979).

11. Application of America Airline, CAB Order 79–10–186 (1979), dissent at 6.

12. *See* Dempsey, *The Rise and Fall of the Civil Aeronautics Board—Opening Wide the Floodgates of Entry,* 11 TRANSP. L. J. 91, 182 n. 434 (1979).

13. HOUSE REPORT, *supra* note 2, at 6.

14. SENATE REPORT, *supra* note 3, at 100 (citations omitted). *See Senate Hearings, supra* note 1, at 109–115, 118–119.

15. *Senate Hearings, supra* note 1, at 339.

16. Freeman and Gerson, *Motor Carrier Operating Rights Proceedings—How Do I Lose Thee?* 11 TRANSP. L. J. 13, 15 n. 3 (1979).

17. *See supra* note 14 (accompanying text).

18. Dempsey, *Erosion of the Regulatory Process in Transportation—The Winds of Change,* 47 ICC PRAC. J. 303, 308 (1980).

19. *See* 49 U.S.C. § 10922 (b) (1) (A) (1980); *Senate Hearings, supra* note 1, at 40 (testimony of A. Daniel O'Neal).

20. No. MC–2860 (Sub No. 148), National Freight, Inc. (Jan. 6, 1977); No. MC–113267 (Sub No. 353), Central and Southern Truck Lines, Inc. (Mar. 30, 1978). DOT also participated vicariously in a pending fitness investigation involving Transamerican Freight Lines, Inc.

21. *See* HOUSE REPORT, *supra* note 2, at 6.

22. *See Senate Hearings, supra* note 1, at 372 (testimony of Sen. Edward Kennedy).

23. Evans, *Deregulation of Airlines Was Hailed as Blessing, Later Cursed as Harmful,* DENVER POST, June 22, 1980, at 41, col. 1.

24. Prior to 1980, the rate of return for the railroad industry had not exceeded 1.5% during the last four years, and had exceeded 4% in the last 20. Note, *Proposed Regulatory Reform in the Area of Railroad Abandonment,* 11 TRANSP. L. J. 213 (1979).

25. *See e.g.,* Chicago & North Western Transportation Company Abandonment, 354 I.C.C. 735 (1978); Seaboard Coast Line Railroad Company—Abandonment between Arcadia and Port Boca Grande, 360 I.C.C. 257 (1979).

26. Gonzales, *Airline Safety, a Special Report*, PLAYBOY (July 1980) 140, 209.

27. *Id.*

28. Dempsey, *supra* note 12, at 158–71.

29. *See Senate Hearings, supra* note 1, at 358 (testimony of Sen. Donald Riegle), 359, 374–75 (testimony of Sen. Edward Kennedy).

30. *Id.* at 425 (testimony of Rep. Milliceut Fenwick).

31. Liberty Trucking Co., Extension—General Commodities, 130 M.C.C. 243 (1978), 131 M.C.C. 573 (1979).

32. P. C. White Truck Line, v. I.C.C., 551 F 2d. 1326 (D.C. Cir. 1977).

33. Donlan, *Over the Long Haul Deregulation Will Open Up New Opportunities for Truckers*, BARRON'S (June 23, 1980), at 11, col. 1–2.

34. *Id.* at 27. col. 1.

35. *Id.*

36. *See id.*, at 11, col. 1. *See Senate Hearings, supra* note 1, at 53 (statement of A. Daniel O'Neal).

37. *Senate Hearings, supra* note 1, at 59 (statement of A. Daniel O'Neal).

38. *Senate Hearings, supra* note 1, at 103 (statement of Bennett Whitlock).

39. Chow, *Economic Regulation of Motor Freight in Foreign Countries*, 47 ICC PRAC. J. 44, 45 (1979).

40. *Id. Senate Hearings, supra* note 1, at 118 (testimony of Bartley M. O'Hara).

41. Dempsey, *supra* note 12, at 91, 181.

42. *Id.* at 182.

43. *See* Adequacy of Railroad Revenue, 362 I.C.C. 794 (1980).

44. *See* e.g., Burlington Northern, Inc.—Control and Merger St. Louis—San Francisco Railway Company, 360 I.C.C. 783 (1980); Kansas City Terminal Railway Company—Directed to Take Over—Chicago, Rock Island & Pacific Railroad Company, Debtor, 360 I.C.C. 718 (1980); Various Railroads—Directed Service—Chicago, Rock Island & Pacific Railroad Company, Debtor, 363 I.C.C. 82 (1980); St. Louis Southwestern Railway Company—Temporary Authority—Chicago, Rock Island & Pacific Railroad Company, Debtor, 360 I.C.C. 760 (1980); Norfolk and Western Railroad Company and Baltimore and Ohio Railroad Company—Control—Detroit, Toledo and Ironton Railroad Company, 360 I.C.C. 122 (1980), 360 I.C.C. 498 (1979); Missouri Pacific Railroad Company—Merger—Missouri Pacific Railroad Company et al., 360 I.C.C. 202 (1979); Acquisition Procedures for Lines of Railroads in Reorganization, 360 I.C.C. 623 (1980).

45. Note, *Proposed Regulatory Reform in the Area of Railroad Abandonment*, 11 TRANSP. L. J. 213 (1979).

46. *See SENATE REPORT, supra* note 3, at 104.

47. Letter from William J. Augello to Jimmy Carter (April 2, 1979).

48. Dempsey, *supra* note 12, at 91, 171–73.

49. HOUSE REPORT, *supra* note 2, at 8.

50. *Senate Hearings, supra* note 1, at 4 (testimony of Sen. Harrison Schmitt).

51. So too, Washington, D.C., has a small manufacturing base and imports a plethora of commodities while exporting little (except, perhaps, red tape and hot air).

52. *Senate Hearings, supra* note 1, at 139 (statement of Henry M. Karel).

53. CAB chairman Marvin Cohen has stated: "From 1970 to 1976, years of tight airline regulation, load factors averaged 52.8 percent. In 1978, the first year

of real pricing freedom, load factors jumped to 61.7 percent. In the first nine months of this year, the domestic trunk load factor was 65.1 percent." Cohen, *Airline Deregulation Is Working*, ROCKY MOUNTAIN NEWS, Jan. 30, 1980, at 39.

54. Between 1976 and 1979, numbers of applications filed increased 234% from 5,968 to 19,961. During the same period, the grant rate increased from 86% to 98.4%. King, *Deregulation by ICC Appears to Hold Down Truck-Rates Inflation*, WALL ST. J., May 9, 1980, at 1, col. 1.

55. For example, Yellow Freight System lost 13.7% of its truckload traffic last year; McLean Trucking lost 26% in the first quarter of the year. *Id.* at 28, col. 1.

56. Evans, *Deregulation of Airlines Was Hailed as Blessing, Later Cursed as Harmful*, DENVER POST, June 22, 1980, at 41, col. 1.

57. *Id.*

58. *Senate Hearings, supra* note 1, at 56 (statement of A. Daniel O'Neal).

59. Dempsey, *The Experience of Deregulation: Erosion of the Common Carrier System*, 13 TRANSP. L. INST. 121, 172–76 (1981).

60. Evans, *Deregulation of Airlines Was Hailed as Blessing, Later Cursed as Harmful*, DENVER POST, June 22, 1980, at 41.

61. *Airlines*, FORBES (Jan. 5, 1981) at 144. The five largest air carriers lost almost $790 million during 1981. Holsendolph, *Low-Cost Airline Now Seeks Fare Curb It Once Opposed*, N.Y. TIMES, Mar. 10, 1982, at 1.

62. *See Airlines Lose $241 Million*, DENVER POST, Apr. 28, 1983. Domestic airline industry losses during this period were as follows:

In 1980 the airline industry suffered its most severe losses in the history of domestic aviation— an astonishing $280 million. The following year domestic carriers surpassed that record by more than 60%, with losses of $454.8 million. In 1982 domestic airline losses were an astounding $733.4 million.

Dempsey, *Affordability, Safety of Airlines May Suffer*, L.A. TIMES, Oct. 11, 1983, at 7.

63. *More Riders, Less Money for US Airlines in 1982*, J. OF COMMERCE, June 17, 1983, at A2.

64. *Frontier Shows Wounds from Cutthroat Fares*, DENVER POST, Apr. 29, 1983. *Airline Profits Are Still on Standby*, BUS. WEEK (May 16, 1983), at 35. Although the airline industry enjoyed a 13.2% gain in traffic in March, the increase had little positive impact on profitability due to the large number of discount fares being offered. As discounts are dropped, industry revenues may grow. Salpukas, *Traffic is Building at Airlines*, N.Y. TIMES, July 7, 1983, at D4. However, some analysts assert the contrary. Alfred Norling, an analyst with Kidder, Peabody, recently said:

I don't see the period of intensive competition lessening. . . . The airline industry will probably suffer from disequilibrium for some time, and I see a turbulent, chaotic, unstable situation affecting the strong carriers as well as the weak ones. To project the thesis of a stable industry, one would have to assume the lessening of competition. And that has to come about by attrition—bankruptcy.

Martindale, *The Economy Gets an OK for Takeoff*, OAG FREQUENT FLYER (July 1983), at 38, 39.

65. *Airlines Move to Straighten Out Their Fares*, U.S. NEWS & WORLD REP.

(May 16, 1983) at 49. Each upward or downward movement of a point in the prime rate represents $30 million to the industry. *See* Andrews, *Stop the Air War—We Want to Get Off*, WASHINGTON POST, Apr. 16, 1983, at A26. The Civil Aeronautics Board reported that for the year ending September 30, 1982, our nation's airlines enjoyed a net aggregate loss, after nonrecurring items, of $827 million. Genoese, *The Damage Done by Airline Deregulation*, N.Y. TIMES, Nov. 3, 1983, at A30.

66. *On a Wing and a Prospectus*, BUS. WEEK (Feb. 14, 1983), at 124. Some carriers exceed this industry average significantly. For example, Eastern Airlines lost almost $160 million between 1979 and 1982, and its debt has grown to 83% of total capitalization. *Why Eastern Is on a Short String*, BUS. WEEK (Apr. 11, 1983), at 116.

"Suicide fare wars have bled the industry to a point at which Standard & Poor's now rates airlines as the riskiest investment category in the nation." Duffy, *Deregulation Affects Safety*, AIRPORT PRESS, Aug. 1983, at 21. Similarly, Frederick W. Bradley, senior vice president of Citibank, expressed these concerns:

The business risk of operating an airline and, therefore, financing an airline, has increased with the U.S. industry's deregulation.... Assuming an economic recovery with modest growth in air traffic, it still appears that the combination of excess capacity and the deregulatory environment that encourages new entrants and breeds price competition will inhibit the ability of some airlines to operate profitably.

Conference Foresees Airline Struggles, AV. WEEK & SPACE TECH. (Sept. 26, 1983) at 44. Edmond S. Greenslet, vice-president of Merrill Lynch, Pierce, Fenner & Smith, agreed with Bradley, anticipating that the airline industry will remain unstable for years.

67. *The Worst Year for U.S. Airlines*, TIME (Feb. 22, 1982) at 46; *The Last Roundup*, FORBES (June 7, 1982) at 62; *El Al's Anguish*, TIME (Nov. 8, 1982) at 59. Recently, Laker's liquidators instituted a $1 billion antitrust suit against eight airlines alleging that their predatory practices contributed significantly to Laker's demise. *See Did They Gang Up on Laker?* NEWSWEEK (Aug. 1, 1983) at 54.

68. Gibney, *Continuing Airline Losses Predicted*, DENVER POST, June 21, 1982, at 3C, Col. 1; *See* Frank, *Airlines*, FORBES (Jan. 4, 1982) at 197–98; *The U.S. Air-Fare Dogfight*, NEWSWEEK (Apr. 19, 1982) at 69; *World Airways Loss Quadrupled in Quarter to $13.3 Million*, WALL ST. J., May 24, 1982. Most industry analysts appear to agree that under deregulation the nation will eventually have fewer major airlines. *See* Mayer, *Only the Strongest Airlines Will Survive*, ROCKY MOUNTAIN NEWS, Oct. 31, 1983, at 60; Nordlinger, *The Turbulent Skies of Airline Deregulation*, DETROIT FREE PRESS, Oct. 10, 1983, at F–1.

69. *A Gift from the Airlines*, NEWSWEEK (Dec. 13, 1982) at 108. To some extent, these losses have been offset by sales of its New York headquarters building ($294 million) and its Intercontinental Hotel Chain ($368 million). *The Worst Year for U.S. Airlines*, TIME (Feb. 22, 1982) at 46; Cuff, *Major U.S. Airlines Buffeted by Fierce Headwinds*, DENVER POST, May 15, 1982, at 11A. During 1982 Pan American lost $485 million—a new U.S. aviation record. The carrier's immediate cash needs were satisfied by two public offerings of secured and unsecured notes— debentures and warrants which totaled $250 million. *Pan Am Chief Sees Bluer Skies*, NEWSDAY, May 11, 1983, at 37.

70. *Airline Woes Catch Up with Delta*, BUS. WEEK (Nov. 8, 1982) at 131. Delta had just suffered its first full-year deficit in 36 years. For the fiscal year ending June 30, 1983, its losses totaled $86.7 million. *Delta Air Posts 4th-Period Loss of $25.5 Million*, WALL ST. J., July 29, 1983, at 4.

71. Davis, *The Great Airline Disaster*, DENVER POST, Feb. 7, 1982, at 1D.

72. *Braniff: First to Fall?*, DENVER POST, June 14, 1982, at 26A.

73. *The Worst Year for U.S. Airlines*, TIME (Feb. 22, 1982) at 46.

74. *Can Lockheed Fly on Defense Alone?* BUS. WEEK (Dec. 21, 1981) at 42. Declining sales have also led to the cancellation of DC–10 production. *See* Sing, *McDonnell Douglas Ends Production of DC 10 Jets*, WASH. POST, Aug. 4, 1983, at C5.

75. Gibney, *Continuing Airline Losses Predicted*, DENVER POST, June 21, 1982, at 3C, col. 1. Braniff's chief executive officer, Howard Putnam, noted:

I think within five to seven years you will have no more than five [out of a current eleven] trunk airlines. Then you will have a whole bunch of Southwest Airlines-type carriers that start out from scratch and work to keep costs in line. As decreed by the law of the jungle, only the strong will survive.

Martindale, *The Economy Gets an OK for Takeoff*, OAG FREQUENT FLYER (July 1983) at 38, 39.

76. Rowen, *Airlines: Competing to the Death*, WASH. POST, Nov. 11, 1982.

77. Holsendolph, *Act to Help Jobless in Industry*, DENVER POST, May 18, 1982, at F1.

78. Burkhardt, *Airlines, Unions Split on Decontrol Results*, J. OF COMMERCE, June 16, 1983, at A2. During the first 18 months of airline deregulation almost 22,000 employees lost their jobs. CIVIL AERONAUTICS BOARD, AIRLINE EMPLOYMENT SYSTEM OPERATIONS OF MAJORS AND SHORT HAUL NATIONALS, 1978–1981 (1981).

79. Davis, *The Great Airline Disaster*, DENVER POST, Feb. 7, 1982, at D1.

80. Rowen, *Airline Deregulation Comes Back to Haunt*, WASH POST, Mar. 14, 1982, at G4, col. 4.

81. American Trucking Ass'n., TRUCKLINE (Dec. 15, 1982).

82. Maynard, *Trucks Losing Fiscal Race*, ATLANTA CONSTITUTION, Nov. 20, 1981.

83. *The High Toll of Quitting the Trucking Business*, NEWSWEEK (Nov. 23, 1982), at 53. Indeed, more carriers would go bankrupt if not for the inhibitions of poorly conceived ERISA legislation.

84. American Trucking Ass'n. TRUCKLINE (Dec. 15, 1982); Lewis, *Edited Account of Enforcement Conference Released by ICC*, TRAFFIC WORLD (Dec. 27, 1982) at 13. Motor carriers accounting for 16% of industry revenues have gone bankrupt since deregulation was inaugurated. Dr. Irwin H. Silberman has predicted that carriers accounting for another 28% of revenues are also candidates for bankruptcy. Statement of Irwin H. Silberman before the Subcommittee on Surface Transportation of the Senate Committee on Commerce, Science and Transportation, Sept. 21, 1982. In 1976, the revenue market share of the 10 largest motor carriers was 37.9%. As deregulation was intensified, that percentage steadily grew, so that by 1982 these carriers accounted for 48.5% of industry revenues. *Id.*

85. R. Roth, Economic and Financial Conditions of the Regulated Motor Carrier

Industry (unpublished monograph, 1983) at 5. Economist Irwin H. Silberman explained the causes of the shakeout: "The precarious position of the industry has developed primarily as a consequence of the interaction of deregulatory pressures (both administrative and regulatory) with the effects of the current severe economic downturn." REGULAR COMMON CARRIER CONFERENCE, TRUCKING DEREGULATION/ECONOMIC RECESSION: THE FACTS! 2 (1983).

Two large carriers were added to these impressive obituaries. Maislin Transport (with annual revenues of some $200 million) and IML Motor Freight (with revenues of $100 million) have entered Chapter 11 proceedings. One of the major leaders of independent owner-operators has predicted that an additional 25–50% of such carriers will likely go bankrupt if the Surface Transportation Act of 1982 is modified. Siegel, *ICC Paves Road to Ruin for Truckers*, WALL ST. J., Oct. 6, 1983, at 26. Additionally, he has suggested that we "get rid of those 'free market freaks' that remain at the ICC and get back to responsible regulation." *Id.*

86. R. Roth, Economic and Financial Conditions of the Regulated Motor Carrier Industry, and 1982 Supplement (unpublished monograph, 1983) at 4.

87. *Id.* at 2.

88. *Id.* at 3–4.

89. In 1981, the carriers enjoyed a one-time tax write-off that reduced the ratio to 60%. *Id.* at 6.

90. *Id.* at 6.

91. *Id.* at 9.

92. *Id.* at 3.

93. Interstate Commerce Comm'n, Press Release (Apr. 11, 1983).

94. Rosenak, *Address before the Motor Carrier Lawyers Ass'n* (Jan. 8, 1983).

95. Maynard, *Trucks Losing Fiscal Race*, ATLANTA CONSTITUTION, Nov. 20, 1981.

96. Petzinger, Jr., *Business Failures Hit Post-Depression High, Tide Expected to Swell*, WALL ST. J., May 24, 1982.

97. Frank, *Airlines*, FORBES (Jan. 4, 1982) at 198.

98. The combination of less tonnage, increased hauling capacity, and lower prices has affected profits. Total net income for the 98 Class I carriers fell from $311.6 million in 1979 to $284.2 million in 1980. Murray, *Turmoil in Trucking*, DUN'S BUS. REV. (May 1982) at 75.

99. Shifrin, *Adams, Kahn Clash on Hill on Air Policy*, WASHINGTON POST, Dec. 10, 1981, at D16; Karr, *Airline Deregulation after Braniff's Fall*, WALL ST. J., June 4, 1982. The Civil Aeronautics Board has argued that the principal causes of growing unemployment in the airline industry are (a) the general state of the economy, (b) fuel price increases, (c) interest expenditure increases, (d) airline income decreases, (e) fleet reequipping with more fuel efficient and larger aircraft, (f) the grounding of DC–10s, and (g) the Professional Air Traffic Controllers Organization strike in 1981. *CAB Plans Employee Reduction Hearings*, AV. WEEK & SPACE TECH. (May 9, 1983) at 33.

100. Brenner, *Airline Deregulation Is Clipping Carrier's Wings*, WALL ST. J., May 24, 1982. Professor Frederick Thayer summarized some of the problems of airline deregulation in these terms:

The advocates of deregulation, including most of the major media, pointed to discount fares as evidence of success, resolutely ignoring financial losses and extremely high fares on nonvacation routes. They even refused to acknowledge the new form of cross-subsidy; to some extent, business travelers were covering the costs of tourist travelers, a cross-subsidy less justifiable than any other.... The basic problem remains as simple as ever. The airlines, whatever their initial image as luxury travel for the pampered rich, are as much a public utility as a city bus company, and must be rearranged into a coordinated system which somehow abolishes head-to-head competition. Americans, unfortunately, are very slow to learn.

Thayer, *Airline Regulation: The Case for a Public Utility Approach*, 18 LOGISTICS & TRANSP. REV. 211, 230 (1972) [hereinafter Thayer].

Proponents of deregulation often blame the failures of deregulation on the recession and fuel prices. While this reasoning seems plausible on the surface, the facts tell a much different story.

Passenger traffic was actually *up* in 1982, the most severe year of the recession. But during 1982 the airline industry lost nearly $1 billion.

According to Daniel May, president and CEO of Republic Airlines, revenue passenger miles for the 12-month period preceding October 1982 were 16% higher than the 12-month period preceding the passage of the Deregulation Act. Clearly, the recession is not the only culprit.

The airline industry suffered from the fuel price increases following the Iranian revolution and the Iran-Iraq war. But over the two year period from May 1981 to April 1983, the price of fuel dropped 17.2 cents, saving the industry $1.51 billion.

Unfortunately, those savings did not show up on the balance sheets of the embattled airlines; they were all sunk into debilitating fare wars.

A brief look at history shows that from 1973 to 1976, a similar four-year period with an oil price shock and a major recession, the airline industry had net income of more than $1 billion for the four years.

Duffy, *Deregulation 5 Years Later*, OAG FREQUENT FLYER (Oct. 1983) at 54, 56.

101. *See The Humbling of OPEC*, TIME (Feb. 7, 1983) at 42.

102. *Oil Price War*, U.S. NEWS& WORLD REP. (March 7, 1983) at 24; *Keeping 'Em Up Is Costing Less*, OAG FREQUENT FLYER (July 1983) at 29.

103. *See Deregulation Breeds an East Coast Air War*, BUS. WEEK (Jan. 26, 1981) at 30; *The Worst Year for U.S. Airlines*, TIME (Feb. 22, 1982) at 46. Julius Maldutis, vice-president of Salomon Brothers, predicted that airline rates wars would continue to plague the industry for three reasons: new airlines' start-up costs were two-thirds lower than those of established carriers; although many new aircraft were delivered during 1983, old planes were generally not being retired; and airline travel agents had been deregulated. *Bankers Claim Air Fare Wars Will Continue*, JOURNAL OF COMMERCE, May 18, 1983, at A2.

Some analysts maintain that no matter what the economy does, no matter how healthy some airlines grow, fare wars are a certainty. As long as some carriers need cash to meet interest payments and payrolls, and as long as upstarts continue to claim their niches in the marketplace, somebody will always be willing to slash prices.

The stronger airlines could decide to end the bloodletting once and for all by starting fare wars designed to force weaker trunks and entrants out of the marketplace forever. That could bring about additional periods of deeply discounted air travel, then a long period of the kind of "price stability" the airlines want so badly.

Martindale, *The Economy Gets an "OK" for Takeoff*, OAG FREQUENT FLYER (July 1983) at 38.

104. Cuff, *Major U.S. Airlines Buffeted by Fierce Headwinds*, DENVER POST, May 15, 1982, at 11A.

105. Rosenak, *Address before the Motor Carrier Lawyers Ass'n.*, (Washington, D.C., Jan. 8, 1983); *ICC Chairman Tells Senate Panel He Favors Early Sunset of Agency*, TRAFFIC WORLD (Dec. 20, 1982) at 27, 64. The ICC has also largely expanded the ability of private carriers to engage in common carriage. *See* e.g., Leasing Rules Modifications, 132 M.C.C. 927 (1982); Lease of Equipment and Drivers to Private Carriers, 132 M.C.C. 756 (1982). *See* Farris & Southern, *Federal Regulatory Policy Affecting Private Carrier Trucking*, 49 ICC PRAC. J. 503 (1982); Borghesani, *Motor Carrier Regulatory Reform and Its Impact on Private Carriers*, 10 TRANSP. L. J. 389 (1978). As of June 1, 1983, the ICC had certificated 25,342 carriers. This represents a 43% increase in the number of carriers holding operating authority since promulgation of the Motor Carrier Act of 1980. The commission gave some 870 carriers nationwide authority, effectively deregulating them from an entry standpoint until the end of time. *See* Statement of George Ziglich before the U.S. Senate Surface Transportation Subcommittee of the Committee on Commerce, Science and Transportation (Sept. 21, 1983).

106. *See Upstarts In the Sky*, BUS. WEEK (June 15, 1982) at 78; *Deregulation Sketches New Patterns for the Airlines*, CHRISTIAN SCIENCE MONITOR (Dec. 30, 1982); *Real PEOPLE, Real Profits*, TIME (Apr. 4, 1983) at 62.

These new air carriers are responsible for less than 5% of the market. Martindale, *Victims of History*, OAG FREQUENT FLYER (December 1983) at 49–50. Indeed, the Air Transport Association estimates that the new carriers are responsible for only 2.4% of the total traffic. Salpukis, *Airlines Adapt to Decontrol*, N.Y. TIMES, Dec. 8, 1983, at D1. Former CAB chairman Alfred Kahn predicts that their market share will probably never exceed "5% of the total travel." Richards, *CAB's Ex-Chairman, Alfred Kahn, Looks at Airline Industry He Helped Deregulate*, WALL ST. J., Oct. 4, 1983, at 35.

107. As former CAB chairman Secor Browne has noted, the principal reason for deteriorating profits is that "although, like other unregulated industries, airlines suffer from recession and inflation, there has been destructive price competition, and overcapacity—that is, too many seats are chasing too few bottoms," Brenner, *Recontrol Air Fares*, N.Y. TIMES, Apr. 14, 1982, at 16. Rowen, *Airlines: Competing to the Death*, WASH. POST, Nov. 11, 1982, at A29.

Professor Frederick Thayer portrays the overcapacity problem under deregulation as follows:

The basic case is easily made for price and capacity regulation of public transportation systems. Suppose, for example, I wish to fly from New York to Los Angeles. Traditionally, three major airlines have offered me seats on flights scheduled in close proximity to meet peak travel demand. In Milton Friedman's already classic phrase, I was "free to choose" one of the three, thereby leaving the other two with empty seats. The 1978 U.S. policy of deregulation encouraged four additional airlines to offer service on the same route. I now have greater "freedom to choose" (seven alternatives), but the result is six empty seats. This problem is inherent to any transportation system organized to provide "head to head" competition, because the service being offered cannot be held in inventory awaiting other customers; service is destroyed by competition itself. It follows that the greater the number of empty seats, the more fuel wasted moving them about, and the higher the cost per passenger actually moved.

There is no way to deal with the empty seat problem except by limiting the capacity (flight frequency) of any single route. In principle, the problem can be minimized only by eliminating direct competition altogether. If a transportation system is to be so operated, a case can be made for public supervision of safety and prices. This is the classic outline of any industry defined as a public utility.

Thayer, *supra* note 100.

Available seat miles, one measure of capacity, for example, actually increased from 425 billion in 1981 to 439 billion in 1982.

In an effort to fill those empty seats the industry resorted to heavy discounting. The number of passengers who traveled on discount fares soared from 57% in 1980 to 78% in 1982. During the first six month of 1983 this percentage rose to 85%

The analysts and executives agree, however, that deregulation did accelerate the trend toward discount fares. As new carriers began flying in key markets across the country, their main strategy for attracting customers was lower fares. And the result was often bitter fare wars.

Salpukis, *Airlines Adapt to Decontrol*, N.Y. TIMES, Dec. 8, 1983, at D1. The overcapacity in the airline industry has been studied by Merrill Lynch, which concluded that by the end of 1982, the world fleet consisted of 6,100 transports, of which 900 would not be needed if the aircraft were operated at a 65% load factor and full utilization. *Conference Foresees Airline Struggles*, AV. WEEK & SPACE TECH. (Sept. 26, 1983) at 44.

108. *ICC Chairman Tells Senate Panel He Favors Early Sunset of Agency*, TRAFFIC WORLD (Dec. 20, 1982) at 27, 64.

109. One of America's major daily newspapers discussed the issue in these terms:

[T]his is a dangerous time for the airline industry.

Airlines have been pulled apart by deregulation and cut-throat fares, by high fuel costs and low passenger loads. The new pressures have punished the carriers, which lost more than $1 billion in the last three years. And they are still hampered by an unfinished air traffic control system, because half of its 14,000 controllers aren't fully qualified.

The airlines and the regulators have to recognize these stresses. They should be aware that these pressures increase the risk of human error and mechanical error. . . . For the airlines today, maximum safety requires maximum regulation.

Safe Skies Require Strict Regulation, USA TODAY, May 12, 1983, at 10A.

110. Columnist Hobart Rowen characterizes the problem in these terms.

An articulate and well-informed minority understands that the free-market issue is a phony when it comes to deregulation of transportation. Unless somebody cuts corners on services, or safety, deregulation doesn't lower prices, overall, to the consumer.

Rowen, *Airline Deregulation Doesn't Work*, WASH. POST, Apr. 8, 1982, at 26.

111. Professor Golbe's study established that profitable railroads have fewer accidents per mile than do unprofitable railroads. Golbe, *Product Safety In a Railroad Industry: Evidence from the Railroads*, 21 ECONOMIC INQUIRY 39 (1983).

112. Gonzales, *Airline Safety, A Special Report*, PLAYBOY (July 1980) at 140, 209.

113. Gibney, *Continuing Airline Losses Predicted*, DENVER POST, June 21, 1982, at 3C, col. 1. Julius Maldutis, Jr., vice-president of Salomon Brothers, estimates that 524 of the 2,005 planes operated by the nation's top 12 carriers are obsolete. *Id.*

114. Brenner, *Recontrol Air Fares*, N.Y. TIMES, Apr. 14, 1982, at 16.

115. Welling, *The Airline's Dilemma: No Cash to Buy Fuel-Efficient Jets*, BUS. WEEK (Sept. 27, 1982) at 65.

116. Air Line Pilots Ass'n, Press Release (June 15, 1983). Testifying before the House Subcommittee on Aviation, ALPA president Henry A. Duffy remarked that "economics and safety cannot be separated." Under regulation, "[a]n additional margin of safety [was established] by exceeding, not just meeting Federal Aviation Administration minimums." But under deregulation, the airline industry "has consistently degenerated to the point of acute anemia." Duffy noted that there are certain industries, such as aviation, "where the pressures of the marketplace and the spirit of free competition are at cross purposes with the national interest." *Id.*

117. Thayer, *The Lowest Fare is Not the Safest*, WASH. POST, May 1, 1982. "Aviation has had a long-established axiom, dating back to the days when "barnstormers' often slept under their aircraft wings, that the first thing to go when cost cutting begins is some maintenance—and consequently some safety." Reiss, *Airline Cost Cutting Has Bearing on Safety, Too*, YOUNGSTOWN VINDICATOR, June 26, 1983, at B14.

118. Rowen, *Airline Deregulation Doesn't Work*, WASH. POST, Apr. 8, 1982.

119. Thayer, *The Lowest Fare is Not the Safest*, WASH. POST, May 1, 1982. The eroding federal role in protecting passenger safety has been described as follows:

FAA's safety function has been affected in a very direct and visible way by deregulation. Because of the growing number of carriers, general aviation inspectors are being used to monitor commercial air carriers. This problem is compounded by the fact that the Civil Aeronautics Board (CAB) is using only a rubber-stamp safety-fitness test for new entrants. CAB is relying on FAA to catch the board's mistakes, and FAA is strapped for manpower.

The pressure of record losses will not go away. Every airline manager is faced with cost/benefit determinations that must be made in the pressure-cooker atmosphere of an industry dominated by news of bankruptcies, real and threatened.

Orders for new, safer, more efficient aircraft are canceled. And the airlines continue to fly old and tired aircraft that should be replaced.

Duffy, *Deregulation 5 Years Later*, OAG FREQUENT FLYER (Oct. 1983) at 54, 56. Similar concerns were raised in an editorial appearing in the *Washington Post*:

[B]udget cuts have reduced the number of FAA safety inspectors by one-fourth. These are the federal employees who monitor the airlines' maintenance and cockpit procedures for safety problems.

Before deregulation, many airline officials and others argued that deregulating prices, routes and entry into the industry would encourage airlines to let cost competition spill over into safety areas. The federal safety agencies, it was said, would not be able to fight effectively the tide of economic incentives unleashed by competition. Airline officials insist, as you might expect, that they don't cut corners on safety. But which are we to believe: the predictions of danger made years ago or the reassurances offered today?

The statistics show that airline accidents have been declining for years. On that there is no argument. The harder question is whether the combination of several current trends might not lead to serious problems in the longer run. Those trends include the FAA budget cuts, the economic pressure on airline wages and operating costs and the increasing technical complexity of the equipment itself.

Safe In the Skies? WASH. POST, Dec. 3, 1983, at A18.

" If any link can be established between financial distress and safety degradation, the bottom 100 constantly recycling commuter carriers referenced above certainly look like prime examples of this relationship." Statement of Henry A. Duffy before the Subcommittee on Aviation of House Committee on Public Works and Transportation, June 15, 1983. However, the FAA seems to have a reputation of imposing sanctions against only the grossest and most conspicuous of violators. Although aircraft having nine or fewer passengers have a 20 times greater accident rate than those carrying 30 or more passengers, the FAA has been accused of diluting the safety standards for such commuter aircraft. *FAA Bends Rules, Says ALPA*, FLIGHT INTERNATIONAL (Nov. 26, 1983) at 1409. Congressman Elliot H. Levitas (D. Ga.) has expressed serious reservations over the performance of the agency:

I'm disappointed in the dismal record of the FAA in regulating aircraft safety. Legislative action will have to be taken unless the agency acts soon. But, I'm afraid, its too little too late now.

Quotelines, USA TODAY, Nov. 3, 1983, at 8A. Other recent concerns have been expressed as a result of the allegedly poor piloting and maintenance procedures of Air Illinois:

The discoveries have heightened concerns about the safety of some financially weak, inexperienced regional airlines that have been assuming a larger role in the nation's passenger service since Congress approved airline deregulation in 1978.... The trend toward small regional airlines taking over routes once flown by major carriers is continuing at the same time that the Federal Aviation Administration, which regulates airline safety, is reducing the number of its inspectors as a result of the administration's budget-cutting efforts.

Major trunk airlines, dropping unprofitable routes, no longer serve 166 American cities. Those cities still have passenger service, however, provided by small carriers, usually flying propeller planes.

Feaver, *Air Illinois Crash Raises Questions about Small-Airline Safety*, WASH. POST, Nov. 28, 1983, at A3. Although government statistics evidence a decline in airline fatalities in recent years, "the experts express some concern that airlines might ... take risky shortcuts amid financial trouble." Karr, *Safety Debate Rages in the Airline Industry As Unions Claim Ailing Carriers Take Risks*, WALL ST. J., Oct. 18, 1983, at 35.

[T]he inescapable conclusion is that an airline cannot spend money it doesn't have to maintain and improve its safety equipment and procedures. In other words, the economic chaos brought on by deregulation will, sooner or later, erode the safety of our commercial air transportation system.

Duffy, *Deregulation Affects Safety*, AIRPORT PRESS (Aug. 1983) at 21.

120. *See* Rowan, *Airlines: Competing to the Death*, WASH. POST, Nov. 11, 1982.

121. *Fares Fair?* TRANSPORT TOPICS (May 24, 1982). Senator Mark Andrews (R-N.D.) noted that "since deregulation air fares across the country have gone up 112%. The consumer price index went up 46% during the same period." Transcript of CBS NEWS FACE THE NATION, Oct. 2, 1983, at 12. Thus, some argue that the aggregate impact of fare changes since deregulation has been a higher increase that that of the rest of the economy.

Long haul flyers may get cheap fares because of excess competition but shorter hauls cost more and some cities have lost service altogether.

What this adds up to in the end is a greater tendency for higher fares overall for everyone— business and leisure travelers.

Seybold, *Airline Deregulation—Is It Good or Bad?* BOSTON SUNDAY GLOBE, Nov. 6, 1983, at T1.

One traveler described the problems of discrimination he encountered in air service as follows:

I recently had to make an emergency flight to Indianapolis from Los Angeles. Would you believe that the cheapest fare was $369 *each way* while, at the same time, you could fly all the way to the East Coast from Los Angeles for anywhere from $149 to $160 each way?

According to my atlas (and my calculator) this means that the flight to Indianapolis and back cost me about 230% of the Los Angeles to New York City fare even though, on a round-trip basis, I covered 26% less distance. I call this either gouging, or your typical East Coast/West Coast bias against mid-America. To add insult to injury, of course, there is no way in the world you can fly *directly* to Indianapolis from Los Angeles. The airlines' idea of "direct" is to cool your heels for a couple of hours somewhere along the way—in either Chicago, St. Louis, or Louisville.

I know that the airlines are in trouble, and it seems to me that this blatant price discrimination in favor of West Coast/East Coast traffic is symptomatic of the shortsightedness that is wrecking the industry—and it couldn't happen to a nicer bunch of folks.

Campbell, *Airline Prices Going on Flights of Fancy*, LOS ANGELES TIMES, Oct. 20, 1983, at 15.

122. *A Gift from the Airlines*, NEWSWEEK (Dec. 13, 1982) at 108.

123. Holsendolph, *Low-Cost Airline Now Seeks Fares Curb It Once Opposed*, N.Y. TIMES, Mar. 10, 1982; *World Airways Loss Quadrupled in Quarter to $13.3 Million*, WALL ST. J., May 24, 1982.

124. Hayes, *The Plight of World Airways*, N.Y. TIMES, Mar. 11, 1982.

125. *A Gift from the Airlines*, NEWSWEEK (Dec. 13, 1982) at 108.

126. *The U.S. Air-Fare Dogfight*, NEWSWEEK (Apr. 19, 1982) at 69.

127. *The Worst Year for U.S. Airlines*, TIME (Feb. 22, 1982) at 46.

128. Curley, *Decontrol of Airlines Shifts Pricing from a Cost to a Competitive Basis*, WALL ST. J., Dec. 4, 1981, at 37.

[I]n July 1980, a citizen of Tulsa, Okla., paid $230 to fly to Los Angeles, or 18 cents a mile, while fare wars enabled a New Yorker to fly to Los Angeles for $99, or 4 cents a mile. Today the Tulsa passenger pays $279 to go to Los Angeles while the New Yorker pays $179.

Rowan, *We Goofed—Let's Regulate Airlines Again*, CHICAGO SUN-TIMES, Oct. 10, 1983, at A25.

129. W. Augello, The Deregulation Disaster (unpublished monograph, 1983). Ironically, it was the experience of California and Texas intrastate carriers that maintained scheduled service at rates significantly below those of their federally regulated interstate counterparts that was emphasized by deregulators to support federal deregulation of air carriage. *See* Kahn, *Applying Economics to an Imperfect World*, 2 REGULATION 17 (1978). *See* G. DOUGLAS & J. MILLER, III, ECO-NOMIC REGULATION OF DOMESTIC AIR TRANSPORT 178 (1974).

130. *DOT's View of Airline Deregulation Challenged by Small Cities, Labor*, TRAFFIC WORLD (June 20, 1983) at 16. Richard B. Keinz, assistant commissioner of the aeronautical division of the Minnesota Department of Transportation, also testified before a subcommittee of the House Public Works Committee that :

It is clear that the objectives of Congress are not being met for many cities and isolated areas. The experience of many cities since the enactment of the Airline Deregulation Act has been a vicious cycle in declining traffic, declining service and rising fares. In part this has been due to a weak economy which has affected these cities and the airlines serving them. To a great extent, however, it has been the result of deregulation.

Id.

131. *Airlines Move to Straighten Out Air Fares*, U.S. NEWS & WORLD REP. (May 16, 1983) at 49. One major newspaper recently published an editorial that described the nation's airline industry as in a "state of crisis," with the result that major carriers are undergoing bankruptcy and reorganization as the "Darwinian process" reaches "full throttle." The editorial goes on to call for "an immediate federal review of the growing airline dilemma before it does indeed balloon into a crisis of national proportion." *The Airlines' Patchwork Crisis*, SEATTLE POST-INTELLIGENCER, Oct. 2, 1983, at A30.

Inconsistent, unreliable, erratic service at prices which vary monthly from ridiculously low to prohibitively high is hardly in the public interest. Neither the business nor the pleasure traveler finds a hint of health in the current air passenger transportation scheme created by Mr. Kahn.

Kissinger, *CAB's Ex-Chief Encounters Turbulence*, WALL ST. J., Oct. 12, 1983, at 32.

132. *See Laker Collapse Facilitates North Atlantic Fare Rises*, AV. WEEK & SPACE TECH. (Feb. 15, 1982) at 31.

133. *Airlines*, FORBES (Jan. 5, 1981) at 144.

134. Rowan, *Airline Deregulation Comes Back to Haunt*, WASH. POST, Mar. 14, 1982, at G4, col. 1.

135. A number of major American corporations have grown increasingly dissatisfied with the inconvenience and cost of commercial air service and have responded by purchasing their own aircraft:

Commercial trips often involve delays while waiting for flights, switching planes or traveling from airports located far from city centers. And the costs rise if employees are forced to stay overnight because air service is limited.

Byrne, *Kimberly-Clark Seeks to Turn Its Shuttle from Wisconsin to Atlanta into an Airline*, WALL ST. J., July 6, 1983, at 27.

136. *The U.S. Air-Fare Dogfight*, NEWSWEEK (April 19, 1982) at 69.

137. *Great Trucking Wars*, DISTRIBUTION (Nov. 1982) at 30.

138. *Id.* Ernest R. Olsen noted that

We now have...in trucking...the same wild climate that existed prior to 1935....Almost anyone can secure authority, charge what he wishes, and operate legally or illegally at will, with little risk of penalty. Large established carriers are getting larger; small and weak carriers are dropping out in substantial numbers....LTL carriers will eventually identify the areas in which they have market monopoly and will act accordingly. Small shippers should be properly armed....The small producers can forget about the railroads; they will serve only volume shippers in the future...The large shipper will command added attention among truckers, with new power to demand reduced rates, as well as special deals.

Policing of Abuses of Economic Power, TRAFFIC WORLD (May 23, 1983) at 6.

139. CIVIL AERONAUTICS BOARD, REPORT ON AIRLINE SERVICE 43–50 (1979). *See* GENERAL ACCOUNTING OFFICE, THE CHANGING AIRLINE INDUSTRY: A STATUS REPORT THROUGH 1981 17 (1982).

140. Berry, *Speakers in "Great Debate" in Detroit Differ in Appraisals of Deregulation*, TRAFFIC WORLD (Nov. 30, 1981) at 18. Between November 1, 1978, and May 1, 1981, 74 communities lost all their previously enjoyed certificated service. CIVIL AERONAUTICS BOARD, COMPETITION AND THE AIRLINES 135 (1982). Declines in federal subsidies will contribute to a further reduction in small community service. *Id.* at 144.

141. Brenner, *Recontrol Air Fares*, N.Y. TIMES, Apr. 14, 1982, at 16. The Civil Aeronautics Board admits that major airlines have reduced the number of city pairs which enjoyed nonstop service prior to deregulation. *Airlines Decreasing Nonstop Service*, AIRPORT PRESS, Aug. 1983, at 10.

The fact is that the deregulation of airlines has ignored one of the fundamental precepts of any modern society, i.e., that transportation is so vital to communities and regions that its adequate maintenance cannot be left strictly to the whims of the marketplace.

The zealots who successfully lobbied for deregulation misled Congress into believing that removal of "public utility" licensing of air service would have only minor effects on the air route map. For example, the Kennedy subcommittee of the Senate was persuaded that, with deregulation, route abandonment by the major trunk carriers would affect "routes that, at the very most, account for one-half of 1 percent" of airline traffic.... The clock cannot be turned back to 1978. But this does not preclude some reasonable modification of deregulation so as to overcome its more serious defects. A first step must be a willingness to stop whitewashing this new regime and to face objectively all its consequences—the bad as well as the good.

Brenner, *Communities Imperiled by Airline Deregulation*, N.Y. TIMES, Dec. 5, 1983, at A18.

142. Havens & Heymsfeld, *Small Community Air Service under the Airline Deregulation Act of 1978*, 46 J. AIR L. & COM. 641, 673 (1981).

As of September 14, 1983, since deregulation was inaugurated frequency of service had increased for 302 communities, remained unchanged for 15, and decreased for 351. Among this 351, 106 have lost all scheduled service, and 44 have lost more than 50% of the service they previously enjoyed. Rowen, *Reiterating the Case for Airline Regulation*, WASH. POST, Oct. 9, 1983, at G1. *See Officials Criticize Essential Service*, AV. WEEK & SPACE TECH. (Aug. 22, 1983) at 26.

143. *See* Duffy, *In Wyoming, You Can't Get There from Here*, DENVER POST, May 14, 1982, at D1.

Service has declined in numerous Essential Air Service markets as well. In Kentucky, for example, available seats departing from Essential Air Service communities have declined 61.3% since deregulation. In Missouri, available seats at Essential Air Service cities are down 27.6% and nonstop destinations have dropped from 30 to 24. And in Nebraska, departures in Essential Air Service communities have dropped 53.9% since deregulation. There are numerous other examples of the loss of service.

This drop in service greatly discriminates against the individual traveler to and from small cities. Because fewer connecting flights are available to and from smaller cities, travelers are often forced to wait or take other modes of transportation, losing both time and money.

In addition, service reductions inhibit growth in those smaller communities. What business wants to locate in a city that has intermittent air service at exorbitant rates? Cutting off the air lifeline from smaller cities effectively cuts off their growth potential.

Duffy, *Deregulation 5 Years Later*, OAG FREQUENT FLYER (Oct. 1983) at 54, 58.

144. *See* 49 U.S.C. sec. 1389 (1980).

145. Chapman, *Airlines Soon Will Find It Difficult to Retain Scarce Subsidy Funds*, TRAFFIC WORLD (Sept. 6, 1982) at 33.

146. Motor Carrier Reform Act of 1980: Report of the Senate Comm. On Commerce, Science, and Transportation, S. Rep. No. 96–641, 96th Cong., 2d Sess. 85 (1980).

147. Panetta, *Commuter Airlines: Taming the Wild Blue*, COLORADO BUS. (Nov. 1979) at 17. Tom Binford, airport manager at Laramie, Wyoming, characterized the problems small and remote communities have faced with commuter airlines:

We've had lots of airlines start up, but they don't seem to last long. Usually an airline is started by some furloughed pilot who mortgages his home, puts a down payment on a plane and goes into business. But in the main, they're undercapitalized and poorly managed and don't last.

Duffy, *In Wyoming, You Can't Get There from Here*, DENVER POST, May 14, 1982, at D1.

148. Urinas, *Bus Deregulation Gains Favor, Worrying Small Towns, Small Operators and Elderly*, WALL ST. J., Aug. 2, 1982.

149. D. Baker, Deregulation: Where We Were: Where We Are; Where We're Going (unpublished address before the Western Traffic Conference, Monterey, Calif., May 23, 1983).

The tragedy is that the people who do and must ride the buses are dependent upon and usually have no other means of obtaining transportation. They are the older, senior citizens who no longer are economically or physically able to own or operate automobiles. Young people and school children, who must depend upon bus transportation. Economically disadvantaged persons, who cannot afford to own or operate automobiles. Businesses in small cities that must have transportation available to attract and keep employees. Persons not owning automobiles that require bus service to visit their doctors, obtain medical services, seek employment, visit relatives or friends.

Id. at 5–6.

For Greyhound, airline deregulation has meant increased competition from new low-cost air carriers, which have undercut bus fares on routes of 100 to 250 miles, important runs for the bus industry. Bus deregulation has meant fare wars with Trailways, Inc., Greyhound's main competitor, and it raises the specter of fare wars with other competitors. "Bus deregulation also means Greyhound can raise fares and eliminate unprofitable runs." Serrin, *How Deregulation Allowed Greyhound to Win Concessions from Strikers*, N.Y. TIMES, Dec. 7, 1983, at A22.

150. *Id.* Interstate deregulation of bus operations has also resulted in a deterioration of service for small communities. *See* Cox, *Bus Service Loss Isolates Julesburg*, DENVER POST, Mar. 14, 1983, at 6A.

151. *What's Happened to Liability Coverage?* HANDLING & SHIPPING MANAGEMENT (December 1982) at 13–14.

152. W. Augello, The Deregulation Disaster (unpublished monograph, 1982) at 2.

153. Investigation of Liability Claims Rules and Practices, CAB Order 76–3–139 (1976); CAB Order 77–3–61 (1977).

154. Augello, *supra* note 152, at 3.

155. *Id. See* generally Berry, *Many Topics Covered at 16th Annual Motor Transportation Law Institute*, TRAFFIC WORLD (Aug. 8, 1983) at 27–28; Butler, *Truck-*

ing Industry Seeks Uniformity In Claims Liability for All Modes, TRAFFIC WORLD (July 18, 1983) at 27.

156.

The call for regulation of railroads, like that for most utilities, arose because the public perceived that competition was imperfect. Many believed that railroads, like gas and electric companies, were natural monopolies, where the market in a given area could best be served by one supplier. But, in the absence of competition, that supplier has to be regulated.

Railroad regulation is older than antitrust regulation, and, in fact, all modern administrative law flows from the ICC model for regulation of railroads. Regulation of the rail lines began in the states, principally the Granger areas where the local elevator and the farmers served by it were dependent upon rail freight service.

Thoms, *Clear Track for Deregulation of American Railroads,* 12 TRANSP. L. J. 183, 186 (1982).

157. *Id.*

158. *See* e.g., Chicago and Northwestern Transportation Co.—Abandonment— Between Clintonville and Eland, WI, 363 I.C.C. 975 (1981). Rail carriers' freedom under deregulation to abandon branch lines has deprived a number of midwestern grain elevators of rail service. Samuelson, *Competition's Mixed Effects,* WASH. POST, Oct. 18, 1983, at E1.

159. Thoms, *supra* note 156, at 210.

160. Feaver, *Major Railroads Poised for Transcontinental Mergers,* WASH. POST, June 19, 1983, at F1. These are 1981 figures. A revenue ton mile constitutes a ton of freight carried one mile. *Id.*

161. The five carriers were the Central of New Jersey, the Lehigh and Hudson River, the Lehigh Valley, the Reading, and the Erie Lackawana. *See* Wilson, *Cloudy Future for Conrail,* PHILADELPHIA INQUIRER, Aug. 21, 1981, at 26; Salpukas, *Turnaround at Conrail,* N.Y. TIMES, Dec. 4, 1981, at 36.

162. A smaller railroad is being assembled by Timothy Mellon, who purchased the Maine Central, the Boston & Maine, and the Delaware and Hudson. Together these railroads traverse almost 4,000 miles. *See* Guilford Transportation Industries, Inc.—Control—Delaware and Hudson Company, 366 I.C.C. 396 (1982); Sept. 18, 1981, at 37; Harkavay, *Mellon to Complete Rail Purchases by Summer,* BOSTON SUNDAY GLOBE, Nov. 1, 1981, at 63.

163. *CSX: Railroading for Fun and Profit,* BUS. WEEK (Nov. 1981) at 51.

164. *See* Florida East Coast Ry. Co. v. United States, 250 F. Supp. 903 (M. D. Fla. 1966).

165. *See* Augello, *supra* note 152, at 3.

166. *See* Norfolk Southern Corporation—Control—Norfolk and Western Railway Company, 366 I.C.C. 171 (1982). Salpukas, *I.C.C. Allows Formation of a Giant Carrier,* N.Y. TIMES, Mar. 26, 1982, at 31, col. 2. Wayne, *A Surprising Move by N.&W.,* N.Y. TIMES, Sept. 3, 1981, at 26; Fingleton, *No Panty Hose,* FORBES (Nov. 9, 1981) at 135.

167. *See* Burlington Northern, Inc.—Control and Merger—St. Louis-San Francisco Railway Co., 366 I.C.C. 862 (1983).

168. *See A Railroad for the Long Haul,* FORBES (Apr. 27, 1981) at 120–26.

169. Union Pacific—Control—Missouri Pacific; Western Pacific, 366 I.C.C. 458 (1982).

170. Paul, *Freight Transportation Is Being Transformed in Era of Deregulation*, WALL ST. J., Oct. 20, 1983, at 18.

171. *See* Note, *The Staggers Rail Act of 1980: Authority to Compete with Ability to Compete*, 12 TRANSP. L. J. 301, 308 (1982).

172. *Id.* at 311–13. 49 U.S.C. § 10709 (1982).

173. Improvement of TOFC/COFC Regulation, 364 I.C.C. 391 (1980). TOFC is "trailer on flat car"; COFC is "container on flat car."

174. Ex Parte No. 346 (Sub. No. 8); *see* 50 ICC PRAC. J. 449 (1983).

175. Ex Parte No. 346 (Sub. No. 7); *see ICC Eyes World Market Competition in Deregulating Export Coal Moves*, TRAFFIC WORLD (June 13, 1983).

176. A rate scheme similar to that of differential pricing (a notion approved in San Antonio, Tex. v. United States, 631 F.2d 831 [D.C. Cir. 1980]) is Ramsey pricing. Rail carriers have suggested that the ICC adopt the principles developed by British economist Frank Ramsey in assessing whether rail rates are just and reasonable. Under Ramsey pricing, shippers are charged a rate that encompasses the variable cost of providing the service, plus a share of fixed costs inversely proportional to the shipper's elasticity of demand for service. Hence, a shipper of coal which enjoyed the alternatives of either coal slurry pipelines or barge transportation in addition to rail service would receive a lower rail rate than would a similarly situated shipper without such transportation alternatives.

The ICC has estimated that 78% of rail costs are "variable," and 22% are "fixed." It is argued that Ramsey pricing will benefit all shippers, because price-elastic shippers will bear some of the fixed costs which, in turn, will reduce the fixed-cost burden for price-inelastic shippers, and theoretically, will result in lower rail rates for the latter.

177. The ICC has proposed guidelines in Ex Parte No. 347 (Sub. No. 1), Coal Rate Guidelines, Nationwide, which would further reduce its role in policing rail rate increases for captive shippers. Essentially, the guidelines provide that rail carriers are free to raise their rates for market dominant traffic up to 14% annually above inflation, unless such rates would exceed the "stand-alone cost" of serving the shipper, increases are attributable to inefficient rail management, or the rail carrier has achieved revenue adequacy.

"Stand-alone cost" is defined by the ICC as the cost that would be incurred by shippers if they were forced to serve themselves. The reproduction of service capabilities (e.g., construction of track, purchase of locomotives and cars) is measured by the current cost of producing equipment or facilities with equivalent capabilities.

Managerial efficiency is insisted upon by the Staggers Rail Act, which encourages rail carriers to earn adequate revenues under "honest, economical and efficient management" 49 U.S.C. § 10704(a)(2). Consideration of this criterion is also suggested by the Long-Cannon amendment to the Staggers Act. The Long-Cannon amendment provides that, in determining whether to investigate a rate, the ICC must assess (a) the amount of the railroad's traffic that does not contribute to going concern value (i.e., variable costs) and the carrier's efforts to minimize it, (b) the traffic that contributes only marginally to fixed costs and the extent to which such rates can be raised, and (c) the impact of the rate increase upon national energy and rail transportation policies. 49 U.S.C. § 10707a(e)(2)(B).

Congress has insisted that the ICC assist the railroads in achieving revenue adequacy. 49 U.S.C. §§ 10704 (a)(2), 10707a(e)(2)(3)(iii). The ICC has addressed the criteria relevant to its determination of "revenue adequacy" in Ex Parte No. 393, Standard for Revenue Adequacy, 358 I.C.C. 844 (1978), 359 I.C.C. 270 (1978), 361 I.C.C. 79 (1978), 362 I.C.C. 199 (1980). The commission concluded that adequate revenues are those which allow rail carriers to earn a return on investment equal to the current cost of capital, so that they would be able to compete with other firms for available sources of financing. Once a carrier has achieved revenue adequacy, the ICC will scrutinize rate increases for market dominant traffic more closely.

The standards adopted by the ICC for determining market dominance have been criticized as

A decision which seriously erodes captive shipper protection by injecting the question of geographic and product competition into evidence as to the existence of market dominance in transportation. Whether a shipper could obtain a commodity from a different source or could substitute a different commodity for the freight at issue simply has no bearing on whether there is effective transportation competition for certain movements.

J. Lema, Remarks before Conference on Coal Transportation (Arlington, Va. 1983). The ICC's recent efforts in this area have been characterized as follows:

The I.C.C. proposed that the railroads should be permitted to charge 15 percent per year more than presently unreasonable rates for coal traffic—above inflation—until a railroad is revenue adequate and possibly beyond. These increases are to be limited only by the utilities' purported "option" to build its own railroad. That is nothing less than total deregulation, because it would set the upper limit at precisely the level at which a shipper would go elsewhere. The I.C.C. has set out to tell the monopoly railroad how best to set an optimum monopoly price. ... The I.C.C. is proposing to turn the clock back 100 years and once more let the robber barons loose on the captive traffic. On its centennial anniversary the I.C.C. will have as its most recent legacy the attempt to recreate the very monopoly conditions which it was established to control 100 years ago.

M. Foldes, Post-Staggers Act, I.C.C. Actions and Shipper Initiatives (address before Conference on Coal Transportation, Alexandria, Va. 1983).

During the past four years, mine prices for coal increased only half as much as the Bureau of Labor's Producers Price Index (PPI) for all commodities. During the same period, rail rates for coal increased one and a half times the PPI—this during a period of severe recession in the American economy. J. Lema, Remarks before Conference on Coal Transportation (Arlington, Va. 1983).

178. Letter from 27 coal company chief executive officers to President Reagan (May 25, 1983), appendix at 2–3.

179. A. Friedlaender, The Dilemma of Freight Transport Regulation, 165 (1969). In all fairness, however, it must be admitted that Ann Friedlaender has long been a proponent of transportation deregulation.

180. The U.S. Air-Fare Dogfight, NEWSWEEK (Apr. 19, 1982) at 69.

181. Speakers in "Great Debate" in Detroit Differ in Appraisals of Deregulation, TRAFFIC WORLD (Nov. 30, 1981) at 18.

182. Sterling, Will Truckers Follow the Airlines' Lead?, GO WEST (July 1982) at 6.

183. Id.

184. The Worst Year for U.S. Airlines, TIME (Feb. 22, 1982) at 46.

185. Mayer, Uncertainty Clouds Future of Airlines, ROCKY MOUNTAIN

NEWS, Apr. 17, 1983, at 98. However, it must be recognized that many air carriers have concluded that no regulation at all would be preferable to the existing governmental environment, or reregulation. As United's chairman, Richard J. Ferris, noted, "the egg of deregulation has been well scrambled and there is no way to unscramble it." Burkhardt, *Airlines, Unions Split on Decontrol Results*, J. OF COMMERCE, June 16, 1983, at A2. *See U.S., Carrier Officials Oppose Reregulation in Spite of Losses*, AV. WEEK & SPACE TECH. (June 6, 1983) at 51. United, the nation's largest air carrier, has long been a vigorous proponent of airline regulation.

E. H. Boullioun, senior vice-president of Boeing, characterized the impact of airline deregulation as stretching the system "beyond the breaking point." He has predicted that the market disruptions engendered by deregulation will probably continue indefinitely. *Boeing Official Cites Dangers of Deregulation*, WASH. POST, Oct. 26, 1983, at D10.

186. *Braniff: First to Fall?* DENVER POST, June 14, 1982.

187. Cook, *Transportation*, FORBES (Jan. 8, 1979), at 56. Nevertheless, even the temporary attributes of airline deregulation may not be repeated in the surface transportation of commodities. As has been indicated, the passenger market is price elastic—lower prices may generate demand for discretionary travelers. However, in the aggregate, the commodities market is almost totally demand-inelastic with respect to the use of transportation services. Between carriers and modes there may be some demand elasticity, but the total market, at any point in time, is virtually finite. Hence, while air passenger deregulation led to price competition that, in turn, enabled air carriers to fill seats that might otherwise have flown empty, deregulation is unlikely to fill empty areas in motor carrier trailers or rail boxcars.

188.

Clearly, there is more at stake than the sanctity of the laws of the marketplace. There is a public interest in assuring that the fundamental ingredients of economic growth are abundant in all regions of our nation, so that the fruits of such growth might be enjoyed by a larger segment of the population. This is, of course, a distribution of wealth concept. A geographic disbursement of economic growth offers the potential for a more equitable distribution of regional growth rates. Moreover, by removing industry from the concentrated urban areas where the industrial revolution was born, the quality of life might ultimately be improved as workers, following industry like a magnet, enable population to become more geographically disparate.

Like communications and energy, transportation is a fundamental component of national, regional, and local economic development. If any of these vital components is deficient, either from a qualitative or quantitative standpoint, investment in industry may relocate elsewhere. Traditionally, it has been thought that these essential industries were too important to be left to the rigors of the marketplace.

Several of these industries were natural monopolies (*e.g.*; the early railroads, telephone, telegraph, gas, and electric companies, and to some extent, television and radio), which if unregulated would produce in lower quantities and at higher prices than would industries in a competitive market. Regulation seeks to substitute what is lacking in the marketplace by insisting that such natural monopolies produce at a lower price and higher volume than they otherwise might.

Recognizing this distinction, virtually every major industrial nation on the planet treats these industries in a manner significantly different from the rest. In most, the industries are owned and operated by the state. In transportation, most of the rail, motor, barge, and air carriers are socialized, even in Western Europe.

In the United States, the services of transportation, communications, and energy have largely been performed by the private sector, with government serving the role of a regulator of a wide variety of activities, weighing and balancing the public interest against what would otherwise be the economic laws of the market place. The government plays a dual and perhaps schizophrenic role—on the one hand, it seeks to stimulate the inherent economics and efficiencies of the regulated industries; on the other, it seeks to protect the public from the abuses which these industries might otherwise perpetrate. For the most part, the United States has been able to avoid nationalizing these industries, for private ownership thereof has, on the whole, proven successful. The major exception is rail passenger service.

Dempsey, *Erosion of the Regulatory Process in Transportation—The Winds of Change*, 47 ICC PRAC. J. 303, 311 (1980).
  189.

The critics [of regulation] seem to misunderstand or consciously avoid one of the traditional objectives of motor carrier regulation: although reasonable rates for the industry as a whole may result in higher profit margins for the larger, more economically efficient carriers, they also protect small, marginally efficient carriers. Protection of small carriers, the preservation of diversity, and the willingness to pay the incremental additional price have all contributed to the fundamental foundations of motor carrier regulation, and have preserved a healthy competitive structure. To turn this practice against . . . the industry, without first addressing the underlying value judgment that "smallness" should be protected for its inherent value in stimulating innovation in service and price and "largeness" must be restricted for its inherent risks in stifling such economic attributes, is to undermine the traditional objectives of regulation without ever stating an acceptable justification for such a radical change in course.

Dempsey, *Rate Regulation and Antitrust Immunity in Transportation: The Genesis and Evolution of this Endangered Species*, 32 AM.U.L. REV. 335, 371 (1983).
Professors Wagner and Dean predict that

To the extent that smaller, less efficient carriers are forced out of business, larger, more efficient companies increasingly may dominate motor carriage. The result may move the industry toward a greater degree of imperfect competition as several large firms dominate. . . . An open-door entry regulation policy may invite a new type of trucker—inexperienced, overconfident, and opportunistic. Many fear an influx of people with little capital, poor or used equipment, and little education coupled with high expectations. Whether such carriers fill a service void is questionable. Although these carriers often cut rates to gain business initially, failures frequently have resulted due to a lack of managerial experience or cost control; prior to that time, however, there is often less need awareness for safety and service. . . . One effect of deregulation is that carriers may lessen service to smaller areas and concentrate on the more lucrative, urban centers.

Wagner & Dean, *A Perspective View toward Deregulation of Motor Carrier Entry*, 48 ICC PRAC. J. 406, 415 (1981) [citations omitted].
  190. Cook, *Transportation*, FORBES (Jan. 8, 1978) at 58–59.
  191. Letter from Richard H. Suddath to Paul S. Dempsey (Apr. 26, 1983).
  192. Chow, *Economic Regulation of Motor Freight in Foreign Countries*, 47 ICC PRAC. J. 44, 45 (1979).
  193. *Id.*
  194. Paul, *Freight Transportation Is Being Transformed in Era of Deregulation*, WALL ST. J., Oct. 20, 1983, at 1.

The key to the railroads' strength is that they have far more cash and fixed assets than other types of carriers, and far less internal competition. While the number of truckers proliferate, the number of railroads shrinks, with the outlook for no more than six to 10 major rail systems serving the U.S. within five years.

Id. at 18.

195. *Id.* at 18. As an example of the railroads' enormous political and economic clout, the article pointed out the industry's success in defeating a congressional proposal to promote coal slurry pipeline construction. "Most coal companies are 'captive' to a single railroad and wanted coal slurry pipelines so as to create a competitive situation." *Id.*

196. *Id.*

197. *The Airlines Hit a Downdraft,* NEWSWEEK (Oct. 10, 1983) at 66. Other commentators have affirmed the move toward concentration: "[E]conomists predict that by 1990 there will be four or five giant airlines and a host of specialized, although not necessarily tiny, ones." *A Painful Transition for the Transport Industry,* BUS. WEEK (Nov. 28, 1983) at 83. *See* Byrne, *United's Expansion on West Coast Threatens Future of Small Airlines,* WALL ST. J., Nov. 16, 1983, at 33.

198. Columnist Hobart Rowen has vigorously called for a reintroduction of regulation:

Transportation is not just any old business. Basically, it's a public utility, which has to be regulated in the public interest. It's time to reregulate the airlines.

Rowen, *Airline Deregulation: A Bankrupt Policy,* WASH. POST, Sept. 29, 1983, at A21. Columnist Carl Rowan echoed these concerns:

It is crucial to America's economic and social well-being, and surely its security, that we have an airlines system that can be relied upon in peace and war.

Congress deregulated our airlines just enough to perpetrate a disaster. Can it admit to an error, and reverse its action of 1978, when so many of its members voted for a debacle? Let us pray. Rowan, *We Goofed—Let's Regulate Airlines Again,* CHICAGO SUN-TIMES, Oct. 10, 1983, at A25. One CAB staff member prepared an impressive analysis of the relevant financial and statistical data and concluded that:

The evidenced structural changes have caused and will continue to cause a higher required overall fare level, generally poorer passenger service, and allow significant price discrimination. It is further evident that fares are not cost-based, and that the industry is becoming less productive and failing to share the expected efficiency gains. . . . Large short-term consumer gains are coupled with tremendous operating and capital losses by the industry. Improved service quality in some markets is offset by lower quality service system-wide. Increased service competition has lowered unit productivity, increasing cost with little gain in efficiency. So far, I do not believe the gains can be shown to outweigh the losses.

Unfortunately, there seems to be little reason to expect the promised benefits of deregulation to come to fruition.

Letter from David B. Richards to James J. Howard and Nancy Landon Kassebaum, (Aug. 20, 1983); *see CAB Staffer Tells Congress Deregulation Is a Failure,* COM-MUTER REGIONAL AIRLINE NEWS, Oct. 10, 1983, at 1; Rowen, *Reiterating the Case for Airline Deregulation,* WASH. POST, Oct. 9, 1983, at G1.

199. Malkin, *Second Thoughts,* HEREFORD'S NORTH AMERICA *(June–Nov. 1982). See also,* Berg, *Needed: A Return to Regulation,* TRAFFIC WORLD (Nov. 1, 1982) at 42.

200. Augello, *supra* note 52, at 10.

A major survey of 309 traffic executives of Fortune 500 companies evidenced little enthusiasm for air cargo deregulation. *Is Airline Deregulation Working?* AIR COMMERCE, Sept. 21, 1983, at 1, 4.

The returns clearly showed that air cargo deregulation has failed to win the broad, unqualified shipper enthusiasm that had been taken for granted by its early proponents.

Although 45 percent cast their vote in favor of deregulation, a large minority (34 percent) preferred a return to some form of the regulation. Considering the fact that 21 percent of the 302 respondents had still not made up their minds on the issue, it can be seen that substantially less than half may be regarded at this time as staunch supporters of deregulation.

Id. at 6.

As the . . . survey . . . appears to indicate, air cargo deregulation has been less than a howling success. Two thirds of the Fortune 500 traffic/distribution executives surveyed reported not having been stimulated by deregulation to the point where they increased their air freight usage. Thirty-four percent want regulation; another 21 percent are undecided.

Id. at 38.

201. *DOT's View of Airline Deregulation Challenged by Small Cities, Labor,* TRAFFIC WORLD (June 20, 1983) at 16–17. This statement was made by Linda A. Puchala, president of the Association of Flight Attendants, before a subcommittee of the House Committee on Public Works and Transportation. She went on to say:

As part of the struggle to survive harsh competition in the deregulated skies, the industry has extended its cost-cutting efforts not only to reducing labor costs, modifying route structures, and trimming passenger service such as food, ticketing, and baggage handling. The airlines are also cutting costs in ways that passengers don't see—ways which reduce the level of safety.

Id. at 17. See Serrin, *Deregulation Called Disaster for Airline Industry,* N.Y. TIMES, Oct. 5, 1983, at B7; Sawyer, *Six Air Unions Urge a Return to Regulation,* WASH. POST, Oct. 5, 1983, at A1; *Air Unions to Ask for "Re-Regulation" of Ailing Industry,* WALL ST. J., Oct. 5, 1983, at 14; *Why Airline Pilots Are Becoming "Street Fighters",* BUS. WEEK (Oct. 31, 1983) at 127.

202. *See* e.g., *Prevention of Transportation Disintegration,* TRAFFIC WORLD (Apr. 4, 1983) at 1; *Experts on Freight Claim Issue Offer Advice in SNFCC Conference,* TRAFFIC WORLD (April 4, 1983) at 19; *National Trucking Lobby Formed to Unmask Anti-Truck Activities,* TRAFFIC WORLD (May 30, 1983) at 23; *End of Deregulation Experiment, Reintroduction of Some Rules Urged,* TRAFFIC WORLD (Aug. 1, 1983) at 21. *Take Another Look at Deregulation,* AIR COMMERCE, Nov. 28, 1983, at 30; Pitts, *Future of Airlines Worries DU Prof.,* DENVER POST, Oct. 3, 1983, at 9A; Dempsey, *Affordability, Safety of Airlines May Suffer,* L.A. TIMES, Oct. 11, 1983, at 7; Dempsey, *Stormy Skies of Deregulation,* CHICAGO TRIBUNE, Oct. 14, 1983, at 19; Dempsey, *Airline Deregulation's Hostile Skies,* DENVER POST, Oct. 17, 1983, at 3B.

203. Muskin, *The Physical Distribution Infrastructure,* TRANSP. QUARTERLY (Jan. 1983); *Deregulation and the Free Market,* TRAFFIC WORLD (Jan. 10, 1983) at 3.

204. Thayer, *supra* note 100, at 228.

4

EFFICIENCY

ALLOCATIVE EFFICIENCY AND PERFECT COMPETITION

In a purely competitive market in which no single producer has market power, consumers purchase goods and services at prices closely approximating their marginal costs of production. In an ideal competitive marketplace, there is no input waste, excess capacity, or "monopoly" profits. In theory, the most efficient producers provide the commodity or service and the public enjoys an efficient allocation of resources.

Prior to deregulation, the consensus among many economists was that removal of governmental barriers to entry and pricing, particularly for airlines and motor carriers, would result in a healthy competitive environment, one perhaps approaching that of perfect competition. Destructive competition, whose purported existence gave birth to regulation of these two industries in the 1930s, was deemed unlikely to occur. A 1978 Senate committee report on federal regulation provided a fairly typical summary of those attributes of destructive competition deemed not likely to surface in a deregulated air and motor carrier industry:

A justification sometimes offered for regulation is that in the absence of regulation competition would be "destructive." In other words, without regulation, an industry might operate at a loss for long periods....When there is excess capacity in a competitive industry...prices can fall far below average cost. This is because individual producers minimize their losses by continuing to produce so long as their variable (avoidable) costs are covered, since they would incur their fixed (overhead) costs whether they produced or not....Similarly, if resources are mobile [as they are in the trucking and airline industries] depressed conditions in an industry or a region would result in the shift of resources to other employments....What is "destructive" about large and long-lasting losses? Some economists have suggested that they would result in long periods of inadequate investment and slow technical progress which in turn might lead to poor service and periodic shortages.... Another scenario that has sometimes been suggested is that periods of large losses will result in wholesale bankruptcies and the shakeout of many small producers with the result that the industry in question becomes highly concentrated in a few large firms.... A third and related notion is the possibility that powerful firms might engage in predation.... "Destructive competition" seems... unlikely in the cases of airlines and trucks.[1]

The trouble is, transportation is simply not the ideal model of perfect competition that many proponents of deregulation insisted it was. There appear to be significant economies of scale and scope, and economic barriers to entry in the railroad, airline, and less-than-truckload (LTL) motor carrier industries. Widespread bankruptcies and mergers have reduced the number of competitors in each mode to the point that major oligopolies now exist. The theory of contestable markets, which posits that if a monopolist or oligopolist begins to earn supracompetitive profits, new competitive entry, or the threat thereof, will restore pricing competition, appears not to be sustained by the empirical evidence. Hence, many carriers are now able to exert market power. In a situation where market power exists, prices rise and/or the level of service deteriorates, excessive wealth is transferred from consumers to producers, and society's resources are misallocated, as consumers purchase alternative products or services it costs society more to produce. In the long run, the pricing competition enjoyed by many users of the transportation network may be lost as a handful of giants come to dominate the industry. These consequences will be addressed more fully below.

PUBLIC POLICY

A word about policy objectives beyond allocative efficiency is in order. Regulation has traditionally been employed to facilitate a number of public policy objectives which either might not find a high priority in the free market, or are necessary to avoid the problems surrounding the existence of imperfect competition. As was said by Vermont Royster, editor emeritus of the *Wall Street Journal*:

[R]egulaton to protect consumers is almost as old as civilization itself. Tourists to the ruins of Pompeii see an early version of the bureau of weights and measures, a place where the townsfolk could go to be sure they weren't cheated by the local tradesmen. Unfortunately a little larceny is too common in the human species.

So regulation in some form or other is one of the prices we pay for our complex civilization. And the more complicated society becomes, the more need for some watching over its many parts. We shouldn't forget that a great deal of regulation we encounter today in business or in our personal lives arose from a recognized need in the past.[2]

Indeed, it was the rate abuses of the monopoly railroads that gave birth to the Granger movement of the 19th century and in 1887 inspired the creation of the nation's first independent federal regulatory agency—the Interstate Commerce Commission. The ICC was vested with jurisdiction to prohibit discrimination in rail rates and require carriers to offer rates which were just and reasonable. The economic problems of destructive competition during the Great Depression led to the expansion of the jurisdiction of the ICC in 1935 to embrace motor carriage[3] and the creation of the Civil Aeronautics Board in 1938 to regulate the airlines.[4] Historical experience with market imperfection was the catalyst for economic regulation at both the federal and state levels.

In the United States, private ownership of the means of production has been deemed to provide the optimum incentives for efficiency in our economy. Nonetheless, the need for government to facilitate the market's ability to accomplish desirable social and economic objectives has long been recognized:

America's economic system is based on the belief that a competitive, free enterprise system is the best means of achieving national economic goals. Among these goals are minimum unemployment, a low rate of inflation, adequate supplies of goods and services, and an increasing standard of living.

In some industries, the operation of the competitive, free enterprise system does not result in attaining these economic goals. This is because these goals sometimes conflict with the principal goal of private business, which is to maximize profits. For example, it may be more profitable for businesses to limit the supply of a product, thereby raising its price, than to produce a large enough supply to satisfy demand for the product. Limiting supply, however, may reduce the number of jobs in the industry, cause inflation, and negatively impact the standard of living....[T]o prevent this from occurring, government regulation may be used as a means of altering the existing market (i.e. economic environment) to achieve economic goals.

Government regulation is also used to achieve political and social goals when the economic system is unable to achieve these goals. These include such goals as national defense, regional development, and social equity. Like economic goals, political and social goals sometimes cannot be achieved through the economic system because they conflict with businesses' goal to maximize profits.[5]

To achieve societal ends other than those resulting from the pursuit of wealth, the regulatory mechanism provides broad perimeters for production and pricing of privately owned firms. Regulation provides an equitable balance of public interest objectives with market imperatives.

For example, regulatory prohibitions against rate discrimination are essential to rectify the problems of imperfect competition. By requiring carriers to charge both small and large shippers the same rate for equivalent shipments, economic regulation prohibits large shippers from using their monopsony power to exact a lower rate, which would give them superior access to the market for the sale of their products. Regulation thereby reduces the economic advantages attributable to size that a large shipper would otherwise enjoy over its smaller rivals. Both small and large shippers thereby enjoy nondiscriminatory access to the transportation infrastructure, and an equal opportunity both to get their goods to market and to compete fairly in that market for the sale of their goods. Hence, the distortions of imperfect competition are mollified by a requirement that there be no rate or service discrimination.

But even if perfect competition existed in transportation (and it does not), society frequently views the achievement of objectives other than allocative efficiency as more important than fidelity to the ideology of laissez faire. For example, one public policy objective that may be enhanced by economic regulation is wealth distribution, or stated differently, a spreading of the opportunity to participate in economic growth to a more diverse group of participants. For example, prohibitions against rate discrimination require carriers to price their services to small communities at or just below marginal cost, facilitating economic growth in all geographic regions. Small towns and rural communities are served by fewer competitors than urban centers, and in the absence of regulation are more prone to the extraction of higher, noncompetitive rates by monopoly or oligopoly carriers flexing their muscles of market power.

The transportation infrastructure is the foundation upon which the rest of commerce is built. Without adequate and reasonably priced transportation services, small towns and rural communities cannot sustain economic growth. Conversely, the social and economic costs to a town or rural community of poor or highly priced service can be devastating. It can impede growth and thereby cause an outmigration of employment opportunities and population. This will be examined in detail in Chapter 9.

An additional public policy objective encouraged by economic regulation is the forced internalization of the costs of personal injury and property damage caused by poor levels of safety attributable to overworked, exhausted labor and deteriorated equipment. Regulation is superior to judicially ordained tort damage awards for injuries in that however well money can ease the pain of injury, economic compensation for injury frequently cannot restore health, and can never restore life. In contrast, regulation attempts to prevent injuries before they occur, thereby protecting the innocent from harm. Safety, too, will be discussed in greater detail in Chapter 7.

In an analogous sense, regulation protects smaller competitors from the predatory practices of larger rivals trying to drive them out of business. Judicial antitrust remedies ordinarily only award economic compensation to those injured by such anticompetitive conduct, and do not restore the lost competitor to the market. Thus, regulation can keep the market flush with small and medium-size competitors engaged in a healthy competitive battle, providing consumers with a high level of service and just, reasonable rates.

But before focusing on these policy objectives, let us examine the empirical evidence of industry concentration occurring since deregulation, which reveals that perfect competition does not exist in the unregulated marketplace.

CARRIER PRODUCTIVITY UNDER DEREGULATION

Although deregulation proponents confidently predicted substantial improvements in carrier productivity from deregulation, their predictions do not appear to have been realized. In fact, productivity of interstate motor carriers has actually declined since federal deregulation began—this despite the introduction of larger and more efficient equipment.[6] Tremendous over-capacity stimulated both by unlimited entry and the predatory struggle for market share has decreased average load factors for general freight motor carriers. Professor Martin Farris prophetically predicted that this would be the result of deregulation prior to the promulgation of the federal Motor Carrier Act of 1980:

The concern over efficiency in the regulated sector is a real paradox. Critics of [economic regulation allege that it produces inefficiences that are exemplified by] ...low load factors in air transportation, empty backhauls in trucking, energy waste, excess capacity, and idle capital all around. To the critics it is obvious that these "wastes of regulation" could be avoided if regulation were abolished and the natural forces of supply and demand were allowed a free hand. The paradox arises in that the solution to these "inefficiencies caused by regulation" is *more* excess capacity, *more* duplication, *more* wasted energy, *more* idle capital, *more* empty back-hauls, and low load factors caused by allowing more competition in entry and price. As more firms entered these markets and competed on a price basis, excess capacity and waste would increase, not decrease.[7]

De facto federal deregulation of the motor carrier industry began under ICC chairman A. Daniel O'Neal nearly three years prior to promulgation of the Motor Carrier Act of 1980. Although productivity for general freight carriers grew by an average of 0.29% annually after 1969, it has declined by 0.21% per year since 1978. In contrast, productivity levels of all manufacturers have increased an average of 2.4% per year since 1975.[8] As a consequence, thousands of motor carriers have gone bankrupt or ceased operations in the post-deregulation era. Many more would likely have joined their ranks were it not for the unfunded pension liability imposed by the Employer Retirement Security Act (ERISA).[9]

Since transportation is an industry particularly susceptible to overcapacity, unconstrained entry must necessarily lead to distress sale pricing in those markets where competition is excessive, at least until waves of bankruptcies wipe out the smaller and weaker rivals.[10] Since deregulation began, motor

Table 4.1
Bankruptcies and Profit Margins for Interstate Motor Carriers Vis-à-Vis Profit Margins for All Manufacturers Since 1978

Year	Motor Carrier Bankruptcies	Motor Carrier Profit Margins	All Man-ufacturers
1978	162	2.92%	5.4%
1979	186	1.97	5.7
1980	382	1.73	4.8
1981	610	1.58	4.7
1982	960	0.77	3.5
1983	1,228	2.37	4.1
1984	1,416	2.24	4.6
1985	1,543	1.74	3.9
1986	1,564	2.64	3.8
1987	1,351	1.57	4.9

carrier profits, as measured by return on equity, have consistently fallen below the average rate of all manufacturers.

BANKRUPTCIES

Dean Stanley Hille has observed that "over-capacity [in the motor carrier industry] coupled with large discounts to powerful shippers have driven down the profitability of carriers to a point where rates of return in the industry are inadequate to attract new capital, and carrier bankruptcies are at the highest level in history."[11]

One source indicates that between 1979 and the first half of 1986, more than 10,000 motor carriers went out of business.[12] Another states that the number of LTL firms dropped from nearly 500 in 1973 to fewer than 150 in 1986.[13] Between 1978 (the year that de facto deregulation of interstate trucking began) and 1986, more than 54% of the LTL trucking companies went out of business, costing 120,000 employees their jobs.[14] The trend of motor carrier bankruptcies and profit margins since deregulation began is noted in Table 4.1.[15]

Note that carrier failures have exceeded 1,000 each year since 1983.[16] This is all the more remarkable in light of the fact that by 1984 the national economic recession had abated and by 1986 fuel prices had declined significantly. As we shall see below, these waves of carrier bankruptcies have created service and pricing instability and a deteriorating margin of safety.

Note also that the profit margins of all manufacturers have been consistently superior to those of interstate motor carriers since deregulation began. Although profit margins for all manufacturers fell during the recession of the early 1980s, the drop was not nearly as drastic as that experienced by the deregulated motor carriers. Today, the profit margin of interstate motor carriers is among the lowest of all American industries.[17]

While manufacturers seem to have rebounded from the depths of the recession of the early 1980s, profit margins in the motor carrier industry began to plummet beforehand and continued after it. Further, despite the record number of bankruptcies, which have absorbed some of the excess carrier capacity, Table 4.1 reveals that the gap between motor carrier profits and those of all manufacturers although narrowing in 1986, grew sharply wider in 1987.

Airlines have also suffered severe losses since deregulation. Deregulation was largely premised on the theory of contestable markets—the notion that there were no significant economies of scale or barriers to entry in the airline industry. New competitors, it was argued, would spring up to challenge the entrenched incumbents, and the industry would become hotly competitive. In the long run, we see how wrong these predictions were.

In the Darwinian scramble for survival and market share unleased by deregulation, hundreds of carriers have gone into bankruptcy, including such darlings of deregulation as Air Florida and Freddie Laker's Skytrain. Like Sir Freddie Laker, Donald Burr's smiling face stared out from the cover of *Time*, an expression of the overwhelming success of airline deregulation that the media initially perceived. But not long thereafter, his airline, People Express, like so many others, was standing on the precipice of bankruptcy and was swallowed by one of the giant megacarriers. Alfred Kahn once pointed to these new upstart airlines as evidence that deregulation was a brilliant success. But most have since dropped from the skies into the social Darwinist grave of bankruptcy. A rash of mergers and bankruptcies has turned the industry into a national oligopoly, and in many markets, a monopoly.

As one careful observer of the airline industry, Melvin Brenner, noted:

The eight years of deregulation comprise the worst financial period in airline history. The cumulative industry operations in those eight years generated a loss of over $7 billion, when interest payments are included with operating expenses.... The deregulation era is the first time that the industry as a whole has recorded a cumulative loss over an eight-year period.... The principal cause of the poor financial results has been the tendency of airlines to engage in *destructive* competition in the absence of regulation—a tendency evident particularly in excess capacity and fare wars....

By failing to cover fixed costs, marginal cost reliance jeopardizes the industry's long term viability.[18]

Ten years after he implemented airline deregulation as President Carter's chairman of the Civil Aeronautics Board, Alfred Kahn admitted, "There is no denying that the profit record of the industry since 1978 has been dismal, that deregulation bears substantial responsibility, and that the proponents of deregulation did not anticipate such financial distress—either so intense or so long-continued."[19]

In one important sense, the economic characteristics of transportation differ from those of most other sectors of the economy and make it inherently vulnerable to overcapacity. If a manufacturer or retailer suffers a period of slack demand, unsold goods can usually be stored and sold another day, when demand improves. In contrast, transportation firms sell what is, in essence, an instantly perishable commodity. Once the truck leaves its loading dock, once the train pulls its boxcars down the track, and once an aircraft taxis down the runway, any unused capacity is lost forever. This inevitably leads to distress sale pricing during weak demand periods, or when excess capacity created by unlimited entry abounds. Hence, the vicissitudes of the market cycle are particularly brutal for transporation. It is as if a grocer was faced with spoilage of all his canned goods on a daily basis—as if they had the properties of open jars of unrefrigerated mayonnaise. He would be forced to have a fire sale every afternoon.

In trucking, things are worse still, for many small, unsophisticated companies do not know what their marginal costs are. Their naivete, or the monopsony bullying tactics of large shippers, can result in underpricing of their services and eventual bankruptcy. In the interim, shippers enjoy a windfall at the expense of motor carrier labor and investors, while trucking productivity and profitability decline. For while the small, unsophisticated trucking companies are hemorrhaging dollars, they are taking traffic away from efficient firms, causing them to bleed as well.

The established, efficient firms respond to such overcapacity by pricing at marginal costs (or sometimes, it has been alleged, by engaging in predatory practices if they can afford it, to hasten the demise of the new entrant).[20] But a company can price at the margin for only so long. It must eventually recover its fixed costs, or it too is doomed. Thus, under deregulation, many small, unsophisticated entrepreneurs have dragged a number of established, efficient companies with them into the Darwinian grave of bankruptcy.

SUBHAULERS UNDER DEREGULATION

Independent owner-operators are also taking an economic beating under deregulation, as the profit margins of the carriers with which they contract are squeezed. These are the small entrepreneurs, the rugged individualists, who own their own tractors and lease their services to common carriers. Of the 300,000 in existence in 1980, the *Wall Street Journal* has estimated that fewer than 100,000 are still on the highway.[21]

Their competitive presence once offered some promise for the notion of new competitive entry and contestability. But the disastrous results of excessive competition have absorbed much of this segment of the industry. As we shall see below, the struggle to survive on the brink of bankruptcy creates a momentum all its own of deferred maintenance and aged equipment, which in turn jeopardizes the safety of those with whom they share the highways.

Subhaulers, comprised mostly of owner-operators, serve as an important supplement to the common carrier system. They give the system needed flexibility and additional capacity, which is particularly valuable during periods of peak demand.

As the prime carriers have been driven against the wall by the overcapacity generated by unlimited entry, and by shippers with monopsony power, rates have been sent tumbling. The squeeze on prime carriers has, quite naturally, squeezed every aspect of their costs, including maintenance, vehicular replacement, labor, and subhaulers. Hence, the tragedy of subhaulers is merely one aspect of a broader picture in which deregulation assaults prime carriers, and the inevitable consequence is that every enterprise affiliated with prime haulers suffers too.

INDUSTRY CONCENTRATION

During the past decade, several major American industries have been subjected to federal deregulation. These include telecommunications, airlines, railroads, bus companies, and motor carriers. The overriding and unmistakable trend that cuts across each of these industries has been an unambiguous movement toward hefty concentration in a remarkably short period of time. Indeed, the economic pressures placed upon carriers by the intensive competition unleashed by deregulation has reduced the number of major competitors through waves of bankruptcies and mergers to the point that several of these industries have become oligopolies.

By the end of 1986, AT&T retained an 82% share of the long-distance telecommunications market, and a near monopoly in the toll-free, big business, and international markets.[22] The six largest airlines increased their passenger share from 73% in 1973 to 84% in 1986.[23] The largest freight railroads in 1978 had merged into seven by 1986.[24] The bus duopoly evolved into a national monopoly with the merger of Greyhound and Trailways. And the top 10 less-than truckload motor carriers accounted for almost 60% of shipments and 90% of industry profits.[25] Let us look more closely at each transport mode.

Motor Carriers

In 1978, the largest four LTL motor carriers enjoyed 20% of the industry's shipments; the top 10 accounted for 39%; and the top 20 for 43%. By early 1985, the top four had 35% (a 75% increase); the top 10 had 60% (a 70% increase); and the top 20 enjoyed 67% of the market (a 56% increase since 1978).[26] By 1988, the four largest LTL carriers enjoyed 40% of the 100 largest carriers' gross revenue, and 48% of its profits. All geographic regions in the nation have experienced increased concentration in the trucking industry since deregulation.[27]

Entry into the LTL industry has proven difficult because of the high costs incurred in developing terminal operations geared to the movement of small shipments. Major LTL trucking companies utilize a network of hub-and-spoke systems which include hundreds of satellite terminals and dozens of large consolidation centers.[28] Professor Nicholas Glaskowsky summarized the considerable economies of scale in the LTL industry:

A modern LTL operation of significant size involves an extensive network of terminals, a computerized management information system, a large number of employees, has a need for a highly skilled management, and must be able to cope with the fact that most of its costs are fixed in the short run and at least semi-fixed in the longer run. For these reasons, the barriers to entry in the LTL sector of the motor carrier industry are high. Accordingly, it is in this sector of the motor carrier industry that there is considerable potential for economic concentration. That potential has been realized dramatically since the industry was deregulated.[29]

These high barriers to entry have effectively prohibited a single new major LTL carrier from emerging since 1978.[30] The only major new entrant into the nationwide less-than-truckload industry since promulgation of the federal Motor Carrier Act of 1980 was Leaseway, which has since abandoned the costly effort.[31] It is somewhat ironic that Leaseway, a vigorous advocate of the philosophy of deregulation, proved incapable of sustaining its presence once freed to compete. The same could be said of Sir Freddie Laker in the airline industry.

Poor levels of productivity, excessive capacity, numerous bankruptcies, significant economies of scale and scope, and economic barriers to entry have caused the number of major LTL carriers to dwindle since deregulation. Concentration flourishes:

The LTL for-hire carrier segment of the industry is *not* atomistic in any sense of the word. A small and still shrinking group of increasingly large firms dominates this traffic nationally. LTL operations *do* have significant operating economies of scale. The established large national LTL carriers *are* the beneficiaries of an almost insurmountable financial barrier to entry.[32] On the basis of the indisputable hard evidence, it is clear that one of the most significant results of deregulation of the motor carrier industry is that *large scale interstate LTL motor carriage has become a closed club with a dwindling number of members*....The rate of growth of interstate LTL traffic concentration since deregulation is without parallel in American business history. It is unquestionably a direct result of motor carrier deregulation, and the increasing concentration of LTL traffic in the hands of a shrinking number of carriers is continuing.[33]

At the other end of the spectrum, smaller interstate trucking companies complain that the large LTL carriers are expanding into regional markets by engaging in predatory pricing; large carriers, it is alleged, use the profits they earn on less competitive long-haul routes to sustain the deep (and sometimes below-cost) discounts offered in short-haul markets. As a consequence, there has been a high failure rate among small and medium-size motor carriers.[34]

The insurance crisis is also contributing to the overwhelming number of bankruptcies in this industry. Small entrepreneurs are encountering significant economic barriers to entry in the high cost (and, in some instances, unavailability) of insurance. Insurance rates appear to be skyrocketing not only because of the national insurance crisis, but also because, in an era of intensive competition in which profits are inadequate, maintenance has been deferred, the margin of safety has deteriorated, and accident rates have soared.

Moreover, with the high failure rate, the capital markets for new trucking ventures are drying up. Hence, the industry may ultimately become even more concentrated and less competitive than it is now as deregulation takes its toll on the small trucking competitors unable to survive the Darwinian economic process. Professor Grant Davis put it this way:

Unlimited competition in trucking was envisioned to result in small units employing highly mobile capital. The growing concentration trend, the financial environment, and carrier market strategy indicate that capital is not mobile, and a finite market is in the process of being dominated by a limited number of carriers. Small shippers dependent upon this segment of the industry for service are virtually "captive," and rates will continue to increase in certain segments of this market.[35]

Railroads

The trend toward concentration cuts across all of the deregulated industries. Since 1980, when Congress passed the Staggers Rail Act, we have witnessed tremendously large railroad mergers. East of the Mississippi there are today but three major railroads: in 1980, the Chessie and Family Lines System merged to become CSX; in 1981, the Norfolk & Western and Southern merged to become the Norfolk/Southern; and during the 1970s, eight railroads in the northeastern United States merged to form Conrail.[36]

West of the Mississippi, only four major railroads exist: in 1980 the

Burlington Northern merged with the Frisco; in 1982 the Union Pacific, Missouri Pacific, and Western Pacific merged; only the proposed Santa Fe/Southern Pacific merger was disapproved by the Interstate Commerce Commission.[37]

The rail industry is today an oligopoly. Seven major firms are responsible for 85% of the nation's revenue-ton miles[38] Moreover, major members of the industry are beginning to purchase their competitors. They are thereby becoming origin-to-destination intermodal megacarriers. For example, the Burlington Northern Railroad is acquiring a half dozen motor carriers.[39] The Norfolk/Southern purchased the nation's largest household goods carrier, North American Van Lines.[40] The Union Pacific purchased the nation's fifth largest motor carrier, Overnite Transportation.[41]

Railroads are also purchasing major pipelines, ocean shipping, and inland water companies. For example, in 1984 CSX Corporation, the nation's second largest railroad, purchased American Commercial Lines, the parent of the nation's largest barge company. CSX acquired Sea-Land Corporation, the nation's largest U.S.-flag ocean carrier. It also bought Texas Gas, which has significant pipeline interests. Burlington Northern has also gone into the pipeline business, purchasing El Paso Natural Gas. And Norfolk/Southern announced its intention to go into the barge business.[42] For the movement of large, bulk commodities, there are few competitive alternatives. And the railroads seem to be buying up most of them.

Airlines

During the Reagan administration, the U.S. Department of Transportation (DOT) regularly reported misleading data about the impact of deregulation. For example, in testimony submitted to a Senate subcommittee, DOT assistant secretary Matthew Scocozza observed, "As you know, aviation operations were deregulated in 1978 and the changes brought by this policy shape today's market. The results? Nine years ago approximately 39 commercial carriers were operating. A recent count estimates that 131 are now in service."[43]

The numbers may be right, but the impression is grossly misleading. Since promulgation of the Airline Deregulation Act of 1978, the airline industry has also become an oligopoly, and in many major markets, a monopoly. While small air carriers have entered, more than 150 airlines have fallen from the skies into bankruptcy.

In January 1986, the five largest airlines accounted for 54% of the domestic passenger market; by 1987, the figure had grown to 72%. Fifteen independent airlines operating at the beginning of 1986 had been merged into six megacarriers by the end of 1987.[44] One commentator challenged DOT's optimistic portrait of new competition under deregulation:

The 11 major airlines have shrunk to eight; the eight former local service carriers are now two and they are trying to merge; the eight original low-cost charter airlines have been reduced to one, through bankruptcy and abandonment; 14 former regional airlines have shrunk to only four; over 100 new upstart airlines were certified by the CAB and about 32 got off the ground and most of those crashed, leaving only a handful still operating; of the 50 top commuters in existence in 1978, 29 have disappeared....Today, the top 50 commuter carriers who constitute 90 percent of that industry are captives of the major carriers, in part or in total owned, controlled, and financed by the giant airlines and relegated to serving the big airlines at their hubs.[45]

Never before has the United States experienced the level of concentration in aviation that we have now. In several cities, a single airline enjoys virtual monopoly domination, with 60–80% of landings, takeoffs, gates, and passengers. These include the hubs of Baltimore (51% US Air), Charlotte (73% Piedmont), Cincinnati (68% Delta), Dayton (64% Piedmont), Detroit (64% Northwest), Houston Intercontinental (72% Texas Air), Memphis (67% Northwest), Minneapolis/St. Paul (82% Northwest), Nashville (60% American), Newark (65% Texas Air), Pittsburgh (83% US Air), Salt Lake City (75% Delta), and St. Louis (82% TWA). Only four of America's hubs are duopolies: Atlanta (95% Delta and Eastern), Chicago (72% American and United), Dallas (87% American and Delta), and Denver (89% Texas Air and United). Since Frontier was absorbed, first by People Express and then by Continental (Texas Air), no hub has had the three-carrier competition theretofore enjoyed by Denver.[46]

Since deregulation, all major airlines have created hub-and-spoke systems, funneling their arrivals and departures into and out of hub airports where they dominate the arrivals, departures, and infrastructure. Deregulation has freed them to leave competitive and smaller markets and consolidate their strength into regional, hub, and market monopolies and oligopolies. As the dust settles upon the bankruptcies and mergers of deregulation we see a horizon devoid of meaningful competition. Even before bankruptcy of Eastern Airlines, nearly two-thirds of city-pair markets were airline monopolies and another 20% were duopolies.

Much criticism has been levied at the Department of Transportation for approving every merger submitted to it since it assumed the Civil Aeronautics Board's jurisdiction over mergers, acquisitions, and consolidations (under section 408 of the Federal Aviation Act) upon the CAB's demise on December 31, 1984. The Airline Deregulation Act of 1978 insisted that the agency guard against "unfair, deceptive, predatory, or anticompetitive practices" and avoid "unreasonable industry concentration, excessive market domination," and similar occurrences which might enable "carriers unreasonably to increase prices, reduce services, or exclude competition."[47] But these admonitions fell on deaf ears at DOT, which never met a merger it didn't like.

DOT approved them all. It approved Texas Air's (i.e., Continental and New York Air) acquisition of both People Express (which included Frontier) and Eastern Airlines (which included Braniff's Latin American routes);[48] United acquisition of Pan Am's transpacific routes; American's acquisition of Air Cal; Delta's acquisition of Western; Northwest's acquisition of Republic: TWA's acquisition of Ozark; and US Air's acquisition of PSA and Piedmont, to mention only a few. This has sharply increased national levels of concentration to the point that the eight largest airlines control 94% of the domestic passenger market.[49] Concentration levels are even more pronounced when one recognizes that before deregulation we had a healthy charter industry that had a significant market share. Under deregulation it has virtually vanished.[50]

The father of airline deregulation, Alfred Kahn, has appeared dismayed by what he characterizes as an "uncomfortably tight oligopoly." He has been particularly critical of the Department of Transportation's permissive approach to airline mergers: "They have been *permitted* by a totally, and in my view indefensibly, complaisant Department of Transportation. It is absurd to blame deregulation for this abysmal dereliction."[51] Certainly, DOT deserves some severe criticism for its abdication of antitrust responsibility to protect the public from excessive concentration.[52]

Clearly, the merger of Northwest and Republic resulted in sharply increased levels of concentration at Minneapolis/St. Paul and Detroit; and equally clearly, the same happened at St. Louis when DOT approved the merger of TWA with Ozark Airlines. But as Table 4.2 reveals, massive hub concentration has occurred at a large number of cities where no merger had a significant impact.

Indeed, the explanation for concentration at all but Detroit, Minneapolis/St. Paul, and St. Louis is not DOT's generous approval of airline mergers, but simply the entry and exit opportunities unleashed by deregulation. Carriers adopting particular cities as hubs have increased frequencies and leased more gates, while incumbent airlines have quietly exited in favor of market dominance opportunities of their own in other hub airports. Kahn is therefore wrong. Freedom to enter and exit markets is the very heart of deregulation, and it is more responsible for concentration at hub airports than is the DOT's "abysmal dereliction," abysmal through it clearly is. The CAB would never have approved the widespread entry and abandonments which produced this massive hub concentration. Nonetheless, the DOT's antitrust delinquency is responsible for national concentration levels which are unacceptable, and which dampen competition by reducing the number of competitors in particular city pairs. Although some city-pair markets are less concentrated than before deregulation, by early 1989 nearly two-thirds of city-pairs were airline monopolies.

One additional observation about concentration levels before and after deregulation is appropriate. Before deregulation, even a high level of concentration could be tolerated because fare levels were regulated. A monop-

Table 4.2
Single-Carrier Concentration at Major Airports Pre and Post Deregulation

Airport	1977	1987
Baltimore/Washington	24.5% US Air	60.0% USAir*
Cincinnati	35.0% Delta	67.6% Delta
Detroit Metropolitan	21.2% Delta	64.9% Northwest
Houston Intercontinental	20.4% Continental	71.5% Continental
Memphis	40.2% Delta	86.7% Northwest
Minneapolis/St. Paul	45.9% Northwest	81.6% Northwest
Nashville Metropolitan	28.2% American	60.2% American
Pittsburgh	43.7% US Air	82.8% US Air
St. Louis-Lambert	39.1% TWA	82.3% TWA
Salt Lake City	39.6% Western	74.5% Delta
AVERAGE	33.8%	73.2%

* Includes Piedmont

Source: Consumer Reports (June 1988), at 362–67.

olist could not reap monopoly profits from a market because the CAB regulated rates, ensuring that they were "just and reasonable." But in a post-deregulation environment these high levels of concentration are a matter of serious concern, for the regulatory mechanism which formerly shielded consumers from price gouging has been eradicated by deregulation, and the theory of contestable markets seems not to be sustained by the empirical evidence of deregulation.[53] Today, there appear to be significant economies of scale in the airline industry.

For several reasons, it is unlikely that a new entrant will emerge to rival the megacarriers. First, the infrastructure of gates, terminal facilities, and (at four of America's busiest airports—Chicago O'Hare, Washington National, and New York's LaGuardia and Kennedy) landing slots have been consumed. There are no gates to lease to a new entrant at 68% of our airports. Even if an incumbent would be willing to lease a gate to an upstart airline (and at an incumbent's hub, few are so willing), the incumbent could nevertheless exact monopoly rents. The decision of the DOT to allow carriers to buy and sell landing slots means that the deeper-pocket carriers can purchase market share and thereby enjoy the market power to reap oligopoly profits.[54]

Second, the largest airlines today own the largest computer reservations systems, from which most tickets are sold. Many critics have argued that not only does such vertical integration offer the incumbents the potential to enjoy various forms of system bias (including screen bias, connecting point bias, and database bias),[55] it gives the incumbents superior access to market information, with which they can adjust the number of seats for which discounts are offered on an hourly basis depending on passenger demand for seats.[56] Moreover, the advantages of being listed in the computer as an "on-line" connection with one of the major airlines has led 48 of the 50 small air carriers to affiliate themselves with the megacarriers, renaming their companies (to, for example, United Express, Continental Express, American Eagle) and repainting their aircraft in megacarrier colors. Of the 31.7 million passengers who aboard regional airlines in 1987, 90% were aboard computer reservations system code-sharing airlines.[57] The small carriers have become, in effect, franchisees of the behemoths of the industry, and are therefore an unlikely source from which new competition will spring. They are also declining in number. The regional airlines, peaking at 246 in 1981, dwindled to 168 in 1987.[58]

Third, large airlines have more attractive frequent flyer programs, which serve as a lure to business travelers, the most lucrative segment of the market. Brand loyalty makes it difficult for a new rival to find a niche, particularly when its frequent flyer program offers free travel to decidedly less exotic destinations.

Fourth, although new entrants enjoyed significantly lower labor costs in the inaugural years of deregulation, the squeeze on carrier profits unleashed by deregulation has forced management to exact serious concessions in terms of labor wages and work rules. Some, like Continental and TWA, have effectively crushed their unions. Thus, the margin of labor cost and productivity between a new entrant and an established airline has been significantly narrowed.

Finally, with 150 airlines having gone bankrupt since 1978, investor confidence in new airline ventures has evaporated. Hence, significant new entry is highly unlikely in the deregulated airline industry.[59]

The dominance by incumbent carriers of gates, terminal space, landing and takeoff slots, computer reservations systems, and the most attractive frequent flyer programs makes it unlikely that new entrants will emerge to challenge the megacarriers. Barriers to entry and economies of scale do exist in the airline industry; the theory of contestable markets, which supplied the intellectual justification for deregulation, has been refuted by an overwhelming body of empirical evidence. After a decade of deregulation, one thing is clear—the oligopoly that resulted from deregulation is here to stay.

That of course, means that the price discounts that many consumers have enjoyed in recent years will likely evaporate. Low fares have stimulated new traffic in the past decade, mostly for vacation travelers flying between large cities served by more than a single carrier. But business travelers and others unwilling to sleep in strange cities on Saturday nights, individuals flying to small towns, or people who, at the last minute, have to fly home for funerals or other emergencies, are ineligible for these discounts. So deregulation's benefits have been unevenly distributed. Pricing discrimination is pervasive.

Kahn once argued that deregulation would bring about cost-based pricing. After a decade of deregulation, pricing seems to reflect the level of competition in any market, not costs. There seems to be a positive correlation between more competition and lower prices, and between fewer competitors and higher prices. With the industry becoming more highly concentrated, prices are ascending.

But even if new entry is unlikely, why should we be concerned with the high level of concentration which has emerged in the airline industry under deregulation? After all, even though Coke and Pepsi dominate the soft drink industry, don't we still have pricing competition between them? Although other American industries are dominated by huge firms, transportation is different in the way it impacts the economy. Melvin Brenner said it best:

> Other industries, even when comprised of only a few large firms, do not usually end up with a one-supplier monopoly in specific local markets. But this can happen in air transportation.
>
> Moreover, because of the nature of transportation, a local monopoly can do greater harm to a community than could a local monopoly in some other industry. This is because transportation is a basic part of the economic/social/cultural infrastructure, which affects the efficiency of all other business activities in a community and the quality of life of its residents. The ability of a city to retain existing industries, and attract new ones, is uniquely dependent upon the adequacy, convenience, and reasonable pricing of its airline service.[60]

Emerging Oligopolies

All deregulated transportation industries—airlines, bus companies, motor carriers, and railroads—are marching to the drum of increased concentration. Each is becoming a monopoly or oligopoly.

Traditionally healthy carriers have been bankrupted or substantially driven out of the transportation industry by the selective rate cutting of major competitors that now dominate the market nationally. Increased concentration created by bankruptcies of small and medium-size competitors increases the probability that the firms remaining will be in a position, unilaterally or collectively, to exercise market power.

As noted above, market power is the ability of one or more firms to maximize profits by maintaining prices above or restricting output below the competitive level for a significant period of time. That results in the transfer of wealth from consumers to producers and is therefore regressive in character. A transportation industry with market power will mean that even the price wars that the nation's largest shippers (and passengers flying between major markets) have enjoyed since deregulation began may be a short-term phenomenon.

Deregulation wasn't supposed to turn out this way. It was supposed to ensure that consumers enjoyed more competition, not less. Its proponents assured us that if an incumbent were to raise its prices in a monopoly or oligopoly market, and thereby enjoy supracompetitive profits, new competitors would be attracted like sharks to the smell of blood, and would reestablish the competitive equilibrium. This was the theory of contestable markets, which was premised upon the false assumption that transportation was inherently competitive and the only barriers to entry were governmental requirements that carriers obtain certificates of public convenience and necessity before being allowed to compete.

The foundation upon which the theory rested has been shattered by an overwhelming body of empirical evidence that proves that economic barriers to entry, significant advantages in terms of traffic density, and economies of scale and scope do exist in the airline, railroad, bus, and LTL trucking industries. The concentration that has inevitably emerged is a natural consequence of the dynamics of deregulation. We will take a more careful look at industry trends toward concentration in Chapter 8.

NOTES

1. *Study on Federal Regulation, Report of the Senate Comm. on Government Affairs*, 96th Cong., 1st Sess. 13–15 (1978).

2. Royster, *"Regulation" Isn't a Dirty Word*, WALL ST. J., Sept. 9, 1987, at 36.

3. P. DEMPSEY & W. THOMS, LAW & ECONOMIC REGULATION IN TRANSPORTATION 7–12 (1986).

4. Dempsey, *The Rise and Fall of the Civil Aeronautics Board—Opening Wide the Floodgates of Entry*, 11 TRANSP. L.J. 95 (1979).

5. COLORADO STATE AUDITOR, PERFORMANCE AUDIT OF THE PUBLIC UTILITIES COMMISSION 14–15 (1988) [hereinafter PUC PERFORMANCE AUDIT].

6. *Oversight of the Motor Carrier Act of 1980: Hearings before the Subcomm. on Surface Transportation of the Senate Comm. on Commerce, Science and Transportation*, 99th Cong., 1st Sess. 96 (statement of Dean Stanley J. Hille) [hereinafter *1985 Senate Hearings on MCA*].

7. Farris, *The Case against Deregulation in Transportation, Power, and Communications*, 46 ICC PRAC. J. 306, 329 (1978) [emphasis in the original].

8. *Panelists Deplore Truck Deregulation, Rate Discrimination at NARUC Confab*, TRAFFIC WORLD (Dec. 1, 1986) at 68–69 [hereinafter cited as *Rate Discrimination*].

9. Dempsey, *Transportation Deregulation—On a Collision Course?* 13 TRANSP. L.J. 329, 346–49 (1984) and N. GLASKOWSKY, EFFECTS OF DEREGULATION ON MOTOR CARRIERS 18–19 (1986).

10. Dempsey, *supra* note 9, at 351.

11. *1985 Senate Hearings on MCA, supra* note 6, at 100.

12. *Rate Discrimination, supra* note 8, at 69.

13. Silberman & Hill, *State of the LTL Industry,* TRANSPORTATION EX-ECUTIVE UPDATE (Mar./Apr. 1988) at 6.

14. Comments of Martin E. Foley before the California PUC En Banc Hearing on Regulation of the State's For-Hire Trucking Industry, at 34 (Feb. 12, 1988) [hereinafter M. Foley].

15. These statistics were compiled by Ron Roth, Director of Statistical Analysis of the American Trucking Associations (Jan. 1988). Profit margins are measured in terms of after-tax earnings as a percentage of gross revenues.

16. *Truckers in Trouble,* INSIGHT (Nov. 3, 1986) at 45.

17. *See* R. Roth, Economic and Financial Conditions of the Regulated Motor Carrier Industry 4 (unpublished monograph, 1983).

18. Brenner, *Airline Deregulation—A Case Study in Public Policy Failure,* 16 TRANSP. L.J. 179, 200–01 (1988) [emphasis in original].

19. Kahn, *Airline Deregulation—A Mixed Bag, But a Clear Success Nevertheless,* 16 TRANSP. L.J. 229, 248 (1988) [citation omitted].

20. Allegations of predatory behavior have been raised by many carriers. *See* e.g., Marnell v. United Parcel Service, 260 F. Supp. 391 (N.D. Cal. 1966) and Broadway Delivery Service v. United Parcel Service, 651 F.2d 122 (2d Cir. 1981), *cert. den.* 454 U.S. 968 (1981).

21. Richards, *Independent Truckers Who Hailed Deregulation Reconsider As a Rate War Rages and Taxes Rise,* WALL ST. J., Mar. 31, 1983, at 50.

22. *Is Deregulation Working?,* BUS. WEEK (Dec. 22, 1986) at 50, 52.

23. *Id.* In the short term, competition unleashed by deregulation reduced the dominance by the largest airlines. Thus, in January, 1986, the five largest airlines accounted for 54.3% of the domestic passenger market. But by June of 1987, after a series of unprecedented mergers, their share had soared to 72.2%. Dempsey, *Antitrust Law and Public Policy in Transportation: Monopoly I$ the Name of the Game,* 21 GA. L. REV. 505, 543 (1987).

24. *Is Deregulation Working? supra* note 22, at 52. *See* Dempsey, *supra* note 9, at 367–68.

25. *Is Deregulation Working?, supra* note 22, at 52.

26. N. GLASKOWSKY, *supra* note 9, at 25.

27. U.S. GENERAL ACCOUNTING OFFICE, TRUCKING REGULATION 11, 14 (1987).

28. *Is Deregulation Working?, supra* note 22, at 53.

29. N. GLASKOWSKY, *supra* note 9, at 25.

30. *Is Deregulation Working?, supra* note 22, at 53.

31. *Id.* at 16.

32. N. GLASKOWSKY, *supra* note 9, at 9 [emphasis in original].

32. *Id.* at 26 [emphasis in original].

33. *Id.*

34. Davis, *Unresolved Issues in U.S. Trucking Regulatory Modernization Debate,* 54 TRANSP. PRAC. J. 163, 171 (1987).

36. Dempsey, *supra* note 23, at 547–48.

37. *Id.* at 548–49.

38. Dempsey, *supra* note 9, at 367.

39. ICC STAFF REPORT NO. 10, at 15 (1986). TRAFFIC WORLD (Aug. 4, 1986), at 36.

40. D. SWEENEY, C. MCCARTHY, S. KALISH, & J. CUTLER, JR., TRANS-PORTATION DEREGULATION: WHAT'S DEREGULATED AND WHAT ISN'T 25–26 (1986).

41. *Union Pacific to Buy Overnite for $1.2 Billion*, WALL ST. J., Sept. 19, 1986, at 3.

42. Dempsey, *supra* note 23, at 551–52.

43. *The Effect of Airline Deregulation on the Rural Economy: Hearings before the Subcomm. on Rural Economy and Family Farming of the Senate Comm. on Small Business*, 100th Cong., 1st Sess. 145 (1987) (statement of Matthew V. Sco-cozza) [hereinafter *1987 Senate Hearings on Deregulation*].

44. Brenner, *supra* note 18, at 180.

45. *1987 Senate Hearings on Deregulation*, *supra* note 43, at 61–62 (testimony of Morten S. Beyer).

46. Dempsey, *supra* note 23, at 592–93.

47. 49 U.S.C. sec. 1302(a)(7). *See* Dempsey, *supra* note 4, at 135.

48. DOT did require that some shuttle routes be sold off in the northeastern corridor, but otherwise the Eastern acquisition by Texas Air passed through un-molested. *See* Dempsey, *supra* note 23, at 538.

49. *Id.*

50. *See* Brenner, *supra* note 18, at 184.

51. Kahn, *supra* note 19, at 234.

52. Dempsey, *supra* note 23.

53. *See* Brenner, *supra* note 18. Even deregulation's most adamant proponents are now beginning to admit this. *See* Levine, *Airline Competition in Deregulated Markets: Theory, Firm Strategy, and Public Policy*, 4 YALE J. REG. 393 (1987); Moore, *U.S. Airline Deregulation: Its Effects on Passengers, Capital, and Labor*, 29 J. L. & ECON. 1 (1986).

54. *See* Hardaway, *The FAA "Buy-Sell" Slot Rule: Airline Deregulation at the Crossroads*, 52 J. AIR L. & COM. 1 (1986).

55. *See* Saunders, *The Antitrust Implications of Computer Reservations Systems*, 51 J. AIR L. & COM. 157 (1985).

56. GENERAL ACCOUNTING OFFICE, AIRLINE COMPETITION: IMPACT OF COMPUTERIZED RESERVATIONS SYSTEMS (1986).

57. *Dereg's Falling Stars*, OAG FREQUENT FLYER (Aug. 1988) at 28.

58. *Id.*

59. *See* Dempsey, *supra* note 23.

60. Brenner, *supra* note 18, at 189.

5

PRICING

Competition has enabled some users (particularly large shippers and discretionary passengers in major airline markets) to enjoy lower prices. But these benefits have been unevenly distributed, for small businesses, small towns, and rural communities pay relatively higher prices for poorer service. Moreover, as noted in Chapters 4 and 8, the unprecedented concentration emerging in all transport modes threatens to make the low prices enjoyed in large, competitive markets a short-term phenomenon.

Deregulation inevitably eradicates some of the important benefits derived from the traditional scheme of economic regulation, including the prohibition against pricing discrimination. As Professors Wagner and Dean have noted, "regulation may better provide for rate equity for various shipper groups among commodities and between geographical regions. It can reduce discrimination."[1] Thus, it is no surprise that deregulation became a catalyst for pricing and service discrimination.

CROSS SUBSIDIZATION

Prior to deregulation there was some amount of cross-subsidization within the transportation industry. While carriers were allowed to serve specified lucrative routes, they were also required to serve less lucrative markets in the geographic territory designated by their operating certificates. Carriers were expected to cross-subsidize losses or meager profits earned from serving small communities with healthier revenues earned from dense, lucrative markets, thereby providing just and reasonable rates to both. Deregulation was designed to end this internal cross-subsidization on grounds that such wealth redistribution created allocative inefficiency.

Actually, cross-subsidization appears merely to have been reversed in direction, rather than eliminated. Today, carriers can extract higher rates from their monopoly and oligopoly markets (typically small and rural communities) to cross-subsidize the losses they are incurring as a result of the intensive competitive battles being waged for market share in dense traffic lanes. The carriers which are ultimately victorious in those price wars stand to reap significant economic rewards once the dust has settled and the competition has been eliminated. Such are the spoils of economic battle.

With the floodgates of deregulation thrown open to new entrants and the advent of unconstrained pricing, carriers have been able to charge predatory rates in competitive markets and cross-subsidize such losses with higher, discriminatory rates in oligopoly and monopoly markets. As we have seen, significant barriers to entry and economies of scale exist in the railroad, airline, and less-than-truckload motor carrier industries, making it possible for survivors to exert market power once competition has fallen by the wayside.

MONOPOLY

The impact of market power is already visible in the rail industry, which is the most heavily concentrated of transport modes, the one with the largest fixed costs, and the one with the most significant economies of scale and barriers to entry. Many shippers of bulk commodities, typically grain and coal, have no realistic alternative to monopoly railroads to get their product to market. There is often no parallel railroad or barge line, and no economically feasible trucking operation. As a consequence, the railroads are free to charge whatever the market will bear. These inflated rates are passed on to consumers in the form of higher electric bills by their coal-fired utilities. The Consumer Federation of America estimates that these excessive charges are costing consumers $1.3 billion a year.[2]

As we saw in Chapter 4, most of the transport modes are becoming oligopolies; but most have not yet acquired the dominant position for many commodities that the railroads have attained. For example, in trucking, many carriers find themselves dwarfed by the economic power of America's largest shippers.

MONOPSONY

Professor Grant Davis has observed that the nation's largest shippers exert monopsony power over trucking companies. By virtue of the economic leverage they wield by conferring or withholding their vast volumes of freight, the *Fortune* 500 can unilaterally dictate rates at (and for cash-starved carriers, below) the marginal costs of trucking companies.[3] Professor James Rakowski agrees:

[A]bout 90 percent of the firms in the LTL general freight industry, including some of the largest firms, are having severe financial difficulty. Firms on the brink of bankruptcy cannot worry about long range planning and marketing studies. Carriers up against the wall need cash for tomorrow (actually the bills are probably long past due), not next week. They must price accordingly to get the traffic, regardless of their costs.[4]

In essence, the problem is one of greatly unequal market power between shippers and truck companies. The technical term for a situation like this is "monopsony." It is in very simplistic terms, something like a buyer side analogy to monopoly. In other words, the buyer rather than the seller has the power to set the price for the product. In the present situation, the large shippers and not the carriers themselves are effectively dictating the level of truck rates in many instances.

With enormous amount of traffic available, these large shippers simply play one carrier off against another until unrealistically low (and unprofitable) rates are offered in order to get the traffic. Conversely, a shipper could simply name a price and, in plain English, tell the carriers to take it or leave it if they do not file a rate at that level.[5]

The secret negotiation of special and discriminatory rate discounts between motor carriers and large-volume shippers has become widespread in deregulated interstate markets.[6] While large-volume shippers often exact substantial discounts from rail and motor carriers for the movement of freight, smaller businesses lack the monopsony power to decree a price lower than the published rate. Further, the published rate is climbing to make up for the substantial discounts demanded by large shippers. Smaller shippers are forced to pay a disproportionate portion of carrier fixed costs while large shippers enjoy generous discounts.[7] Hence, America's deregulated industries are robbing Peter to pay Paul.

Here, too, concentration exacerbates the problem of discriminatory pricing. The deregulated transportation industries are becoming oligopolies as the larger carriers consolidate their operations and smaller carriers collapse into bankruptcy. With fewer competitive alternatives to get their goods to market, smaller shippers today pay more for poorer service.[8]

DISCRIMINATION

Deregulation has created an environment in which widespread discrimination by airlines and motor carriers favors urban markets and large-volume shippers, while penalizing smaller shippers and rural communities. One ICC study in California found that shippers in small towns were paying up to 40% more for motor carrier service than shippers in larger communities.[9]

In a sense, the big become bigger and the small become smaller. It is no wonder, then, that America's largest companies clamor for still more deregulation, for it is they that are the principal beneficiaries of pricing and service discrimination. In earlier periods of American political history, such concentrations of wealth and power would have mandated governmental intervention, not regulatory regression.

Professor Donald Harper has noted that the ability of small shippers to compete against larger rivals is hindered by relatively higher freight rates.[10] Hence, discriminatory transportation costs contribute to the economies of scale that larger entrepreneurs enjoy throughout the American economy.[11] The higher cost of access to the stream of commerce endured by small shippers places them at a competitive disadvantage vis-à-vis their larger rivals. Assuming all other factors are equal, the large manufacturer with relatively (and in many cases, significantly) lower transportation costs will be able to market products at a lower price than a smaller counterpart. Deregulation facilitates this discrimination. These deleterious economic consequences have a broader social impact, for small businesses create most of America's jobs.

A small shipper recently summarized the impact of transportation deregulation upon smaller enterprises in testimony before the U.S. House of Representatives: "the benefits promised by the Motor Carrier Act of 1980 have not reached the medium and small shipper. Small shippers are receiving discounts substantially below what the large shippers enjoy. Our markets are shrinking."[12] Dean Hille's survey of small Missouri shippers appears to confirm these conclusions.[13]

Interstate deregulation of motor carriers has been described as a "disaster" by many small shippers.[14] Professor Harper notes that "[t]he chief victim of [deregulation] is the small shipper who has little bargaining power with carriers, whose traffic is not as "desirable" to the carriers as that of larger shippers, and who cannot practically enter into private carriage for financial or other reasons."[15]

In Professor David Huff's study comparing interstate and intrastate freight rates in Texas,[16] it was demonstrated that published intrastate rates for shipments of 20,000 pounds were significantly lower than corresponding interstate rates for the same commodity classifications, weights, and distances.[17] Looking beyond the published rates, Dr. Huff examined the interstate and intrastate rates actually charged Texas shippers in 1985 and found that the intrastate rates averaged 4.4 cents per pound, while corresponding interstate rates averaged 7.1 cents per pound.[18] Thus, regulated intrastate rates were 59.5% lower than deregulated interstate rates.[19]

The difference is even more pronounced when truckload rates are computed separately. For shipments of less than 500 pounds, Dr. Huff found that interstate rates were 186% higher than intrastate rates.[20] Based on such findings, he concluded that "an important expectation among those advocating the deregulation of the trucking industry is that rates will decline. The specific facts in Texas as well as historical developments in deregulated markets such as in interstate commerce and in California indicate that such an expectation is erroneous except for the small minority of shippers interested in large truckload shipments."[21]

Pricing discrimination may cause serious injury to those enterprises or geographic regions disfavored by the pricing scheme. The U.S. Supreme Court has observed that "discriminatory rates . . . may affect the prosperity and welfare of a State . . . .They may stifle, impede, or cripple old industries and prevent the establishment of new ones."[22] Dabney Waring, a nationally recognized transportation economist, has echoed these sentiments: "Discrimination, preference or prejudice, favoring one region, one industry, one person (or one type of region, industry, or person) can have an extremely disruptive effect on the dispersion of population and industry."[23]

Today, most states prohibit motor carrier discrimination in intrastate rates, charges, and classifications between shippers. Such provisions are fundamental if small shippers and small communities are not to suffer relatively higher rates than their larger counterparts.

The one area in which the average consumer has had direct experience with deregulation is airline transportation. Here, widespread discrimination is practiced against business and other nondiscretionary travelers in favor of vacation travelers, and against small towns in favor of large, competitive markets. We will examine the comprehensive impact of pricing and service discrimination upon small towns and rural communities in Chapter 9. But a few examples will illustrate the point.

For example, the airline rate from Dubueque to Chicago is $1 per seat-mile while the fare from New York to Los Angeles is 3.3 cents per seat-mile.[24] A round-trip coach ticket between International Falls, Minnesota, and Minneapolis/St. Paul is 86 cents a seat-mile; between Washington, D.C., and Minneapolis/St. Paul, the fare is 27 cents a seat-mile.[25] The trip from Madison, Wisconsin, to St. Louis costs $225 one way, while a ticket from New York to Los Angeles via St. Louis is only $199.[26] Hence, rather than reflecting marginal costs, air fares are instead reflecting the level of competition in a given market. These fares take from the poor who fly between small towns and give to the urban rich in competitive battles waged for domination of the larger, more lucrative markets. Moreover, unprecedented concentration in this industry is sharply reducing the number of markets in which effective competition exists.

Growing consumer irritation with the deregulated airline industry is reflected in public opinion polls. In 1984, when consumers were asked "Should airlines be allowed to raise or lower their fares on their own, or should they be required to get government permission?", only 35% believed that they should be required to get the government's permission. However, as consumers became more acquainted with deregulation, they became less enamored with it. In 1987, when asked the same question, almost half were willing to opt for more government rate regulation.[27] Alfred Kahn now admits that the time has come to consider price ceilings in markets dominated by a single carrier.[28]

PRICE SAVINGS

Most proponents of deregulation focus on the significant price reductions enjoyed by consumers during the past decade. Some, like Alfred Kahn, insist that fares have dropped 30%, adjusted for inflation.[29] But Kahn's figures run from 1976, before he was appointed chairman of the CAB, and two years before promulgation of the Airline Deregulation Act. More realistic are figures recently announced by DOT secretary (and deregulation proponent) James Burnley, who says that as of 1988 fares have dropped 13% since deregulation, adjusted for inflation.[30]

Ticket prices have dropped, on average, but there are nonetheless several questions which remain:

- What has happened to air fares paid by that segment of the market that cannot take advantage of pricing discounts?
- Do these reports of price reductions take into account the fact that airline ticket prices were falling in the decades preceding deregulation, or that fuel prices have fallen significantly since the mid–1970s?
- What are the opportunity costs of the tremendous delays and circuitous routing which dominates the deregulated airline industry?
- With the industry becoming a national oligopoly and prices rising, are these pricing discounts consumers have enjoyed only a short-term phenomenon?
- Aren't we comparing apples and oranges? Even if prices are down, the product we purchase is inferior to that which we could purchase a decade ago?

High Prices

Not all consumers have benefitted from average fare reductions. Indeed, full fares have risen 156% since 1978, double the rate of growth of the Consumer Price Index.[31] Business travelers who refuse to sleep in a strange city on a Saturday night, individuals who must travel immediately and cannot purchase a ticket days or weeks before departure, and individuals flying to small towns are not finding the bargains enjoyed by the discretionary traveler in the New York-Los Angeles market.

Long-Term Trends

Melvin Brenner's study of the airline industry revealed that fares in constant dollars had been declining steadily since the early 1960s.[32] He points out that there is no reason to conclude that this long-term trend would have stopped abruptly in the absence of deregulation.[33] Hence, at least some of the price decline would have occurred even had deregulation not happened, as a result of long-term productivity gains. Deregulation cannot take all the credit.

Moreover, no study that this author has seen takes into account the sharp fall in fuel prices in the mid–1980s, a cost savings for which deregulation can take no credit. Fuel prices are a significant component of aircraft operational costs.

Opportunity Costs

If we take into account only the ticket price, we ignore the full cost to society of air travel. In particular, we miss the significant opportunity costs of air travel—the time we lose stranded at airports, imprisoned in aircraft, or routed through circuitous hub connections. All of these costs have increased significantly under deregulation. The widely acclaimed Brookings Institution study on airline deregulation claimed that consumers save $6 billion annually as a result of deregulation, of which approximately $4 billion is attributable to opportunity cost *savings*.[34] Ostensibly, business travelers save time because they have more frequencies from which to choose. It is fair to say that most business travelers, if polled, would find such an assumption implausible.

In fact, one source recently reported that opportunity *costs* (not savings) of $3.2 billion a year are incurred because of air travel delays.[35] One who files regularly must intuitively find the latter figure more realistic. The Brookings study has been discredited.[36]

Note too, that even accounting for lost time, for which there is some equivalent dollar measure, we do not take into account the other, less measurable, costs to society of deregulation. The aggravation and anxiety many travelers feel today because of delays, congestion, and a narrower margin of safety cannot easily be calculated. Neither can the deafening sound of aircraft takeoffs and landings at congested hub airports.

The Emerging Oligopoly

Chapters 4 and 8 point out that the overall trend of deregulation is toward an oligopoly of megacarriers. As the dust settles on a horizon devoid of meaningful competition, prices are ascending. Even Alfred Kahn admits that prices are likely to rise.[37] Hence, the pricing benefits many consumers enjoyed under deregulation are a short-term phenomenon. As the industry becomes more highly concentrated, prices are rising.

Service

Service is the subject of the next chapter, but a few words are appropriate here. Today, the product we buy when we purchase air transportation is decidedly inferior to what we could buy before deregulation. A decade ago, we could buy only one class of service, and it was very good, and a bit

Table 5.1
The World's Top 20 Airlines

Rank	Airline	Score
1.	Singapore Airlines	75.4
2.	Japan Air Lines	71.0
3.	Cathay Pacific	70.2
4.	Thai International	64.7
5.	SAS	64.4
5.	Swissair	64.4
7.	Lufthansa	62.4
8.	KLM	60.9
9.	Air New Zealand	56.9
10.	Quantas	56.2
11.	El Al	53.3
12.	Finnair	52.0
13.	Ansett	46.7
14.	British Airways	46.4
15.	Air France	46.2
16.	Korean Air	46.0
17.	Delta	41.4
18.	American	41.3
19.	Aer Lingus	38.1
20.	United	35.1

Source: Conde Nast Traveler (Nov. 1988), at 26.

expensive. Today, we can only buy a much poorer class of service, and for some of us, it is very cheap.

To pose an analogy, a decade ago we could buy steak. Steak is very tasty, but a bit expensive. Today we can only buy horse meat. Consumers save billions of dollars eating horse meat, but it doesn't taste quite right.

Service on American airlines has degenerated universally. Indeed, according to one periodical that specializes on travel (see Table 5.1), only three U.S. carriers made the top 20 of the world's best airlines, with our best airline placing 17th.

In conclusion, what we purchase today is a decidedly poorer product that we could buy before deregulation, and the decline has been nearly universal. To compare the price we pay for air service now with then, without taking into account that we buy less now than then, is to compare apples and oranges.

NOTES

1. Wagner & Dean, *A Prospective View toward Deregulation of Motor Common Carrier Entry*, 48 ICC PRAC. J. 406, 413 (1981). *See also* Wagner, *Exit of Entry Controls for Motor Common Carriers; Rationale Reassessment*, 50 ICC PRAC. J. 163, 172–73 (1983).

2. *$1.3 Billion in Rail Overcharges*, CURE NEWSLETTER (June 1985) at 1.

3. *Oversight of the Motor Carrier Act of 1980: Hearings before the Subcomm. of Surface Transportation of the Senate Comm. on Commerce, Science and Transportation*, 99th Cong., 1st Sess. 234 (statement of Prof. Grant M. Davis) [hereinafter *1985 Senate Hearings on MCA*].

4. *Id.* at 247 (statement of Prof. James P. Rakowski).

5. *Id.* at 249.

6. *See* Betz, *Taking the Crooked Route*, DISTRIBUTION (Apr. 1986) at 69.

7. *See 1985 Senate Hearings on MCA, supra* note 3, at 241 (statement of Prof. Grant M. Davis).

8. Dempsey, *Small Towns Are Withering*, DENVER POST, Jan. 2, 1988.

9. Butler, *ICC and DOT Charged With Duplicity for Allegedly "Burying" Rate Study*, TRAFFIC WORLD (June 13, 1983) at 21.

10. *1985 Senate Hearings on MCA, supra* note 3, at 278 (statement of Prof. Donald V. Harper).

11. COALITION FOR SOUND GENERAL FREIGHT TRUCKING, THE RATIONALE FOR TRUCKING REGULATION: EXPOSING THE MYTHS OF DEREGULATION 6 (1986).

12. *Id.* at 9.

13. *1985 Senate Hearings on MCA, supra* note 3, at 94 (statement of Dean Stanley Hille).

14. *Panelists Deplore Truck Deregulation, Rate Discrimination at NARUC Confab*, TRAFFIC WORLD (Dec. 1, 1986) at 68.

15. *1985 Senate Hearings on MCA, supra* note 3, at 283 (statement of Prof. Donald V. Harper).

16. D. HUFF, PERSPECTIVES ON THE REGULATION OF TRUCKING IN TEXAS (1987).

17. *Id.* at 53.

18. *Id.* at 59.

19. *Id.* at 60.

20. *Id.*

21. *Id.* at 51.

22. Georgia v. Pennsylvania R.R., 324 U.S. 439, 450 (1945).

23. Waring, *Motor Carrier Regulation—By State or by Market?* 51 ICC PRAC. J. 240–41 (1984).

24. *Effect of Airline Deregulation on the Rural Economy: Hearings before the Subcomm. on Rural Economy and Family Farming of the Senate Comm. on Small Business,* 100th Cong., 1st Sess. (testimony of John J. Nance).

25. *Id.* at 41 (statement of Robert W. Anderson).

26. Dempsey, *Fear of Flying Frequently,* NEWSWEEK (Oct. 5, 1987) at 12.

27. McGinley, *Bad Air Service Prompts Call for Changes,* WALL ST. J., Nov. 9, 1987, at 28.

28. *Ex-Official Suggests Lid on Air Fares,* ROCKY MOUNTAIN NEWS, Nov. 5, 1987, at 100.

29. Carroll, *Higher Fares, Better Service Are Forecast,* USA Today, Oct. 24, 1988, at B1.

30. *Airline Deregulation under Fire,* DENVER POST, Sept. 23, 1988, at 4A.

31. Ott, *Industry Officials Praise Deregulation, But Cite Flaws,* AV. WEEK & SPACE TECH. (Oct. 31, 1988) at 88.

32. Brenner, *Rejoinder to Comments by Alfred Kahn,* 16 TRANSP. L.J. 253, 255 (1988).

33. *Id.* at 256.

34. S. MORRISON & C. WINSTON, THE ECONOMIC EFFECTS OF AIRLINE DEREGULATION 33 (1986).

35. *Gridlock!,* TIME (Sept. 12, 1988) at 52, 55.

36. *See* Brenner, *Airline Deregulation—A Case Study in Public Policy Failure,* 16 TRANSP. L.J. 179, 222–24 (1988).

37. Kahn, *Airline Deregulation—A Mixed Bag, But a Clear Success Nevertheless,* 16 TRANSP. L.J. 229, 236 (1988).

6

SERVICE

A decade has elapsed since the federal government launched its grand experiment in transportation deregulation. The outlines of a consistent trend are becoming visible in all deregulated industries—airlines, railroads, and trucking, bus, banking, and telephone companies. While deregulation has created a class of beneficiaries, small businesses and consumers in small towns and rural communities are not among them. Today, they pay higher prices for poorer service.

Transportation deregulation has meant isolation for many of America's rural communities. With the *de facto* elimination of the common carrier obligation (which traditionally insisted that carriers provide service to all points described in their operating certificates), interstate carriers have been free to reduce their level of service to less lucrative communities and focus their energies and equipment on more profitable market opportunities. The Performance Audit of the Colorado Public Utilities Commission reached these conclusions:

> One clear pattern emerges from the studies on the impacts of deregulation in different public utility industries: small communities and rural areas have often paid a heavy price. Many small communities and rural areas have lost all of their passenger transportation services; many others have had their services reduced significantly. In addition, the costs of both passenger transportation and telephone services have increased, often substantially, in these areas.
>
> The implications of the loss of services and increases in costs to small communities are significant. Many of these communities are trying to attract new businesses and keep existing businesses and residents from moving away.[1]

Attracting new investment becomes increasingly difficult for these communities when transportation services are poor and prices are high. This chapter briefly examines the impact of deregulation of each of the major transport modes upon small towns and rural communities (about which more will be said in Chapter 9), before examining the universal decline of airline passenger service since deregulation.

Since promulgation of the Bus Regulatory Reform Act of 1982, 4,514 communities have lost bus service, while only 896 have gained it. The big losers have been small communities. Indeed, 3,432 of the towns which have lost service have a population of 10,000 or less.[2] When Greyhound began its inaugural rounds of service cessation and reduction in 1982, 90% of the towns affected had fewer than 10,000 residents.[3]

The *New York Times* reports that "[t]he trend toward cuts in service is continuing at a rapid pace, with dozens of communities throughout the Middle West facing possible loss of their last means of public transportation."[4] Senator Larry Pressler (R-S.D.) notes that "[b]us deregulation has had a devastating impact on rural America....Low-income families and the elderly are disproportionately affected because it is they who most heavily rely on the service."[5] With the Greyhound-Trailways merger, the bus duopoly became a monopoly. Can higher prices be far down the road?

Railroads have also taken advantage of the abundant opportunities provided by deregulation to abandon small towns. Railroads used the exit opportunities in the Transportation Act of 1958 to shed themselves of most of the nation's passenger trains.[6] Since enactment of the Staggers Rail Act of 1980, the focus has been on freight discontinuances; more than 1,200 communities have lost rail service.[7] The tragedy is that the loss is usually permanent—once the rails are ripped off their ties, they are almost never replaced.

The airline industry provides yet another example of the impact on small community service resulting from deregulation. The result of airline deregulation "is that many small communities have experienced a drastic reduction or deterioration in air service."[8]

Congress deregulated the industry with the promulgation of the Airline Deregulation Act of 1978. In the first year of deregulation, 260 cities suffered a deterioration in air service, a disproportionate number of them being small towns.[9] Seventy communities which were receiving some service lost all of it.[10] In the first two years of deregulation, more than 100 communities lost all scheduled service.[11]

Professors Stephenson and Beier note that "deregulation has accelerated the withdrawal from smaller communities and . . . there has been a concomitant reduction in the frequency of direct flights in those markets."[12] This is indeed a surprising consequence of deregulation, since section 419 of the Airline Deregulation Act of 1978 provided for a 10-year program of federal subsidies to attempt to preserve essential air service to small communities. Since deregulation began, approximately 140 small towns have lost all air service. In 190 more, the larger airlines have disappeared, replaced by smaller commuter carriers offering inferior levels of comfort, convenience, and safety.[13]

Clearly, there has been a qualitative deterioration of service for small communities.[14] With the use of smaller aircraft, several communities enjoy more frequent departures, but suffer a decrease in the number of seats.[15]

Many passengers complain that the smaller, unpressurized aircraft used by the commuter airlines are less comfortable.[16] They are certainly less safe. Depending upon how it is measured, commuter airlines have a safety record 3–30 times worse than that of established jet airlines.[17] Author John Nance summarized the reasons for the deterioration of safety resulting from the substitution of inferior commuter carrier service for scheduled airlines:

The aircraft [commuter airlines] fly are usually less sophisticated, largely unpressurized, and much smaller than main-stream jetliners. Many are devoid of not only restrooms, they are also devoid of radar, devoid of decent cockpit communications, devoid of sophisticated flight instruments, devoid of those elements that are part of the safety buffer which all of us as Americans have come to expect of our air transportation system, whether we are boarding in a rural area or not.

In addition [most] of these aircraft . . . fly at altitudes most vulnerable to weather hazards and potential mid-air collisions. They are maintained by less sophisticated maintenance departments, they are flown by less experienced pilots, usually the first airline job of their career.[18]

Passengers also appear to be less satisfied with the service schedules and flight delays of commuter airlines.[19]

Small towns lie remotely scattered under the dark and cloudy skies of deregulation, where not enough sunlight falls to give passengers a glimpse of the supersaver discounts prevalent in major markets.[20] With the airline industry becoming an oligopoly (the top five carriers dominate 72% of the domestic passenger market), passengers in small towns find their service reduced to a single airline providing circuitous connections out of a major hub and charging whatever the market will bear.[21]

Even deregulation proponent Thomas Gale Moore admits that 40% of small communities have suffered both a loss of air service and a disproportionate increase in ticket prices since deregulation began.[22] Similarly,

Professor Addus observes that "[a]s a result of airline deregulation . . . fares for traveling between small points have increased rapidly; and commuter air carrier fares are reported to be particularly high in most cases."[23] Assessing the quantitative and qualitative impacts, it has been noted that "small communities are receiving markedly worse air service than existed prior to deregulation."[24]

Under section 419 of the Airline Deregulation Act of 1978, small community subsidies were to last until 1988. In 1985, 142 communities were receiving subsidized service under the program.[25] Most will likely lose air service altogether if federal economic subsidies dry up.

The loss of service has an unhealthy ripple effect throughout the economy of each of these communities. As one commentator has noted, "besides increasing transportation costs for companies already doing business in many small communities, the impact of deregulation is decreasing the attractiveness of locating new businesses in these communities."[26] A survey of executives of the 500 largest American corporations reveals that 80% would not locate in an area which did not have reasonably available scheduled airline service.[27]

Not only has airline service into and out of small towns deteriorated, the national system of air travel is significantly worse than that which existed prior to deregulation. Even travelers who can get a super-saver fare find that the product they buy today is decidedly inferior to that which they purchased before deregulation.

Flying has become a miserable experience. The planes are aged, delayed, cancelled, and overbooked, our luggage disappears, and the food is less than succulent. Chronic delays, missed connections, near misses, and circuitous routing are all products of hub-and-spoking, adopted by every major airline. Too often, we find ourselves stranded in airports or imprisoned in aircraft, waiting endlessly to get to our destinations. America has suffered billions of dollars in opportunity costs as a result of these delays. Travel delays in 1986 alone cost airlines $1.8 billion in extra operating expenses, and cost consumers $3.2 billion in lost time.[28]

Consumer abuses do not stop with miserable service. Under deregulation, management philosophy in the airline industry is dominated by the predatory insight of P. T. Barnum: "There's a sucker born every minute."

Without government oversight, airlines freely engage in imaginative forms of consumer fraud, including bait-and-switch advertising, deliberate overbooking, unrealistic scheduling, and demand-based flight cancellations. As the *Wall Street Journal* observed:

Complaints about service are at an all-time high, with flight delays and cancellations provoking protest chants and even violence among angry passengers. The alarming rise in reported midair near-collisions has sharpened demands for improved safety.

Meanwhile, mergers have given some carriers so much market clout that fliers are seeing the consumer benefits of deregulation eroded.[29]

Some commentators have asserted that airline deregulation has resulted in significant economic benefits to the consuming public. A Brookings Institution study maintained that these savings were as much as $6 billion, comprised of fare discounts and opportunity cost savings realized as a result of "improved service convenience [to business travelers] attributable to the accelerated development of hub-and-spoke operations and to frequence improvements in low-density markets."[30] The overall import of the study was that airline service had not declined since deregulation began and had actually improved because of additional frequencies.

By focusing on the number of flights in larger markets as the dominant measure of airline service, the Brookings study appears to have missed what frequent flyers see. Whatever the improvements in the rate structure since deregulation, the consensus of most of what is written about airlines in this environment is that service has declined significantly. Moreover, the epidemic of delays which pervades the airline industry seems actually to have imposed significant opportunity costs, not benefits. As Melvin Brenner noted:

The very increase in hub-and-spoke frequencies which played so large a part in the study's calculations has been an important contributor to the congestion and delays which by 1987 had become a matter of widespread concern. While reducing the time interval between *published* departure time, the increased hub-and-spoke frequencies have increased the actual *delay* time at the gate, and in runway queues— a form of lost time that is especially costly to business traveler productivity.[31]

Moreover, the product which consumers now purchase is today, on average, decidedly inferior to what they could purchase before deregulation. A recent survey of consumers reveals that almost 50% believed that airline service had declined since deregulation; less than 20% said service had improved. Among the complaints: late departures, crowded seating, long lines at check-in, unappetizing food, overbooked aircraft, and an unacceptably long wait for baggage.[32] Another survey, this one of 15,000 frequent flyers, found even more negative attitudes on the impact of deregulation upon air service: 68% said that deregulated air service was "less convenient and enjoyable," while only 19% thought it more convenient and enjoyable.[33] Still another survey, this one of 461 members of the Executive Committee (a group of corporate presidents and chief executives), revealed that 36% had lost job efficiency because of air travel delays.[34]

These results parallel those obtained by the U.S. Department of Transportation. DOT data reveal that consumer complaints about airline delays, congestion, overbooking, bumping, missed connections, lost baggage, cancellations, and deteriorating food have soared in recent years.[35] During the first six months of 1987, DOT received 15,621 consumer complaints, a 144% increase over the same period one year earlier.[36] The top 10 complaints, in order of number registered, were:

- *Flight Problems*: Cancellations, delays, or any other deviation from schedule.
- *Baggage*: Claims for lost, damaged, or delayed baggage; charges for excess baggage; carry-on problems; and difficulties with airline claim procedures.
- *Refunds*: Problems in obtaining refunds for unused or lost tickets or fare adjustments.
- *Customer service*: Rude or unhelpful employees, inadequate meals or cabin service, and treatment of delayed passengers.
- *Reservations, ticketing and boarding*: Airline or travel agent mistakes in reservations and ticketing; problems in making reservations and obtaining tickets due to busy phone lines or waiting in line; delays in mailing tickets; and problems boarding the aircraft (except oversales).
- *Oversales*: All bumping problems, whether or not the airline complied with DOT oversale regulations.
- *Other*: Cargo problems, security, airport facilities, claims for bodily injury, and other miscellaneous problems.
- *Fares*: Incorrect or incomplete information about fares, discount fare conditions and availability, overcharges, fare increases, and the level of fares in general.
- *Smoking*: Inadequate segregation of smokers from nonsmokers, failure of the airline to enforce no-smoking rules, and objections to the rules.
- *Advertising*: Ads that are unfair, misleading, or offensive to consumers.[37]

A recent editorial in the *Washington Post* summed up what many firmly perceive to be the results of deregulation: "Airline Service Has Gone to Hell."[38] Why? One authority on services marketing said, "It's one of those terrible debt spirals. Without profit, there can be no service and no safety."[39]

Admittedly, some consumers are paying less for air service than they did before deregulation. Those who have benefitted most are vacation (discretionary) travelers in large markets served by several carriers. Business travelers flying between small towns served by only a single carrier have not benefitted from fare reductions. And today, both vacation and business travelers are often routed through a circuitous hub connection, consuming more time in both aircraft and airports in a decidedly less pleasurable fashion than before deregulation. For many, opportunity costs have increased since deregulation began. Moreover, what we buy today is a poorer product for our money.

Why has the unregulated market not corrected this deterioration in service? Some suggest that service deterioration is attributable to the decline in profitability of firms caused by the "destructive competition" unleashed by deregulation.[40] Hence, carriers don't have the resources to staff flights with more flight attendants than FAA minimums, to staff ticket counters or baggage areas adequately, to provide better food, to avoid deliberate overbooking or unrealistic scheduling, or even to clean aircraft properly. While some airlines are worse than others, the decline appears to be nearly universal.

Another explanation of the market's failure may be reflected in the nature of the item being sold. When consumers purchase a manufactured product, they can examine it in a retail store before spending their money, pulling it off the shelf, turning it over, and making some assessment of its quality. But when consumers buy a service like transportation, its definition beyond a mere description of "the movement of my body from A to B" is more amorphous.

When booking a flight, most consumers do some price shopping. Where a competitive alternative exists, there has been some measure of pricing competition under deregulation, and those who price shop often opt for the lower fare. Frequent flyers who have been through the ordeal of a hub connection may ask for a nonstop if one is available, or a one-stop, if one is not. But beyond that, how many consumers ask "(1) what kind of aircraft is being flown, how old is it, and when was it last overhauled; (2) how often is this flight late, and by how much, on average; (3) by what percentage of passengers do you usually overbook the flight; (4) what percentage of bags are usually lost on the flight, and if you don't lose them, how long will I have to wait at destination for my bags; (5) how many flight attendants are on board; (6) what's for dinner, and how tasty is it; (7) what's the average wait in the line at the airport; (8) how crowded is the flight and the waiting lounge at the gate; (9) how much knee and leg room do you give me between seats; and (10) how comfortable is the seat?" Because most of these questions are not asked by consumers before they purchase their tickets, the market has not responded to consumer desires for better service.

The U.S. Department of Transportation has authority to protect consumers from many of these evils, including deliberate overbooking, unrealistic scheduling, and fraudulent ("bait and switch") advertising. But the Reagan administration's DOT was reticent to do much of anything to correct market failure.

Another consideration which increasingly impacts both service and fare levels is the level of industry concentration that has emerged under deregulation. With fewer carriers, with some traffic lanes and hubs now a monopoly or oligopoly, and with no government agency to protect consumers, it is quite likely that as time passes prices will rise and service will decline further.

MOTOR CARRIERS

Because of the glut of capacity in the trucking industry and the fact that the overwhelming majority of states continue to regulate intrastate motor carriage and enforce the common carrier obligation, we have not yet seen wholesale motor carrier abandonments of small communities. We may see them yet if more states abandon their regulatory responsibility to protect the public interest. As indicated above, evidence already exists of widespread price discrimination against small shippers, particularly those located in rural areas and small towns.

The economic impact of isolation is rippling perniciously throughout rural America, making it increasingly difficult for small towns to attract new investment, or indeed, to dissuade existing businesses from leaving. The downward economic spiral inevitably leads to an outmigration of youth as small towns wither on the vine.[41] We will examine the impact of deregulation upon small towns and rural communities in greater detail in Chapter 9.

NOTES

1. COLORADO STATE AUDITOR, PERFORMANCE AUDIT OF THE PUBLIC UTILITIES COMMISSION 39 (1988).

2. Letter from ICC Chairman Heather J. Gradison to Senator Larry Pressler (Sept. 8, 1986).

3. Charlier, *Small-Town America Battles a Deep Gloom As Its Economy Sinks*, WALL ST. J., Aug. 4, 1988, at 1, 6.

4. Robbins, *Dependent on Buses, Midwestern Towns Fight Cuts in Service*, NEW YORK TIMES, Oct. 14, 1986, at A14.

5. *Id.*

6. Dempsey, *The Dark Side of Deregulation: Its Impact on Small Communities*, 39 ADMIN. L. REV. 445, 450–53 (1987).

7. Dempsey, *Punishing Smallness*, CLEVELAND PLAIN DEALER, Dec. 12, 1987, at 15A.

8. Note, *Airline Deregulation and Service to Small Communities*, 57 N. DAK. L. REV. 607, 608 (1981).

9. *See* CIVIL AERONAUTICS BOARD, REPORT ON AIRLINE SERVICE 43–50 (1979).

10. Meyer, *Section 419 of the Airline Deregulation Act: What Has Been the Effect on Air Service to Small Communities?* 47 J. AIR L. & COM. 151, 181 (1981).

11. Havens & Heymsfeld, *Small Community Air Service under the Airline Deregulation Act of 1978*, 46 J. AIR L. & COM. 641, 673 (1981).

12. Stephenson & Beier, *The Effects of Airline Deregulation on Air Service to Small Communities*, 20 TRANSP. J. 54, 57 (1981).

13. Dempsey, *With Deregulation, Big Get Bigger*, PHILADELPHIA INQUIRER, Dec. 19, 1987, at 9A.

14. *See* GENERAL ACCOUNTING OFFICE, DEREGULATION 73 (1985) [hereinafter cited as GAO REPORT].

15. *Id.* at 73; Meyer, *supra* note 10, at 181.

16. Oster, Jr. & Zorn, *Deregulation and Commuter Airline Safety*, 49 J. AIR L. & COM. 315–16 (1984).

17. *See* Oster, Jr. & Zorn, *Airline Deregulation, Commuter Safety, and Regional Air Transportation*, 14 GROWTH AND CHANGE 3, 7 (1983).

18. Effect of Airline Deregulation on the Rural Economy: Hearings before the Subcomm. on Rural Economy and Family Farming of the Senate Comm. on Small Business, 100th Cong., 1st Sess. 81–82 (testimony of John J. Nance).

19. *See* Ahmed, *Air Transportation to Small Communities: Passenger Characteristics and Perceptions of Service Attributes*, 38 TRANSP. Q. 15, 21 (1984).

20. Dempsey, *Life since Deregulation: It Means Paying Much More for Much Less*, DES MOINES REGISTER, Dec. 30, 1987.

21. Dempsey, *Fear of Flying Frequently*, NEWSWEEK (Oct. 5, 1987).

22. Moore, *U.S. Airline Deregulation: Its Effects on Passengers, Capital, and Labor*, 24 J. L. & ECON. 1, 15, 18 (1986).

23. Addus, *Subsidizing Air Service to Small Communities*, 39 TRANSP. Q. 537, 548 (1985).

24. Meyer, *supra* note 10, at 182. *See also* S. TOLCHIN & M. TOLCHIN, DISMANTLING AMERICA: THE RUSH TO DEREGULATE 245–46 (1983).

25. GAO REPORT, *supra* note 14, at 31–32.

26. Meyer, *supra* note 10, at 175.

27. Dempsey, *supra* note 6, at 458.

28. *Gridlock!*, TIME (Sept. 12, 1988), at 52, 55.

29. McGinley, *Bad Air Service Prompts Call for Changes*, WALL ST. J., Nov. 9, 1987, at 28.

30. S. MORRISON & C. WINSTON, THE ECONOMIC EFFECTS OF AIRLINE DEREGULATION 33 (1986).

31. Brenner, *Airline Deregulation—A Case Study in Public Policy Failure*, 16 TRANSP. L.J. 179, 223 (1988).

32. *The Big Trouble with Air Travel*, CONSUMER REPORTS (June 1988), at 362–63.

33. Brenner, *supra* note 31, at 223.

34. *Gridlock!*, *supra* note 28, at 55. Many said they took the precaution of arriving in a city on the night before an appointment rather than risk flight delays or cancellations, thereby saddling their firms with the cost of a hotel room. *Id.*

35. Brenner, *supra* note 31, at 223.

36. Coleman, *No Silver Lining Expected to Brighten Airlines' Stormy Skies*, MARKETING NEWS (Sept. 25, 1987) at 1.

37. *Id.*

38. Rowen, *Airline Service Has Gone to Hell*, WASHINGTON POST, July 23, 1987, at A21. *See also* Dempsey, *Consumers Pay More to Receive a Lot Less*, USA TODAY, July 16, 1987, at 8A.

39. Coleman, *supra* note 36.

40. *See* Brenner, *supra* note 31.

41. Dempsey, *Deregulation's First Decade*, JOURNAL OF COMMERCE, Dec. 18, 1987, at 8A.

7

SAFETY

Serious questions exist as to whether an unhealthy transportation industry can be a safe industry. One of the dangers of poor or nonexistent profits for transportation firms is the natural tendency of management to curtail costs. Among those which can be significantly diminished are maintenance costs, including mechanic's wages, spare or replacement parts, and idle vehicle time lost during inspections and maintenance.

RAILROADS

Unsatisfactory profits in the rail industry under regulation led it to defer maintenance on equipment and trackage as a matter of policy. The result was a series of derailments, often causing loss of human life.[1] Deregulation has enabled railroads to extract monopoly profits from captive consumers of bulk commodities such as coal and grain. This has significantly improved their economic posture and made it possible for them to upgrade deteriorated track and roadbed and purchase new rolling stock, all to the substantial benefit of their level of safety. Hence, a carrier's economic health seems to bear a positive correlation with its level of safety.

AIRLINES

Conversely, for airlines and motor carriers the economic strains created by the intensive pricing competition unleashed by deregulation have had a deleterious effect upon carrier safety. Carriers earning inadequate profits cut costs where they can, by deferring maintenance or replacement of defective equipment, or by pushing labor beyond federal safety standards.[2]

The father of airline deregulation, Alfred Kahn, now admits that the margin of safety has "possibly" narrowed since 1978, although fatality statistics do not yet reflect it.[3] Of course, if the body count were the only measure of victory, we would have won the war in Vietnam.

Although passenger fatalities have not ascended to the levels one would expect in such an environment, every other measure of safety paints a different picture. As was explained in Chapter 4, deregulation has severely squeezed the profit margin of America's airlines. This has, quite naturally, deprived carriers of the resources to reequip with new aircraft or maintain the wide margin of safety the public previously enjoyed. Since deregulation, the average age of our nation's aircraft fleet has grown sharply. Expenditures for maintenance and the number of mechanics per aircraft have been reduced. The number of near misses has soared. For example, 1987 saw the highest number of aircraft accidents since 1974.[4] The average age of cockpit crew members is the lowest since deregulation began, and the standards for hiring and the duration and quality of their training have declined.[5] For example, in 1983 a prospective pilot needed 2,300 hours of flight time and uncorrected 20/20 vision to be hired by one of the major airlines. Today, one needs only 800 hours of flight time and (for all but one airline) only correctable vision to be hired by a major carrier, and only 100 hours to be hired by a commuter carrier. The Continental Airlines DC–9 crash in Denver during a takeoff in a snowstorm in 1987 was piloted by a 26-year old individual with less than 37 hours of flight time in a DC–9, while the captain had only 33 hours. Before deregulation, 80% of pilots had experience as a military pilot; today only half do.

Because of the competitive pressures unleashed by deregulation, overall industry financial performance has declined to the point of inadequacy, despite the fact that the recession of the early 1980s has abated and fuel prices have fallen. In many instances, these competitive pressures have had beneficial impacts upon carrier productivity; management has been forced to engage in hard negotiations to reduce labor costs and inefficient work rules.

But cost cutting may well have had a deleterious impact on the margin of safety. For example, pilots are now pushed to fly more hours with less rest. While working longer for less pay increases efficiency, it can induce fatigue, which has a negative impact upon safety. Today, fatigue is responsible for two operational errors per week—errors such as pilots falling asleep in the cockpit, landing on the wrong runway, or wandering out of assigned flight paths. Legitimate concerns have also been raised over the problem of the age and poor maintenance of jets flown by unhealthy airlines, which lack the financial resources to reequip with modern aircraft or properly maintain their aging fleets.[6] This is particularly a concern in the commuter airline industry, seemingly plagued by endless bankruptcies, where used, recycled aircraft dominate the fleets of the smaller carriers.[7] Professor Frederick Thayer reminds us that "safety always has suffered when airlines were largely unregulated."[8]

Table 7.1
Number of Mechanics Per Aircraft

Airline	1982	1987
American	16.6	15.6
Continental	14.6	13.0
Delta	21.3	14.9
Eastern	22.1	16.9
Northwest	11.6	12.4
Pan Am	27.4	28.2
Piedmont	13.0	9.7
TWA	30.9	25.7
United	17.8	21.2
US Air	12.4	11.8
AVERAGE	18.77	16.94

Source: Wall Street Journal, July 19, 1988, at 25.

Ninety-seven percent of airline pilots believe that deregulation has had a deleterious effect on airline safety.[9] Among the problems identified are: "lagging and inadequate maintenance; pressure to avoid delays; lowered hiring and experience standards for new pilots; increased use of waivers and exemptions from safety rules; increased flying hours for pilots; [and] the profusion of new, inexperienced airlines."[10] One out of every five pilots was involved in a near miss during a recent 24 month period, and only 25% of those were reported to the FAA.

As aircraft become older, airlines should spend 2% more on maintenance per year, on average. But rather than spending more on aircraft maintenance America's airlines are spending less, while the fleet has grown steadily older. According to the U.S. Department of Transportation, the amount of resources devoted by commercial airlines to aircraft maintenance fell 30% during deregulation's first six years.[11] A survey of commercial airline pilots reveals that almost half believe that their companies defer maintenance for an excessive period of time.[12] As Table 7.1 reveals, the number of mechanics per aircraft has declined more than 10% on average for the major airlines in the past five years.

Today, most carriers lack the resources to replace their aging fleets of aircraft. As a consequence, the average age of the industry's geriatric jets grew 21% from 1979 to 12.53 years in 1988.[13] Today, more than half the

Table 7.2
Airline Fleet Averages in Years

American	11.14
Continental	11.96
Eastern	14.49
Delta	9.76
Northwest	14.54
Pan Am	14.67
TWA	15.14
United	14.43
US Air	11.58
Piedmont	10.25

Source: "Aging Jets Problem Discussed Years Ago," *Rocky Mountain News*, May 8, 1988, at 32.

2,767 jets in service are 16 years old or older.[14] Table 7.2 provides the average aircraft ages of the 10 largest carriers.

The new low fares which have been offered in larger, competitive markets during the last decade have stimulated significant new passenger demand. Between 1978 and 1987, departures for major airlines increased by 27%.[15] With airlines funneling their flights into "hub and choke" bottlenecks and scheduling takeoffs and landings through a narrow window of time and space, near misses are soaring.[16] The flight paths of the nation's major airports are heavily congested during peak periods. There were 584 near misses during 1984, 758 in 1985, 839 in 1986, and 610 for the first half of 1987 alone.[17]

All of this has placed serious strains on the air traffic control system at a time when it is least capable of handling the surge in demand. In 1981, President Reagan fired 11,000 members of the Professional Air Traffic Controllers Organization (PATCO) for striking, leaving it with only a third of its work force, and the Federal Aviation Administration (FAA) has yet to replace them all.[18] Not only is the system understaffed, many airports and navigational facilities are equipped with obsolete and aging equipment. Operational errors, or mistakes by controllers, increased by 20% during the first half of 1987 over the same period one year earlier.[19]

The level of public and media concern over the trimmed margin of safety has turned up the heat on the Federal Aviation Administration to become

Table 7.3
FAA Outstanding Fines

United	$1,262,100
Hawaiian	1,169,000
Continental	982,130
Eastern	893,500
Braniff	518,000
American	421,250
Northwest	371,000
Pan Am	264,500
US Air	166,100
Delta	147,250
Midway	128,000
TWA	118,000
Southwest	56,500
America West	1,500
Alaska	1,000

Source: McGinley, "Fifteen Airlines Face FAA Fines Totaling about $6.5 Million for Alleged
    Violations," *Wall Street Journal*, May 12, 1988, at 4.

more vigilant in enforcing its safety regulation mandate, something it was lethargic in doing during the early years of the Reagan administration. Table 7.3 reveals, significant fines have recently been levied on the major airlines.

Nonetheless, the Federal Aviation Administration recently came under fire in a report prepared by the Office of Technology Assessment (OTA).[20] It found that the FAA was understaffed in the number of inspectors, controllers, and technicians it employs, and maintained inadequate programs to improve the performance of aircraft crews, air-traffic controllers, and mechanics. It urged the FAA to continue surprise inspections and, in particular, to engage in intensive and extensive oversight of the commuter airline industry "during the shakeout expected over the next few years."[21]

It also had a few words of criticism for the airline industry. OTA found that although all airlines profess adherence to high safety standards, there are significant variations in corporate cultures and maintenance procedures. Professed adherence to safety "means one thing to a financially well-off airline with an ample number of landing slots at airports, but something else to a financially strapped airline that must choose between spending money on discretionary maintenance on aircraft and buying new slots."[22] OTA concluded that "while airline officials are concerned about safety, financial considerations drive many industry decisions and will continue to do so as strong competition exists among the airlines."[23] Further, "many airlines have lowered hiring standards, [and] increased pilot and mechanic duty time.[24]

Why then, have the fatality levels not reflected the industry's miserable economic environment? There are two reasons. First, the aircraft themselves are overengineered. Even if maintenance is deferred and a critical system fails, usually a back-up system will fill the void until the plane can land. Even if the plane becomes a convertible, as did that 737 Aloha Airlines jet in Hawaii, a good pilot can still land it safely. Second, there is a higher level of vigilance in the cockpit than there has been been. Hub and spoking creates intense congestion, and pilots know if they don't keep a sharp eye out, a near miss could become an actual hit. Moreover, pilots are overwhelmingly concerned about the deterioration of maintenance under deregulation. They watch more carefully for mechanical problems than they ever have. Thus, we have been spared the tragedies that the economic imperatives of deregulation suggest. Let us hope that we continue to be so lucky.

MOTOR CARRIERS

Similar conclusions have been reached by academicians who have studied the motor carrier industry. For example, Professor Daryl Wyckoff found a positive correlation between motor carrier regulation and safety; regulated carriers displayed a superior safety and compliance record vis-à-vis unregulated motor carriers.[25]

Approximately 4,500 people died in accidents involving heavy trucks in 1986. Odds are 40 to 1 that the car occupant rather than the truck driver will die in these highway catastrophes.[26] An overwhelming body of evidence suggests that trucking safety has deteriorated sharply since deregulation.

As discussed in Chapters 4 and 5, motor carriage does not operate in a purely competitive environment. Large shippers enjoy and exert monopsony power—the ability to dictate pricing discounts unavailable to smaller rivals.

Hence, small shippers become saddled with the fixed costs of operation. That disparity of bargaining power (which demands pricing discrimination), coupled with unlimited entry (and the glut of capacity resulting therefrom), has made it difficult even for well-managed and efficient motor carriers to earn a reasonable return on investment. The losses have to be borne by someone. They have come out of the hides of labor and investors, and from deferred maintenance. Drivers must now drive longer hours to earn the same income. Firms with inadequate profits lack the resources to invest in new equipment, or repair aged equipment. As a consequence, trucking accidents have soared under deregulation. Virtually every objective study of highway safety has concluded that the rate of truck-related accidents, fatalities, and injuries has increased dramatically since deregulation began, at a pace higher than the increase in truck miles traveled.

A study commissioned by the American Automobile Association (AAA) concludes that because there are few other areas in which to cut costs, motor carriers whose profit margins are squeezed have little alternative but to "run older equipment, pay less in wages, work drivers longer, and/or skip on maintenance."[27] Professor Glaskowsky reached similar conclusions, noting that "after five years of deregulation three trends are fairly clear: (1) the equipment fleet of the motor carrier industry is aging, (2) a lot of maintenance (expense) is being deferred, and (3) the motor carrier accident rate is increasing."[28]

Indeed it is. Because carrier profits have been so severely squeezed, the average age of equipment on the highway has increased dramatically since deregulation.[29] In 1978, when *de facto* deregulation began, the median age of trucks operating on the highway was six years; by 1986, that had risen to 7.5 years.[30] Economically distressed carriers simply haven't the resources to invest in replacing (and in some instances, repairing) aged equipment. As Professor Garland Chow observed, "the carrier which eventually goes bankrupt spends less on safety and maintenance, has older equipment and depends on owner operators more than carriers not going bankrupt. As these financially distressed carriers approach their eventual demise, they spend even less on safety [and] new equipment."[31]

It is not only the carrier exiting the unregulated market which poses a serious safety hazard on the highway. New, undercapitalized, shoe-string operators who naively believe that they can compete in the "big leagues" are also a threat. Professors Corsi and Fanara, Jr., examined the impact of the Motor Carrier Act of 1980 upon safety and concluded that new entrants have accident rates between 27% and 33% higher than established carriers.[32]

As wages are reduced by financially strapped carriers, drivers have a strong economic incentive to stay on the highway beyond the maximum hours established by the federal government, sometimes pumped up on amphetamines.[33] The result has been sharply increased rates of trucking accidents and related deaths and injuries. Daust and Cobb found a "relationship between federal economic deregulation and the substantial rise in safety related incidence [as well as a] cause-and-effect relationship of driver fatigue and unqualified drivers on traffic crash occurrences."[34] An AAA study reveals that driver fatigue is the probable or primary cause of 41% of heavy truck accidents.[35] As one driver noted:

In 10 years of driving I have had no employer who expected less than twice the legally allotted number of hours. Many drivers . . . must constantly break the law to keep their jobs. The resulting fatigue is the truck driver's real enemy and the true killer on the highway. . . . If the same official zeal [over drug abuse by drivers] were focused on shippers and employers who demand outlawry from drivers, the first step will have been taken toward reducing [the number of truck-related fatalities]. Until then, shippers will expect 68-hour trips from California to Boston, and profit will be made because drivers disregarded the law. More important, public safety will continue to be jeopardized.[36]

The Bureau of Motor Carrier Safety of the U.S. Department of Transportation reported an 18% increase in trucking accidents from 1983 to 1984.[37] That is the largest increase since 1972.[38] The American Insurance Association reports that the accident rate for interstate motor carriers increased from 2.65 per million miles in 1983 to 3.06 in 1984, and to 3.39 for the first half of 1985.[39] *Fortune* magazine found that both the age of trucks on the highway and the number of truck accidents have soared since promulgation of the Motor Carrier Act of 1980, and reached these conclusions:

The growing safety problem is a lesson in the perils of deregulation . . . .Deregulation compounded the problems [of highway safety] by creating economic circumstances that made trucking far more dangerous. Price competition forced hundreds of large and medium-size companies out of business. The smaller outfits and independent owner-operators who took their place are nimbler, but these new entrants have a hard time making money. . . . To stay in business, the small operator must run each rig at least 120,000 miles a year—more than 300 miles every day. . . . In today's competitive climate, the numbers often do not add up. . . . Result: Many hard-pressed truckers have plenty of incentive to spend excessive hours at the wheel and to overlook expensive maintenance requirements . . . .[A]s many as one in three long-haul drivers resort to illegal drugs to help cope with grueling hours on the road . . . .Even a drug-free driver may be a menace on the highway because of the sorry condition of his vehicle. Roadside inspections conducted in various states in the past year regularly turned up serious problems in 30% to 40% of trucks pulled over.[40]

Nationwide surveys performed under the Federal Motor Carrier Safety Assistance Program concluded that of the 366,400 trucks checked in 1985, 29% were insufficiently safe to drive on the highway. In 1986, safety inspectors in New York and Connecticut, operating under the federal program, ordered as many as 60% of the trucks off the highway as unsafe.[41] Professor Beilock, after surveying truck drivers in Florida, reached the following conclusions:

Compared to those who see less difficulty, almost six times as many drivers respond that it has become more difficult to drive safely since 1980, the year the trucking industry was legislatively deregulated under the Motor Carrier Act. Although many reasons are given for increased difficulty, an appreciable number are symptoms of root causes connected with deregulation. Reasons which are or potentially deregulation-related are mentioned quite prominently by the 85 percent who specified a reason or reasons.[42]

Each of these independent studies points to a common conclusion: there has been a significant deterioration in the level of safety of motor carriers since federal deregulation began. There are reasonable grounds to believe that rate deregulation and safety deterioration are interrelated. As was revealed by Professor Glaskowsky's comprehensive study on the impact of deregulation upon motor carriers:

Many aspects of deregulation are subject to disagreement and debate as to their effects, but safety is not one of them. Safety costs money where transportation operations are concerned and it was inevitable that deregulation would put much financial pressure on many motor carriers. Corners are being cut by financially strapped carriers and the accident rate is rising. This was a clearly foreseeable consequence of deregulation.[43]

Equipment maintenance is another major factor. Firms without adequate returns simply haven't adequate resources for such continuing maintenance items as brakes and tires. In recent years, state inspections around the nation have seen a dramatic increase in the number of trucks pulled out of service as unsafe to be on the highway because of illegal vehicles or drivers. Moreover, the average age of trucks on the highway has grown steadily every year of federal deregulation. The bottom line is that the principal cause of the deterioration of safety under deregulation is the economic anemia unleased by overcapacity and the market power of large shippers.

Let's go a bit deeper and look at the problem of externalities. Take a typical large manufacturer with a private fleet subsidiary of its own trucks and trailers. It will make sure that this subsidiary will earn a reasonable return on investment sufficient to allow it to maintain its equipment so as to avoid the potential liability that would be inspired by shoddy maintenance and overworked drivers. Now, suppose the large manufacturer tenders some freight to a common carrier. It has no incentive to ensure that the common carrier earns a reasonable return on investment, for any highway accident becomes a liability problem for the carrier, not the manufacturer. Instead, the manufacturer has an incentive to cut the common carrier's profit margin to the bone so as to maximize its wealth, the public be damned! With its own private fleet, the manufacturer cannot externalize the price the public pays for its greed, in terms of injuries and fatalities on the highway; with a common carrier, it can. So to avoid the spillover effects upon third parties not participating in the transaction for either the sale of transport services or the goods the manufacturer sells in the market, responsible regulation is required.

Moreover, even if litigation were somehow able to force internalization of the injury innocent human beings bear (and for the reasons just expressed, it is not), litigation would be a poor alternative to regulation in that courts award monetary relief; even a generous jury award for damages cannot restore lost health or life. In contrast, regulation can prevent injury before it occurs, and this is a significant benefit indeed.

Targeted safety programs help. But unless the state is prepared to put a highway patrol officer in every cab, it cannot hope to thwart the economic imperatives of inadequate returns mandated by deregulation.

Too many of us have seen the crushed accordions of twisted steel and bent chrome on our interstate highways that were passenger automobiles before they were squashed by huge diesel-powered trucks pulling giant trailers. The kinetic energy released by a 40-ton tractor-trailer unit moving at 55 mph is approximately 16 million foot-pounds, or about 4,000 times the energy released by a high-powered rifle.[44] It is quite capable of compressing a compact car into a glob of steel almost the size of a suitcase.

One source reports that "[v]irtually all studies of accident, fatality, and injury rates found that rates are increasing more for trucks than for other types of vehicles and at a pace higher than the increases in truck miles traveled."[45] An overwhelming body of evidence demonstrates that the motor carrier industry suffers from critical economic anemia under deregulation and that truck-related carnage on the highways has soared since the early 1980s.

Despite the evidence, some deregulation proponents dogmatically insist that no one has proven conclusively that economic deregulation causes safety deterioration. One is reminded of the argument by tobacco companies that no one has established a conclusive link between cigarette smoking and cancer.

No one has been able to step forward with conclusive evidence to prove (or for that matter, disprove) either proposition. Nonetheless, public policy suggests that the burden of proof ought reasonably to be placed on the constituency which, common sense suggests, is harming innocent people.[46]

Simply put, if a carrier hasn't the economic resources to replace worn equipment, it will have little choice but to defer maintenance, leave the truck rolling on the highway, and hope the next load or two will improve its economic position. This, indeed, was the explicit practice of the unhealthy railroad industry under regulation. The economic imperative of survival in the Darwinian market suggests the same for the unhealthy trucking industry under deregulation. The fact is, human beings are being maimed and killed in increasing numbers in truck-related accidents on our highways.

Only a change in the economic lot of carriers will improve highway safety. Not until motor carriers earn a reasonable return on investment will they have the resources to maintain their equipment properly, or replace it with newer trucks. Not until drivers earn a decent living will they be spared endless hours behind the wheel pumped up on amphetamines. Prudently administered economic regulation can, by controlling entry, constrict excess capacity and thereby enhance carrier productivity. By regulating rates, it can ensure that efficient and well-managed carriers earn a return on investment sufficient to maintain and upgrade equipment to safe levels. By holding the Damocles sword of license revocation over their heads, the regulatory commission can ensure that sufficient resources are spent to enhance safety.

NOTES

1. Professor Golbe's study established that profitable railroads have fewer accidents per mile than do unprofitable rail carriers. Golbe, *Product Safety in a Regulated Industry: Evidence from the Railroads*, 21 ECON. INQUIRY 39 (1983).

2. Dempsey, *Transportation Deregulation—on a Collision Course?* 13 TRANSP. L.J. 329, 352 (1984).

3. Kahn *Airline Deregulation—A Mixed Bag, But a Clear Success Nevertheless*, 16 TRANSP. L.J., 229, 251 (1988).

4. *Air Safety Record Worst since '74*, CHICAGO TRIBUNE, Jan. 13, 1988, at 5.

5. Thomas & McGinley, *Airlines' Growth, Pilot Shortage Produce Least Experienced Crews in Nine Years*, WALL ST. J., Nov. 20, 1987, at 28.

6. Welling, *The Airline's Dilemma: No Cash to Buy Fuel-Efficient Jets*, BUS. WEEK (Sept. 27, 1982) at 65. P. DEMPSEY, LAW & FOREIGN POLICY IN INTERNATIONAL AVIATION 90 (1987).

7. Dempsey, *supra* note 2, at 354 n.100.

8. Rowen, *Airline Deregulation Doesn't Work*, WASHINGTON POST, Apr. 8, 1982, at A27.

9. Duffy, *View from Cockpit is Clearly Negative*, DENVER POST, Dec. 7, 1987, at 2E.

10. *Id.*

11. Fischetti & Perry, *Our Burdened Skies*, 23 IEEE SPECTRUM 36, 79 (1986).

12. *Id.*

13. Valente, Harris, Jr., & McGinley, *Should Airlines Scrap Their Oldest Planes for Sake of Safety?*, WALL ST. J., May 6, 1988, at 1.

14. *Id.*

15. *Skies Safe Today, But Turbulence is Brewing*, ROCKY MOUNTAIN NEWS, May 4, 1988, at 37.

16. Dempsey, *Cross Your Fingers, Hope Not to Die*, CHICAGO TRIBUNE, Aug. 28, 1987, at 28.

17. *Increasing Near-Midair Incidents Spur Drive to Improve ATC Performance*, AV. WEEK & SPACE TECH. 21 (1987).

18. Morganthau, *Year of the Near Miss*, NEWSWEEK (July 27, 1987) at 20.

19. Molinari, *How Safe is the Air Traffic Control System?* USA TODAY, Nov. 1987, at 12–13.

20. OFFICE OF TECHNOLOGY ASSESSMENT, SAFE SKIES FOR TOMOR-ROW, SUMMARY (1988) [hereinafter OTA REPORT ON AIRLINE SAFETY].

21. *Id.* at 13.

22. McGinley, *Congressional Report Warns Air Safety May Be Imperiled without Swift Action*, WALL ST. J., July 28, 1988, at 35.

23. OTA REPORT ON AIRLINE SAFETY, *supra* note 20, at 11.

24. *Id.* at 12.

25. MOTOR CARRIER ACT OF 1980: REPORT OF THE SENATE COMM. ON COMMERCE, SCIENCE AND TRANSPORTATION, S. REP. No. 96–641, 96th Cong., 2d Sess. 85, 100 (1980).

26. Labich, *The Scandal of Killer Trucks*, FORTUNE (Mar. 30, 1987) at 85.

27. F. BAKER, SAFETY IMPLICATIONS OF STRUCTURAL CHANGES OC-CURRING IN THE MOTOR CARRIER INDUSTRY 15 (1985) [hereinafter cited as AAA SAFETY STUDY].

28. N. GLASKOWSKY, EFFECTS OF DEREGULATION ON MOTOR CAR-RIERS 32 (1986).

29. AAA SAFETY STUDY, *supra* note 27, at 17. N. GLASKOWSKY, *supra* note 28, at 32.

30. Comments of Martin E. Foley before the California PUC En Banc Hearing On Regulation of the State's For-Hire Trucking Industry, at 25 (Feb. 12, 1988).

31. Chow, *Deregulation, Financial Condition and Safety in the General Freight Trucking Industry*, in NORTHWESTERN UNIVERSITY CONFERENCE PRO-CEEDINGS, TRANSPORTATION DEREGULATION AND SAFETY 629 (1987).

32. Corsi & Fanara, Jr., *Effects of New Entrants on Motor Carrier Safety*, in NORTHWESTERN UNIVERSITY CONFERENCE PROCEEDINGS, TRANS-PORTATION DEREGULATION AND SAFETY 561 (1987).

33. AAA SAFETY STUDY, *supra* note 27, at 16.

34. Daust & Cobb, *The Relationship between Economic Deregulation of the Motor Carrier Industry and Its Effects On Safety*, in NORTHWESTERN UNI-VERSITY CONFERENCE PROCEEDINGS, TRANSPORTATION DEREGULA-TION AND SAFETY 785 (1987).

35. AAA FOUNDATION FOR TRAFFIC SAFETY, A REPORT ON THE DE-TERMINATION AND EVALUATION OF THE ROLE OF FATIGUE IN HEAVY TRUCK ACCIDENTS (1985). For purposes of this study, fatigue was defined as more than 15 consecutive hours of on-duty or defined activity time. *Id.* at 2.

36. Barton, *A Trucker's Road to Safety and Sanity*, WALL ST. J., Dec. 22, 1987, at 20.

37. COALITION FOR SOUND GENERAL FREIGHT TRUCKING, THE RA-TIONALE FOR TRUCKING REGULATION: EXPOSING THE MYTHS OF DE-REGULATION 15 (1986) [hereinafter cited as MYTHS OF DEREGULATION].

38. N. GLASKOWSKY, *supra* note 28, at 32.

39. *Id.*

40. Labich, *supra* note 26, at 85–86.

41. Hanley, *60% of Trucks Fail New York Area Inspections*, N.Y. TIMES, Oct 8, 1986, at B1.

42. R. BEILOCK, 1986 MOTOR CARRIER SAFETY STUDY vi (1986).

43. N. GLASKOWSKY, *supra* note 28, at 33.

44. *Id.* at 32.

45. COLORADO STATE AUDITOR, PERFORMANCE AUDIT OF THE PUBLIC UTILITIES COMMISSION 34–35 (1988).

46. For an excellent analysis of the impact of deregulation upon highway safety, *see* D. BAKER, COMMON SENSE RELATIONSHIP BETWEEN MOTOR CARRIER ECONOMIC REGULATION AND HIGHWAY SAFETY (1987).

8

CONCENTRATION

In 1987, the United States celebrated its centennial of economic regulation of transportation. The establishment of our nation's first independent regulatory agency, the Interstate Commerce Commission (ICC), in 1887 was motivated largely by the need to shield the public against the monopoly abuses of the railroads. Only three years later, Congress expanded its arsenal of statutory weapons against monopolies and other anticompetitive activities with the promulgation of the Sherman Act of 1890.[1] Antitrust laws were established to preserve the competitiveness of the marketplace by thwarting concentration of market power and thereby promoting efficiency in the allocation of resources.[2]

If market failure was the catalyst for the establishment of the transportation regulatory agencies—the ICC in 1887 and the Civil Aeronautics Board (CAB) in 1938—*regulatory* failure would become the catalyst for their demise.[3] Beginning in the late 1970s, Congress promulgated a series of comprehensive reform bills designed to inject increased levels of competition into the transportation industry.[4] Presidents Carter and Reagan followed suit by appointing individuals vehemently dedicated to deregulation to the transportation regulatory agencies.[5] These agencies—the ICC,[6] the CAB,[7] and the Department of Transportation (DOT)[8]—accepted their new mission with zeal, often exceeding their less ambitious statutory authorizations.[9]

It was thought that enhanced competition would give consumers of air, rail, and motor carrier services the range of price and service options dictated by demand, as reflected in votes of dollar approval in the marketplace. Commentators had blamed regulatory failure for the inefficiencies of the industry, excessive service competition, and inadequate pricing competition.[10] In theory, the new range of consumer choices was to produce an allocation of resources superior to that which existed under regulation.

In the short run, deregulation has made the air and motor carriers highly competitive. Even the rail industry has tended to price its services competitively when necessary to meet the inroads made by its rival modes, the trucks and barges. Thus, deregulation has meant a more attractive pricing structure for many consumers and shippers, particularly in intensely competitive markets such as heavily traveled corridors or large-volume movements.[11] The profit margins of many air and motor carriers, however, have been squeezed (while railroads have become more profitable), forcing management to enhance efficiency, increase productivity, and lower costs or face bankruptcy.[12] Although deregulation has lowered entry barriers into the airline and motor carrier industries, the stress on the small and medium-size competitors has meant bankruptcy for many.[13] Predatory practices by their larger competitors have allegedly contributed to this trend.[14]

The behemoths of the air, rail, and motor carrier industry have targeted smaller competitors for acquisition, while the smaller have merged among themselves to stave off extinction. There has been an unprecedented wave of intramodal and intermodal mergers, purchases, acquisitions, and consolidations. This atmosphere of "merger mania," coupled with the bankruptcies and retrenchments of the weak, threatens the vigorous competition that has benefitted some consumers of transportation services.

This chapter assesses the principal legal and economic developments since deregulation began from an antitrust and public policy perspective. Major mergers of airlines until recently had to be approved by the DOT, while those in the rail and motor carrier industries must be approved by the ICC. Despite statutory admonitions that suggest caution,[15] with but two exceptions, the agencies have been exceedingly generous in their willingness to acquiesce in these anticompetitive endeavors.[16] Each decision has been a step toward increased concentration. Most new entrants have failed to achieve significant market shares,[17] and even those that have, like People Express in the airline industry and Leaseway in the less-than-truckload motor carrier industry, have been forced to retrench.[18]

If this trend continues unabated, the resultant monopolies and oligopolies will be the death knell of meaningful competition, perhaps leading to a return to the market problems that preceded regulation. For the regulatory agencies, devotion to deregulation appears to mean not only the destruction of economic (entry and pricing) regulation in all its forms, but the elimination of meaningful antitrust regulation as well. An examination of the major steps taken toward concentration since deregulation became a reality should make this clear.

AIRLINE CONCENTRATION

Air Carrier Mergers, Consolidations, and Acquisitions of Control since Deregulation

The trend toward concentration in the deregulated airline industry has visibly accelerated.[19] The acquisitions of: Pan American World Airways' (Pan Am's) transpacific operations by United Airlines; Republic Airlines by Northwest Orient Airlines; Ozark Air Lines by Trans World Airlines (TWA); People Express, Frontier, Continental, and Eastern Airlines by Texas Air Lines; Western Airlines by Delta Air Lines; and Piedmont Airlines by US Air may signal the beginning of the end of the vigorous pricing competition that many consumers have enjoyed in our nation's largest passenger markets since the late 1970s.

The first strong wave of merger activity occurred in the years immediately following promulgation of the Airline Deregulation Act of 1978.[20] In 1979, North Central Airlines and Southern Airways joined to become Republic Airlines, which acquired Hughes Airwest the following year for $45 million. Also in 1980, Frank Lorenzo's Texas International Corporation began a hostile takeover bid for National Airlines. Texas International failed in that bold effort, but enjoyed a $47 million profit as it sold its shares of National to Pan Am, which itself acquired National for $400 million. The nation's two major all-cargo carriers, Flying Tigers and Seaboard, also consolidated during this early period.

More recently, Texas Air has vigorously attempted to acquire airlines ailing in the fierce headwinds of deregulation. It succeeded in a hostile $100 million takeover attempt of Continental Airlines, then danced that carrier through subchapter 11 bankruptcy proceedings to shed its union contracts. And although Texas Air failed in its 1985 bids to acquire Frontier and TWA, in 1986 it succeeded in signing a $675 million merger agreement with Frank Borman's Eastern. The merged company inherited Eastern's massive $2.5 billion debt as well as a $9.5 million fine imposed by the Federal Aviation Administration for 73,373 alleged safety violations. Eastern had been an acquiring carrier itself in 1983, when it purchased bankrupt Braniff Airline's Latin American routes for $30 million.

In acquiring Continental, People Express, Frontier, and Eastern, Texas Air became the largest airline in the United States. Only the Soviet Union's Aeroflot flew more aircraft. Texas Air dominated the lucrative New York–Washington shuttle service, which had heretofore been highly competitive. Prior to the merger, Texas Air's subsidiary, New York Air, and Eastern held 420 takeoff and landing slots at tightly controlled New York LaGuardia and Washington National airports. The Department of Justice stated that anticompetitive effects could be felt in as many as two dozen additional markets.[21] Texas Air thus agreed to sell a number of slots and gates in this market to struggling Pan Am.

For its part, TWA avoided Texas Air's frontal assault, but corporate raider Carl Icahn subsequently devoured TWA. In 1986, Icahn also concluded a $224 million agreement to acquire Ozark. Both TWA and Ozark operated hubs at St. Louis. Combined, the carriers controlled 56 of the 74 available gates at St. Louis' Lambert International Airport. The merged airline controls 76% of the airport's gates and 86% of passenger enplanements.

Also in 1986, at a price to Northwest Orient of $884 million, the merged Northwest Orient and Republic became one of America's largest airlines. The merged company now controls 51 of the 63 gates at Minneapolis/St. Paul International Airport. The merger enhanced concentration in Detroit as well, dominating more than 60% of passenger enplanements in that city. Indeed, the Justice Department alleged that competition could suffer in some 85 markets.[22]

United is another of the industry's growing powers. In 1985, the industry behemoth purchased half of Frontier's aircraft and concluded an agreement to buy the remainder of Frontier's operations in 1986. United had acquired Hertz Rent-a-Car in 1985. It was already among the most vertically integrated of American airlines, owning Westin Hotels and Apollo, the nation's largest computer reservations system. United also bought all of Pan Am's transpacific routes, corresponding aircraft, and ground facilities in the fall of 1985 for $750 million. It purchased Hilton International Hotels, a company formerly owned by TWA. It subsequently divested itself of its non-airline subsidiaries to stave off a hostile acquisition.

United's proposed acquisition of Frontier ultimately fell through, ostensibly because of United's inability to conclude a labor agreement covering Frontier's employees. People Express, the only major entrant into the industry since deregulation began, had only recently acquired Frontier, but was forced to put it in subchapter 11 bankruptcy reorganization to stem losses totaling $10 million a month.[23] In late 1986, airline maverick Frank Lorenzo announced his intention to acquire People Express and its subsidiaries, Frontier, Britt, and PBA, for $298 million. During the same time period, Atlanta-based Delta caught the merger virus and announced an $860 million purchase of Salt Lake City-based Western Airlines. And in 1987, US Air followed suit by purchasing Piedmont Airlines for $1.6 billion.

A host of smaller merger transactions have also been consummated in recent years: Midway Airlines acquired Air Florida; US Air bought PSA, Pennsylvania, and Suburban Airlines; Southwest Airlines purchased Muse Air; American acquired Air Cal; Piedmont Airlines absorbed Henson, Jet Stream International, and Empire Airlines; Pan Am purchased Ransome Airlines; Texas Air bought Rocky Mountain Airways; Delta acquired 20%

Figure 8.1
Major Air Carrier Mergers, Acquisitions, Purchases and Consolidations Since Promulgation of the Airline Deregulation Act of 1978

		Market share* 1989	1988	1987
American	AMERICAN	16.6	15.2	13.8
Air Cal				
United	UNITED	16.2	16.4	16.9
Pan Am (transpacific routes)				
Texas International	TEXAS AIR	15.9	19.3	19.0
Continental				
New York Air				
Frontier--People Express				
Britt				
PBA				
Braniff (Latin America)--Eastern				
Rocky Mountain				
Delta	DELTA	13.3	12.0	12.2
Western				
Northwest	NORTHWEST	9.6	8.9	10.3
North Central--Republic				
Southern				
Hughes Airwest				
TWA	TWA	7.2	7.4	8.2
Ozark				
US Air	US AIR	7.2	7.2	7.1
PSA				
Empire--Piedmont				
Henson				
Pan Am	PAN AM	5.9	7.1	6.3
National				
Ransome				

* Percentage market share as measured by revenue passenger miles as of July, 1987.

Sources: *Business Week*, Oct. 5, 1987, 40; *Wall Street Journal*, Mar. 10, 1989, A8.

of Atlantic Southeast Airlines and Comair; and Air Wisconsin merged with Mississippi Valley Airlines, to mention only a few.[24]

Figure 8.1 graphically depicts the major airline mergers that have been proposed or consummated since deregulation and the resulting market shares of the major carriers.[25]

The Texas Air-Eastern, TWA-Ozark, Northwest Orient-Republic, Texas Air-People/Frontier, and Delta-Western mergers announced in 1986 portend reduced competition at the major U.S. hubs of Newark, St. Louis, Minneapolis/St. Paul, Denver, and Detroit. Moreover, more than 60% of U.S. airports have no available gates for new entrants.[26]

Yet analysts speculate that still more airline mergers may be in the offing as obesity becomes epidemic. Industry giants such as United and American are described as potential suitors. Pan Am, Southwest, Midway, and America West have been labeled as potential targets. Carl Icahn admits that despite its acquisition of St. Louis-based Ozark, TWA will have to merge with another airline in the near future to be successful, for it needs new aircraft and another domestic hub.[27] A continuation of these consolidations and acquisitions could well reduce the industry to one dominated by only four or five megacarriers within a few years. The statutory public interest and antitrust policies however, reveal the apparent indifference by the DOT to the harm that may result from an overly concentrated industry.

Airline Mergers under the Federal Aviation Act

Section 408 of the Federal Aviation Act of 1958[28] confers jurisdiction on the federal government to approve consolidations, mergers, and acquisitions of control of an air carrier by a "person substantially engaged in the business of aeronautics."[29] Prior to 1985, this authority was held by the CAB, which "sunset" on December 31, 1984.[30] The DOT's authority expired on January 1, 1989, when such responsibilities were transferred to the U.S. Department of Justice.[31]

Under amendments added by the Airline Deregulation Act of 1978,[32] neither the CAB (prior to 1985) nor the DOT (thereafter) could approve any transaction that would result in the creation of a monopoly.[33] The DOT could not approve a transaction "the effect of which in any region of the United States may be substantially to lessen competition" unless it concluded both that the anticompetitive effects were outweighed by the probable effect of the transaction in meeting significant transportation needs *and* that these needs could not be satisfied by reasonably available alternative means whose effects are materially less anticompetitive.[34] Under section 414 of the Federal Aviation Act, the DOT could exempt a transaction approved under section 408 from the antitrust laws where it concluded that such exemption was required by the public interest.[35]

Antitrust and Public Interest Analysis by the Civil Aeronautics Board

The first merger approved after the promulgation of the Airline Deregulation Act was that of North Central and Southern. In the *North Central-Southern Merger Case*, the CAB dodged the question of whether section 408 includes both a public interest and an antitrust test.[36] It also refused to grant section 414 antitrust immunity, finding insufficient evidence that such an exemption was required by the public interest.[37] The latter precedent has been followed in all subsequent CAB and DOT decisions.[38] For example, in the *Baniff South American Route-Transfer Case*,[39] the CAB noted:

Post-deregulation act Board decisions have emphasized that a grant of immunity is extraordinary relief, appropriate only upon a strong showing by the proponents that it is necessary to permit the transaction to proceed or that it is required in the public interest. Antitrust exposure is a normal risk of doing business in an unregulated competitive environment and is consistent with our reliance on competition to the maximum extent possible.[40]

The CAB subsequently made up for its rather cautious initial advance into the realm of deregulation with its lengthy decisions regarding alternative acquisition bids for National Airlines. Texas International's application was approved but never consummated, while Pan American's bid was approved and concluded.[41] These decisions provided extensive guidelines for future analysis of antitrust and public interest in airline mergers.[42]

The administrative law judge decided that the combined statistical market shares created by the Texas International-National merger would exceed the percentage limits allowed under the Supreme Court's approach in *United States v. Philadelphia National Bank*,[43] particularly in the Houston-New Orleans market.[44] The judge concluded that the merger would be unlawful under section 7 of the Clayton Act.[45] On intra-agency appeal, the CAB rejected both the administrative law judge's exclusive reliance on market-share statistics to analyze anticompetitive effects and his emphasis on precise geographic markets.[46] The CAB felt that exclusive reliance on concentration statistics would not reflect the realities of the new competitive environment because it would ignore the ease of entry into most of the city-pair markets that had been fostered by deregulation.[47]

Instead of relying on *Philadelphia Bank*, the CAB chose to follow the guidance of the Supreme Court decision in *Brown Shoe v. United States*,[48] which promoted a functional approach to antitrust.[49] To assess whether a proposed merger would substantially lessen competition, *Brown Shoe* suggested defining geographical and product markets, and analyzing each to determine market share,[50] cross-elasticity of demand between the product and its substitutes, and barriers to entry.[51] This functional approach was reinforced by *United States v. General Dynamics*,[52] a Supreme Court decision rendered subsequent to *Philadelphia Bank*.[53]

Armed with the functional approach to the antitrust standard in section 408, the CAB could now avoid heavy reliance on market-share data and emphasize other factors such as entry constraints. As the CAB said in *Pan American World Airways-Texas International-National Airlines Acquisition*:[54]

The use of market share data has not been found particularly helpful in establishing the probable competitive performance of individual city-pair markets, and one must look at other factors. . . . Those factors include direct constraints on airport entry (such as slot or gate shortages or impediments imposed in response to environmental problems), the potential that an apparently dominant position at a given airport or city might create an entry barrier, or that dominance (or "shared dominance") at numerous hubs within a region could inhibit entry into markets within that area, or that a pattern of similar market shares over a network of routes could create a potential for tacit collusion.[55]

It concluded that regulatory barriers were nonexistent and new entry had been successful in many markets after deregulation.[56] In so doing, the CAB pitted the new competitive opportunities unleashed by deregulation against market-share statistics.[57]

The CAB also considered potential competition in assessing proposed mergers or acquisitions. Under section 7 of the Clayton Act,[58] if one of the merger partners has the potential to enter into a market in the future, a merger may be proscribed even though the party is not competing there currently.[59] The CAB developed two theories. If firms expected that one of the merging partners would enter a market served by the other if profit opportunities became sufficiently appealing, then there was "perceived potential competition" holding prices and profits down.[60] Similarly, "actual potential competition" suffered when "a substantial reduction of competition [would] result from the loss through merger of a firm with the ability to make a procompetitive entry into a noncompetitive market."[61] In the CAB's view, it should be concerned about potential competition only if entry into a market was expensive or difficult.[62] Because federal licensing restrictions had largely been eliminated and entry barriers were thus perceived to be low, the CAB required a showing of special conditions proving loss of potential competition before it would disapprove a merger on those grounds.[63] Thus, reduced to its simplest terms, the emerging functional approach to antitrust consisted of three elements: the level of concentration, barriers to entry, and the availability of potential entrants.[64]

The CAB settled the dilemma left unresolved by the *North Central-Southern Merger Case*[65] in the *Pan American World Airways-National Acquisition Case*[66] by concluding that section 408 did indeed include both a public interest test and a separate antitrust test.[67] Thus, a merger could be disapproved for failure to satisfy the public interest even though it posed no significant antitrust problems, and the antitrust and public interest considerations of section 408 required separate standards of analysis.[68] The *Pan Am-National Acquisition Case* also made clear that the public interest test was to include the competitive considerations set forth in section 102, and that market shares were only one of a number of factors to be evaluated in assessing the anticompetitive consequences of a proposed consolidation.[69]

The result of the *Pan-Am National Acquisition Case* was that the CAB approved Pan Am's proposed acquisition of National Airlines on the condition that National's London-Miami route not be included in the transaction.[70] Using the functional antitrust analysis, the CAB concluded that while the relevant markets would increase in concentration, the increase would be offset by liberalized freedom of entry into the European markets and competition from foreign airlines.[71] The London-Miami route was considered a separate market because of severe entry restrictions.[72] If the route were part of the acquisition, the three-firm market-share concentration would have been 95.5%. The statistical anticompetitive effects of the transfer were not outweighed by other factors, such as ease of entry, so Pan Am was allowed to serve the route only until another carrier could be selected.[73]

Similarly, in the proposed Eastern-National merger, the CAB held that the level of concentration revealed by market-share statistics was not outweighed by other factors.[74] The proposed merger involved extensive route overlaps and combined market shares averaging 79% in five regional markets.[75] If Eastern had not moved to dismiss its application, the CAB might have disapproved it. Although its focus would have been on entry barriers rather than on market shares, the CAB had acknowledged that large market shares might be of significant concern on a national level.[76]

The next merger application filed with the CAB involved two local carriers, Republic and Hughes Airwest. Since there were no objections, the CAB accepted the statements of the two applicants that they were not potential competitors and approved the merger.[77] This was the first proceeding in which the CAB utilized the newly promulgated part 315 of its Procedural Regulations allowing processing of a merger application in a show-cause proceeding, without a hearing.[78]

In 1980, the CAB investigated an allegation that Texas International had acquired control of National Airlines prior to CAB approval of the acquisition.[79] Under section 408, ownership of 10% of the shares of an airline constitutes a per se controlling interest.[80] Texas International had filed an application under section 408 to purchase 25% of National Airlines and place the shares in a voting trust.[81] Under the proposed voting trust, Texas International retained the power to vote on major changes.[82] Assuming that the trust would be approved, Texas International jumped the gun on purchasing shares. Much to its surprise, the CAB disapproved the voting trust.[83] Texas International scrambled to revise it to a mirror trust arrangement. The carrier's acquisitions exceeded the 10% limit during the interim period, but the CAB considered the rapid revision of the trust sufficient to avoid prosecution.[84]

Continental and Western Airlines first attempted to merge in 1979. Concerns about constraints at Denver's Stapleton Airport (which was near capacity) and the airports in San Diego, San Francisco, and Los Angeles (which were faced with serious noise problems) led the CAB to disapprove the merger.[85] Defining the western United States as the relevant geographic market, the CAB felt that the merger would result in a duopoly in the region, with only United providing major competitive service.[86]

Continental and Western again attempted to merge in 1981. This time, the CAB gave its blessing, noting that all airlines could expand their route structures with the advent of deregulation.[87] It reiterated its policy of using a functional approach in antitrust analysis,[88] but abandoned its reliance on regional market definitions, emphasizing instead the importance of entry barriers.[89] When Continental and Western had attempted to merge in 1979, there were three airports where new entry was constrained. That situation had changed.[90] The only obstacle in 1981 seemed to be that a new entrant into Denver would have difficulty developing a hub operation radiating from Stapleton Airport.[91] The CAB concluded that a potential competitor did not have to be able to develop a hub operation to pose a threat of a competitive response to an unreasonable increase in prices or a decline in output by the existing competitors.[92] Despite CAB approval, the Continental-Western merger was effectively blocked by Texas International's hostile acquisition of Continental.[93]

The CAB focused on the same issues in reviewing Texas International's takeover of Continental.[94] Market-share concentration was deemphasized as merely a useful preliminary indicator that could be potentially misleading in some airline markets.[95] No entry barriers existed, and there was both actual or potential competition.[96] The approved transaction was not considered profitable, but there were other potential entrants available to replace a weakened competitor should it be forced to exit.[97] The CAB expressly refused to substitute its judgment for that of airline management.[98] Its approach effectively narrowed the public interest analysis of issues other than competition. In the CAB's view, its assessment of the public interest was to be based on reasonable standards, not speculation on "every conceivable adverse consequence."[99] The CAB felt that it was not required to make a merger more difficult under the public interest test than it would be under the antitrust analysis alone.[100]

The public interest criterion did play a role in the *Braniff South American Route-Transfer Case*.[101] Immediately prior to its collapse in 1983, Braniff sought to transfer its South American routes to Eastern for six years in return for $30 million. The CAB first addressed the antitrust standard.[102] Longstanding tradition and many relevant bilateral air transport agreements permitted only one U.S.-flag carrier in many markets, and there were serious restrictions on fares and operations. In short, there were solid barriers to entry accompanied by little potential for competition. The CAB, however, did not perceive the route transfer as changing the competitive situation; it simply substituted one carrier for another.[103] Hence, antitrust analysis was blocked. The CAB performed a detailed analysis of the public interest items of section 102 of the Federal Aviation Act of 1958 and approved the transfer on public interest grounds alone.[104]

Antitrust and Public Interest Analysis by the DOT

The DOT assumed the CAB's regulatory authority over airlines on January 1, 1985.[105] It has followed the two-part analysis inaugurated by the CAB, assessing whether the proposed transaction could be either anticompetitive or contrary to the public interest. Yet the DOT's essential policy in reviewing section 408 transactions has been that "the public interest is best served by allowing market forces to operate without unnecessary regulatory interference."[106] This standard appears to constitute a more narrow interpretation of the public interest than that embraced by the CAB.[107]

In the *Southwest Airlines-Muse Air Acquisition Show Cause Proceeding*,[108] the DOT held that the anticompetitive effects of a merger should be assessed by evaluating the impact of the transaction in the relevant city-pair and national markets.[109] Embracing the functional analysis of antitrust issues, the DOT downplayed the market-share concentration in Dallas and Houston. It felt that sufficient actual or potential competition existed in those markets, despite the fact that new entry was constrained at the Houston Hobby and Dallas Love Field Airports.[110] In the DOT's estimation, the significant barriers to entry at these two airports were offset by access to the outlying Houston Intercontinental and Dallas/Fort Worth International airports, irrespective of differences in costs, quality, or consumer preferences.[111]

Southwest had already been charged with engaging in predatory pricing; a merger would arguably increase its ability to continue that practice. Opponents argued that this made the merger inconsistent with the public interest.[112] The DOT claimed discretion to exclude issues not fundamental to its analysis, but went on to note that "vigorous competition was not predation," and that excessive fares should produce new entrants into the market.[113] It did not explore other public interest issues in depth except to say that a merger or acquisition would not be approved or disapproved on the basis of its financial consequences.[114]

The "failing company" doctrine was introduced as the DOT's rationale for approval. Under this approach, "acquisitions or mergers that would otherwise be prohibited by the antitrust laws as anticompetitive can be permitted, if business failure of the acquired company is highly probable and other conditions are met."[115] The DOT listed four elements important to the application of the failing company doctrine, the first three of which it considered essential: (1) the acquired airline must be on the "brink of collapse"; (2) the acquired airline must have little realistic prospect of emerging from bankruptcy proceedings as an operating company; (3) the failing company must have made good faith efforts to find a reasonably available less anticompetitive offer of acquisition and failed; and (4) the acquisition must not be for an anticompetitive purpose.[116] According to the DOT, the final element need only be satisfied "to some extent."[117] The DOT then concluded that Muse's precarious financial condition placed this acquisition within the standards of the failing company doctrine even if the merger were otherwise deemed anticompetitive.[118]

In November of 1985, the DOT approved the acquisition of Frontier by People Express.[119] The DOT first found that any increase in market-share concentration did not have to translate into a substantial reduction in competition in the national or city-pair markets.[120] Because People-Frontier was an end-to-end merger, it would not substantially reduce competition nationally. It also would not reduce competition in city-pair markets. The DOT emphasized that even if competition were reduced, no significant barriers to entry existed, and there were many actual and potential competitors available to offset market-share concentration.[121]

Public interest factors were given little emphasis in the People Express-Frontier decision. The DOT concluded that the Airline Deregulation Act of 1978 "substantially curtailed the scope of . . . public interest review under section 408."[122] This conclusion ignored the contrary CAB precedent that a separate, and potentially more stringent, public interest test was required under the act.[123]

The next application that the DOT considered required public interest analysis to help rationalize approval. It involved a foreign route transfer with significant barriers to entry and high market-share concentration. United sought approval to take over Pan Am's United States-Asia routes and corresponding aircraft and facilities, but the Department of Justice Merger Guidelines suggested disapproval.[124] The Merger Guidelines employ the Herfindahl-Hirschman statistical analysis of market-share concentration that establishes benchmarks regarding when to challenge a transaction.[125] The Justice Department's calculations on the Pacific route transfer exceeded those benchmarks in all the relevant markets.[126]

The DOT, however, discounted the arguments based on the guidelines, concluding that an increase in market-share concentration in a merger or acquisition created only an inference of lessened competition.[127] Because there were significant entry barriers that would not offset the market-share concentration, the DOT changed the focus of its competition analysis to an analysis of market power.[128] The DOT defined market power as the ability of a single firm or several firms colluding to decrease output below or raise prices above competitive levels.[129] It identified two factors to consider in assessing market power: the concentration in the relevant markets, and the structure and operation of those markets.[130] Along with the new antitrust test, the DOT placed the burden on the opponent of the transaction to demonstrate *actual* harm to competition.[131]

Contemporary Airline Consolidations and Proposed
Merger Legislation

During 1986, 25 airlines were involved in 15 mergers. The most significant involved applications from Northwestern Airlines to acquire Republic, from Texas Air to acquire Eastern and People Express/Frontier, from TWA to acquire Ozark, and from Delta to acquire Western.[132] In the Northwest-Republic, Texas Air-Eastern, and TWA-Ozark merger proceedings the Justice Department levied opposition, but recommended approval of Texas Air's acquisition of People/Frontier and Delta's acquisition of Western.

Until recently, the Justice Department has, in its analysis of airline industry mergers, acquisitions, and consolidations, employed a more traditional antitrust analysis, one more skeptical than that embraced by the DOT regarding the ability of new entrants to restore the competitive equilibrium after a consolidation is consummated. The Justice Department began with the presumption that section 408 of the Federal Aviation Act of 1958 is sufficiently analogous to Section 7 of the Clayton Act that its Merger Guidelines should be applied so as to prevent the creation or enhancement of market power.[133]

Employing this analysis, the Justice Department expressed concern that Texas Air's acquisition of Eastern would result in a reduction of competition in 33 city-pair markets, including the slot-constrained markets in Washington, D.C.-New York; Washington, D.C.-Boston; and New York-Boston.[134] Indeed, the two carriers flew 100% of the scheduled flights between New York's LaGuardia and Washington's National airports.[135]

Similarly, the Justice Department found that if Northwestern acquired Republic, competition would be reduced in 42 markets, all but four of which radiated from the carriers' common hubs at Minneapolis/St. Paul (26 cities) and Detroit (12 cities).[136] In 26 of the 42 markets, the merger would result in the consolidation of the only nonstop carriers, thereby eliminating all existing competition. In 29 additional markets, the combined carriers would have more than 80% of existing capacity. Although the Justice Department had conceded that even large market shares could be tolerated if entry barriers were low and competitors could be expected to enter expeditiously should incumbent firms charge supracompetitive prices,[137] it concluded that new entry was unlikely for the reason that a hub at one endpoint would be necessary to provide competitive service.[138] Non-hub carriers would not be likely to restore competition because they lacked the ability to attract overhead, beyond-flow passengers.[139] Its extreme northerly location made Minneapolis/St. Paul an unattractive site for a hub of a new entrant.[140]

Nevertheless, the DOT approved the merger in August, 1986.[141] While acknowledging the extensive overlapping of the two carriers' routes, the DOT concluded that sufficient competition would remain after the merger to restrain Northwest-Republic from raising fares above competitive levels.[142] In so holding, the DOT rejected the administrative law judge's recommendation for the imposition of LPP's (Labor Protective Provisions).[143]

In a move that stunned the airline industry, the DOT initially disapproved Texas Air's acquisition bid for Eastern in August of 1986.[144] The two airlines had overlapping service in 33 city-pairs; combined market shares in those areas ranged from 24.6% to 79.3%.[145] Texas Air sold some landing and takeoff rights to Pan Am at three congested northeastern airports for $65 million, which prompted the Justice Department to withdraw its objections.[146] Although the DOT has final authority on the approval of airline mergers, it was not expected to block one that the Justice Department had approved.

The DOT stated that its disapproval was based on Pan Am's inability to secure a sufficient number of takeoff and landing slots at New York's LaGuardia Airport to provide hourly service during peak periods in the New York–Washington shuttle market.[147] Only Eastern and New York Air (a Texas Air subsidiary) provided competitive shuttle service. The merger would remove a competitor unless Pan Am secured a sufficient foothold to compete.

Apparently the DOT was more concerned with the inadequacy of landing and takeoff slots than with the unavailability of gates that exists as a result of the DOT-approved Northwest-Republic merger at Minneapolis/St. Paul and the TWA-Ozark merger at St. Louis. Perhaps congressional and media criticism of airline mergers prompted the DOT to take a nominal position against at least one of the proposed mergers. At any rate, the DOT invited Texas Air to restructure the transaction (perhaps either by offering to sell New York Air or more slots to Pan Am, thereby retaining competition in the New York-Washington shuttle market) and resubmit it for approval.[148] Analysts correctly predicted that this decision would slow, but not stop, Texas Air's acquisition of Eastern.[149] After Texas Air sold Pan Am enough landing slots to operate 15 daily round-trips in the Washington National-New York LaGuardia-Boston Logan markets, the DOT approved Texas Air's $676 million acquisition of Eastern.[150]

With respect to TWA's proposed acquisition of Ozark, the Justice Department noted that competitive service would be reduced or eliminated in 30 city-pairs.[151] In 18 of the 30, the two carriers had 100% market share.[152] The combined carrier would control 76% of the gates at St. Louis's Lambert International Airport, and 86% of its enplanements.[153] Hence, a potential competitor would have difficulty entering the market.

Nevertheless, the DOT approved the application.[154] TWA's $250 million acquisition of Ozark results in a single carrier providing service between 27 pairs of cities, including certain routes to and from Cleveland, Indianapolis, and Milwaukee. On 11 other routes, competition was reduced from three competitors to two. The Justice Department alleged that TWA could have merged with almost any other airline and posed fewer antitrust problems while still accomplishing the other economic benefits it sought.[155]

After deregulation, Denver became the only city in the United States in which three carriers—United, Continental, and Frontier—shared competing hubs. As a consequence, passengers originating from, destined to, or passing through Denver enjoyed bargain-basement fares. It was thought that United's acquisition of Frontier from ailing People Express would end the low fares because the number of competing hub carriers was reduced to two at Stapleton International Airport.

In order to reduce antitrust opposition to its proposed acquisition of Frontier, United announced plans to sell 12 of Frontier's 24 gates to the city for $22 million, so that the gates could be redistributed to other carriers. However, 12 gates is inadequate to support the inauguration of a major hub rival. United then failed to conclude an agreement with the Air Line Pilots Association to integrate Frontier employee wages into the higher United wage scales, thereby failing to satisfy one of its contractual conditions for acquisition of Frontier from People Express. It appeared that if United would not consummate the purchase agreement, Frontier would be dismembered through bankruptcy liquidation or sold to some third-party airline. People Express, which was losing approximately $10 million monthly in Frontier operations, grounded its jets and contemplated placing Frontier in chapter 11 bankruptcy reorganization proceedings in order to review its options.[156]

Along rode "white knight" Frank Lorenzo, who, through Texas Air, offered to purchase all of People Express, including bankrupt Frontier, for $298 million.[157] The merger would give Texas Air 70% of the boardings at People's hub, Newark International Airport,[158] and 35% of the flights and gates at Frontier's hub, Stapleton International Airport in Denver.[159] The purchase would also saddle heavily leveraged Texas Air with $750 million in additional debt, raising its total debt and lease obligations to more than $4.5 billion[160]—a debt-to-equity ratio of 82%, well above the industry average of 53%.[161] With the acquisitions of Eastern, People Express, and Frontier, Texas Air would become the largest carrier in the free world (and second only to the Soviet Union's Aeroflot), flying 590 jets as compared to United's 361, with major hubs at Atlanta, Denver, Houston, Kansas City, Miami, New York, and Newark.[162]

Lorenzo's policy seemed to be that, under deregulation, carriers must become large in order to survive. By offering frequent flights to America's largest cities, having passengers connect at its hubs, and coordinating the frequent-flyer programs, reservations systems, and route schedules of its subsidiaries, Texas Air hoped to achieve significant economies of scale.[163]

The Justice Department supported Texas Air's acquisition of People Express/ Frontier, saying that it could not establish that the acquisition would "substantially lessen competition."[164]

Even traditionally conservative Delta Air Lines, which has not acquired an airline since 1972, joined the stampede by announcing an agreement to purchase Western Airlines for $860 million in the fall of 1986.[165] Because this was an end-to-end merger of a large eastern and small western carrier, it did not raise significant anticompetitive concerns. Delta, the nation's fifth largest airline, maintains major hubs at Atlanta and Dallas/Ft. Worth and secondary hubs at Boston, Cincinnati, and New York. Western's principal hub was Salt Lake City, with a secondary hub at Los Angeles. The Justice Department urged the DOT to approve the merger.[166]

As a result of these unprecedented mergers of the nation's airlines, the top five air carriers enjoy 82.3% of industry capacity (see Table 8.1).

When measured by revenue passenger miles (see Table 8.2), these mergers give the top seven airlines 84.4% of the market.

Table 8.1
Major Airlines' Domestic Market Share After Consummation of Mergers (in percentages, based on capacity)[167]

Texas Air Corp.	24.3%
Continental Airlines	4.9%
New York Air	.8%
Eastern Airlines	12.0%
People Express	5.0%
Frontier Airlines	1.6%
United Airlines	17.5%
Delta Air Lines	15.5%
Delta Air Lines	11.4%
Western Airlines	4.1%
American Airlines	15.1%
Northwest-Republic Airlines	9.9%
Total	82.3%

Table 8.2
Major Airlines' Market Share After Consummation of Proposed Mergers (in percentages, based on revenue passenger miles through July, 1986)[168]

Texas Air	20.1%
Eastern	9.6%
Continental	5.4%
People Express	3.3%
Frontier	1.2%
New York Air	0.6%
United	15.7%
American	13.5%
Delta	11.9%
Delta	8.8%
Western	3.1%
Northwest	9.4%
Northwest	6.6%
Republic	2.8%
TWA	8.1%
TWA	7.2%
Ozark	0.9%
Pan American	5.7%
US Air	3.0%
Total	84.4%

In January 1986, the top five airlines accounted for 54.3% of the domestic passenger market when measured in revenue passenger miles. By July of 1987, the top five dominated 72.2% of the market.[169] An article in *Fortune* magazine summarized the implications of these trends:

The long-term goal of the acquisition-minded airline is to become a supercarrier with strategic advantages that will make it impregnable in the territories it serves.... The industry's major analysts predict that ultimately only a half dozen or so big national carriers will still be flying, along with several strong regional airlines and a scattering of small commuter operations....Alfred Kahn...is talking these days like a man who thinks he may have helped create Frankenstein's monster. "The number of carriers in a market is the main factor in keeping prices down," he says. "If carriers in a city are reduced from two to one, I get worried." The possibility that other carriers might come in is not sufficient protection for consumers.[170]

A bill was introduced in the House of Representatives in 1986 to transfer federal authority to approve airline mergers from the DOT to the Justice Department.[171] The sponsor of the bill, Representative Dan Glickman, said:

Consumers will lose in the end if a few companies are allowed to control the market. If we don't take any action to slow this trend and subject airline industry mergers to the same antitrust reviews that other industries are subjected to, airline travelers, particularly in less densely populated areas, will face a drastic loss of services.[172]

The DOT's airline merger authority was transferred to the Justice Department on January 1, 1989.[173] Unfortunately, its ultimate decision not to oppose Texas Air's acquisitions of Eastern or People Express/Frontier despite lingering anticompetitive issues raises a question of whether the Justice Department would provide superior protection.

Under section 414 of the Federal Aviation Act, antitrust immunity could have been granted in any of the mergers or acquisitions discussed.[174] In the *North Central-Southern* decision, the CAB declared that antitrust immunity was discretionary and would not be granted unless it was "necessary to permit the transaction to go forward and . . . only when the Board determines that it is required in the public interest.[175] Antitrust immunity was requested in only a few cases after that decision and was consistently denied.[176] Denying antitrust immunity in the *Braniff South American Route-Transfer* decision, the CAB said, "antitrust exposure is a normal risk of doing business in an unregulated competitive environment and is consistent with our policy of reliance on competition to the maximum extent possible."[177]

Under the DOT's regulations, applicants could seek either comprehensive antitrust immunity, or immunity only from private treble damages.[178] The DOT would grant immunity only to the "extent necessary for the transaction to go forward."[179] Any immunity that was granted would have a termination date and would not be automatically renewed.[180] The DOT was not been any more inclined to grant antitrust immunity than the CAB.[181]

Since no antitrust immunity has been granted since deregulation, all of the transactions since then have been potentially subject to prosecution for violations of the Sherman and Clayton antitrust acts. DOT airline merger, acquisition, and consolidation orders are subject to judicial review.[182] However, as the CAB said in the *North Central-Southern* merger decision, "where . . . the Board has found that the merger is not anticompetitive, it is doubtful that a court would entertain a challenge on the same Clayton Act grounds.[183] Furthermore, although the Justice Department has opposed airline mergers in regulatory proceedings before the DOT, it appears reluctant to engage in judicial prosecution of antitrust violations.[184]

In 1986, Congress had before it a bill entitled the Merger Modernization Act.[185] Section 7 of the Clayton Act presently provides that a merger that may "tend to create a monopoly" may be blocked.[186] If the Merger Modernization Act had passed, Section 7 would have been amended to provide that a merger may be blocked only if there is a "significant probability" that the merger "will" increase the capabilities of the company to exercise market power.[187] The bill's language coincided with the DOT's focus on market power antitrust analysis, suggesting that the DOT may have implemented the Merger Modernization Act *de facto*.[188]

The House of Representatives passed a resolution in December of 1985 opposing the Justice Department's Merger Guidelines.[189] Attorneys general from all 50 states have adopted stricter merger guidelines than those used by the Justice Department.[190] The most recent wave of airline mergers and acquisitions is potentially highly anticompetitive. Yet it seems doubtful that measures will be taken soon enough to head off the accelerated urge to merge. Analysts project that, left unchecked, the industry may eventually be "dominated by five or six national carriers, a 'handful' of regional carriers, and 'new entrants will cease to exist.' "[191]

The purpose of the Airline Deregulation Act of 1978 was to decrease government's influence in the airline industry. The CAB was mindful of this goal and its vanishing role in the regulatory process, but its decisions on earlier merger applications made at least a stab at protecting against anticompetitive effects. The CAB expected vulnerability to the antitrust laws to even the score.

It would have been prudent for the responsible agencies to increase antitrust protection as economic deregulation accelerated but, instead, they essentially eliminated it. In later decisions on merger applications, the agencies seemed to manipulate antitrust analysis to justify approval of almost any merger. More lenient antitrust standards are being applied administratively without statutory amendment. The applicants are becoming bolder in proposing increasingly anticompetitive mergers and are meeting only "cotton candy" opposition.[192]

RAIL HORIZONTAL AND VERTICAL INTEGRATION

The Trend toward Rail Oligopoly

After more than a decade of serious and comprehensive merger activity, the nation is left with but seven major rail carriers, which together are responsible for 86% of revenue ton miles and 93% of the industry's profits.[193] The proposed Santa Fe Railroad-Southern Pacific Railroad and Norfolk/Southern Railroad-Conrail consolidations, had they been approved by the ICC and Congress, respectively, would have reduced the major railroads to five.

Conrail is the only major northeastern carrier,[194] itself the result of a 1973 merger between Penn Central Railraod and five smaller railroads.[195] Penn Central was the product of an earlier merger between the Pennsylvania and New York Central Railroads. There are only two large railroads south of Conrail—the CSX Railroad and the Norfolk/Southern. The CSX resulted from the 1980 merger of the Chessie and the Family Lines.[196] The Chessie was the product of a 1963 merger between the Chesapeake and Ohio, the

B & O, and the Western Maryland Railroads. The Family Lines resulted from the 1971 merger of the L & N Railroad and the Seaboard Coast Line, which was likewise the product of a 1967 merger of the Seaboard Air Line and the Atlantic Coast Line. The Norfolk/Southern resulted from the 1981 merger between the Norfolk & Western and the Southern Railroads[197] and operates some 18,000 miles of track extending into 20 states and Ontario, Canada.[197]

The four large western railroads are the Burlington Northern, the Union Pacific, the Southern Pacific, and the Atchison, Topeka & Santa Fe Railroads. The Burlington Northern represents a 1980 merger of the BN and Frisco Railroads. The BN was produced from the 1970 merger of the Great Northern, the Northern Pacific, the Chicago, Burlington & Quincy, and the Spokane, Portland & Seattle Railroads. Today, the Burlington Northern serves 25 states and two Canadian provinces. The 1982 Tri-Pac merger of the Union Pacific, Western Pacific, and Missouri Pacific Railroads combined an even larger system.[198] The merger consolidated approximately 21,000 miles of track extending from Salt Lake City, Omaha, Kansas City, St. Louis, Chicago, Dallas/Ft. Worth, El Paso, and New Orleans to the west coast. In 1983, the Santa Fe and Southern Pacific announced plans to merge and form the nation's third largest railroad. Together the holding companies have some 26,000 miles of track in the west and southwest and assets exceeding $10 billion.[199]

Figure 8.2 graphically depicts the major rail mergers that have been proposed or consummated in recent decades.

Secretary of Transportation Elizabeth Dole recommended that Congress sell the nation's 85% interest in Conrail to the Norfolk/Southern Corporation for approximately $2.1 billion. The combined carriers would have had a route system extending over 31,500 miles of track in 24 states, extending from Montreal and Boston in the east, Chicago, Kansas City, and St. Louis in the west, and Memphis, New Orleans, and Jacksonville in the south.[200] The Antitrust Division of the Justice Department objected on grounds that the proposed acquisition would have a substantial anticompetitive effect in more than 100 markets in 21 states served by the combined railroads.[201]

One commentator predicted that these seven railroads will likely be merged into as few as three by the early 1990s: "Over the next decade, a combination of mergers driven by intense competition between trucks and railroads will result in a few—probably three—super railroads. Dozens of small branch lines, operated by private owners or state governments, will provide feeder service."[202]

Smaller railroads have also caught the merger virus. Guilford Transportation Industries, owner of the Maine Central Railroad, acquired the Boston & Maine Railroad[203] and the Delaware and Hudson Railway.[204] The Soo Line Railroad consumed much of the bankrupt Milwaukee Railroad,[205] and

Figure 8.2
Major Railroad Mergers, Acquisitions and Consolidations Since 1960

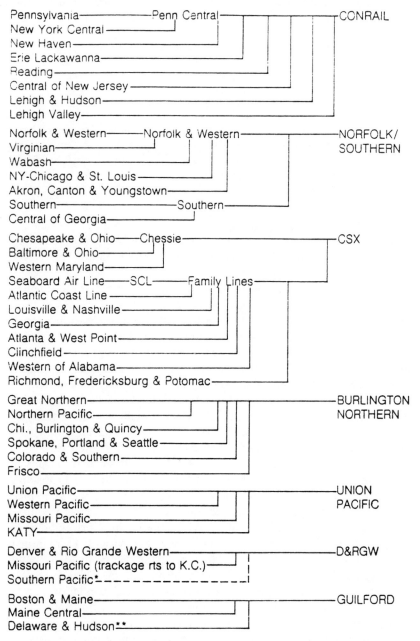

* Originally merged into the Santa Fe, but ICC disapproved the merger and ordered divestiture; merger into D&RGW pending ICC approval.

** In bankruptcy; operated under service order by the New York, Susquehanna & Western.

the Canadian National and Canadian Pacific Railways received ICC approval to acquire the Canada Southern Railway from Conrail.[206] The Union Pacific proposed to buy the Missouri-Kansas-Texas Railroad for $110 million.[207]

Senator Larry Pressler has expressed concern over the merger activity in the railroad industry:

Mergers proliferate. Since the passage of Staggers, the number of major railroads has declined from 12 to 8, and there are 2 more major rail mergers pending today.

As major railroads continue to consolidate, many of the marginal lines become increasingly threatened. Macrodecisions made in corporate board rooms naturally focus on main line operations [while lighter density lines are abandoned] ....Mergers and abandonments will certainly create more captive shippers who are forced to rely upon one rail line.[208]

In August 1986, the Department of Agriculture produced a study that concluded that rail rates for the shipment of grain would have increased significantly had the Norfolk/Southern-Conrail and/or Santa Fe-Southern Pacific mergers been consummated.[209]

Given the liberalized approach of the contemporary ICC, railroads have also been aggressive in acquiring competing or alternative modes of transportation.[210] For example, in 1984 CSX Corporation, the nation's second largest railroad, acquired American Commercial Lines, which owns the nation's largest barge line.[211] This was the first ICC approval of a rail acquisition of an inland water carrier in 73 years. It was approved despite the fact that in some cases the two routes "parallel[ed] each other to a significant degree."[212] CSX has also acquired Sea-Land Corporation, the nation's largest U.S.-flag ocean carrier, which specializes in the transportation of intermodal containers, for $800 million.[213] For $1 billion, CSX also purchased Texas Gas, which has significant pipeline interests.

Similarly, the Burlington Northern purchased El Paso Natural Gas for $700 million. It has also established BN Motor Carriers, Inc., as a subsidiary to control its trucking units, acquired Victory Freightway, and announced plans to take over five to eight small regional motor carriers. In addition to its proposal to acquire Conrail for $1.2 billion, the Norfolk/Southern purchased North American Van Lines from Pepsico for $315 million in 1985. Norfolk/Southern also held a large interest in Piedmont Aviation and announced its intention to go into the barge business in the Delaware Bay.[214]

As early as 1970, the *Nadar Report* criticized the deregulation-minded ICC because it failed "to consider the impact of major rail mergers on the shipping public, despite the legal requirement to do so, and has generally rubber-stamped merger requests."[215] An examination of the statutory criteria governing rail purchases, mergers, acquisitions, and consolidations shows that this criticism is even more valid under deregulation.

Antitrust and Public Interest Standards in Rail Mergers

The Southern Pacific Railroad acquired the stock of the Central Pacific Railroad in 1899, but in 1922 the Supreme Court held that the merger violated section 1 of the Sherman Act of 1890 and ordered divestiture.[216] Congress promptly responded by promulgating the Transportation Act of 1920,[217] which vested the ICC with authority to approve carrier mergers and shielded approved transactions from the prohibitions of the Sherman Act and all other laws.[218] With the promulgation of the Motor Carrier Act of 1935,[219] Congress added motor carriers to the jurisdiction of the ICC, subjecting them to the requirements of the Interstate Commerce Act,[220] including its merger approval requirements and antitrust shield opportunities.[221]

Today, a regulated surface carrier must obtain ICC approval before it may "(1) purchase, lease or operate the properties of another carrier; (2) consolidate or merge with another carrier; or (3) acquire control of another carrier through stock ownership, management or otherwise."[222] The ICC may approve a merger or acquisition of control that it finds to be "consistent with the public interest."[223] Congress has specified five factors for the ICC to consider in assessing whether the merger of two Class I railroads is consistent with the public interest:

- The effect of the proposed transaction on the adequacy of transportation to the public
- The effect on the public interest of including, or failing to include, other rail carriers in the area involved in the proposed transaction
- The total fixed charges that result from the proposed transaction
- The interest of carrier employees affected by the proposed transaction
- Whether the proposed transaction would have an adverse effect on competition among rail carriers in the affected region[224]

In promulgating the Railroad Revitalization and Regulatory Reform Act of 1976 (the "4-R Act"),[225] Congress instructed the ICC to encourage "efforts to restructure the [rail industry] on a more economically justified basis."[226] The legislative history of the 4-R Act reflects that it is "intended to encourage mergers, consolidations, and joint use of facilities that tend to rationalize and improve the Nation's rail system."[227] Paradoxically, the 4-R Act also requires the ICC to "ensure the development and continuation of a sound rail transportation system with effective competition among rail carriers and with other modes."[228] In the legislative directives expressed by the National Transportation Policy,[229] Congress insists that the ICC "avoid undue concentrations of market power."[230]

A long line of court decisions requires the ICC to consider the antitrust laws in its analysis of whether the public interest is satisfied by a proposed merger.[231] In another context, the U.S. Supreme Court acknowledged that antitrust principles contribute "understandable content to the broad statutory concept of the public interest."[232] In *McLean Trucking Co. v. United States*,[233] the Supreme Court succinctly characterized the appropriate weight to be accorded antitrust law in merger proceedings:

[T]he Commission must estimate the scope and appraise the effects of the curtailment of competition which will result from the proposed consolidation and consider them along with the advantages of improved service, safer operation, lower costs, etc., to determine whether the consolidation will assist in effectuating the over-all transportation policy.[234]

In another landmark decision, *Florida East Coast Railway v. United States*, a lower federal court established precedent that has been widely followed.[235] The court held that although the ICC must take national antitrust policy into account in assessing proposed carrier mergers, it need not employ the sophisticated antitrust analysis required in cases prosecuted under section 1 of the Sherman Act or section 7 of the Clayton Act.[236] Indeed, the court determined that the ICC may approve a merger that would fail under the antitrust laws, even one that might create a limited monopoly, so long as it concludes that these undesirable consequences are outweighed by important public benefits.[237]

Hence, the ICC does not sit as an antitrust court; it has statutory obligations to consider public interest values beyond the anticompetitive effects of the transaction. The ICC must balance the anticompetitive effects of a proposed transaction against its anticipated benefits.[238] It may approve consolidations that might otherwise violate the antitrust laws, and, conversely, it may disapprove transactions that would not violate antitrust standards.[239] At the same time, ICC approval of merger or consolidation confers automatic approval under the antitrust laws.[240]

In 1981, the ICC issued a policy statement on rail consolidations that attempted to identify appropriate criteria for assessing the considerations the commission deemed to constitute public interest.[241] The ICC announced a balancing test, weighing "the potential benefits to applicants and the public against the potential harm to the public."[242] The policy statement declared that the ICC "will consider whether the benefits claimed by the applicants could be realized by means other than the proposed consolidations that would result in less potential harm to the public."[243] Among the potential benefits of rail consolidations are operating efficiencies resulting from an elimination of redundant facilities that create a more financially sound competitor in the existing markets.[244] Mergers may also be the only feasible means of entering new markets.[245]

At the same time, the ICC has recognized that the National Transportation

Policy requires it to "take even greater care to identify harmful competitive effects and to mitigate those effects where possible."[246] Rail mergers have deleterious effects upon the public where they reduce present or future intra- or intermodal competition and harm essential services:

If two carriers serving the same market consolidate, the result would be the elimination of the competition between the two. Even if the consolidating carriers do not serve the same market, there may be a lessening of potential competition in other markets. While the reduction in the number of competitors serving a market is not in itself harmful, a lessening of competition resulting from elimination of a competitor may be contrary to the public interest.[247]

A consolidation may injure essential service where, for example, the resulting projected traffic shifts are so significant that the competitor's essential transport services are no longer economically viable.[248]

Rail Merger Conditions

The Interstate Commerce Act specifically allows the ICC to impose conditions upon approved merger transactions to mitigate the deleterious effects of the transaction upon the public.[249] The three types most frequently imposed are those that protect competing carriers, require inclusion of other rail carriers,[250] or protect labor.[251] The latter is required in all mergers by the Interstate Commerce Act.[252] A court recently summarized the scope of the conditions traditionally imposed upon rail carriers to protect competing lines:

Over the years, the Commission has frequently imposed conditions on mergers to guard against potential anticompetitive effects. For example, before a merger, there is one railroad, X, carrying goods between points A and B, and two railroads, Y and Z, carrying goods between points B and C. After the merger, there is now one railroad, XY, stretching all the way from point A to point C, and one line, Z, still operating only between B and C. In this new competitive environment, and absent any restrictions, the new railroad, XY, might insist that all shippers send their goods on its single-line haul from point C to A and not on the joint-line haul using railroad Z from C to B and then railroad XY from B to A. Railroad Z would then be forced out of its old market.

To avoid this result, the Commission has traditionally imposed conditions on mergers which essentially require consolidated railroads to continue the same relationships with the other railroads as existed before the merger. First imposed in 1922, these conditions were finally distilled to a set of six standard conditions in a 1950 consolidation case, Detroit, Toledo & Ironton R. Co. Control, 275 I.C.C. 455, 492. Since 1950, these so-called "DT & I conditions" have been imposed on most mergers, sometimes combined with special conditions to deal with unique or difficult situations

The Commission has interpreted the DT & I conditions to require, among other things, "rate equalization." This means that consolidated carriers must refrain from charging rates on their new, single-line routes that are any lower than the rates on competing joint-line routes in which they also participate. To allow otherwise, in the Commission's view, would result in the "commercial closing" of the joint-line routes and a decrease in inter-railroad competition because shippers would automatically send their products on the cheaper route.[253]

In 1982, the ICC declared that "DT & I" conditions were no longer in the public interest and would not be imposed in future rail mergers.[254] It also announced that "DT & I" conditions would be removed retroactively from consummated mergers in which they had been imposed.[255] The Sixth Circuit Court of Appeals reversed this latter decision, insisting that the ICC hold an "individual hearing on each previously approved merger before it can find that revocation of 'DT & I' conditions imposed on that merger is appropriate."[256]

The ICC has recently ordered the transfer of trackage rights as a condition of approval to ameliorate the anticompetitive consequences of approved mergers on competing railroads. For example, in the Union Pacific-Missouri Pacific-Western Pacific merger, the Denver & Rio Grande Railroad received trackage rights between Pueblo, Colorado, and Kansas City, Missouri; the Southern Pacific received access to St. Louis from Kansas City; and the MKT Railroad was given such rights on several other routes.[257]

Rail Acquisitions of Competing Modes of Transport

Acquisitions of Motor Carriers

The Interstate Commerce Act states that the ICC "may approve [a rail application to acquire a motor carrier] only if it finds that the transaction is consistent with the public interest, will enable the rail carrier to use motor carrier transportation to public advantage in its operations, and will not unreasonably restrain competition."[258] Traditionally, the ICC interpreted this provision to allow only the acquisition of motor carriers providing operations "auxiliary and supplemental" to rail services and not to authorize the acquisition of motor carriers having unrestricted operating rights in the absence of "special circumstances."[259]

Hence, the ICC traditionally interpreted the Interstate Commerce Act to permit rail carriers to hold non-rail-related motor carrier operating authority only when warranted by compelling public need for service not offered by existing motor carriers.[260] The purpose of Congress' general prohibition on dual authority, as upheld by the Supreme Court,[261] was to protect motor carriers from domination by their more powerful competitors, the railroads.[262] As the ICC explained: "The main purpose for the policy...was to prevent the railroads from acquiring motor operations through affiliates and using them in such a manner as to unduly restrain competition of independently operated motor carriers."[263]

In 1982, the ICC abandoned the special circumstances doctrine in the issuance of unrestricted operating authority to motor carrier subsidiaries of railroads.[264] In 1983, the Denver & Rio Grande became the first rail carrier to receive unrestricted operating rights for its trucking subsidiary.[265] In 1986, Burlington Northern, Inc., a railroad holding company, received ICC approval to acquire six motor carriers.[266] That same year, the ICC approved the Norfolk/Southern Railway's $370 million acquisition of North American Van Lines, the nation's largest household goods carrier.[267] In 1986, Union Pacific Corporation announced an agreement to acquire the nation's fifth largest motor carrier, Overnite Transportation Co., for $1.2 billion.[268]

In an important opinion rendered in the fall of 1986 in *International Brotherhood of Teamsters v. ICC (Teamsters I)*,[269] the Court of Appeals for the District of Columbia Circuit held the ICC's eradication of the special circumstances doctrine inconsistent with the provisions of the Interstate Commerce Act governing rail acquisition of motor carriers.[270] The act imposes a tripartite test upon such transactions: (1) they must be in the "public interest"; (2) they must "enable the rail carriers to use motor carrier transportation to public advantage in its operations"; and (3) they must "not unreasonably restrain competition."[271] The second element of that test led the court to remand the ICC's approval of Norfolk/Southern's acquisition of North American Van Lines.[272]

Applying the methodology announced earlier by the Supreme Court in *Chevron U.S.A., Inc. v. Natural Resources Defense Council, Inc.*,[273] the District of Columbia Circuit found the first and third criteria sufficiently ambiguous that it could rely on the ICC's interpretation.[274] However, the court deemed the second criterion precise enough to reflect a clear congressional intent regarding the question at issue: that "rail carriers . . . be allowed to acquire only motor carriers that would be useful in rail operations."[275] In its 1984 policy statement, the ICC had erroneously concluded that the statutory requirement would be satisfied if the acquired motor carriers would be used in its "overall transportation operations."[276] Because many of North American's operations were, and would continue to be, unrelated to supplementing rail services, the rail acquisition violated the statute's requirement that railroads may acquire motor carriers only for purposes of improving rail operations.[277]

After remand, a curious rider was attached to antidrug legislation in the closing days of the Ninety-ninth Congress. The rider effectively grandfathered approval of any acquisition of a motor carrier by a railroad agreed to before the District of Columbia Circuit's opinion in *Teamsters I*.[278] Apparently the several railroads that had such acquisitions challenged in the courts utilized their political power to open the window wide enough for them to pass through.

Shortly thereafter, the ICC sought withdrawal of the *Teamsters I* opinion on grounds that the legislation had turned it into a mere advisory opinion, the acquisition issue was moot, and the question was nonjusticiable. In *International Brotherhood of Teamsters v. United States (Teamsters II)*,[279] the court declined to withdraw its prior opinion on grounds that there were other unresolved issues appropriate for remand. But in light of the supervening legislation, it reversed those portions of its decision relevant to section 11344(c).[280] Nonetheless, the two decisions appear to revive the "special circumstances" doctrine, at least for rail acquisitions not shielded by the 1987 antidrug legislation.[281]

Acquisitions of Water Carriers

Two sections of the Interstate Commerce Act govern rail acquisitions of water carriers. The first is the general provision applicable to all mergers or acquisitions of control not involving two Class I railroads. The ICC must approve the transaction unless it concludes that:

1. As a result of the transaction, there is likely to be a substantial lessening of competition, creation of a monopoly, or restraint of trade in freight surface transportation in any region of the United States.
2. The anticompetitive effects of the transaction outweigh the public interest in meeting significant transportation needs.[282]

The second section is more specifically directed to water carrier acquisitions. No carrier may acquire a competing water carrier unless, with respect to carriers that do not operate via the Panama Canal, the ICC concludes that such acquisition "will still allow that water common carrier or vessel to be operated in the public interest advantageously to interstate commerce and that it will still allow competition, without reduction, on the water route in question."[283]

In 1984, the ICC approved CSX's $725 million acquisition of American Commercial Lines, Inc., which had as a subsidiary the nation's largest inland water carrier, notwithstanding the fact that there was extensive intermodal competition between the two.[284] In June of 1986, CSX acquired Sea-Land Corporation for $800 million.

Recent Major Proposals for Railroad Consolidations

In 1986, two major rail consolidation proposals were considered: the purchase of Conrail by the Norfolk/Southern and the merger of the Santa Fe and Southern Pacific. The former required the approval of Congress, because 85% of Conrail's stock was held by the government. The latter required approval by the ICC.

Norfolk/Southern-Conrail

In 1968, the Pennsylvania, New York Central, and New Haven Railroads merged to become the nation's largest transportation company—the Penn Central Railroad. The declining industrial base of the "rust belt," competition from competing modes, union "featherbedding," mismanagement, a deteriorating physical plant, and regulatory inertia led to Penn Central's disintegration.[285] In 1970, the Penn Central filed for bankruptcy. That year, Congress passed the Emergency Rail Services Act of 1970,[286] creating $125 million in loan guarantees.[287] This bandage proved insufficient to stop the hemorrhaging of dollars. In 1974, Congress again responded by passing the Regional Rail Reorganization Act of 1973 (the "3-R Act"),[288] providing authorization of between $1 billion and $1.5 billion in federal subsidies and loan guarantees and merging most of Penn Central and major portions of the lines of Central of New Jersey, Lehigh Valley, Lehigh & Hudson, Pennsylvania-Reading Seashore, and Ann Arbor Railroads with short sections of the Reading and Erie-Lackawanna Railroads, to create the Consolidated Railroad Corporation (Conrail).[289]

In the ensuing years, Conrail consumed more than $7.5 billion in federal revenue, but it began to turn the corner in 1981, earning profits of $39.2 million. The following year, Conrail was free of federal funding and earned $174.2 million. In 1983, it realized net income of $313 million. It earned over half a billion dollars in 1984 and earned $442 million in 1985.[290]

In 1984, the DOT invited bids for Conrail's purchase. Fourteen bids were submitted, all but one of which assumed that the government would forgive the $7 billion debt. In 1985, Secretary of Transportation Elizabeth Dole chose the Norfolk/Southern's bid, originally for $1 billion for the 85% held by the government and $325 million for the 15% held by Conrail labor.[291]

The Justice Department objected on grounds that the acquisition would adversely affect competition in more than 100 markets in 39 countries and 21 states, with the most severe deleterious impact along an east-west corridor between St. Louis and Chicago in the west and Buffalo and Pittsburgh in the east.[292] As in its opposition to several of the contemporary airline mergers, the Justice Department was concerned that enhanced concentration could lead to market power:

"Market power" is the power of a firm or firms to raise the price of a product or service in a specific market above a competitive level for a significant period of time without fear that existing competitors or new entrants will make such a price increase unprofitable by expanding their output or charging a lower price. When only a few firms in a market into which entry is difficult account for most of the sales of a product, they may either explicitly or implicitly coordinate their actions to eliminate rivalry on price and non-price variables. When firms exercise market power in this way, the result is a transfer of wealth from buyers to sellers and a misallocation of resources that harms the economy. Therefore, a merger that would eliminate a significant competitor in an already highly concentrated market into which entry is difficult may enhance the ability of the remaining firms to exercise market power.[293]

The Senate approved the $1.2 billion purchase offer in 1985, but the House balked.[294] Norfolk/Southern then increased its bid to $1.9 billion.[295]

When the House of Representatives had failed to act favorably upon Secretary Dole's proposal to sell Conrail to the Norfolk/Southern by the summer of 1986, congressional approval of the merger appeared unlikely. In late August 1986, Norfolk/Southern withdrew its $1.9 billion offer to purchase the government's 85% share of Conrail. Conrail was subsequently ordered privatized with a public offering of equity and debt, optimistically projected to produce some $3 billion.[296]

Santa Fe-Southern Pacific

The Justice Department argued that a Santa Fe-Southern Pacific merger similarly posed severe anticompetitive consequences in the west, midwest, southwest, and southeast, where the two carriers have virtually parallel lines.[297] The proposed merger would have had an adverse effect on 6.2 million tons of freight, particularly among such commodities as agricultural products, manufactured food products, chemicals, paper products, motor vehicles, primary metals, petroleum products, nonmetallic minerals, and lumber in the following geographic regions:

- Transcontinental moves between California and the midwest, southeast, and northeast
- Moves between California and the Texas Gulf coast, and shorter moves within this corridor
- Moves between the midwest and Texas/southwest points
- Moves originating in the Pacific Northwest and terminating in Arizona and Southern California[298]

In reducing intermodal competition, the proposed merger would have eliminated the most effective constraint on a rail carrier's ability to increase its rates. The Justice Department views motor carriers as an inadequate competitor for large-volume bulk movements over long distances; entry by another railroad is virtually impossible. Hence, the merged railroad could exert significant market power in this territory.[299]

Here again, the Justice Department expressed its concern with the adverse impact of market power:

A merger can increase market power by creating a sole seller (a monopolist) of a product or service with no good substitute that can raise price by restricting its output or by creating a dominant firm that can raise price even in the presence of a number of fringe competitors. A merger can also facilitate the exercise of market power by reducing the number of selling firms and thereby increase the likelihood that in certain circumstances—depending upon the size of the market shares, the ease with which new entry can occur and other factors—the firms can either explicitly or implicitly coordinate their actions to approximate the performance of a monopolist.[300]

In a move that stunned the industry, the ICC disapproved the Santa Fe-Southern Pacific merger application, which had been pending for two and a half years.[301] The merger was rejected largely because of the long stretches of parallel tracks operated by the two carriers between Los Angeles and El Paso and in California's San Joaquin Valley. As ICC commissioner Malcolm Sterrett said, "common sense should tell us if any proposal fails to meet the statutory guidelines, this case should be it."[302] This was the first major rail merger disapproved by the ICC in more than two decades,[303] and the decision may well reflect the strong political pressure generated by the storm of protests by captive shippers against rail monopoly abuses and the further diminution of competition engendered by increased concentration.

In its opinion, the ICC was critical of internal Santa Fe and Southern Pacific documents indicating that the "purpose of the merger was to achieve market power."[304] Santa Fe's objective was to "seek an affiliation with a major western carrier so as to gain significant market power and potential Staggers Act benefits."[305] The Santa Fe was subsequently acquired by the Denver & Rio Grande Western Railway.

Legislative Proposals for Relief against Monopoly Rail Abuses

Although shippers in some regions of the nation enjoy competitive transportation services, in others rail is the only viable transport mode. This problem is particularly acute in long-distance shipments of large-volume bulk commodities, such as coal or grain. Too often, there is no competing barge or pipeline service, and air and motor carrier transport is prohibitively expensive. With the merger mania that has swept the industry, the parallel rail roadbeds are also disappearing.

Many shippers are left at the mercy of the unilateral pricing decisions of the railroads. The Staggers Rail Act, while intended to enhance the profitability of the rail industry, also reflected a strong congressional concern for the protection of market-dominant traffic against monopoly ratemaking abuses.[306] Nevertheless, the ICC has ignored this objective.[307] As a consequence, rail rates for the movement of coal and grain have outpaced the nation's rate of inflation, resulting ultimately in higher prices for consumers.[308]

If such monopoly abuses arose in another sector of the service economy, consumers could still rely on the antitrust laws to provide relief.

But transportation has been singled out as exempt from most private antitrust remedies under the archaic notion that the ICC exists "to strike a fair balance between the needs of the public and the needs of regulated carriers."[309]

In the landmark decision of *Keogh v. Chicago & Northwestern Railway*,[310] the Supreme Court held that private shippers may not recover treble damages from railroads in an antitrust action over ICC-approved rates.[311] Furthermore, injunctive relief against surface transportation companies pursuant to section 16 of the Clayton Act is available only to the Justice Department with respect to any subject matter within ICC jurisdiction.[312] Post-Staggers Act enforcement of antitrust legislation against railroads has been anything but robust.[313]

ICC jurisdiction over carrier mergers is plenary, and ICC approval confers automatic antitrust immunity over these transactions.[314] Federal courts, by and large, have been unwilling to reverse ICC decisions in this area.[315] Hence, in a regime of lax antitrust scrutiny, carrier mergers, consolidations, and acquisitions proliferate while competition suffers.

Two major legislative proposals have been introduced to remedy the imbalance in favor of the railroads. In March of 1986, the House Judiciary Committee reported favorably on the proposed Railroad Antimonopoly Act.[316] The bill would have amended the Clayton Act by adding a new section 9, making it "unlawful for an owner rail carrier to deny to any shipper or receiver, or to another established rail carrier on reasonable terms, the use of a sole railroad facility for the shipment of a bulk commodity if such denial has the effect of monopolizing."[317] Actual (not treble) damages and injunctive relief were the sole remedies available under the bill.[318] The proposed act, however, was set aside in favor of a proposal sponsored by Consumers United for Rail Equity (CURE).[319]

The Consumer Rail Equity Act, the CURE bill,[320] would provide more specific legislative guidance to the ICC on implementation of the ratemaking provisions of the Staggers Rail Act. It would constrict the ICC's ability to deregulate the rail industry by administrative fiat and insist that the agency protect captive shippers against exorbitant rail rates.[321] The bill also provides that the ICC shall order reciprocal switching, through-route agreements, and terminal facility use agreements to assure competitive transportation.[322] In the fall of 1986, however, an effort to add the CURE provisions as a rider to the Conrail privatization legislation narrowly failed in the House Committee on Energy and Commerce. Some congressmen, although sympathetic with the plight of captive shippers, were reluctant to add unrelated language which might jeopardize the Conrail sale and risk a presidential veto.[323]

Both bills are likely to be resurrected in future legislative sessions. House Energy and Commerce Committee chairman John Dingell has described the ICC as "brain dead."[324] He has vigorously criticized the agency for years of "incompetence or indifference, probably both."[325] Under President Reagan, the ICC was chaired by Heather Gradison, who publicly called for the agency's abolition.[326] Despite legislative requirements to the contrary, she did not believe that the ICC should set carrier rates even where the shippers suffered from market dominance by the railroads.[327]

As Supreme Court Justice Felix Frankfurter observed at the 75th anniversary of the ICC, "institutions do not die, they commit suicide."[328] Perhaps by regulating in a manner that raises the ire of those the agency was statutorily commissioned to protect, the present commissioners hope to swell the ranks of those who will scream for its demise. As this author has noted elsewhere, "if an agency decides to perform its function irresponsibly, those members of the public which have traditionally benefited from regulation will ultimately view deregulation as a lesser vice than irresponsible regulation, and themselves call for the death of the beast which has devoured the benefit of the regulatory burden."[329]

Should the ICC be abolished, captive shippers would be left without a forum in which to adjudicate their complaints against the unilateral pricing demands of the increasingly concentrated railroad industry. If the ICC's remaining responsibilities were transferred to the DOT, as the Reagan administration proposed, the net result would be little better, as the DOT seems to have a strong bias in favor of rail interests. The only hope for such shippers seems to be a strong legislative mandate for the ICC, and the appointment of commissioners less passionately dedicated to deregulation ideology.

MOTOR CARRIER CONCENTRATION

A motor carrier merger, consolidation, or acquisition of control requires approval by the ICC.[330] Unlike the regulatory environment surrounding airline acquisitions, the purchase of 10% of the target carrier's stock does not constitute presumptive control and thus require approval. Indeed, purchases of up to 36% of a carrier's stock have been held in certain circumstances not to constitute control.[331]

When Congress promulgated the Staggers Rail Act, it redefined the criteria for mergers of railroads by adding a fifth criterion, in effect codifying the common-law rule that the ICC must consider "whether the proposed transaction would have an adverse effect on competition,."[332] The other four criteria had been applicable to both motor and rail carriers. In redefining the merger criteria for railroads, Congress inadvertently removed motor carriers from the Interstate Commerce Act's requirements. This rather sloppy legislative draftsmanship persisted when Congress added section 21 of the Bus Regulatory Reform Act of 1982 (the Bus Act),[333] which reinstated the traditional four criteria for motor passenger carriers, but was silent as to motor carriers of property.[334] The ICC seized the opportunity to further its deregulatory agenda by construing the obscure congressional intent to warrant consideration of motor property carrier mergers under the statute's less vigorous public interest criterion and the standards identified for mergers of non-Class I railroads.[335]

Although the ICC proposed that Congress authorized it to exempt motor carriers from all of the approval requirements of the Interstate Commerce Act, the Bus Act, in fact, only allows the ICC to exempt carriers from the finance approval requirements.[336] Under the Bus Act, the ICC may exempt classes of carriers or transactions from the finance requirements if it finds that regulation of such classes would not be necessary to carry out the requirements of the National Transportation Policy.[337] To grant an exemption, the ICC must find that the transaction is of limited scope or that finance regulation is unnecessary to protect shippers from the abuse of market power.[338]

Although the ICC assured Congress that it did not anticipate employing the exemption authority in major transactions that might have possible anticompetitive effects,[339] it promulgated a rule effectively exempting motor carriers from all finance proceedings.[340] In 1984, the ICC issued a blanket exemption for most motor carrier mergers, consolidations, and acquisitions. Opposing parties may protest approval of the proposed transaction only if they are employees who will be adversely affected if it is consummated or they believe that the transaction will be anticompetitive in effect.[341]

Motor carrier deregulation began with ICC initiatives in the late 1970s, then accelerated with the promulgation of the Motor Carrier Act of 1980 and the president's appointment of commissioners zealously dedicated to comprehensive deregulation.[342] The combined impact of deregulation and concentration in the motor carrier industry has been as follows: [343]

- The 10 most profitable carriers in 1984 accounted for over 80% of all general freight carriers' profits.
- Between 1979 and 1983 the 75 largest general freight carriers increased their share of Class I less-than-truckload revenues from 79.2% to 88.2%.
- During this same period, the four largest carriers increased their market share from 26.4% to 30.6%, with the largest carrier increasing its share from 9.1% to 10.1%.

Moreover, with the advent of Canadian deregulation, the U.S. industry concentration may spill over the border and engulf all of this continent north of the Rio Grande.[344]

CONCLUSION: THE OLIGOPOLY IS HERE TO STAY

During the Carter administration, when deregulation of the airline industry was first proposed by the CAB, a number of small and medium-sized carriers expressed fear that the long-term result of deregulation would be an industry oligopoly dominated by a few large carriers.[345] The CAB dismissed these fears as unfounded.[346]

In the early Reagan administration, as the airline industry suffered the worst losses in its history and bankruptcies became epidemic, commentators predicted that "the number of major airlines will probably be reduced to five or six within the next few years."[347] But the CAB, and its successor, the DOT, continued to resist the empirical evidence suggesting a trend toward greater concentration. As recently as October 1986, Professor Robert Hardaway scoffed at those who warned that the industry would come to be dominated by giants: "Critics resisted deregulation on the theory that it would . . . result in industry concentration, and, eventually, oligopolization. Deregulation in large measure has proved the inaccuracy of these predictions."[348] With consolidations of the magnitude of Northwest-Republic, Texas Air-Eastern, TWA-Ozark, Texas Air-People/Frontier and Delta-Western announced in 1986 alone, one wonders how much longer the skies will remain competitive under deregulation.

Concentration through mergers and bankruptcies is an unfortunate consequence of the competitive market forces unleashed by deregulation. The airline industry is more subject to distress sale pricing than most, because it markets a product that is, in essence, instantly perishable. Once an aircraft rolls down the runway, any empty seats are lost forever; they cannot be warehoused and sold another day as can, say, canned beans. In an era of distress sale pricing, unless carriers have deep pockets, they become candidates for bankruptcy or acquisition. In an era of lax antitrust enforcement, oligopoly may be the ultimate result of this trend as the stronger carriers drive the weaker out through a social Darwinist process of predatory pricing. Those not driven out are gobbled up through the increasingly popular process of mergers and acquisitions.

In the short run, deregulation meant a more competitive marketplace where consumers were given a wider choice of price and service options. Braniff became the first major casualty of improvident management after deregulation, and its bankruptcy served as a warning of what was to come. Carrier management and labor, which had grown fat and lethargic under regulation, were forced to tighten their belts. Lower ticket prices and increased industry productivity were indeed considerable benefits of airline deregulation.

But deregulation has not been without its costs. Low fares have been unevenly distributed in favor of America's major non-hub cities, where the competition has been most intense for market share. There is a positive correlation between higher ticket prices and fewer competitors. Transcontinental fares are sometimes lower than the price of flying less than half the distance to a small city.

Passenger convenience has waned. Today's airline traveler is flown on crowded aircraft that are funneled into congested hubs. Flights are chronically delayed and passengers are served cardboard food.[349] Despite this, one feels lucky when not stranded by overbooking, as so many are.

Stockholders and employees have also been stranded in the icy headwinds of deregulation. In the early years of deregulation its advocates were slow to accept any blame, pointing fingers at the economic recession and wildly escalating fuel prices. The recession is now over and aviation fuel prices have been sent crashing through the floor, as have wages for many employees.

Consolidations will inevitably reduce competition in many markets, thereby forcing prices up. Airline profitability (and hopefully its margin of safety) will increase, but so will fares. The short-term price wars some consumers have enjoyed since deregulation will become a thing of the past in many markets.

The traveling public deserves a safe, efficient, and healthy airline industry providing an adequate level of service at a reasonable price. With the demise of the CAB, government no longer assures that these public interest values will be protected.[350] In the absence of economic regulation, only responsible enforcement of our antitrust laws will ensure that consumers enjoy the efficiencies and economies available in a competitive marketplace and are not burdened by the regressive extraction of monopoly or oligopoly profits. Although the social Darwinists can celebrate the net result of deregulation, consumers have been taken for a ride.

The public will have been ill-served by deregulation should the trend toward an oligopoly of megacarriers be realized. If air, rail and motor carrier deregulation is construed broadly to embrace not only reform of economic regulation, but erosion of antitrust standards as well, then concentration most surely is inevitable.[351] With the market power engendered by increased concentration, transportation prices will rise while service declines; wealth will be transferred from consumers to producers.[352]

Under conditions where only a few dominant firms exert market power, producers may maximize their profits by increasing prices and/or reducing service. Because consumers are forced to pay more than a competitive price for the service, they may substitute less desirable alternatives for it. These may include alternatives that cost society more to produce. For example, consumers may be able to drive to business or vacation destinations at a price lower than that charged by monopoly airlines, even though the cost of air transportation may be lower. This results in a misallocation or waste of society's resources and a reduction in the satisfaction level of consumers.[353] Moreover, concentration may be undesirable for a reason reflecting democratic values—concentration of economic power may lead to concentration of political power as well.[354]

The unprecedented wave of mergers, acquisitions, and consolidations unleashed since deregulation has created an oligopoly in which the top eight airlines control 94% of the American passenger market;[355] the top seven railroads dominate approximately 86% of the rail revenue ton miles and 93% of the industry's profits;[356] and the top 10 less-than-truckload motor carriers transport more than 60% of the freight and enjoy more than 90% of general freight profits.[357] Moreover, the Greyhound-Trailways bus duopoly has become a merged monopoly under deregulation.

What is even more distressing is that for certain regions of the nation there is but a single carrier. For shippers dependent upon rail transportation, the northeast is dominated by Conrail; the southeast by Norfolk/Southern and CSX; and the west by the Burlington Northern, Union Pacific, Santa Fe, and Southern Pacific. In the contemporary era, many cities are dominated by a single airline (see Table 8.3).

Table 8.3
Airline Hubs in Which a Single Carrier Enjoys More Than 60% of Market Share

City	Carrier
Charlotte	US Air
Detroit	Northwest
Houston	Texas Air
Memphis*	Northwest
Minneapolis/St. Paul*	Northwest
Newark	Texas Air
Pittsburgh*	US Air
Salt Lake City	Delta
St. Louis*	TWA

*In these cities, the incumbent airline enjoys more than 75% of market share.[358]

Shortly after US Air consolidated its operations around the Pittsburgh hub, it raised its ticket prices.[359] Similarly, after the DOT approved the Northwest/Republic merger, the carrier announced a nearly 15% reduction in scheduled departures from its Minneapolis/St. Paul hub.[360]

US Air and Northwest/Republic were not alone. Once the merger dust began to settle in the fall of 1986, United, American, Delta, and TWA announced 5% fare increases from their hubs of Chicago, Dallas, and St. Louis.[361] Within weeks, these carriers announced a second round of across-the-board increases of an additional 5%.[362] Further increases followed. Such is the inevitable consequence of industry concentration.[363] As a former industry executive observed: "It's obvious that a major motive behind many of the airline mergers is to eliminate the competition....Carriers are trying to achieve the market dominance that, among other things, will give them better control over their prices."[364]

The DOT, in approving all the mergers submitted to it, has optimistically assumed that new carrier entry will reestablish competition in the market-place lost as a result of these consolidations. In fact, much of deregulation was premised on the theory of contestable markets. Theoretically, if a producer of a commodity or service is earning supracompetitive profit, new entrants should be attracted to the industry like sharks to the smell of blood.[365] Proponents of deregulation enthusiastically pointed to the discount passenger fares inaugurated by the new airlines—first by Laker Skytrain, then by Air Florida and People Express—as reflecting the consumer benefits of deregulation.[366] But the first two are bankrupt and the third was near bankruptcy when it was absorbed by Texas Air. Since promulgation of the Airline Deregulation Act of 1978, some 150 carriers have declared bankruptcy or ceased operations.[367] The fact remains that new entrants, like Midway and America West, have not made significant inroads into passenger share.

The same is true in surface transportation. The only major entrant into the less-than-truckload motor carrier market, Leaseway, has since retreated. And where is the entrepreneur who has the vast resources it would take to lay track for a new major railroad?

Despite the optimistic projections of both the Carter and Reagan de-regulators, new market entry in the airline, railroad, or less-than-truckload motor carrier industries is not likely to reestablish competition of the level enjoyed by consumers during the first few years of deregulation.[368] The advantages enjoyed by the nation's largest airlines provide a useful example.

Landing Slots, Gates, and Terminal Facilities. With 100,000 flights per day, American airports are so congested that landing and takeoff ceilings have been imposed at four of the nation's busiest airports: Chicago O'Hare, Washington National, New York LaGuardia, and New York Kennedy.[369] Under rules recently promulgated by the DOT, carriers are free to own, buy, or sell these takeoff and landing slots.[370] This, of course, allows the incumbent airline to enjoy the monopoly or oligopoly rents realized on this scarce resource either by raising ticket prices to supracompetitive levels or by selling slots at high premiums. Moreover, 68% of the nation's leading airports have no terminal space available for new entrants. At half of these, subleasing of gates is impractical because of either high incumbent utilization or exorbitant rates for subleases.[371] Hence, the infrastructure at the nation's most attractive hubs has by now been locked up by the megacarriers and can only be secured at exorbitant prices or through expensive litigation. For example, Southwest Airlines was forced to seek DOT assistance to wrestle a gate from TWA at St. Louis's Lambert International Airport,[372] where, since the TWA-Ozark merger, TWA enjoys a robust 83% market share.[373]

In the post-deregulation era, numerous carriers have consolidated their operations into hub-and-spoke systems whereby flights are fun-neled into a single airport where passengers change planes for their ultimate destinations. Any new entrant attempting to inaugurate point-to-point service into an incumbent's hub is at a competitive disadvantage. It cannot hope to keep its capacity as full as the incumbent rival, which is able to tap overhead, beyond-segment passengers. Domination of a hub may enable a carrier to exert market power with respect to flights entering or leaving it, maximizing its profits by raising prices or lowering levels of service.

Computer Reservations Systems. Two of the nation's largest airlines, United and American, own the nation's two largest computer reservations systems (CRS), Apollo and Sabre, respectively. Approximately 70% of travel agents use one of these two systems, and more than 90% of travel agents book their customers' flights through a CRS. Competitors have alleged that the CRS-parent carriers (1) program the computers to show a strong bias in favor of their airlines, thereby leading agents to book more flights aboard them, (2) charge unreasonably high rates to unaffiliated competitors for participation in the CRS, and (3) utilize information acquired from their CRS to gain an unfair competitive advantage.[374] Another advantage of sophisticated computer systems is the ability of carriers to target promotional fares to only those numbers of passengers needed to fill empty seats and to respond daily (even hourly) to capitalize on growing or declining market demand or the raising or lowering of fares by competitors, thereby maximizing revenue. Some analysts have said that the demise of People Express was partially attributable to its lack of a sophisticated computer system to meet the flexibility of its larger competitors.

Frequent Flyer Programs. The business passenger, whose demand is less price-elastic than that of the vacation traveler, is the most lucrative member of the air passenger market. The larger carriers have been able to build up brand loyalty, not only by their ability to serve all major geographic destinations, but also by offering free travel and related benefits as a reward for accumulating mileage on the airline. Since small carriers cannot offer the spectrum of more exotic travel destinations, they have little hope of inducing the business traveler to join a free-travel program.

Labor Costs. Regulation had created an environment where labor wages, staffing levels, and work rules were more generous than those available to new entrants once deregulation was inaugurated. In the early years of deregulation, new entrants were able to offer comparatively low prices reflecting their significantly lower labor costs vis-à-vis incumbents. But since then, incumbent carriers have successfully lowered labor costs and improved productivity to the point that the short-term competitive advantage held by the nonunion, minimally staffed upstarts is no longer as significant. Carriers such as United, American, and Piedmont now have two-tier pay scales, with lower wages for newly hired workers, and they have exacted wage and work-rule concessions from existing employees.[375] Continental and TWA have gone further and effectively broken some of their unions.

Investor Confidence. With 150 airlines having gone bankrupt since promulgation of the Airline Deregulation Act of 1978, and average airline profitability lower than most industries, the capital markets for new airline ventures began to dry up.[376] The transportation industry is more subject to distress sale pricing than most, and this makes the vicissitudes of the marketplace particularly brutal for transportation companies. Those with deeper pockets can better weather the storm.

All of this has led former CAB chairman and deregulation guru Alfred Kahn to worry that the industry may be evolving into an "uncomfortably tight oligopoly."[377] Even the traditionally pro-deregulation *Economist* perceived the danger:

A more fundamental issue for debate is whether deregulation itself was a mistake....[M]any now fear that the government's dead hand may be replaced by a cartel of five or six monster airlines, which would be in a strong position to quash competition and raise fares.
  This may indeed by happening. Many smaller airlines and some not so small have been driven to take shelter under the wings of the giants with which they cannot compete.[378]

And several of the original proponents of deregulation now concede that, after nearly a decade of deregulation, the empirical evidence fails to sustain the theory of contestable markets.[379]

Three agencies have been heavily involved in the contemporary merger mania in the transportation industry. The DOT has jurisdiction to put a halt to anticompetitive airline mergers, acquisitions, and consolidations, but has yet to do so. Its unconditional approval of the Northwest-Republic and TWA-Ozark mergers, the ones that raised the most serious anticompetitive concerns, established precedent that made it exceptionally difficult to disapprove the proposed airline mergers that followed, such as US Air's acquisition of Piedmont. DOT secretary Elizabeth Dole's recommendation that Conrail be sold to Norfolk/Southern is consistent with the philosophy that government should treat proposals by management warmly. The ICC has prevented rail intermodal and intramodal consolidation in only one case—the Santa Fe-Southern Pacific consolidation proposal. While the Justice Department has raised serious objections in several of the pending consolidation hearings, it has yet to fight an approved merger in the courts, despite the fact that, at least with respect to airline consolidations, no antitrust immunity has been conferred.[380] Indeed, criminal prosecution of antitrust violations arising from mergers and monopolies appears to have been "all but abandoned."

At a time when traditional pricing and entry regulation is being diminished (for railroads), eroded (for motor carriers), or abolished (for airlines), antitrust regulation must be correspondingly enhanced if the public is to enjoy a competitive marketplace. Mergers, acquisitions, and consolidations, while sometimes increasing carrier efficiency, should be scrutinized carefully by government, lest they result in an abuse of market power.[381]

The Reagan administration seems not to have had a consistent antitrust policy.[382] Schizophrenia is reflected in: the Justice Department's position in favor of the Texas Air-Eastern and United-Frontier acquisitions, and against the Northwest Orient-Republic, TWA-Ozark, Santa Fe-Southern Pacific, and Norfolk/Southern-Conrail mergers; the Department of Transportation's position in favor of the Northwest Orient-Republic and Norfolk/Southern-Conrail mergers, and its temporary disapproval of the Texas Air-Eastern acquisition; and the Interstate Commerce Commission's approval of the numerous rail acquisitions of competing modes of transportation, and its disapproval of the Santa Fe-Southern Pacific merger. The automatic antitrust shield of ICC-approved rail and motor carrier mergers is inconsistent with the discretionary antitrust shield of the CAB/DOT in the airline sector, and should be repealed. This would enable the judiciary to scrutinize all mergers under the Sherman and Clayton Antitrust Acts, and perhaps create some rational scheme of consistency in this patchwork of permissiveness.

The contemporary urge to merge reflects several realities. First, carrier management perceives that when the dust settles in the Darwinian marketplace, only the strong will survive, and the largest members will dominate the industry. Second, acquisition of a rival is often a less expensive means of growing than gradually opening up new markets through internal expansion. For example, purchasing a small or medium-size airline results in the acquisition of its aircraft at premium prices; new aircraft are expensive, and their relative fuel efficiency is less significant in this era of low fuel prices. Acquisition may also be the only way to acquire landing slots, gates and/or terminal facilities in a congested market. Third, the candy store is open; the antitrust mood in Washington, D.C., has never been more permissive in this century. No prior administration would have approved concentration of this magnitude. Hence, carriers are scrambling to consolidate while the window is still open.[383] The industrial marketplace is "dominated by a blizzard of unrestricted mergers and acquisitions."[384] Fourth, the psychology of the stampede is to join or be trampled by the hooves of the charging beasts. All of this culminates in a trend toward consolidation which, if not soon abated, will have deleterious economic effects upon all of us who consume transportation services—and we all do, directly or indirectly.

NOTES

1. Ch. 647, 26 Stat. 209 [current version at 15 U.S.C. §§ 1–7 (1982)]. The Sherman Act was passed principally to stifle the growth of monopolies because of their deleterious effect upon competition. The statutory arsenal of antitrust enforce-

ment remedies was significantly supplemented with the promulgation of the Clayton Act of 1914, ch. 323, 38 Stat. 730 [current version at 15 U.S.C. § 18 (1982)].

2. Stated differently, "Congress ... enacted the antimerger laws largely to prevent firms from using mergers to obtain greater market power, raise prices, and thereby acquire some consumer surplus from purchasers of the products." Fisher, Lande, & Vandeale, *Afterword: Could a Merger Lead to Both a Monopoly and a Lower Price?*, 71 CALIF. L. REV. 1697 (1983). But *see* Lande, *Wealth Transfers as the Original and Primary Concern of Antitrust: The Efficiency Interpretation Challenged*, 34 HASTINGS L.J. 65 (1982) (proposing that the objective of antitrust laws is to distribute wealth rather than promote efficiency).

3. *See* generally S. BREYER, REGULATION AND ITS REFORM (1982).

4. This legislation included the Railroad Revitalization and Regulatory Reform Act of 1976 ("4-R Act"), Pub. L. No. 94–210, 90 Stat. 31 (codified as amended in scattered sections of 15, 31, 49 U.S.C.); the Air Cargo Deregulation Act, Pub. L. No. 95–163, 91 Stat. 1278 (1977) (codified in scattered sections of 49 U.S.C.); the Airline Deregulation Act of 1978, Pub. L. No. 95–504, 92 Stat. 1705 (codified as amended in scattered sections of 49 U.S.C.); the International Air Transportation Competition Act of 1979, Pub. L. No. 96–192, 94 Stat. 35 (1980) (codified in scattered sections of 49 U.S.C.); the Motor Carrier Act of 1980, Pub. L. No. 96–296, 94 Stat. 793 (codified as amended at 18 U.S.C. § 1114 (1982) and in scattered sections of 49 U.S.C.); the Staggers Rail Act of 1980, Pub. L. No. 96–448, 94 Stat. 1895 (codified as amended in scattered sections of 11, 45, 49 app. U.S.C.); the Household Goods Transportation Act of 1980, Pub. L. No. 96–454, 94 Stat. 2011 (codified at 26 U.S.C. § 250 (1982), 28 U.S.C. § 2343 (1982), 39 U.S.C. § 5201 (1982), and in scattered sections of 49 U.S.C.); the Bus Regulatory Reform Act of 1982, Pub. L. No. 97–261, 96 Stat. 1102 (codified at 15 U.S.C. § 776 (1982), 26 U.S.C. § 250 (1982), 39 U.S.C. § 5201 (1982), and as amended in scattered sections of 49 U.S.C.); the Civil Aeronautics Board Sunset Act of 1984, Pub. L. No. 98–443, 98 Stat. 1703 (codified at 16 U.S.C. § 18b (1982), 31 U.S.C. § 3726 (1982), 44 U.S.C. § 3502 (1982), and in scattered sections of 5, 7, 10, 15, 26, 39, 49 U.S.C.). *See* generally P. DEMPSEY & W. THOMS, LAW AND ECONOMIC REGULATION IN TRANSPORTATION (1986).

5. *See* Dempsey, *Transportation Deregulation—On a Collision Course?* 13 TRANSP. L. J. 329, 339 (1984).

6. The ICC, established in 1887, was the nation's first independent regulatory commission. *See* Dempsey, *Entry Control under the Interstate Commerce Act: A Comparative Analysis of the Statutory Criteria Governing Entry in Transportation*, 13 WAKE FOREST L. REV. 729–30 (1977).

7. The CAB was established in 1938. *See* Dempsey, *The International Rate and Route Revolution in North Atlantic Passenger Transportation*, 17 COLUM. J. TRANSNAT'L L. 393, 413 (1978).

8. Unlike the ICC and CAB, which were established as independent regulatory agencies under Article I, Section 8 of the Constitution (which vests in Congress the power to regulate interstate and foreign commerce), the DOT is an executive branch agency subject to the direct political will of the president.

9. *See* Dempsey, *Congressional Intent and Agency Discretion—Never the Twain Shall Meet: The Motor Carrier Act of 1980*, 58 CHI. [-] KENT L. REV. 1, 29–34 (1981); Dempsey, *Erosion of the Regulatory Process in Transportation—*

The Winds of Change, 47 ICC PRAC. J. 303, 317–18 (1980); Dempsey, *The Interstate Commerce Commission—Disintegration of an American Legal Institution*, 34 AM. U.L. REV. 1, 33–35 (1984); Dempsey, *The Rise and Fall of the Civil Aeronautics Board—Opening Wide the Floodgates of Entry*, 11 TRANSP. L. J. 91, 123–27 (1979); Kretsinger, *The Motor Carrier Act of 1980: Report and Analysis*, 50 UMKC L. REV. 31, 36, 47 (1981).

   10. Professor Alfred Kahn argued that because the airline industry is inherently competitive, the effort of the CAB in the four decades following its creation to restrain pricing competition led to "irrational service inflation." A. KAHN, THE ECONOMICS OF REGULATION 211, 213 (1966). In Kahn's words, airlines had a tendency to compete not only "in adopting the most modern and attractive equipment and in the frequency with which they schedule flights, but also in providing comfort, attractive hostesses, in-flight entertainment, food and drink." *Id.* at 211. Excessive scheduling and other offerings of wastefully higher levels of service caused marginal costs to begin to rise to the level of passenger fares. The upward pressure on costs squeezed profit margins and led the industry to ask the CAB for a repeated series of additional fare increases, causing ticket prices to spiral upward. While a high level of service might be desirable to some, Dr. Kahn would prefer the test of the competitive marketplace:

That test requires that customers be provided with a sufficient variety of price-quality combinations—consistent with efficient production—so that each can register a free and tolerably well-informed monetary appraisal of the quality differentials that are offered....The reason why it is questionable that the service improvements produced by competition in the airline industry have been worth the cost is that the [CAB's] restrictions on *price* competition have denied consumers the alternative of less sumptuous service at prices reflecting its lower cost. They have therefore not had the opportunity to determine whether the better quality is in their collective judgment worth the higher cost of providing it.

Id. at 216. A subcommittee chaired by Senator Edward Kennedy agreed. It concluded that although the airline industry was potentially highly competitive, the CAB had restricted pricing competition and stifled new entry. Although consumer fares were high, airline profits were low because excessive service competition exacerbated costs. It argued that with pricing and entry freedom, carriers could provide service with higher load factors at significantly reduced ticket prices. S. REP. NO. 1374, 94th Cong., 1st Sess. 12–14 (1975); *see also* Dempsey, *The Rise and Fall, supra* note 9, at 116–17; Jones, *Government Price Control and Inflation: A Prognosis Based on the Impact of Controls in the Regulated Industries*, 65 CORNELL L. REV. 303, 313–24 (1980); note, *Competitive Policy in Airline Deregulation*, 28 AM. U.L. REV. 537, 554–55 (1979).

   The competition unleased by deregulation did lead to lower ticket prices for consumers and higher load factors in the late 1970s. For a short while, many carriers enjoyed higher profit margins. *See* generally E. BAILEY, D. GRAHAM, & D. KAPLAN, DEREGULATING THE AIRLINES 60–66 (1985); S. BREYER, REGULATION AND ITS REFORM 197–221 (1982); S. BREYER & R. STEWART, ADMINISTRATIVE LAW AND REGULATORY POLICY 674–97 (1985); Levine, *Revisionism, Revisited? Airline Deregulation and the Public Interest*, 44 LAW & CONTEMP. PROBS. 179 (1981).

   11. However, small businesses, small towns, and rural communities have not

fared well under deregulation. Today, they pay higher prices for poorer service. Dempsey, *The Dark Side of Deregulation: Its Impact on Small Communities*, 39 ADMIN. L. REV. 445 (1987).

12. The squeeze on profits engendered by the increased competition unleashed by deregulation has strongly motivated airline management to insist on higher levels of efficiency, enhanced productivity, and lower labor costs. The confrontation between management and labor in this industry since deregulation has been fierce. Nevertheless, the industry as a whole had become lethargic under regulation. Hence, the disciplines imposed by the Darwinian marketplace have led to higher levels of carrier efficiency, an improved allocation of resources, and lower prices for many consumers. Indeed, freedom to lower (and raise) prices has enabled carriers to tap the price elasticities of the marketplace to maximize profits on the nondiscretionary (e.g., business) traveler and fill seats that might otherwise have flown empty with the discretionary (e.g., vacation) traveler. In less competitive markets, prices have generally been set higher than those in highly competitive markets. In the early years of deregulation a number of carriers enjoyed healthier profits since deregulation. *See* generally Hardaway, *Transportation Deregulation (1976–1984): Turning the Tide*, 14 TRANSP. L. J. 101 (1985).

13. *See infra* notes 23–27 and accompanying text.

14. *See infra* note 112 and accompanying text.

15. *See infra* note 34 and accompanying text.

16. The two exceptions are the ICC's disapproval of the Southern Pacific-Santa Fe Railroad merger and the DOT's temporary disapproval of Texas Air's acquisition of Eastern Air Lines, both occurring in August of 1986.

17. *See infra* text accompanying notes 366–67.

18. *See infra* text accompanying notes 23–24.

19. One commentator confidently, but inaccurately, predicted that the first merger wave of the late 1970s was a "passing phenomenon" and that mergers would not continue to be an attractive option among domestic carriers. *See* Eads, *Airline Competitive Conduct in a Less Regulated Environment: Implications for Antitrust*, 28 ANTITRUST BULL. 159, 179–83 (1983). Similarly, former CAB chairman Marvin Cohen noted that "[s]ince airlines can now grow by acquiring aircraft and hiring new personnel in a buyer's market, there seem to be few reasons to expand by merger and thus combine (and perhaps compound) the labor and other problems of the two merging carriers." Cohen, *The Antitrust Implications of Airline Deregulation*, 28 ANTITRUST BULL. 131, 139 (1983); *see also* White, *Economies of Scale and the Question of "Natural Monopoly" in the Airline Industry*, 44 J. AIR L. & COM. 545–46 (1979).

For other analyses of the merger movement, *see* Keyes, *Notes on the History of Federal Regulation of Airline Mergers*, 37 J. AIR L. & COM. 357 (1971); Phillips, *Airline Mergers in the New Regulatory Environment*, 129 U. PA. L. REV. 856 (1981).

20. Pub. L. No. 95–504, 92 Stat. 1705 (codified as amended in scattered sections of 49 U.S.C.).

21. *See* Preliminary Comments of the United States Department of Justice, Application of Texas Air and Eastern Airlines, DOT No. 43825 (Mar. 21, 1986) [hereinafter Preliminary Comments in Texas Air-Eastern].

22. *See* Comments of the United States Department of Justice, NWA-Republic

Acquisition Case, DOT No. 43754 (Mar. 28, 1986) [hereinafter Comments in NWA-Republic].

23. Heavy overbooking and flight cancellations led many passengers to complain about People Express service. Indeed, the DOT reported that People Express had the highest ratio of complaints (10.3 per 100,000 passengers in the first quarter of 1986) of any major airline. *See* Carley, *Many Travelers Gripe about People Express, Citing Overbooking,* WALL ST. J., May 19, 1986, at 1, col. 6.

24. *See* Bean, *Piedmont Air Makes It Big in Small Cities,* WALL ST. J., June 23, 1986, at 6, col. 1; Deals, USA TODAY, July 11, 1986, at 4B, col. 1

25. As measured by revenue passenger miles as of July, 1987. BUS. WK., Oct. 5, 1987, at 40.

26. According to an Airport Operators Council international survey, 60 of the 88 U.S. airports have no unleased terminal space for new entrants. Thirty-one have oversaturation of leased space or offer excessive rates to sublessees. *See Report of the Airport Access Task Force: Hearing before the Subcomm. on Investigations and Oversight of the House Comm. on Public Works and Transportation,* 98th Cong., 1st Sess. 71 (1983).

27. *Icahn Says TWA Had up to 30 Million in July Pre-Tax Profit,* WALL ST. J., Aug. 14, 1986, at 5.

28. Pub. L. No. 85–726, 72 Stat. 731 (codified as amended in scattered sections of 14, 15, 16, 31, 40, 48, 49, 50 U.S.C.).

29. 49 U.S.C. app. § 1378(b) (1982).

30. *See* 49 U.S.C. app. § 1551 (Supp. III 1985). Mergers were often employed by the CAB as a means of rescuing failing airlines by consolidating them with healthier carriers. Under the pre–1978 legislation, CAB approval automatically conferred antitrust immunity. *See* Keyes, *supra* note 19, at 368–78.

31. *See* 49 U.S.C. app. § 1551(a) (7) (Supp. III 1985).

32. Pub. L. No. 95–504, 92 Stat. 1705 (codified as amended in scattered sections of 49 U.S.C.).

33. 49 U.S.C. app. § 1378(b) (1) (A) (1982).

34. *Id.* § 1378 (b) (1) (B). The "public interest" criteria is set forth in the Airline Deregulation Act's declaration of policy in section 102. 49 U.S.C. app. § 1302 (1982). Similarly, section 7 of the Clayton Act prohibits mergers and acquisitions where "in any line of commerce in any section of the country, the effect of such acquisition may be substantially to lessen competition, or to tend to create a monopoly." 15 U.S.C. § 18 (1982).

35. 49 U.S.C. app. § 1384 (1982); *see* generally Beane, *The Antitrust Implications of Airline Deregulation,* 45 J. AIR L. & COM. 1001 (1980); note, *Public Interest under the Federal Aviation Act of 1978 and the Airline Deregulation Act of 1978,* 4 NORTHRUP U.L.J. 83 (1983).

36. 82 C.A.B. 1 (1979).

37. *Id.* at 6.

38. For a review of the early merger cases in the post-Airline Deregulation Act environment, *see* note, *The Airline Merger Cases: CAB Application of Clayton Act § 7 after Deregulation,* 12 TRANSP. L.J. 139 (1980). *See also* P. DEMPSEY & W. THOMS, *supra* note 4, at 245–51.

39. 102 C.A.B. 103 (1983).

40. *Id.* at 115 (footnote omitted).

41. *See* National Airlines, Acquisition, 84 C.A.B. 408 (1979); *see* generally Keyes, *A Preliminary Appraisal of Merger Control under the Airline Deregulation Act of 1978*, 46 J. AIR L. & COM. 71, 78–83 (1980).

42. *See infra* notes 54–76 and accompanying text.

43. 374 U.S. 321, 363–66 (1963).

44. *See* National Airlines, Acquisition, 84 C.A.B. at 422. The administrative law judge found that the two-firm market share would be approximately 50%. *Id.*

45. *Id.*

46. *Id.* at 422–33; *see also* Cohen, *supra* note 19, at 135.

47. National Airlines, Acquisition, 84 C.A.B. at 422–23.

48. 370 U.S. 294 (1962).

49. *See* National Airlines, Acquisition, 84 C.A.B. at 424. The CAB also extensively relied on United States v. Marine Bancorporation, 418 U.S. 602 (1974), where the Court used a functional approach in a civil case. *Id.* at 431.

50. *See* note, *Airline Merger Cases, supra* note 38, at 143. Because of the unique nature of airline service, the geographic market was early defined as city-pairs in which the merging carriers presently compete or in which they are a potential entrant. *See* National Airlines, Acquisition, 84 C.A.B. at 418. In subsequent decisions, the CAB identified four alternative geographical markets for analysis—city-pair markets, hub markets, regional markets, and the national market. In the Continental-Western Merger Case, 90 C.A.B. 1 (1981), however, it abandoned the regional analysis in assessing airline mergers. *Id.* at 2. As the CAB explained:

Scheduled air transportation service is provided between a specific origin point and a specific destination point. The aggregation of traffic into broad geographic regions ignores the differing service characteristics of the city pairs or clusters of city pairs in a region and the varying capabilities of airlines to serve particular types of routes. Such an approach is therefore at odds with the "functional" analysis that we require, whose central inquiry is whether the merger will permit the exercise of market power by decreasing service or raising fares above competitive levels in any relevant market.

Id at 4. The CAB also refused to consider individual airport concentrations as a part of the geographic market where a city is served by more than a single airport.

51. *See Brown Shoe*, 370 U.S. at 319–22. The *Brown Shoe* Court emphasized that the principal criterion for determining whether items fall within the same product market for purposes of antitrust analysis is whether they are reasonably interchangeable, or whether there exists cross-elasticity of demand with its substitutes. *Id.* at 325. Earlier CAB cases had defined the product as "scheduled air passenger transportation service between a specific origin point and a specific destination point." National Airlines, Acquisition, 84 C.A.B. at 418. The CAB rejected consideration of charters, air taxis, surface modes of transportation, or alternative forms of communications as within the relevant product market. *Id.* The CAB reasoned that "scheduled air carriers were specialized vendors with distinct customers and that scheduled air service had distinct characteristics." *Id.*

52. 415 U.S. 486 (1974).

53. *Id.* at 494–504.

54. 84 C.A.B. at 408.

55. *Id.* at 420.

56. *Id.* at 419. In a subsequent proceeding, the CAB noted:

We have adopted a functional approach instead of the more traditional market share analysis because the mobility of airline resources allows carriers that do not serve particular city-pairs to insure competitive performance on those routes. Higher concentration, as measured by market shares, will not necessarily mean a reduction in competition if other carriers or potential new entrants can respond to anti-competitive activities of the merged carrier.

Continental-Western Merger Case, 90 C.A.B. 1, 4 n.8 (1981).

57. *See* National Airlines, Acquisition, 84 C.A.B. at 425.

58. Ch. 323, 38 Stat. 730 (1914) (codified as amended in scattered sections of 15, 18, and 29 U.S.C.).

59. *See* 15 U.S.C. § 18 (1982).

60. National Airlines, Acquisition, 84 C.A.B. at 428.

61. *Id.*

62. *Id.* at 436.

63. *Id.* at 431, 435.

64. *Id.* at 433.

65. *See supra* text accompanying notes 36–37.

66. 84 C.A.B. 408 (1979).

67. *Id.*

68. *See* note, *Airline Merger Cases, supra* note 38, at 150.

69. *Id.* at 158.

70. 84 C.A.B. at 462.

71. *Id.* at 450.

72. *Id.* at 452–54.

73. *Id.* at 461–62. In 1980, the bilateral air transport agreement between the United States and the United Kingdom was amended to allow two U.S.-flag carriers to serve the Miami-London market, and thus Pan Am was permitted to retain the route. *See* Cohen, *supra* note 19, at 136.

74. Eastern Acquisition of National, 84 C.A.B. 1210 (1979).

75. *See* note, *Airline Merger Cases, supra* note 38, at 149–51.

76. *See* Brodley, *Antitrust Policy under Deregulation: Airline Mergers and the Theory of Contestable Markets*, 61 B.U.L. REV. 823, 839–40 (1981).

77. *Id.* at 842 n.89.

78. *See* 14 C.F.R. § 315 (1980). For a discussion of the show cause proceeding, see note, *Airline Merger Cases, supra* note 38, at 151–52.

79. *See* Texas Int'l-National Acquisition/Enforcement Case, 85 C.A.B. 1 (1980).

80. The Federal Aviation Act of 1958 established a presumption that ownership of more than 10% of the voting stock of the air carrier constituted control of it. 49 U.S.C. app. § 1378(f) (1982 & Supp. III 1985). The CAB has recognized that smaller ownership interests may also constitute control. *See* Allegheny Airlines, Enforcement Proceeding, 41 C.A.B. 743, 744–45 (1964). Ordinarily, the acquiring carrier seeks DOT approval of a voting trust in which voting stock in excess of 10% will be held pending resolution of the section 408 acquisition application. *See* e.g., Application of Texas Air Corp. for Approval of a Voting Trust Agreement, No. 85–10–9, slip op. (D.O.T. Oct. 2, 1985); Texas Int'l-National Acquisition, 85 C.A.B. at 4.

81. *See* Texas Int'l-National Acquisition, 85 C.A.B. at 4.

82. *Id.* at 4 n.11.

83. *Id.* at 6.

84. *Id.* at 7.

85. Continental-Western Merger Case, 83 C.A.B. 967 (1979).

86. *Id.* at 968.

87. *See* Continental-Western Merger Case, 90 C.A.B. 1, 2 (1981).

88. *Id.* at 4. n.8.

89. *Id.* at 5.

90. *Id.* at 4.

91. *Id.* at 6.

92. *Id.* at 3–16.

93. *See* Cohen, *supra* note 19, at 138. After Western lost its opportunity to merge with Continental, it sought approval to merge with Wien Airlines. *See* Bergt-Western-Wien Acquisition/Control Case, 92 C.A.B. 253 (1982). However, Neil Bergt was the chief executive officer of both Wien and Alaska International Airlines (AIA). The CAB approved the proposal conditioned on Mr. Bergt's being insulated from controlling AIA for 18 months. As a consequence, the merger was never consummated. *See* Cohen, *supra* note 19, at 138–39.

94. *See* Texas Int'l-Continental Acquisition Case, 92 C.A.B. 70 (1981).

95. *Id.* at 76.

96. *Id.* at 77.

97. *Id.* at 80.

98. *Id.* at 81.

99. *Id.* at 75.

100. *Id.* at 81.

101. 102 C.A.B. 103 (1983).

102. *Id.* at 110–12.

103. *Id.* at 111.

104. *Id.* at 112–14.

105. *See supra* note 30 and accompanying text.

106. Application of Texas Air Corp. for Approval of a Voting Trust Agreement, No. 85–10–9, slip op. at 3 (D.O.T. Oct. 2, 1985); *see also* Joint Application of Texas Air Corp. and Trans World Airlines, No. 85–8–16, slip op. at 4–5 (D.O.T. Aug. 6, 1985); Application of People Express, Inc. for Approval of a Voting Trust Agreement, No. 85–10–78, slip op. (D.O.T. Oct. 28, 1985).

107. Although the DOT restructured and recodified the CAB's regulations on mergers and acquisitions [*see* 49 C.F.R. § 303 (1986)], the changes were largely procedural. The DOT did not significantly amend preexisting CAB regulations. Theoretically, its antitrust approach was to follow CAB precedent. There were procedural changes, however. Previously, the applicant had to submit "documents relating to any potential adverse impact of the merger caused by an increase in operating costs or a decrease in the quality or quantity of air service." Saying, "we will not second guess carrier management decisions regarding the down-side risk of transactions," the DOT eliminated this requirement. Implementation of the Civil Aeronautics Board Sunset Act of 1984: Transfer of Antitrust Authority Under Sections 408, 409, 412, and 414 of the Federal Aviation Act of 1958 From the Civil Aeronautics Board to the Department of Transportation, 50 Fed. Reg. 31,134, 31,136 (1985) [hereinafter Transfer of Antitrust Authority].

Applications for mergers, acquisitions, or consolidations must be served on the DOT, the Justice Department, and any interested person so requesting. 50 C.F.P. § 303.03 (1986). It is the duty of interested parties to monitor the DOT's lists of proceedings. *Id.* § 303.41 Section 408 requires the DOT to hold a hearing before approving or disapproving an application. The DOT concluded that because section 408 did not specify what kind of hearing was required, a less formal, show cause proceeding would satisfy the requirement where material fact issues are not in dispute. *See* Transfer of Antitrust Authority, *supra*, at 31,139. The DOT used such a show cause proceeding in approving Southwest Airlines' acquisition of Muse Air after concluding that oral hearings were "not necessary to resolve issues of law, policy or discretion" and that there were no material disputed issues of fact. Southwest Airlines-Muse Air Acquisition Show Cause Proceeding, No. 85–6–79, slip op. (D.O.T. June 24, 1985) [hereinafter DOT No. 85–6–79].

108. DOT No. 85–6–79.

109. *Id.* at 3 [citing Storer Broadcasting v. United States, 351 U.S. 192 (1956)]. The DOT has stated, however, that the absence of "significant barriers to entry in the domestic airline industry means that even large market shares do not show that a market will not perform competitively." Application of People Express, Inc. for Approval of Acquisition of Control, 2 AV. L. REP. (CCH) 22,381 (D.O.T. Nov. 20, 1985).

110. *See* DOT No. 85–6–79, slip op. at 20.

111. *Id.*

112. *Id.* at 10.

113. *Id.*

114. *Id.* at 19.

115. *Id.* at 21.

116. *Id.*

117. *Id.*

118. *Id.*

119. *See* Application of People Express, Inc. for Approval of Acquisition of Control, 2 AV. L. REP. at 14,461.

120. *Id.* at 14,463.

121. *Id.*

122. *Id.*

123. *See supra* text accompanying notes 66–67, 101–04.

124. United States Department of Justice Merger Guidelines, 49 Fed. Reg. 26,827 (1984).

125. *Id.* at 26,830–31.

126. *See* Pacific Division Transfer Case, 2 AV. L. REP. (CCH) 22,382 (D.O.T. Oct. 31, 1985).

127. *Id.*, at 14,473.

128. *Id.* at 14,467, 14,483–91.

129. *Id.* at 14,467, 14,480.

130. *Id.* at 14,466–67.

131. *Id.* at 14,480.

132. *See Airline Executive Finds Mergers Pending at DOT Threaten Competition*, 50 ANTITRUST & TRADE REG. REP. (BNA) 713 (Apr. 24, 1986) [hereinafter *Executive*]; Russell, *Flying among the Merger Clouds*, TIME (Sept. 29, 1986) at 56.

133. *See* Fed. Reg. 26, 827, 830–31 (1984). Market power is the ability of one or more firms to maintain prices above or restrict output below the competitive level for a significant period of time. In the absence of market power, consumers

purchase goods and services closely approximating their marginal costs of production. Thus, in an ideal competitive marketplace there is no input waste, excess capacity, or monopoly profit. The most efficient producers provide the commodity or services, and the public enjoys an efficient allocation of resources. In a situation where market power exists, prices rise and/or the level of service deteriorates, excessive wealth is transferred from consumers to producers, and society's resources suffer from misallocation. *See* Direct Testimony and Exhibits of the United States Department of Justice, NWA-Republic Acquisition Case, DOT No. 43754 (Mar. 27, 1986) [hereinafter Testimony in NWA-Republic]; Hardaway, *The FAA "Buy-Sell" Slot Rule: Airline Deregulation at the Crossroads*, 52 J. AIR L. & COM. 1, 16 (1986) [citing P. SAMUELSON, ECONOMICS 461 (8th ed. 1976)]. Professor Hardaway describes Professor Samuelson's analysis of the problem in these terms:

> In a market where an incumbent firm faces such a nonhorizontal demand curve, profit maximization occurs not at the most efficient social pricing level (*i.e.*, where price equals marginal cost), but rather at the point where marginal *revenue* equals marginal cost. Because this results in a price higher than marginal cost, optimum efficiency goes unachieved because "society does not get quite as much of [the firm's] good as it really wants in terms of what that good really costs society [to] produce."

Id. at 16–17 (footnotes omitted).

Increased concentration in a market resulting from acquisitions, purchases, consolidations, or mergers increases the probability that the firms remaining will be in a position, unilaterally or collectively, to exercise market power. As explained in *Testimony in NWA-Republic:*

> [I]f a market is concentrated (*i.e.*, a large share of the market is supplied by a small number of firms), then it is more likely that firms can exercise market power for several reasons. First, the fewer the firms, the greater their degree of interdependence. With few firms, a change in one firm's price of sales affects the other firms' sales to a greater degree than if there are many firms. Recognizing that interdependence, a firm may be less likely to reduce prices since it is more likely other firms will follow and therefore the price-cutting firm would not expect to take business away from its rivals. Furthermore, the larger the share of the market held by a firm, the smaller (in percentage terms) an output restriction must be for that firm to achieve a particular price increase, all else equal. Finally, the fewer the number of firms, the easier it is for them to coordinate and enforce a collusive reduction in output to increase price. Thus, as a market becomes more concentrated, there is an increased likelihood that prices will rise and output will be reduced.

Testimony in NWA-Republic, *supra* DOJ Exh. T–2, at 5 (testimony of Gloria J. Hurdle).

Empirical research in the post-deregulation environment has demonstrated a positive correlation between concentration and higher air fares. *See e.g.,* E. BAILEY, D. GRAHAM, & D. KAPLAN, DEREGULATING THE AIRLINES 164 (1985); Graham, Kaplan, & Sibley, *Efficiency and Competition in the Airline Industry*, 14 BELL J. ECON. 118, 128–37 (1983). It is the purpose of the antitrust laws to prohibit the deleterious results of concentration. 49 Fed. Reg. 26,284 (1984). To measure concentration, the Justice Department utilizes the Herfindahl-Hirschman Index, which consists of the sum of the squares of the market shares, multiplied by 10,000. The methodology gives greater weight to the larger firms. *See* 49 Fed. Reg. 26,827, 26,830–31 (1984).

Since market power can only be exercised in the context of a market, antitrust analysis usually begins with defining the relevant market. A relevant market is ordinarily deemed to constitute both a product and the geographic area in which it is sold. The Justice Department has urged that specific city-pair markets should be the appropriate subjects of concern. *See* e.g., Horizon-Cascade Acquisition Show Cause Proceeding, No. 86–1–43, slip op. at 7 (D.O.T. Jan. 22, 1986); Piedmont-Empire Acquisition Show Cause Proceeding, No., 85–12–17, slip op., at 5–6 (D.O.T. Dec. 9, 1985); Southwest Airlines-Muse Air Acquisition Show Cause Proceeding, No., 85–6–79, slip op. (D.O.T. June 24, 1985); Texas Int'l-Continental Acquisition Case, 92 C.A.B. 70, 77 (1981). The Justice Department also defines the "product market" as various service levels of air transportation, with an emphasis upon nonstop service. *See* Comments in NWA-Republic, *supra* note 22.

134. *See* Preliminary Comments in Texas Air-Eastern, *supra* note 21.

135. *Id.*

136. *See* Comments in NWA-Republic, *supra* note 22.

137. *See* United States v. Waste Management, Inc., 743 F.2d 976, 982–83 (2d Cir. 1984) [citing United States Department of Justice Merger Guidelines, 49 Fed. Reg. 26,827 (1987)].

138. Comments in NWA-Republic, *supra* note 22.

139. Overhead passengers are those originating from or destined to points beyond the relevant city-pair market.

140. The Justice Department gave this example to explain its position:

[Assume] there are 50 local passengers per day on city pair A-B. A new entrant providing service equivalent to that of the incumbent can expect to attract at most 50 local passengers per day. The hub carrier, however, might also attract 100 additional passengers destined for its numerous hub destinations; the non-hub entrant will attract no such passengers. The new entrant cannot fly an equally-efficient 200-seat aircraft on the city pair because its load factor would be only 25 percent versus the hub carrier's 75 percent. The new entrant thus faces a prohibitive disadvantage.

Comments in NWA-Republic, *supra* note 22, at 18 n.13.

141. *See* NWA-Republic Acquisition Case, 2 AV. L. REP. (CCH) 22,390 (D.O.T. July 31, 1986).

142. *Id.* at 14,547.

143. *Id.* at 14,553–54.

144. *See U.S. Move Signals More Airline Mergers*, WALL ST. J., May 21, 1986, at 6, col. 1 [hereinafter *Signals*].

145. *See Division Urges Caution to DOT in Texas Air Bid To Acquire Eastern*, 50 *ANTITRUST & TRADE REG. REP.* (BNA) 539 (Mar. 27, 1987).

146. *See Signals, supra* note 144; Thomas, *Texas Air Move Means Unit Faces Seeking New Niche*, WALL ST. J., May 15, 1986, at 41, col. 1.

147. *See* Joint Application of Texas Air Corp. & Eastern Air Lines, Inc., No. 86–9–53, slip op. at 1 (D.O.T. Sept. 18, 1986).

148. *See* Texas Air-Eastern Acquisition Case, 86–6–77, slip op. (D.O.T. Aug. 26, 1986).

149. *See Texas Air's Plan to Buy Eastern Blocked by U.S.*, WALL ST. J., Aug. 27, 1986, at 3, col. 1.

150. *See* Joint Application of Texas Air Corp. & Eastern Air Lines, Inc., No. 86–10–2, slip op. (D.O.T. Oct. 1, 1986).

151. *See* Preliminary Comments of the United States Dept. of Justice, Application of Trans World Airlines & Ozark Air Lines, DOT No. 43837 (Apr. 4, 1986) [hereinafter Comments in Trans World-Ozark].

152. *See* e.g., *Antitrust Division Is Concerned over TWA's Bid to Acquire Ozark*, 50 ANTITRUST & TRADE REG. REP. (BNA) 640 (Apr. 10, 1986).

153. Comments in Trans World-Ozark, *supra* note 151.

154. Trans World Airlines-Ozark Airlines Acquisition Case, 2 AV. L. REP., (CCH) 22,392 (D.O.T. Sept. 12, 1986).

155. *See* Comments in Trans World-Ozark, *supra* note 151.

156. *See* Cohen & Koten, *People Express Delays Filing on Frontier Air*, WALL ST. J., Aug. 26, 1986, at 3, col,. 1; Koten & Williams, *People Express Again Delays any Move on Bankruptcy-Law Filing for Frontier*, WALL ST. J., Aug. 27, 1986, at 2, col. 3.

157. *Texas Air Corp. Agrees to Buy People Express*, WALL ST. J., Sept. 15, 1986, at 3, col. 1 [hereinafter *Texas Air Corp. Agrees*]. Texas Air purchased People Express and its subsidiaries for less money than People Express paid for Frontier the preceding year.

158. *See* Hayes, *Texas Air's Bold Bargaining*, N.Y. TIMES, Sept. 16, 1986, at D1, col. 3.

159. *See* Pasztor & Carley, *People Express Bid by Texas Air Clears a Hurdle*, WALL ST. J., Oct. 2, 1986, at 2, col. 2.

160. *See* Thomas, *Purchase of People Express Would Add $750 Million of Debt to Texas Air Corp.*, WALL ST. J., Sept. 16, 1986, at 3, col. 2.

161. Hayes, *supra* note 158.

162. *See Texas Air Corp. Agrees*, *supra* note 157, at 3, col. 1.

163. Thomas, *supra* note 160, at 3, col. 2.

164. Pasztor & Carley, *supra* note 159, at 2, col. 2.

165. *See Delta To Buy Western Air for $860 Million*, WALL ST. J., Sept. 10, 1986, at 3, col. 1.

166. *See* Pasztor, *Delta Air's Bid for Western Air Clears a Hurdle*, WALL ST. J., Oct. 3, 1986, at 14, col. 1; *see also* Anderson, Carroll, & Glickman, *Delta Courts Western Air with $860M*, USA TODAY, Sept. 10, 1986, at 2B, col. 2.

167. *Texas Air Corp. Agrees*, *supra* note 157, at D1.

168. Russell, *supra* note 132, at 56, 57.

169. *See What's Standing between US Air and Piedmont*, BUS. WK., Oct. 5, 1987, at 40.

170. Labich, *Why Bigger Is Better in the Airline Wars*, FORTUNE, Mar. 31, 1986, at 52, 55.

171. *See* H.R. 4734, 99th Cong., 2d Sess. (1986).

172. *House Bill Would Move Authority Over Airline Mergers to Justice Department*, 50 ANTITRUST & TRADE REG. REP. (BNA) 819 (May 8, 1986).

173. *See* H.R. 4734, 99th Cong., 2d Sess. (1986).

174. *See* 49 U.S.C. § 1384 (1982).

175. 82 C.A.B. at 7.

176. *See supra* notes 37–38 and accompanying text.

177. 102 C.A.B. at 115.

178. *See* 14 C.F.R. § 303.05(a) (1986).

179. Transfer of Antitrust Authority, *supra* note 107, at 31,136 (quoting section 414 of the Federal Aviation Act).

180. *Id.*

181. *See supra* note 38 and accompanying text.

182. *See* 49 U.S.C. § 1486(a) (1982).

183. 82 C.A.B. at 8.

184. *See* Middleton, *"New Antitrust" Era Takes Shape*, NAT'L L.J., Jan. 13, 1986, at 1.

185. H.R. 4247, 99th Cong., 2d Sess. (1986). More recently, it has been introduced as S. 635, 100th Cong., 1st Sess. (1987).

186. 15 U.S.C. § 18 (1982).

187. S. 635, 100th Cong., 1st Sess. (1987).

188. *See supra* text accompanying notes 128–31.

189. *See* H.R. Res. 303, 99th Cong., 1st Sess. (1985). For a summary of the contemporary DOT Merger Guidelines, *see* note, *Mergers under the Reagan Justice Department: Redefining Section 7 of the Clayton Act*, 11 J. LEGIS. 421 (1984).

190. *See* Middleton, *supra* note 184, at 8.

191. *Executive*, *supra* note 132, at 713 (quoting H. Pareti, president and chief executive officer of Presidential Airways, Inc.).

192. All fluff and no substance.

193. *See* Feaver, *Major Railroads Poised for Transcontinental Mergers*, WASHINGTON POST, June 19, 1983, at F1. These are 1981 figures. A revenue ton mile represents "a ton of freight carried one mile." *Id.* For a history of the development of the seven major rail carriers, see Dempsey, *supra* note 5, at 367–68.

194. Timothy Mellon, who purchased the Maine Central, the Boston & Maine, and Delaware & Hudson Railroads is assembling a smaller northeastern railroad. Together these railroads traverse almost 4,000 miles. *See* Guilford Transp. Indus., Inc.—Control—Delaware & Hudson Ry., 366 I.C.C. 396, 397 (1982); Harkavy, *Mellon to Complete Rail Purchases by Summer*, BOSTON SUNDAY GLOBE, Nov. 1, 1981, at A28, col. 1.

195. Those five carriers were the Central of New Jersey, the Lehigh and Hudson River, the Lehigh Valley, the Reading, and the Erie Lackawanna Railroads. For a discussion of Conrail, *see A Turnaround for Conrail*, N.Y. TIMES, Dec. 4, 1981, at D1, col. 3.

196. *See CSX: Railroading for Fun and Profit*, BUS. WK., Nov., 30, 1981, at 80.

197. *See* Norfolk Southern Corp.—Control—Norfolk and W. Ry., 366 I.C.C. 171 (1982); Fingleton, *No Panty Hose*, FORBES, Nov. 9, 1981, at 132; Salpukas, *I.C.C. Backs N. & W. Link to Southern*, N.Y. TIMES, Mar. 26, 1982, at D1, col. 3; Wayne, *A Surprising Move by N. & W.*, N.Y. TIMES, Sept. 3, 1981, at D1, col. 3. This was the first merger of two Class I railroads to be approved after promulgation of the Staggers Rail Act of 1980. *See infra* note 274 and accompanying text.

198. *See* Union Pac., Pacific Rail Sys. and Union Pac. R.,R.—Control—Missouri Pac. Corp. and Missouri Pac. R.R., 366 I.C.C. 458 (1982), *aff'd in part and rev'd in part sub nom.* Southern Pac. Transp. Co. v. ICC, 736 F.2d 708 (D.C. Cir. 1984), *cert. denied sub nom.* Kansas City S. Ry. v. United States, 105 S. Ct. 1171 (1986).

199. Paul, *Freight Transportation Is Being Transformed in Era of Deregulation*,

WALL ST. J., Oct. 20, 1983, at 1, 18. A smaller merger was also concluded in 1985, involving the merger of the Chicago, Milwaukee, St. Paul, and Pacific Railway into the Soo Line. Machalaba, *Railroads May Be Forced to Cut Costs after ICC Rejection of Proposed Merger*, WALL ST. J., July 28, 1986, at 5.

200. Koenig & Machalaba, *Norfolk Southern Faces Number of Challenges to Its Conrail Purchase*, WALL ST. J., Feb. 11, 1985, at 1, col. 6.

201. See TRAFFIC WORLD, Feb. 4, 1985, at 11.

202. Feaver, *Major Railroads Poised for Transcontinental Mergers*, WASHINGTON POST, June 19, 1983, at F1.

203. See Guilford Transp. Indus., Inc.—Control—B & M Corp., 366 I.C.C. 292 (1982).

204. See Guilford Transp., Indus., Inc.—Control—Delaware & Hudson Ry., 366 I.C.C. 396 (1982).

205. See In re Chicago, Milwaukee, St. Paul & Pac. R.R., 784 F.2d 831, 832 (7th Cir. 1986).

206. *Oversight of the Staggers Rail Act of 1980: Hearings before the Subcomm. on Surface Transportation of the Senate Comm. on Commerce, Science, and Transportation*, 99th Cong., 1st Sess. 24 (1985) [hereinafter cited as *Staggers Act Oversight*].

207. Fling, *Here Come the Truckbusters*, FORBES, June 30, 1986, at 86, 87; Keeney, *Union Pacific-KATY Merger Proposal Submitted for Commission Approval*, TRAFFIC WORLD, Nov. 24, 1986, at 43.

208. *Staggers Act Oversight*, supra note 206, at 30–31 (statement of Sen. Pressler).

209. *Study Finds Rate Rises in Two Railroad Mergers*, TRAFFIC WORLD, Aug. 18, 1986, at 27.

210. See Machalaba, *Railroads Seek To Become Megacarriers*, WALL ST. J., Sept. 25, 1986, at 6, col. 1.

211. See Crounse Corp. v. ICC, 781 F.2d 1176, 1180 (6th Cir.), *cert. denied*, 107 S. Ct. 290 (1986).

212. *Id.* at 1181.

213. See *CSX and Sea-Land File Formal Merger Proposal before the Commission*, TRAFFIC WORLD, July 21, 1986, at 20; McGinley, *CSX's Purchase of Sea-Land Gets Go-Ahead*, WALL ST. J., Feb. 12, 1987, at 4, col. 1. For a review of the legal issues surrounding intermodal transportation, see J. MAJONEY, INTERMODAL FREIGHT TRANSPORT 25–41 (1985); Dempsey, *The Contemporary Evolution of Intermodal and International Transport Regulation under the Interstate Commerce Act*, 10 VAND. J. TRANSNAT'L L. 505 (1977); Dempsey, *Foreign Commerce Regulation under the Interstate Commerce Act: An Analysis of Intermodal Coordination of International Transportation in the United States*, 5 SYRACUSE J. INT'L L. & COM. 53 (1977).

214. See TRAFFIC WORLD, Apr. 30, 1984, at 23. Norfolk/Southern held 17.7% of the stock of Piedmont Aviation as of April 1984. *Id.*

215. R. FELLMETH, R. BERENBIEM, G. BILLOW, R. BRADSKY, A. KEAR, E. PACHNIAK, & J. ROWE, THE INTERSTATE COMMERCE OMISSION: THE RALPH NADER STUDY GROUP REPORT ON THE INTERSTATE COMMERCE COMMISSION AND TRANSPORTATION 314 (1970).

216. See United States v. Southern Pac. Co., 259 U.S. 214 (1922).

217. Ch. 91, 41 Stat. 456 [current version at 49 U.S.C. § 10101 (1982 & Supp. III 1985)].

218. *See* 49 U.S.C. § 11341 (1982). Three years later, the ICC approved the Southern Pacific-Central Pacific merger with certain conditions designed to remove the opportunity for restraints of competition. *See* Control of Central Pac. by Southern Pac., 76 I.C.C. 508 (1923).

219. Ch. 498, 49 Stat. 543 (current version in scattered sections of 49 U.S.C.).

220. Ch. 104, 24 Stat. 379 (1887) [current version at 49 U.S.C. §§ 501–26, 3101–404, 10101–11916 (1982)].

221. *See* 49 U.S.C. §§ 11344, 10706 (1982); *see also* P. DEMPSEY & W. THOMS, *supra* note 4, at 216.

222. P. DEMPSEY & W. THOMS, *supra* note 4, at 214 [citing 49 U.S.C. § 1604(i) (1982)].

223. 49 U.S.C. § 11344(c) (1982).

224. *Id.* § 11344(b) (1). The standards governing the mergers of non-Class I railroads are slightly different. *Id.* § 11344(d) (1982 & Supp. III 1985). The fifth factor was added by the Staggers Rail Act of 1980, Pub. L. No. 96–448, § 228(a), 94 Stat. 1895, 1931 [codified at 49 U.S.C. § 11344(b) (1) (e) (1982)], and actually represents no change in prior law, but rather codifies preexisting federal common law on the subject. *See*, e.g., Union Pac. Rail Sys., and Union Pac. R.R.—Control—Missouri Pac. Corp. and Missouri Pac. R.R., 366 I.C.C. 459, 483 (1982) [citing Norfolk Southern Corp.—Control—Norfolk & W. Ry., 366 I.C.C. 171, 190 (1982)], *aff'd in part and rev'd in part sub nom.* Southern Pac. Co. v. ICC, 736 F.2d 708 (D.C. Cir. 1984), *cert. denied*, 469 U.S. 1208 (1986).

225. Pub. L. No. 94–210, 90 Stat. 31 (codified as amended in scattered sections of 15, 31, 45, 49 U.S.C.).

226. 45 U.S.C. § 801 (a) (2) (1982).

227. S. REP. NO. 499, 94th Cong., 1st Sess. 20 (1975), reprinted in 1976 U.S. CODE CONG. & ADMIN. NEWS 14, 34. For a discussion of railroad merger procedures, *see* P. DEMPSEY & W. THOMS, *supra* note 4, at 230–33.

228. 49 U.S.C. § 10101a(4) (1982).

229. Pub. L. No. 95–473, 92 Stat. 1337 [codified as amended at 49 U.S.C. §§ 10101—11915 (1982)].

230. 49 U.S.C. § 10101a(13) (1982).

231. *See infra* notes 232–37 and accompanying text.

232. FMC v. Aktiebolaget Svenska Amerika Linien, 390 U.S. 238, 244 (1968).

233. 321 U.S. 67 (1944).

234. *Id.* at 87.

235. 259 F. Supp. 993 (M.D. Fla. 1966), *aff'd*, 386 U.S. 544 (1967).

236. *Id.* at 1000–01, 1004.

237. *Id.* at 1005–15; *see* P. DEMPSEY & W. THOMS, *supra* note 4, at 217–25.

238. *See* Norfolk Southern Corp.—Control—Norfolk & W. Ry. and Southern Ry., 336 I.C.C. 171, 191 (1982).

239. *See* United States v. ICC, 396 U.S. 491, 508–09 (1970).

240. *Id.* at 504; 49 U.S.C. § 11341(a) (1982). Section 16 of the Clayton Act denies private parties a remedy with respect to any matter subject to the jurisdiction of the ICC. *See* 15 U.S.C. § 26 (1982). The ICC also has jurisdiction to enforce

section 7 of the Clayton Act with respect to mergers that might significantly lessen competition. *Id.* § 21(a); *see also* P. DEMPSEY & W. THOMS, *supra* note 4, at 208. The ICC's antitrust immunity has been broadly construed. *See*, e.g., United States v. Navajo Freight Lines, 339 F. Supp. 554 (D. Colo. 1971).

241. *See* Railroad Consolidation Procedures, 366 I.C.C. 75 (1982) [current version at 49 C.F.R. § 1180.1 (1986)].

242. 49 C.F.R. § 1180.1(c) (1986). The ICC has long had an obligation "to consider the effect of the merger on competitors and on the general competitive situation in the industry in light of the objectives of the national transportation policy" and to balance the deleterious impact of any diminution of competition against the benefits the public may enjoy from the transaction. McLean Trucking Co. v. United States, 321 U.S. 67, 87 (1944); *see also* Seaboard Air Line R.R.—Merger—Atlantic Coast Line R.R., 320 I.C.C. 122, 127–30 (1963).

243. 49 C.F.R. § 1180.1(c) (1986). The standard is strikingly similar to that embraced by Congress in the Airline Deregulation Act of 1978. *See supra* note 34 and accompanying text.

244. *See* 49 C.F.R. § 1180.1(c) (1) (1986).

245. *Id.*

246. Union Pac., Pacific Rail Sys., and Union Pac. R.R.—Control—Missouri Pac. Corp. and Missouri Pac. R.R., 366 I.C.C. 459, 502 (1982), *aff'd in part and rev'd in part sub nom.* Southern Pac. Co. v. ICC, 763 F.2d 708 (D.C. Cir. 1984), *cert denied sub nom.* Kansas City S. Ry. v. United States, 105 S. Ct. 1171 (1986).

247. 49 C.F.R. § 1180.1(c)(2)(i) (1986).

248. *Id.* § 1180.1(c)(2)(ii) ("A service is essential if there is a sufficient public need for the service and adequate alternate transportation is not available").

249. *See* 49 U.S.C. § 11344(c) (1982).

250. *Id.*

251. *Id.* § 11347 (Supp. III 1985).

252. *Id*; 49 C.F.R. § 1180.1 (f) (1986); *see also* Brotherhood of Locomotive Eng'rs v. ICC, 761 F.2d 714 (D.C. Cir. 1985) (ICC exceeded its authority by exempting participants to rail consolidations from protections statutorily afforded railroad employees without specifying necessity to justify waiver of the statute), *cert. granted*, 475 U.S. 1081 (1986); McGinness v. ICC, 662 F.2d 853 (D.C. Cir. 1981) (ICC lacks authority to relieve any carrier of obligations to rail employees during rail merger that are imposed by statute).

253. Detroit, Toledo & Ironton R. Co. v. United States, 725 F.2d 47, 49 (6th Cir. 1984) (footnote & citation omitted). The six conditions specified in 1950 were as follows:

1. That under applicant's control, [the merged carrier] shall maintain and keep open all routes and channels of trade via existing junctions and gateways, unless and until otherwise authorized by us.
2. The present neutrality of handling traffic inbound and outbound by [the merged carrier] shall be continued so as to permit equal opportunity for service to and from all lines reaching the rails of those carriers without discrimination as to routing or movement of traffic and without discrimination in the arrangement of schedules or otherwise.
3. The present traffic and operating relationships existing between [the merged carrier], on the one hand, and all lines connecting with their tracks, on the other, shall be continued insofar as such matters are within the control of the applicants.

4. [The merged carrier] shall accept, handle, and deliver all cars inbound and outbound, loaded and empty, without discrimination in promptness or frequency of service as between cars destined to or received from competing carriers and irrespective of destination or route of movement.

5. Applicants shall not do anything to restrain or curtail the right of industries located on [the merged carrier] to route traffic over any or all existing routes and gateways.

6. Any party or any person having an interest in the subject matter may at any future time make application for such modification of the above conditions, or any of them, as may be required in the public interest, and jurisdiction should be retained to reopen the proceeding on our own motion for the same purpose.

Id. at 49 n.1 [quoting Detroit, Toledo & Ironton R. Co. Control, 275 I.C.C. 455, 492 (1950)].

254. *See* 49 C.F.R. § 1180.1(d)(1) (1986). For a carefully reasoned criticism of the ICC's approach, *see* Tye, *Post-Merger Denials of Competitive Access and Trackage Rights in the Rail Industry*, 53 TRANSP. PRAC. J. 413, 426–27 (1986).

255. 49 C.F.R. § 1180.1(d)(2) (1986).

256. Detroit, Toledo & Ironton R. Co. v. United States, 725 F.2d at 51.

257. *See* e.g., Union Pac., Pacific Rail Sys., and Union Pac. R.R.—Control—Missouri Pac. Corp. and Missouri Pac. R.R., 366 I.C.C. 459, 572, 580, 566–72 (1982), *aff'd in part and rev'd in part sub nom.* Southern Pac. Co. v. ICC, 736 F.2d 708 (D.C. Cir. 1984), *cert. denied*, 469 U.S. 1208 (1986).

258. 49 U.S.C. § 11344(c) (1982).

259. Pennsylvania Truck Lines, Inc., Acquisition of Control of Barker Motor Freight, Inc., 5 M.C.C. 9, 11 (1937). For an excellent analysis of these principles, *see* Erenberg & Kasson, *Railroad-Motor Carrier Intermodal Ownership*, 12 TRANSP. L.J. 75, 82–91 (1981).

260. *See* e.g., Rock Island Motor Transit Co.—Purchase—White Line Motor Freight Co., 40 M.C.C. 457 (1946) (granting motor carrier permit to railroad subsidiary on condition that carrier only perform service auxiliary to rail transport), *rev'd sub nom.* Rock Island Motor Transit Co. v. United States, 90 F. Supp. 516 (N.D. Ill. 1949), *rev'd*, 340 U.S. 419 (1951); Kansas City S. Transp. Co., Common Carrier Application 10 M.C.C. 221 (1938) (denying motor carrier permit to company that made agreement with railway to share facilities, customers, and revenue), *modified*, 28 M.C.C. 5 (1941); Pennsylvania Truck Lines, Inc.—Acquisition of Control of Barker Motor Freight Lines, Inc., 1 M.C.C. 101 (1936) (denying authorization of rail carrier's purchase of motor freight company); *cf.* 49 U.S.C. § 11344(c) (1982) (ICC may approve and authorize rail carrier's application for transaction involving motor carrier only if transaction is consistent with public interest, will enable rail carrier to use motor carrier transportation to public advantage, and will not unreasonably restrain competition).

261. *See* American Trucking Ass'ns v. United States, 364 U.S. 1 (1960) (upholding National Transportation Policy goal of preventing railroads from invading trucking industry); American Trucking Ass'ns v. United States, 355 U.S. 141 (1957) (affirming ICC's authority to impose restrictions on railroad operation of motor carriers but finding it to be merely policy and not a rigid limitation).

262. *See* Beardsley, *Integrated Ownership of Transportation Companies and the Public Interest*, 31 GEO. WASH. L. REV. 85, 92–96 (1962) (discussing development of congressional policy concerning railroad ownership of non-rail carrier authority).

263. Rock Island Motor Transit Co. Common Carrier Application, 63 M.C.C. 91, 102 (1954).

264. *See* Applications for Motor Carrier Operating Authority by Railroads and Rail Affiliates, 132 M.C.C. 978 (1982).

265. *See* Johnson, *Seven Transportation Megatrends for the Late 1980s*, 58 TRANSP. PRAC. J. 164, 177–78 (1986).

266. *See* ICC, STAFF REPORT NO. 10, at 15 (1986). In August 1986, BN received approval to acquire Stoops Express, Inc., Wingate Trucking Co., Inc., and Taylor-Maid Transportation, Inc. through its subsidiary, Burlington Northern Motor Carriers, Inc. It had already acquired Monkem Co., Inc., Monroe Trucking, Inc., and Victory Freightway System. *See Three More BN Truck Buys Authorized by Commission without Formal Scrutiny*, TRAFFIC WORLD, Aug. 4, 1986, at 36.

267. *See* D. SWEENEY, C. MCCARTHY, S. KALISH, & J. CUTLER, JR., TRANSPORTATION DEREGULATION: WHAT'S REGULATED AND WHAT ISN'T 25–26 (1986).

268. *See* Machalaba & Williams, *Union Pacific to Buy Overnite for $1.2 Billion*, WALL ST. J., Sept. 19, 1986, at 3, col. 1; McGinley & Machalaba, *ICC Clears Union Pacific's Plan to Buy Overnite Transportation for $1.2 Billion*, WALL ST. J., Sept. 16, 1987, at 5, col. 1.

269. 801 F.2d 1423 (D.C. Cir. 1986).

270. *Id.* at 1430–31.

271. 49 U.S.C. § 11344(c) (1982).

272. International Bhd. of Teamsters v. ICC, 801 F.2d at 1427.

273. 467 U.S. 837 (1984).

274. International Bhd. of Teamsters v. ICC, 801 F.2d at 1423–26.

275. *Id.* at 1427.

276. Acquisition of Motor Carriers by Railroads, Ex parte No. 438, slip op. (I.C.C. July 27, 1984).

277. International Bhd. of Teamsters v. ICC, 801 F.2d at 1430. For discussion of the reaction to this ruling, *see* McGinley, *Norfolk Southern Pact with Trucker Faces Rehearing*, WALL ST. J., Oct. 1, 1986, at 15, col. 1.

278. Anti-Drug Abuse Act of 1986, Pub. L. 99–570, § 3403, 100 Stat. 3207, 3309.

279. 818 F.2d 87 (D.C. Cir. 1987).

280. Footnote 2, however, appears to embrace a restrictive interpretation of the statute, limiting the acquisition of motor carriers to those to be used "only as an adjunct to rail movements." *Id.* at 89 n.2. For an excellent review of this area of the law, and a strong argument that the statute should not be so interpreted, *see* Andrews, *Intermodal Acquisitions after BN and* Teamsters: *A Case Study in Judicial Re-Regulation*, 37 YOUR LETTER OF THE LAW 9 (1987).

281. In an opinion highly critical of the Interstate Commerce Commission, the District of Columbia Circuit also circumscribed the ICC's ability to approve intermodal acquisitions through the exemption mechanism. Regular Common Carrier Conference v. United States, 820 F.2d 1323 (D.C. Cir. 1987).

282. 49 U.S.C. § 11344(d) (1982 & Supp. III 1985).

283. *Id.* § 11321(a), (b).

284. *See* Crounse Corp. v. ICC, 781 F.2d 1176 (6th Cir.) (affirming the ICC's decision), *cert. denied*, 107 S. Ct. 290 (1986); D. SWEENEY, C. MCCARTHY, S. KALISH, & J. CUTLER, JR., *supra* note 267, at 26–27.

285. *See* generally Thoms, *Clear Track for Deregulation: American Railroads, 1970–1980,* 12 TRANSP. L.J. 183, 201–06 (1982).

286. Pub. L. No. 91–663, 84 Stat. 1975 (1971) [codified as amended at 45 U.S.C. § 661 (1982)].

287. *Id.*

288. Pub. L. No. 93–236, 87 Stat. 985 (1971) [codified as amended in 45 U.S.C. §§ 701–92 (1982) and 49 U.S.C. §§ 10361–64, 10710 (1982)].

289. *Id.; see also* Conant, *Structural Reorganization of the Northeast Railroads,* 43 ICC PRAC. J. 207, 211 (1976).

290. *See* Brookes, *Is This any Way to Sell a Railroad?,* INSIGHT, Sept. 15, 1986, at 51.

291. *See* Machalaba & Koenig, *As Conrail Gets Ready to Go Public, It Still Faces a Rough Road,* WALL ST. J., Feb. 4, 1987, at 1, col. 8.

292. *See* Letter from J. Paul McGrath to Elizabeth H. Dole (Jan. 29, 1985).

293. *Id.* at 2.

294. *See supra* note 291 and accompanying text; Koenig, *Conrail Public Offering Might Not Meet Congress's Goal of Raising $1.7 Billion,* WALL ST. J., Feb. 18, 1987, at 20, col. 1.

295. *See* Brookes, *supra* note 290, at 51.

296. *See New Sale Plan to Return Conrail to Private Sector Circulated in Congress,* TRAFFIC WORLD, Aug. 11, 1986, at 66. Congress anticipated that the public offering would result in revenues of $1.7 billion for the federal government's 85% share, plus an additional $300 million contribution to the Treasury from Conrail's $1 billion in cash reserves., *See* Karr, *Plan to Sell Conrail Clears House Hurdle But Other Provisions May Imperil Bill,* WALL ST. J., Sept. 17, 1986, at 64, col. 1; Sandler, *Conrail Offering's Underwriters Will Do Well, But Outlook for Issue's Investors Is Less Certain,* WALL ST. J., Sept. 30, 1986, at 67, col. 3.

297. *See* Post-Hearing Brief of the United States Department of Justice, Santa Fe-Southern Pacific Merger Case, ICC No. 30400, at 4–5 (Oct. 21, 1985).

298. *Id.*

299. *Id.* at 3–4.

300. *Id.* at 13.

301. Santa Fe-Southern Pacific management contemplated an ICC or judicial appeal requesting reversal or legislative relief. *See* Ettorre, *Schmidt Says SFSP Is Considering Seeking Bill Overriding ICC Vote,* TRAFFIC WORLD, Aug. 11, 1986, at 31.

302. *ICC Rejects Merger of Santa Fe and Southern Pacific Railroads,* WALL ST. J., July 25, 1986, at 3.

303. Some industry analysts have concluded that the ICC may be sending a message to the industry "that such major mergers are no longer a viable avenue that railroads can travel to achieve cost-cutting objectives." Poos, *ICC May Have Sent Message to Rails in Denying SF-SP Railroad Merger,* TRAFFIC WORLD, Aug. 4, 1986, at 16. However, since there are only seven major railroads left in the United States, significant merger opportunities are less than abundant.

304. Wastler, *SFSP Document Helped Persuade ICC Merger Would Be Anticompetitive,* TRAFFIC WORLD, Oct. 13, 1986, at 7.

305. *Id.* [quoting memorandum by then-Santa Fe Industries chairman John J. Schmidt (May 16, 1983)]. The merger was refiled and again disapproved by the ICC in 1987. *ICC Reaffirms Its Rejection of Merger of Santa Fe, Southern Pacific Railroads,* WALL ST. J., July 1, 1987, at 3, col. 3.

306. Pub. L. No,. 96–448, 94 Stat. 1895 (1980) (codified in scattered sections of 11, 45, 49, and 49 app. U.S.C.).

307. *See* generally Eckhardt, *The Western Coal Traffic League Case: Condoning ICC Eschewal of Rail Monopoly Ratemaking*, 13 TRANSP. L.J. 307 (1984); Freeman, *The Ties That Bind: Railroads, Coal, Utilities, the ICC, and the Public Interest,* 14 TRANSP. L.J. 1 (1985).

308. For example, between 1976 and 1983, rail rates from the movement of coal increased, in constant dollars, by 54%; during the same period the mine-mouth price of coal decreased by 15%. Dempsey, *Transportation Deregulation—On a Collision Course?*, 13 TRANSP. L.J. 329, 369–71, 388–90 (1984). For many utilities that burn this abundant domestic resource to produce electricity, transportation accounts for 60–70% of the delivered price of coal. *Id.* at 370. Consequently, the net result of ICC abdication of its statutory responsibilities is higher prices for consumers of electricity.

309. Trans Alaska Pipeline Rates Cases, 436 U.S. 631, 653 (1978) (upholding the ICC's authority to suspend rates for the transportation of oil and to establish maximum interim rates).

310. 260 U.S. 156 (1922).

311. *Id.* at 162. The *Keogh* doctrine was recently reaffirmed in Square D Co. v. Niagara Frontier Tariff Bureau, Inc., 476 U.S. 409 (1986). *See also In re* Wheat Rail Freight Rate Antitrust Litig., 759 F.2d 1305 (7th Cir. 1985) (finding railroad carriers impliedly immune from antitrust liability for rates approved by the ICC), *cert. denied*, 106 S. Ct. 2275 (1986); *see* generally Dempsey, *Rate Regulation and Antitrust Immunity in Transportation: The Genesis and Evolution of This Endangered Species*, 32 AM. U.L. REV. 335, 359–60 (1983).

312. *See* Dempsey, *supra* note 311, at 356.

313. The author has been able to locate but a single criminal antitrust action brought since 1980 against a railroad. *See* United States v. Baltimore & Ohio R.R., 538 F. Supp. 200 (D.D.C. 1982) (denying motions to dismiss criminal proceeding for conspiracy in unreasonable restraint of trade in the shipment of iron ore on Lake Erie).

314. *See* Dempsey, *supra* note 311, at 356.

315. For example, the ICC has adopted a definition of market dominance that evaluates whether intermodal competition, intramodal competition, product competition, or geographic competition exists. If any one of the four exists, the ICC concludes that the traffic in question is not market-dominant, and therefore the jurisdictional threshold does not exist. *See P. DEMPSEY & W. THOMS, supra* note 4, at 164–65. This rather liberal and pro-rail interpretation of the Staggers Act jurisdictional threshold was upheld in Western Coal Traffic League v. United States, 719 F.2d 772 (5th Cir. 1983), *cert. denied*, 466 U.S. 953 (1984). The ICC has also proposed that railroads are free to raise their rates until stand-alone costs are achieved. Essentially, this allows upward pricing movement by the carrier until it would become economically feasible for the shipper to construct its own railroad to get its commodities to market. This deregulatory effort was upheld in Potomac Electric Power Co. v. ICC, 744 F.2d 185 (D.C. Cir. 1984).

316. H.R. 1140, 99th Cong., 1st Sess. (1985); *see also* Calderwood, *The Railroad Antimonopoly Act—A Bill Whose Time Has Come*, TRAFFIC WORLD, Apr. 14, 1986, at 40. For the legislative history of H.R. 1140, see H.R. REP. NO. 559, 99th

Cong., 2d Sess. (1986). *See* generally Marshall & Cook, *Issue of Cost Recovery in the Debate over Competitive Access*, 15 TRANSP. L.J. 9 (1986).

317. H.R. 1140, *supra* note 316.

318. *Id.*

319. CURE is a consortium of entities disturbed by what they perceive to be excessive transportation rates unilaterally dictated by the railroads and the unwillingness of the ICC to afford captive shippers regulatory protection from these monopoly abuses. CURE is dominated by shippers of coal and grain—the electric utilities, the coal companies, and agricultural enterprises.

320. H.R. 4096, 99th Cong., 2d Sess., 132 CONG. REC. 7233 (1986). Similar bills were introduced in 1987. *See* S. 676, 100th Cong., 1st Sess. (1987); H.R. 1393, 100th Cong., 1st Sess. (1987).

321. *See* H.R. 4096, *supra* note 320,

322. *Id.*

323. Letter from Representative Dan Schaefer to Paul Stephen Dempsey (Sept. 29, 1986).

324. Dingell, *Florio Challenges ICC Record*, CURE NEWSLETTER, Apr. 1986, at 1.

325. *Id.*

326. *See ICC Chairman Gradison Delivers Progress Report on Where Agency's Headed*, TRAFFIC WORLD, Sept. 15, 1986, at 30.

327. *See* Gilles, *ICC Planning to Continue "Hands Off"*, GREAT FALLS (Montana) TRIBUNE, July 30, 1986, at 16.

328. F. FRANKFURTER, OF LAW AND LIFE AND OTHER THINGS THAT MATTER 245 (1965).

329. Dempsey, *supra* note 5, at 378; *see also* Dempsey, *The Interstate Commerce Commission*, *supra* note 9, at 50–51 (discussing impropriety of major public policy changes being made by political appointees rather than legislative representatives).

330. 49 U.S.C. § 11343(a) (1982).

331. *See* e.g., Maine Cent. R.R. v. Amoskeag Co., 360 I.C.C. 147 (1979); *see also* 49 U.S.C. § 10102 (1982) (defining "control").

332. 49 U.S.C. § 11344(b)(1)(E) (1982).

333. Pub. L. No. 97–261, 96 Stat. 1102 (codified in scattered section of 15, 26, 39, 49 U.S.C.).

334. *See* 49 U.S.C. § 11344(b)(2) (1982).

335. *See* Red Ball Motor Freight, Inc.—Control and Merger—Spector Industries, Inc., 127 M.C.C. 737 (1980). For the public interest criterion, *see* 49 U.S.C. § 11344(d) (1982 & Supp. III 1985). For the non-Class I railroad merger standards, *see* 49 U.S.C. § 11344(c) (1982). The criteria governing the sale of dormant operating authority have also been eased. *See* Central Transport, Inc.—Purchase (Portion)—Piedmont Petroleum Prods., Inc., 127 M.C.C. 284 (1978); *see* generally P. DEMPSEY & W. THOMS, *supra* note 4, at 237–41.

336. *See* 49 U.S.C. § 11343(e) (1982).

337. *Id.* § 11343(e)(1)(A) (citing section 10101 for 1982 National Transportation Policy).

338. *Id.* § 11343(e)(1)(B).

339. *See* Exemption of Transactions under 49 U.S.C. § 11343, 48 Fed. Reg. 26,485, 26,488 (1983) [Taylor, chairman, concurring in part, dissenting in part; referring to letter from ICC to Congress (June 8, 1982)].

340. *See* 49 C.F.R. § 1186 (1986). "Evaluating the relationship between the proposed industry-wide exemption and the national transportation policy, the ICC concluded that transactions such as mergers, consolidations, and acquisitions generally promote efficiency and allow carriers to compete more efficiently." Exemption of Transactions, *supra* note 339, 48 Fed. Reg. at 26,486. Discussing its recent experience with individual exemptions, it reasoned that the regulatory scheme it was operating under impeded such transactions. *Id.*

The ICC also concluded that detailed scrutiny of mergers, acquisitions, and consolidations was not necessary to protect shippers from market power abuses. *Id.* It found that the eased entry provisions and small capital requirements would ensure that there would be many carriers actively competing for business. *Id.* at 26,486–87. The ICC alleged that reduced regulation had already resulted in more authorized carriers and greater competition rather than concentration of market power. *Id.* at 26,487.

Under the ICC's proposal, parties proposing section 11343(a) transactions still would have to file a notice with the ICC requesting exemption., *Id.* The ICC would merely review the notice for accuracy and publish it in the *Federal Register. Id.* This rule removes the ICC's obligation to monitor individual transactions in an in-depth manner. The ICC's interpretation transforms Congress' limited exemption provision into a general policy of nonregulation. It is unclear under the rule what the ICC would or could do if it perceived a concentration of market power or abuses of such power.

341. *See* 49 C.F.R. § 1186 (1986); Exemption of Certain Transactions Under 49 U.S.C. § 11343, 49 Fed. Reg. 48,314 (1984); Modification of Small Carrier Transfer, Carriers of Property, 50 Fed. Reg. 6348 (1985); Katzman, *The Bus Regulatory Reform Act of 1982: What It Does and How It Works*, 52 TRANSP. PRAC. J. 221, 249–50 (1985). In January 1986, the ICC denied a request to reconsider its decision to exempt financial transactions of motor carriers of property. The Transportation Lawyers Association had urged the ICC to add to its list of anticompetitiveness or adverse effects upon employees a complaint on grounds that the proposed transaction was inconsistent with the National Transportation Policy. *See* Exemption of Certain Transactions Under 49 U.S.C. § 11343, Ex parte No. 55, slip op. (I.C.C. Jan. 9, 1986). But *see* Regular Common Carrier Conference v. United States, 820 F.2d 1323 (D.C. Cir. 1987) (limiting the ICC's power to exempt intermodal acquisitions from regulatory approval).

342. Pub. L. No. 96–296, 94 Stat. 793 [codified at 49 U.S.C. §§ 502–26, 10101–11914 (1982)].

343. D. SWEENEY, C. MCCARTHY, S. KALISH, & J. CUTLER, JR., *supra* note 267, at 172.

344. The effect of U.S. deregulation on Canada is a contemporary question surrounding motor carriage. Congress expressed concern with Canadian entry barriers in the promulgation of the Bus Act. Section 6 of that act imposed a two-year moratorium on the issuance of motor carrier operating authority to Canadian and Mexican enterprises, which could be lifted by the president if he concluded that it was in the national interest to do so and notified Congress accordingly. *See* 49 U.S.C. § 10932(1) (1982 & Supp. III 1985). This provision was passed primarily as a response to allegations that with U.S. regulatory reform, Canadian and Mexican carriers could easily obtain entry into the United States, while U.S. carriers had a

more difficult time securing operating authority to serve Canada and faced a virtually impossible task securing authority to serve Mexico. (Article 27 of the Mexican Constitution prohibits noncitizens from owning interests in road transport enterprises.) President Reagan partially lifted the Canadian moratorium on September 20, 1982, on signing the Bus Act into law, and completely lifted it the following month. *See* 47 Fed. Reg. 41,721, 54,053 (1982). The statute includes a prophylactic remedy, providing that any modification of the ban must be delayed for 60 days if the foreign government's policy "substantially prohibits grants of authority" to U.S. carriers. 49 U.S.C. § 10927(1)(2)(A) (Supp. III 1985).

345. *See* Dempsey, *The Rise and Fall, supra* note 9, at 131–32.

346. *See* Las Vegas-Dallas/Ft. Worth Nonstop Service Investigation, 77 C.A.B. 482, 483 (1978); Oakland Service Case, 78 C.A.B. 593, 595 (1978).

347. Gibney, *Continuing Airlines Losses Predicted*, DENVER POST, June 21, 1982, at 3C, col. 1. Braniff's chief executive officer, Howard Putnam, noted:

I think within five to seven years that [there will be] five [out of a current eleven] trunk airlines. Then you will have a whole bunch of Southwest Airlines-type carriers that start out from scratch and work to keep costs in line. As decreed by the law of the jungle, only the strong will survive.

Martindale, *The Economy Gets an OK for Takeoff*, OAG FREQUENT FLYER, July 1983, at 38–39. Columnist Hobart Rowen noted that the "airline industry under deregulation is on a course where competition is being wrung out by the creation of an oligopoly of a few remaining large airlines. The public is not being served by this process." Rowen, *Airlines: Competing to the Death*, WASHINGTON POST, Nov. 11, 1982, at A27, col. 2; *see also* Dempsey, *supra* note 5, at 383–84.

348. Hardaway, *supra* note 133, at 9–10. For an earlier expression of the same theme, *see* Hardaway, *supra* note 12, at 141–43.

349. *See* Dempsey, *Consumers Pay More to Receive a Lot Less*, USA TODAY, July 16, 1987, at 8A, col. 5; Dempsey, *Cross Your Fingers, Hope Not to Die*, CHICAGO TRIBUNE, Aug. 28, 1987, at 27, col. 1; Dempsey, *The Crowded, Dangerous Skies of Airline Deregulation*, SEATTLE TIMES, Sept. 4, 1987, at A11, col. 1; Dempsey, *The Discomforting Turbulence of Airline Deregulation*, TAMPA TRIBUNE, Aug. 9, 1987, at 1C, col. 2.

350. *See* generally Dempsey, *Turbulence in the "Open Skies": The Deregulation of International Air Transport*, 15 TRANSP. L.J. 305 (1987).

351. Former CAB chairman Marvin Cohen has warned:

Some current proponents of deregulation seem to view antitrust as another government regulation to be minimized or eliminated. Actually, vigorous antitrust enforcement will be crucial to the deregulatory process. If deregulation is to succeed, antitrust lawyers and economists will have to play a significant role in assuring that entry barriers remain low, that natural monopoly positions are not abused, and that the airline industry continues to be functionally competitive.

Cohen, *supra* note 19, at 158.

352. Not all commentators agree with this conclusion. According to one,

Regulation may not be necessary to prevent monopoly abuses, even in [a] "natural monopoly" situation. If the barriers to entry into this market are relatively low, then the existence of a number of potential entrants (most likely existing firms serving other markets, but quite possibly new firms), ready to enter the market if profitable opportunities arise, can keep the natural monopolist's prices and profits close to competitive levels....[T]he barriers to entry in airline markets...appear to be quite low, and the number of potential entrants quite high. Thus, there may well be little room for monopoly abuse, even in small airline markets which can support only one carrier at efficient scale.

White, *supra* note 19, at 548 (footnotes omitted).

353. *See* T. MORGAN, J. HARRISON, & P. VERKUIL, ECONOMIC REG-ULATION OF BUSINESS 14 (1985); R. POSNER, ECONOMIC ANALYSIS OF LAW 201 (2d ed. 1977).

354. *See* T. MORGAN, J. HARRISON, & P. VERKUIL, *supra* note 353, at 15.

355. *See* Dempsey, *Consumers Pay More*, *supra* note 349, at 8A, col. 5.

356. *Is Deregulation Working?* BUS. WK., Dec. 22, 1986, at 50, 52.

357. *Id.*; *see* N. GLASKOWSKY, EFFECTS OF DEREGULATION ON MOTOR CARRIERS 9, 25–26 (1986); Dempsey, *The Deregulation of Intrastate Transportation*, 39 BAYLOR L. REV. 1, 12–16 (1987).

358. *See* Dempsey, *The Carnage of Airline Deregulation*, HOUSTON CHRON-ICLE, July 30, 1987, at 27, col. 1; Kilman, *An Unexpected Result of Airline Decontrol Is Return to Monopolies*, WALL ST. J., July 20, 1987, at 1, col. 1; Rowen, *Airline Service Has Gone to Hell*, WASHINGTON POST, July 23, 1987, at A21, col. 1.

359. *See* Koten, *Increased Fares, Fewer Flights Are Likely Results of Airline Mergers*, WALL ST. J., Sept. 17, 1986, at 33, col. 4.

360. *Id.*

361. *See* Carley, *Airline Capitalize on Increased Travel, Falling Competition to Raise Some Fares*, WALL ST. J., Oct. 2, 1986, at 4, col. 2.

362. *See* Koten, *Major Airlines Plan Fare Hike Later in Month*, WALL ST. J., Oct. 14, 1986, at 35, col. 3

363. "With more than 80% of passenger traffic now in the hands of the industry's seven largest carriers, consumer groups and some government officials have expressed concern that increased industry concentration could bring an end to some of the low fares that have been such a boon to travelers." *Id.*

364. *Id.*

365. But *see* R. POSNER, *supra* note 353, at 208 (discussing how this motivation may be frustrated by various factors).

366. *See* Hardaway, *supra* note 12, at 141–45.

367. Russell, *supra* note 132, at 56.

368. The Carter administration's CAB believed that the airline industry had "relatively insignificant economies of scale, low barriers to entry, reasonably elastic demand, and highly mobile resources." Dempsey, *The Rise and Fall*, *supra* note 9, at 130–31; *accord* Oakland Service Case, 78 C.A.B. 593 (1978).

369. *See Turbulent Times*, ECONOMIST, Sept. 6, 1986, at 28.

370. High Density Traffic Airports: Slot Allocation and Transfer Methods, 50 Fed. Reg. 52,180 (1985) (to be codified at 14 C.F.R. pt. 93).

371. Hardaway, *supra* note 133, at 49.

Typically...gates and terminal facilities are the subject of long-term leases required by airport proprietors to support revenue-bond financing of these facilities. Baltimore/Washington airport, for example, has control over only four of twenty-seven gates at its main terminal. The remaining gates are locked into long-term leases until the year 2003. A large number of the leases give the airline lessee total control of counter space and gates, whether used or not. In other instances, incumbent airlines own or jointly own terminal space, further restricting airport proprietors' authority to transfer underutilized space from one carrier to another. New entrants thus can obtain gates only in the rare case where a gate is available for lease or where a competitor will sublease the gate space, usually for an extravagant fee.

Id. at 45–46 (footnotes omitted).

372. *See* Koten, *supra* note 359, at 33.

373. Ott, *Mergers Allow Domination of Individual Airports*, AV. WEEK & SPACE TECH., Sept. 29, 1986, at 27.

374. *See* GENERAL ACCOUNTING OFFICE, AIRLINE COMPETITION: IMPACT OF COMPUTERIZED RESERVATION SYSTEMS (1986); McGinley, *U.S. Probes Airline Reservation Systems over Complaints They Curb Competition*, WALL ST. J., Feb. 3, 1987, at 14, col. 1.

375. *See* Russell, *supra* note 132, at 57.

376. *Id.* at 56–57. For an amusing, but painfully accurate picture of the contemporary environment, *see* Buchwald, *The Benefits of Competition*, DENVER POST, Sept. 23, 1986, at 5B.

377. Kahn, *Despite Waves of Airline Mergers, Deregulation Has Not Been a Failure*, DENVER POST, Aug. 31, 1986, at 3g.

378. *Turbulent Times, supra* note 369, at 28.

379. *See* generally Levine, *Airline Competition in Deregulated Markets: Theory, Firm Strategy, and Public Policy*, 4 YALE J. REG. 393 (1987); Moore, *U.S. Airline Deregulation: Its Effect on Passengers, Capital, and Labor*, 29 J. L. & ECON. 1 (1986).

380. One commentator seems to urge the DOT to play a stronger role in litigating the antitrust issues:

In light of the CAB's strong *laissez-faire* approach in approving the merger of Continental and Western, it seems highly unlikely that the Board will disapprove any future mergers . . . .Perhaps merger opponents, including the United States Department of Justice, will now attempt to circumvent Board merger policy by challenging airline mergers in the courts. Such collateral attacks are indeed possible, because the CAB has not once granted antitrust immunity since deregulation.

Note, *Airline Merger Cases, supra* note 38, at 158–59 (footnote omitted).

381. Middleton, *supra* note 184, at 1.

382. *Antitrust's New School*, NEWSWEEK, Apr. 7, 1986, at 61.

383. *See* Pasztor, *U.S. Move Signals More Airline Mergers*, WALL ST. J., May 21, 1986, at 6, col. 1.

384. *New Era for Antitrust?* NEWSWEEK, Jan. 27, 1986, at 46.

9

SMALL TOWNS AND RURAL COMMUNITIES

In recent years, Congress has promulgated major legislation designed to reform the regulatory environment for the passenger transportation industry. These statutes include the Airline Deregulation Act of 1978 and the Bus Regulatory Reform Act of 1982.[1] Almost two decades before these legislative measures, Congress enacted the Transporation Act of 1958, which significantly liberalized the ability of railroads to respond to market forces and discontinue passenger service.

This comprehensive legislative agenda, coupled with the presidential appointment of individuals fervently dedicated to market theory to head the regulatory agencies (i.e., the Interstate Commerce Commission (ICC), the Civil Aeronautics Board (CAB), and the Department of Transportation (DOT)), has meant that deregulation has swept through this industry rather more comprehensively than it would have had less ideological agency heads been in charge of its implementation.[2]

Any responsible effort to develop prudent public policy with respect to an industry as important to the nation's economy as transportation must attempt to objectively assess the costs and benefits of the new legislative environment. Various forms of deregulation have now had a decade to run their course (and rail passenger liberalization has had three). It would seem, then, to be an appropriate time to reflect on the impact of deregulation, not only upon the industries which have been deregulated, but also upon those members of the traveling public who rely upon their services. Unfortunately, the literature criticizing the previous regime of regulation and applauding the benefits of deregulation tends to gloss over one of deregulation's major costs—its impact upon individuals who reside in America's small towns and rural communities.[3]

Admittedly, the impact upon these constituencies has varied depending upon the mode of transportation involved. In part, these differences reflect the inherent characteristics of each mode and the extent to which each has been deregulated.[4] For these reasons, this chapter will segregate its findings among the several modes—railroads, airlines, and bus companies—and in that order, since that is the order in which passenger service has been deregulated.

Here and there, where appropriate, projections will be made as to the potential impact of telephone deregulation upon these constituencies. The question of telecommunications deregulation is an important one now being addressed by a number of state legislatures and public utility commissions (PUCs).[5] The empirical evidence surrounding transportation deregulation may shed some light on the potential impact of open entry (in interlata toll and local telephone services) upon the ability of telephone companies to fulfill their traditional rate averaging and rural service obligations.

There are, of course, important differences between the two industries— transportation and communications.[6] To mention only two, telecommunications is more strongly driven by the dynamics of emerging technology and has larger fixed costs than all the transport modes, except perhaps, the railroads.

Nevertheless, the traditional statutory and regulatory regimes governing both are somewhat parallel. Modes of transportation and telecommunications are defined by statute as "common carriers," which have long been regulated at both the federal and state levels.[7] Both have traditionally had "universal service" (or common carrier) obligations imposed upon them,[8] to serve all within their operating territories in a nondiscriminatory fashion in terms of both service and pricing.[9] Industry spokesmen in both transportation and communications repeatedly warned that deregulating entry would lead to "cream-skimming," with competitors attracted to their most lucrative markets like sharks to the smell of blood.[10] This would undermine one of economic regulation's most important objectives—that companies cross-subsidize losses incurred in serving rural or small users of the service with profits earned from more lucrative market opportunities, so as to ensure that the largest number of consumers enjoy access to the system at a reasonable price.[11]

These traditional public policy objectives have been sharply eroded for transportation companies by deregulation. Let us explore the impact of this erosion upon a cluster of interests regulation was created to protect.

ORIGINS OF ECONOMIC REGULATION

The legislative history of economic regulation is replete with public policy concerns over access by small and rural communities to the common carrier system. As we saw in Chapter 2, federal economic regulation of American industry began in earnest in 1887 with the creation of the nation's first independent regulatory agency, the Interstate Commerce Commission.

Transportation was the first American industry to be regulated and, paradoxically, the first to be significantly deregulated.

In an early point in our history, it was recognized that the economic development of the interior of the North American continent required that a transportation infrastructure be built. Railroads were encouraged to lay track to the west with the economic incentives of generous federal and state land grants, loans, bonds, purchases of stock, and remission of taxes.[12] But not long after the tracks were laid, farmers began to object to the excessively high rates being charged by the monopoly railroads for grain movements to eastern markets.[13]

It was, in large part, a pre-Populist agrarian political movement that brought about economic regulation. The Grangers succeeded first in securing legislation in several states requiring railroads to charge "just and reasonable" rates, and prohibiting rate and service discrimination. The U.S. Supreme Court had no difficulty sustaining the lawfulness of economic regulation in its seminal decision of *Munn v. Illinois*:[14]

[I]t has been customary in England from time immemorial, and in this country from its first colonization, to regulate ferries, [and] common carriers... and in so doing fix a maximum charge to be made for the services rendered.... [W]hen private property is "affected with a public interest, it ceases to be *juris privati* only."... Property does become clothed with a public interest when used in a manner to make it of public consequence, and affect the community at large.... [Common carriers stand] in the very "gateway of commerce," and, take a toll from all who pass. Their business most certainly "tends to a common charge, and is becoming a thing of public interest and use."[15]

Congress filled the void in interstate regulation in 1887 with the Act to Regulate Commerce. The statute established the ICC and gave it jurisdiction to ensure that rail rates were both nondiscriminatory, and just and reasonable. Hence, the protection of small shippers and small communities from the extraction of exorbitant profits by the railroads was a major purpose of the legislation. It was also, in part, a response to the abuses of laissez faire and the excessive concentrations of wealth and power that had resulted from it.

Market failure again become the catalyst for economic regulation during the Great Depression. Excessive capacity engendered by economic collapse and unlimited entry depressed freight rates and caused thousands of motor carrier bankruptcies during the 1930s. Our elected representatives feared that a continuation of that trend might lead to a deterioration of service and higher prices for small shippers and rural communities, while the surviving carriers concentrated on high-revenue traffic lanes.[16] Therefore, Congress expanded the ICC's authority over surface transporation by adding bus and trucking companies to its jurisdiction with the promulgation of the Motor Carrier Act of 1935.

In 1938, Congress added airlines to the regulatory scheme, creating another transportation regulatory agency, the Civil Aeronautics Board. One of the major proponents of the legislation, Colonel Edgar Gorrell, noted that, "in spreading out into the regions of light-density traffic and developing smaller communities, the small lines have performed an incalculable service to the country. It must be assured, through certificates, that they may continue to perform such a service, and they must be given an opportunity to protect themselves against even the possibility of oppressive competition."[17] Hence, entry regulation was imposed upon the infant airline industry, in part so that small communities would have access to this emerging mode of transport.

In 1940, Congress promulgated the first "National Transportation Policy." Among its principal objectives was "the establishment and maintenance of reasonable charges for transportation services, without unjust discriminations, [or] undue preferences or advantages . . . all to the end of developing, coordinating, and preserving a national transportation system . . . adequate to meet the needs of the commerce of the United States.[18] This cumulative body of legislation reflects a strong congressional policy that the public be protected against pricing and service discrimination.

DEREGULATION LEGISLATION AND ITS IMPACT UPON SMALL TOWNS AND RURAL COMMUNITIES: TALES FROM THE DARK SIDE

In 1979, before the full impact of air and bus deregulation had been felt, and prior to the contemporary farm crisis,[19] Senator Roger Jepsen painted a rather drab portrait of rural America:

Approximately 34 percent of the U.S. population—some 85 million people—and 52 percent of the Nation's poor, live outside metropolitan areas.

Many of these rural residents—especially the rural poor, elderly, handicapped, and young—are isolated and immobile, and face extreme difficulties in gaining access to jobs, health care, social services, shopping, recreation and friends . . . .

Fifteen percent of rural households, 57 percent of the rural poor, and 45 percent of the rural elderly do not own an automobile . . . .

Only 31 percent of the Nation's 20,000 towns with a population of 50,000 or less are served by a public transit system . . . .

Intercity bus lines serve only about half of the Nation's towns of 50,000 or less . . . .

An estimated 60 percent of places less than 2,500 population have no taxi service. . . . Rural residents must travel farther than their urban counterparts to gain access to medical care and essential social services—for example, 20 percent of rural residents as compared to 10 percent of urban residents, must travel more than half an hour to medical care.[20]

However bleak things may have looked when Senator Jepsen spoke these words in 1979, they were to grow progressively worse during the ensuing years.

Legislation giving carriers flexibility to abandon service to small communities has come in three major waves. The Interstate Commerce Commission was vested with the power to reverse state PUC denials of rail passenger discontinuances in 1958; by 1970, the ICC was virtually taken out of the business altogether with the creation of Amtrak. Similarly, with the promulgation of the Airline Deregulation Act of 1978 and the sunset dissolution of the Civil Aeronautics Board on December 31, 1984, there is hardly anything left of domestic airline economic regulation.[21] Under the provisions of the Airline Deregulation Act, state jurisdiction over intrastate air service is totally preempted. And the Bus Regulatory Reform Act of 1982 gave the ICC jurisdiction to reverse PUC denials of bus discontinuances and rate increases. Let us examine each of these statutes in greater detail, and the impact each has had upon small towns and rural communities.

The Transportation Act of 1958

In 1929, some 20,000 passenger trains provided daily intercity service in the United States.[22] Almost every town and village in the nation enjoyed rail passenger service. But after World War II, railroads found passenger service increasingly unprofitable, and wanted out. Under section 1(18) of the Interstate Commerce Act, they could apply to the ICC for a certificate of "public convenience and necessity" (PC&N) to abandon the entire line.[23] Under the statute, the ICC must consider whether the abandonment "will have a serious, adverse impact on rural and community development."[24] The impact of a rail abandonment upon a community was, and is, devastating, for when the line is gone, it is usually gone forever. Many of the ghost towns of the west owe their demise to the decision of the railroads to terminate service.[25] And since promulgation of the Staggers Rail Act of 1980, rail lines have been disappearing from rural areas at an accelerated rate.[26]

But to rail companies, the wholesale abandonment of particular lines was often not an attractive alternative during the 1950s, because freight service operating over them was frequently profitable. Passenger demand for rail service began to decline after World War II, principally because of a loss of traffic to the competing modes (i.e., airplanes, buses, and automobiles). Trucking competition for freight also intensified, making the cross-subsidy more difficult to maintain. Hence, railroads filed applications with the state regulatory commissions requesting permission to discontinue specific passenger trains. These applications would sometimes be denied by the state PUCs, on grounds that the railroad's overall operations, its intrastate operations, and/or its combined freight and passenger operations over the involved line were profitable, and the public's need for the service outweighed the carrier's economic losses in providing it. The PUCs viewed railroads as common carriers with a duty to provide a reasonable level of service to the communities through which they pass.

The railroads sought legislative relief from the economic burden of using freight profits to cross-subsidize passenger losses. Congress responded with the Transportation Act of 1958, which added section 13a to the Interstate Commerce Act.[27] The statute allows the Interstate Commerce Commission to reverse PUC denials of rail discontinuance applications if the ICC concludes that such action is warranted by the PC&N, and that a continuation of the service would "constitute an unreasonable burden on the interstate operations of the carrier or on interstate commerce."[28]

The first opportunity for the U.S. Supreme Court to review the application of these statutory provisions involved an ICC reversal of a decision of the North Carolina Utilities Commission to disapprove the Southern Railway's proposal to discontinue the last pair of trains between Greensboro and Goldsboro, North Carolina.[29] Between 1951 and 1956, the state Utilities Commission had approved 42 of the 44 rail discontinuance proposals that had been filed. Although rail passenger demand had declined over the line, and the cost of providing passenger service was three times its revenue, the North Carolina Utilities Commission found that the Southern Railway was a healthy carrier, that its combined freight and passenger operations over this line were profitable, and that it had done little to market its passenger service. Although the state Utilities Commission had approved the Southern's prior proposals to discontinue two other pairs of trains, it found a strong public interest in retaining the last pair serving the market. But the Supreme Court sided with the ICC, finding that where the public demand for service is not great, the ICC need give little or no weight to the carrier's overall prosperity in reversing a state's denial of a rail discontinuance application.[30]

With this expansive interpretation given the new statute by the U.S. Supreme Court, rail discontinuances of passenger service became robust. Less concerned with the impact of the loss of service upon local populations, the ICC was significantly more liberal in granting rail discontinuance proposals than the states had ever been.[31] Under ICC review, the number of passenger trains fell by 60% between 1958 and 1970.[32] By 1970, only 360 intercity trains were left.[33]

Congressional concern over the rapidly shrinking intercity rail network led it to promulgate the Rail Passenger Services Act of 1970, which allowed railroads to terminate their passenger operations by turning them over to a newly formed federally subsidized corporation, Amtrak.[34] Amtrak began operation on May 1, 1971, with 225 trains. During the conversion from private to Amtrack service, another 500 communities lost intercity passenger train service.[35]

In recent years, efforts to diminish government's role in the market have been expanded to embrace not only economic deregulation but also elimination of federal subsidies in transportation. Throughout the Reagan administration, every White House budget proposal has moved to constrict or eliminate Amtrak's funding. A significant reduction in federal subsidies to Amtrak would force it to terminate service over all of its routes except, perhaps, the Boston-Washington run.[36]

Amtrak today serves more than 500 communities in the United States. That is more cities than are served by all the airlines combined. Of the communities served by Amtrak, 119 have no scheduled airline service;[37] if the present small community air subsidy program is terminated, that figure will likely jump to 161. Another 96 Amtrak-served communities have no scheduled intercity bus service; 40 have neither air nor bus service.[38] And unlike the alternative modes of transportation, rail passenger service is almost never impeded by inclement weather. Also, among Amtrak's passengers are a disproportionate number of low-income and elderly travelers who cannot or will not take an alternative form of transporation.[39]

Today, with the skeletal intercity system that Amtrak provides, the United States compares poorly with the rest of the industrialized world in terms of rail passenger service. Professor William Thoms has observed, "with the exception of the heavily traveled Boston-Washington corridor, service levels on American passenger trains are the worst in the world."[40]

Hence, deregulation of rail passenger service has enabled railroads to shed themselves of a money-losing operation, a relatively small portion of which has been replaced by taxpayer subsidies, while thousands of small communities have been pruned from the system. Let us examine the similar experiences of air and bus carriers.

The Airline Deregulation Act of 1978

Senator Jim Sasser recently pointed out the important role that the transportation infrastructure has played in supporting economic development in America:

[I]n the 19th century... if you lived in an area of water or river transportation, you flourished. Along came the railroad and it appeared to have the power of economic life or death over cities.... Now, a strong case can be made that air service has the same impact on economic development of a region that river traffic or rail access had in an earlier era.[41]

The airline industry was the second major passenger transportation industry to be deregulated, with the promulgation of the Airline Deregulation Act (ADA) of 1978. In that bill, airline exit requirements were significantly liberalized. All but the last carrier in a market is free to leave at will. Congress recognized that such policies might have a deleterious effect upon the provision of service to small communities, and therefore added section 419 to the Federal Aviation Act, which provides a 10-year program of federal subsidies for air service to small communities.[42] The ADA's policy statement specifies that it is the purpose of the new legislation, *inter alia*, to maintain "a comprehensive and convenient system of continuous scheduled airline service for small communities and isolated areas, with direct Federal assistance where appropriate."[43]

But many proponents of deregulation had discounted the likelihood that it would lead to any significant service reductions for small communities. A Senate subcommittee chaired by Edward Kennedy reviewed 327 "losing" city pairs served by United Air Lines; the U.S. Department of Transportation examined 160 "losing" pairs served by Eastern Air Lines. Both found that only about two dozen of the markets were served on a mandatory basis, and that in most of these, more service was provided than required by the CAB. It was predicted that in the remaining markets, if the trunk carrier pulled out, a commuter or local service carrier would fill the void, in most cases without a subsidy.[44] Thus, it was alleged that small communities had little to fear from deregulation.

But there was good reason to fear a reduction in service. Even though the CAB had jurisdiction prior to deregulation to prohibit service abandonments it deemed inconsistent with the public interest, between 1960 and 1978 it had approved the abandonment of 173 communities (or an average of 9.6 per year).[45]

Under deregulation, the trend sharply accelerated. In the first year of deregulation, 260 cities suffered a deterioration in air service, a disproportionate number of them being small towns.[46] Seventy communities which were receiving some service lost all of it.[47] By the second year, more than 100 communities had lost all their scheduled service.[48] So, while abandonments averaged 9.6 per year before deregulation, they soared to more than 50 per year during deregulation's first two years.

More recent statistics are nearly as grim. The U.S. General Accounting Office noted that "[b]etween October 1978 and October 1984, the scheduled air service network shrank from 632 cities to 541, as the number of nonhub communities with scheduled air service decreased by 91 (23 communities gained service during the period while 114 lost service)."[49] Professors Stephenson and Beier note that "there is evidence that deregulation has accelerated the withdrawal from smaller communities and that there has been a concomitant reduction in the frequency of direct flights in those markets."[50] This is indeed a surprising consequence of deregulation, since the Airline Deregulation Act of 1978 provided for a 10-year program of federal subsidies designed to preserve essential air service to small communities. Let us take a closer look at precisely what types of service losses have been endured under deregulation.

Proponents of deregulation, when assessing its impact upon small communities, tend to emphasize the increased number of departures many have enjoyed.[51] Since 1978, 410 markets have been abandoned by larger airlines flying jet aircraft.[52] Many had service restored by commuter airlines, flying smaller aircraft, sometimes landing more frequently.[53] But while departures may have increased for some small communities, there appears to have been a significant reduction in the number of available seats.[54] By 1984, 225 airports had suffered more than a 50% decline in available seats, including some 119 airports that lost service completely.[55] Moreover, a number of rural states have experienced a reduction in departures as well as seats since deregulation began.[56]

Many passengers complain that the smaller, unpressurized aircraft flown by commuter and local service carriers are less comfortable than the jets they replaced.[57] They are certainly less safe. Depending upon how it is measured, commuter airlines have a safety record 3 to 37 times worse than established airlines flying jet aircraft.[58]

Passengers also appear to be less satisfied with service schedules and waiting times.[59] With larger carriers concentrating on hub and spoke operations, small communities lost their direct flights to most large cities.[60] In the first two years of deregulation, 63% of small communities having certificated service experienced reductions in nonstop service.[61] Hence, air travel has become a more circuitous adventure for many passengers.[62] Assessing the quantitative and qualitative impacts, it has been noted that "smaller communities are receiving markedly worse air service than existed prior to deregulation."[63] Clearly the comfort, convenience, and level of safety of air service for small communities has deteriorated.[64]

Even Thomas Gale Moore, a nationally recognized proponent of deregulation, admits that 40% of small communities have suffered a loss of air service since deregulation began, while ticket prices have increased disproportionately for them.[65] Many sources agree with this assessment. The Congressional Research Service found that fares in smaller markets are now substantially higher than those offered prior to deregulation.[66] Professor Addus adds that, "as a result of airline deregulation . . . fares for traveling between small points have increased rapidly; and commuter air carrier fares are reported to be particularly high in most cases."[67]

These results appear to be consistent around the nation. After deregulation, passenger fares in California rose between 38% and 103% as service to small communities deteriorated.[68] The Upper Midwest Council concluded that passenger fares at smaller hubs in the midwestern states rose between two and four times the rate of fare increases at larger hubs.[69] In the Dakotas, the Carolinas, Mississippi, New Mexico, Rhode Island, Tennessee, and West Virginia, the results were the same; a parade of witnesses before several congressional committees provided example after example of the discriminatory fares and deteriorating service resulting from deregulation.[70]

Prior to deregulation, air fares had been set below marginal costs in short-haul markets, and above cost in longer-haul markets. For example, under the CAB's 1969 mileage-based formula, passengers flying 100 miles paid 70% of cost, while passengers flying 1,300 miles paid 109% of cost.[71] The airlines were forced to cross-subsidize losses incurred in serving small communities with profits earned in serving larger markets.[72]

Federal subsidies for service to small communities were scheduled to expire in 1988, but were saved by Congressional appropriations that year.[73] Nearly 150 communities today receive subsidized service under the section 419 program.[74] Most will lose air service altogether if Congress allows federal subsidies to dry up.

The loss of service will ripple perniciously throughout the economy of each of these communities. A survey of the top 500 firms in America reveals that 80% of them will not locate their facilities in an area which does not have easily accessible air transportation.[75] By increasing transportation costs and decreasing accessibility, deregulation is having a deleterious effect upon the ability of small communities to attract new investment (or indeed, to keep existing businesses from leaving).[76] Similar conclusions reached by the Southern Growth Policies Board has been summarized as follows:

[There is an important trend] in economic development...toward greater growth in the nonmanufacturing or service sector, especially in the higher-technology industries. These firms rely...heavily on recent technological advances in communications and information systems, and good air service has become an essential ingredient in their location decisions. Air service is as important to these firms as electricity and telephone communications; and in this sense, air service should be considered a public utility...[77]

Susan and Mark Tolchin, in their comprehensive assessment of the impact of deregulation, reached similar conclusions, addressing the external costs of service deterioration:

The real problem with economic deregulation is that the transportation system, the airwaves, and the banks are national resources, affecting many segments of the population with no immediate connection to the affected industries. A bankrupt airline can leave a city without adequate air transportation, damaging that city's ability to compete in the business community and reducing the quality of life for its residents. In that sense, the traditional lines between economic and social deregulation become blurred. A bankrupt airline, the development of a ghost town, and the closing of a company represent upheavals with such enormous impact that some measure of public protection is more than justified. And who else but a public agency can serve as the ultimate arbiter, stabilizing the kind of erratic market conditions that brought about the creation of these agencies in the first place?[78]

The Bus Regulatory Reform Act of 1982

With the passenger trains having vanished from rural America, and with commercial aircraft no longer landing at many small-town airports, the only means of public intercity transport left was the bus.

Prior to its deregulation, industry officials quite candidly predicted that deregulation would result in a drastic reduction in service to small communities. Harry Lesko, president of Greyhound, said that "Eighty-nine percent of our routes are subsidized by the bread-and-butter primary routes. ... [I]f we are to keep our lines running and the scheduled miles operating on the primary routes to satisfy the high-density population factors, the rural areas are going to have to suffer because they're straining the main line system."[79] Similarly, Charles Webb, president of the National Association of Motor Bus Owners, argued that "[t]he one conclusive argument against removal of controls on entry by motor carriers of passengers stems from their obligation to provide service to thousands of small cities and towns and to vast rural areas without profit or at a loss, and from the fact that it would be unconscionable either to permit new entrants to skim the cream of traffic or to authorize existing carriers to discontinue bus service to thousands of communities having no other form of public transportation."[80] Nevertheless, as with allegations of cross-subsidy made by the airlines prior to deregulation, these too were discounted by congressional committees considering deregulation.[81]

The Bus Regulatory Reform Act of 1982 gave bus companies significant new freedom to abandon or discontinue service and to raise fares. These provisions follow the pattern for railroads established by section 13a, discussed above, allowing the ICC to reverse state PUC denials, and thereby largely preempting state jurisdiction over the question.[82] Note that while bus companies are free to appeal state denials of discontinuance applications or proposed rate increases to the ICC, the public enjoys no corresponding right to appeal when the state grants the discontinuance or rate increase.

The ICC has taken an extremely liberal approach to deregulation here as well.[83] It has placed the burden of proving that a bus discontinuance will impose an unreasonable burden on interstate commerce upon those opposed to it, who are least likely to have access to the relevant information to prove it.[84] In reversing the Oklahoma Corporation Commission's denial of a bus discontinuance application (on grounds that many communities would be left without alternative means of public tranpsort), the ICC held that "the policy of the Bus Act ... favors exit from unprofitable routes and the reduction or elimination of cross-subsidies wherever possible."[85] As a commissioner of the New York Department of Transportation noted, "in case after case ... the ICC has shown a total disregard and lack of concern for the welfare of the riding public."[86]

Since promulgation of the 1982 Bus Act, carrier abandonments have been little short of breathtaking:

An ICC survey of bus companies after only 11 months of deregulation found that 1,294 locations were reported as having been dropped or proposed to be dropped from intercity routes. That is almost 10 percent of all the communities directly served by intercity buses at the time of deregulation.

Of these 1,294 locations, 776 lost all of their intercity service. The vast majority of those communities have less than 10,000 residents. In less than 1 year, almost 1 million people lost their bus service.... [B]etween 1975 and 1982, the number of communities receiving bus service declined at an annual rate of 3.3 percent. In the 2 years following enactment of the Bus Act, that rate has tripled; three times as many communities are losing intercity bus service now than before deregulation. Prior to deregulation, the average number of service terminations to communities was 147 per year; since deregulation, that rate has increased over 200 percent, to over 300 terminations per year.

A figure that makes an even more telling statement of the effect of deregulation is the ratio of service terminations to service initiations. The proponents of deregulation claimed that reducing entry barriers as well as exit barriers would be in the public interest. While it does not appear to have worked out that way, the DOT study found that before deregulation service terminations outnumbered service initiations almost 4 to 1. Since 1982, however, that figure has more than doubled. Specifically, for every community that receives new service, 8.6 communities lose their service.[87]

Hence, in less than a year after deregulation, more than a thousand communities in 40 states lost all their bus service.[88] In 1983, Greyhound alone proposed to eliminate 4,300 miles of service to more than 1,300 stops in 43 states.[89] Greyhound and Trailways (which together dominate 80% of the regular route passenger market) used their new freedom to boost intrastate fares, in some cases as much as 25%.[90] Today, there exists a high incidence of rate discrimination, by which passengers from small communities pay relatively higher rates than their urban counterparts.[91]

By late 1986, 4,514 communities had lost bus service, while only 896 had gained it. The big losers have been small communities; 3,432 of the towns which have lost service have a population of 10,000 or less.[92] The vast majority now have no alternative means of intercity public transport.[93] The loss of bus service not only adversely affects passengers dependent upon personal transportation, but also eliminates express small parcel service for small businesses.

Trailways announced plans to abandon all of Colorado, Montana, Nebraska, South Dakota, Wyoming, and much of Kansas.[94] One source notes that "[t]he trend toward cuts in service is continuing at a rapid pace, with dozens of communities throughout the Middle West facing possible loss of their last means of public transport."[95] The Illinois Commerce Commission has concluded that "the effect of the Act on rural and small city Illinois has been severe, [with] whole areas of nonmetropolitan Illinois...taken from the state bus network, without compensating gains in the more populated regions."[96] Senator Larry Pressler notes that "[b]us deregulation has had a devastating impact on rural America....Low income families and the elderly are disproportionately affected because it is they who most heavily rely on the service."[97] Professor Thoms agrees:

Arrayed against the duopoly of the bus system are customers who are in no position to bargain at arm's length. Bus travelers are often poor people with no alternatives. Many do not own cars. Many are too young, too old, or too infirm to drive.... Deregulation of air and rail...has meant that many cities, towns and rural areas have lost scheduled service.[98]

CONCLUSION: "YOU CAN'T GET THERE FROM HERE"

Transportation, communications, and energy are the foundation upon which the rest of commerce is built. Government policies can have a powerful influence in locational decisions and economic development by virtue of the role they play in the "construction, subsidy, taxation and regulation of carriers and the means of communications."[99]

Trade routes are the arteries of the economic system, linking every city, town, and hamlet to the life blood of commerce.[100] Transportation and economic development are mutually interdependent—transportation improvements stimulate economic growth, and that growth, in turn, increases the demand for transportation.[101] The converse is also true. The absence of reasonably priced transportation will stifle economic development and cause a region's economy to spiral downward.[102] These features distinguish the infrastructure industries from most others in the economy, and explain one of the major reasons why such services have been regulated since an early point in Anglo-American history. In order for the vast rural pockets of this nation to have a healthy economy, small towns must have nondiscriminatory access to them, or they will be isolated from the mainstream of commerce and wither on the vine.

Economic regulation has traditionally protected public interest values that might not find a high priority in the marketplace. It has treated common carriers (e.g., the airlines, railroads, and bus and telephone companies) as industries imbued with a unique responsiblity to satisfy the needs of the public for universal service. Small communities as well as large (and small businesses as well as large) have traditionally been required to be served at a nondiscriminatory price.[103] While the invisible hands of the marketplace have made most of the decisions regarding the level of service and prices to be provided, regulatory agencies have traditionally made a few, establishing the metes and bounds of performance, so as to protect the public interest.[104]

Regulation imposes upon common carriers both a burden and a benefit. The burden is the obligation to provide an adequate level of service to all geographic areas within their operating territory, at reasonable prices. Traditionally, this approach has fostered a distribution of wealth policy, whereby somewhat higher profits earned from the larger users of the system have cross-subsidized below-cost pricing to relatively smaller or more remotely located users. In return for providing this benefit to small communities, the regulated enterprise has been granted a franchise of operating authority which shields it from competitive entry and "cream-skimming" by rivals.

How has this changed under deregulation? The president of the South Dakota Chamber of Commerce put it this way: "The federal government's deregulatory steps of the last decade governing milk prices, railroads, trucking, airlines and telephone service have resulted in higher prices and reduced service."[105] Such are the demons that leapt out of Pandora's box of deregulation.[106] And they were unleashed at a time when America's rural areas were reeling from the most disastrous economic environment for agriculture since the Great Depression.[107] The combination of deregulation and the farm crisis will ensure the degeneration of many small towns into "rural ghettos."[108]

To a European observer, the fact that the richest and most powerful nation on Earth has allowed its transportation infrastructure to disintegrate must appear almost incomprehensible. In Europe, intercity trains provide efficient and expeditious passenger service to all large and medium-sized cities, and many, many small villages as well. North of the Alps, you can set your watch by their departures.[109] The train station is the heart of most European cities, where passengers can find a convenient link to urban subways, streetcars, or buses. And the buses of the Postal Telephone and Telegraph (PTT) service in most countries provide a reliable link to virtually every hamlet in Europe.

In Europe, much of the transportation and communications infrastructure is governmentally subsidized. In the United States, too, public subsidies have been offered to ameliorate the political opposition to deregulation by legislators representing rural constituencies. Yet, in the long term, we see that they become impossible to maintain by a federal government unable to balance its budget. Small-community airline subsidies may eventually expire under the budget-cutting imperatives of a $2 trillion national deficit. And, probably sooner rather than later, Amtrak will disappear as its subsidies are terminated. In America, these days, if the market doesn't provide it, it usually doesn't exist.[110]

Under deregulation, the service obligations of common carriers have become impossible to maintain. The most lucrative markets have become flooded with entrants, thereby squeezing carrier profits and making exit from marginal markets inevitable.[111] Today, when a passenger asks for a ticket to Bountiful, the clerk must answer, "You can't get there from here."[112] And if telecommunications follows the same route, residential consumers will pay higher prices for poorer service.

And so, the trains, jets, and buses have disappeared from much of rural America. Ultimately, those without the private automobile will be left stranded. The economic base of isolated communities will become increasingly difficult to sustain. Without adequate transportation and communications services, many towns in America's heartland will slowly die.

NOTES

1. Other such transportation deregulation legislation involving the movement of freight, as opposed to passengers, includes the Railroad Revitalization and Regulatory Reform Act of 1976, the Air Cargo Deregulation Act of 1977, the Staggers Rail Act of 1980, the Household Goods Transportation Act of 1980, the Motor Carrier Act of 1980, and the Freight Forwarder Deregulation Act of 1986.

2. See Dempsey, *The Interstate Commerce Commission: Disintegration of an American Legal Institution*, 34 AM. U. L. REV. 1 (1984); Dempsey, *Congressional Intent and Agency Discretion—Never the Twain Shall Meet: The Motor Carrier Act of 1980*, 58 CHI. KENT L. REV. 1 (1982); and Dempsey, *The Rise and Fall of the Civil Aeronautics Board—Opening Wide the Floodgates of Entry*, 11 TRANSP. L. J. 91 (1979).

3. See e.g., Hardaway, *Transporation Deregulation (1976–1984): Turning the Tide*, 14 TRANSP. L. J. 101, 106 n. 17 (1986), and articles cited therein. See also S. BREYER, REGULATION AND ITS REFORM (1984).

4. For example, railroads, being tied to their track, are the least flexible of the several modes; airlines are addicted to airports; bus companies are far more flexible in their service capabilities, rolling over asphalt and concrete wherever poured. From an economic perspective, railroads have the highest fixed costs and buses the lowest. The buses are the most fuel-efficient mode for short distances, and the railroads for long.

5. FCC chairman Mark Fowler has urged the states to join a three-year experiment in deregulation, pursuant to which telephone companies would be free to eliminate subsidies for local residential service, raise rates, and enter new businesses without prior approval by state or federal agencies. Fowler, Halprin & Schlichting, *"Back to the Future" A Model for Telecommunications*, 38 FED. COMM. L.J. 145 (1985).

6. For example, under federal deregulation, "evidence is mounting, especially in the airlines, railroads, trucking, and long-distance telephone service, [of a] striking increase in concentration." *Is Deregulation Working?*, BUS. WEEK (Dec. 22, 1986) at 50.

7. See e.g., MacAvoy & Robinson, *Winning by Losing*, 1 YALE J. REG. 1 (1983).

8. See Basedow, *Common Carriers—Continuity and Disintegration in United States Transportation Law*, 13 TRANSP. L.J. 1, 3–14 (1983).

9. See Dempsey, *Rate Regulation and Antitrust Immunity in Transportation*,

32 AM. U. L. REV. 335, 345–49 (1983); W. JONES, REGULATED INDUSTRIES (2d ed. 1975).

10. *See* generally, A. KAHN, vol. 2, THE ECONOMICS OF REGULATION 220–46 (1971).

11. *See* MacAvoy & Robinson, *Losing by Judicial Policymaking: The First Year of the AT&T Divestiture*, 2 YALE J. REG. 225 (1985).

12. P. DEMPSEY & W. THOMS, LAW & ECONOMIC REGULATION IN TRANSPORTATION 7 (1986).

13. *Id.* at 8–9. *See* D. BOWERSOX, P. CALABRO, & G. WAGENHEIM, INTRODUCTION TO TRANSPORTATION 164 (1981).

14. 94 U.S. (4 Otto) 113 (1877).

15. *Id.*

16. Dempsey, *supra* note 9, at 344.

17. Quoted in Dempsey, *Rise and Fall, supra* note 2, at 108.

18. 49 U.S.C. preceding sec. 1 (1975); 49 U.S.C. sec. 10101 (1986). A similar policy was subsequently promulgated for air transport. 49 U.S.C. sec. 1302 (1975).

19. Today, America's agricultural heartland is undergoing the worst economic crisis in half a century, with 2,000 family farms going "belly up" every week. *See* Walljasper, *Little Cell on the Prairie*, THE NATION (Oct. 25, 1986) at 402. Almost 30% of the nation's farms are on the road to bankruptcy. *Bitter Harvest*, NEWS-WEEK (Feb. 18, 1985) at 52.

20. *Oversight on Rural Transportation: Hearings before the Subcomm. on Rural Development of the Senate Comm. on Agriculture, Nutrition, and Forestry*, 96th Cong., 1st Sess. 26–27 (1980).

21. For a review of airline regulation in foreign commerce, *see* P. DEMPSEY, LAW & FOREIGN POLICY IN INTERNATIONAL AVIATION (1987).

22. W. THOMS, REPRIEVE FOR THE IRON HORSE 12 (1973).

23. Dempsey, *Entry Control under the Interstate Commerce Act: A Comparative Analysis of the Statutory Criteria Governing Entry in Transportation*, 13 WAKE FOREST L. REV. 729, 734 (1977).

24. 49 U.S.C. sec. 10903(a).

25. *See* e.g., Abandonment of Branch Line by Colo. & So. Ry., 72 I.C.C. 315 (1922).

26. *See* Thoms, *Clear Track for Deregulation—American Railroads, 1970–1980*, 12 TRANSP. L. J. 183, 187 (1982). ICC policies on rail abandonments have become dramatically more permissive since 1979, so that the number of denials in the 1980s have been reduced to an insignificant portion of cases decided. T. KEELER, RAILROADS, FREIGHT AND PUBLIC POLICY 105 (1983). For a criticism of the ICC's lax approach, *see* Georgia Public Service Commission v. United States, 704 F.2d 538 (5th Cir. 1983). Since the Staggers Act was passed, the ICC has granted 1,298 abandonment applications and denied 26. Appendix to letter from ICC Office of Transportation Analysis director Leland Gardner to Paul S. Dempsey (Mar. 16, 1987). This is a grant rate of more than 98%.

"Almost 5,000 miles of rail lines are closed each year.... The small towns that dot America's farm belt are being abandoned by railroad companies." Dorgan, *Disappearing Railroad Blues*, THE PROGRESSIVE (Aug. 1984) at 32. Shippers that have lost rail service, but have been able to secure alternative transportation, have suffered an average 83% increase in transport costs. Ernst & Whinney, SHIP-

PER RESPONSES TO RAIL SERVICE LOSS: AN ASSESSMENT OF CASE STUDIES 1 (1981).

27. *See* Peterson, *An Economic Analysis of Statutory Changes in Rail Carrier Entry and Exit,* 13 TRANSP. L.J. 189, 210–13 (1984).

28. 49 U.S.C. sec. 10909.

29. Southern Ry. Co. v. North Carolina, 376 U.S. 93 (1964).

30. *Id.*

31. Thoms, *supra* note 26, at 197.

32. *Id.* at 191; P. DEMPSEY & W. THOMS, *supra* note 12, at 73.

33. W. THOMS, *supra* note 22, at 12.

34. *Id. See* Johnson, *Lessons from Amtrak and Conrail,* 49 ICC PRAC. J. 247, 250–51 (1982).

35. Letter from W. Graham Claytor, Jr., to Paul Stephen Dempsey (Mar. 3, 1987) [hereinafter cited as Claytor Letter].

36. *Reagan Puts the Brakes on Amtrak,* BUS. WEEK (Mar. 30, 1981) at 83.

37. *Amtrak Reauthorization: Hearings before the Subcomm. on Surface Transportation of the Senate Comm. on Commerce, Science and Transportation,* 99th Cong., 1st Sess. 74 (statement of W. Graham Claytor, Jr.).

38. Claytor Letter, *supra* note 35. The airline figure is based on availability of such service within a 30-mile radius of city center for communities east of the Mississippi, and a 50-mile radius west of the Mississippi. *Id.*

39. *Amtrak's Struggle to Stay on Track,* NEWSWEEK (June 3, 1986) at 50.

40. Thoms, *supra* note 26, at 196.

41. *The Economic Impact of Federal Airline Transportation Policies on East Tennessee: Hearings before the Sen. Comm. on the Budget,* 99th Cong., 1st Sess. 19 (1985) [hereinafter cited as *Economic Impact of Federal Airline Policies*].

42. 49 U.S.C.A. sec. 1389 (Supp. 1987). *See* Comment, *Commuter Airlines and the Airline Deregulation Act of 1978,* 45 J. AIR L. & Com. 685, 692–98 (1980), and Dempsey, *Erosion of the Regulatory Process in Transportation,* 47 ICC PRAC. J. 303, 310 (1980).

43. 49 U.S.C. sec. 1302(a)(8).

44. E. BAILEY, D. GRAHAM, & D. KAPLAN, DEREGULATING THE AIRLINES 112 (1985).

45. CIVIL AERONAUTICS BOARD, COMPETITION AND THE AIRLINES 135 (1982).

46. *See* CIVIL AERONAUTICS BOARD, REPORT ON AIRLINE SERVICE 43–50 (1979).

47. Meyer, *Section 419 of the Airline Deregulation Act: What Has Been the Effect on Air Service to Small Communities?,* 47 J. AIR L. & COM. 151, 181 (1981).

48. Havens & Hemsfeld, *Small Community Air Service under the Airline Deregulation Act of 1978,* 46 J. AIR L. & COM. 641, 673 (1981).

49. GENERAL ACCOUNTING OFFICE, DEREGULATION 29 (1988) [hereinafter GAO REPORT].

50. Stephenson & Beier, *The Effects of Airline Deregulation on Air Service to Small Communities,* 20 TRANSP. J. 54, 57 (1981).

51. E. BAILEY et al., *supra* note 44, at 123; R. NOLL & B. OWEN, THE POLITICAL ECONOMY OF DEREGULATION 59 (1983).

52. *See* GAO REPORT, *supra* note 49, at 19.

53. Dempsey, *Rise and Fall, supra* note 2, at 178 n.428.

54. Ott, *Upper Midwest Mulls Service Options*, AV. WEEK & SPACE TECH. (July 12, 1982) at 35–36.

55. M. BRENNER, J. LEET, & E. SCHOTT, AIRLINE DEREGULATION 98 (1985).

56. *Id.* at 36, and GAO REPORT, *supra* note 49, at 34.

57. Oster, Jr. & Zorn, *Deregulation and Commuter Airline Safety*, 49 J. AIR L. & COM. 315–16 (1984).

58. *See* Oster, Jr. & Zorn, *Airline Deregulation, Commuter Safety, and Regional Air Transportation*, 14 GROWTH AND CHANGE 3, 7 (1983) and Meyer, *supra* note 47, at 631 n. 222. The National Transportation Safety Board has concluded that the commuter airlines accident rate of 1.48 fatalities per 100 million passenger miles is 37 times worse than that of scheduled airlines. *The Puddle-Jump Problem*, NEWSWEEK (Oct. 23, 1978) at 76 [hereinafter cited as *Puddle-Jump Problem*]. The GAO has found the accident rate for commuters to be seven times higher than the rate for the large scheduled airlines, and the rate for air taxis to be 18 times higher. *FAA Passenger Regulation of 9-Seat and under Passenger Aircraft: Hearings before the Subcomm. on Investigations and Oversight of the House Comm. on Public Works and Transportation,* 98th Cong., 1st Sess. 3 (1985) (testimony of Oliver W. Krueger). *See Congress Wrestles with Air Safety Concerns*, 43 CONG. Q. 2293 (Nov. 9, 1985).

59. *See* Ahmed, *Air Transportation to Small Communities: Passenger Characteristics and Perceptions of Service Attributes*, 38 TRANSP. Q. 15, 21 (1984).

60. *See* Warren, *Changing Air Transportation Services for Smaller Metropolitan Regions*, 38 TRANSP. Q. 245, 265 (1984).

61. Stephenson & Beier, *supra* note 50, at 56–57.

62. *Flying the Deregulated Skies*, AV. WEEK & SPACE TECH. (July 5, 1982) at 9.

63. Meyer, *supra* note 47, at 182. *See also* S. TOLCHIN & M. TOLCHIN, DISMANTLING AMERICA: THE RUSH TO DEREGULATE 245–46 (1983).

64. Dempsey, *supra* note 42, at 304–06.

65. Moore, *U.S. Airline Deregulation: Its Effects on Passengers, Capital, and Labor*, 24 J. L. & ECON. 1, 15, 18, 28 (1986).

66. Quoted in *Economic Impact of Federal Airline Policies, supra* note 41, at 5 (testimony of Sen. Jim Sasser). The U.S. General Accounting Office also found that "passengers in many lightly traveled, short-distance city pairs did not benefit from lower fares." GAO REPORT, *supra* note 49, at v, 51–52.

67. Addus, *Subsidizing Air Service to Small Communities*, 39 TRANSP. Q. 537, 548 (1985).

68. R. Brozoski, Airline Deregulation in California (California PUC, Transportation Division, Oct. 1981); O'Lone, *PUC Statement Contested by Airlines*, AV. WEEK & SPACE TECH. (Jan. 28, 1980) at 37. The California result is particularly interesting in light of the fact that its intrastate experience prior to deregulation was pointed to as model of the benefits that could be realized by deregulation. *See* note, *Is Regulation Necessary? California Air Transportation and National Regulatory Policy*, 74 YALE L.J. 1416 (1965); Edles, *The Strategy of Regulatory Change*, 49 ICC PRAC. J. 626, 628 (1982).

69. Ott, *supra* note 54, at 36.

70. *See Economic Impact of Federal Airline Policies, supra* note 41. *Field Hearing on Aviation Matters: Hearings before a Subcomm. of the Senate Comm. on Appropriations*, 98th Cong., 2d Sess. (1984). *See also Impact of Airline Deregulation on Service to Small and Medium Sized Communities: Hearings before the Subcomm. on Aviation of the Senate Comm. on Commerce, Science, and Transportation*, 96th Cong., 1st Sess. (1979).

71. GAO REPORT, *supra* note 49, at 22.

72. "The historical cross-subsidy policy resulted in some communities getting air service they otherwise would not have. The fare formula benefited passengers in short-distance or lightly traveled markets because they generally paid fares below the cost of the service they received." *Id.* at 23.

73. *See* M. BRENNER et al., *supra* note 55, at 102.

74. *See* GAO REPORT, *supra* note 49, at 31–32.

75. *Economic Impact of Federal Airline Policies, supra* note 41, at 12–13 (testimony of Eugene Joyce).

76. Meyer, *supra* note 47, at 175. *See Puddle-Jump Problem, supra* note 58; and *When the Jets Stopped Flying at Bakersfield*, BUS. WEEK (Nov. 5, 1979) at 106. Many observers agree. "Deregulation has brought inconveniences to many and a sense of isolation to others, touching the lives of businessmen wanting connections to the national transportation system, and of vacationers.... Threat of further air service losses, at least disruptions, at the scheduled conclusion of federal subsidies, has been an additional psychological blow to communities seeking to develop or even maintain current status." Ott, *supra* note 54, at 36.

77. *Economic Impact of Federal Airline Policies, supra* note 41, at 16–17 (testimony of William Willis).

78. S. TOLCHIN & M. TOLCHIN, *supra* note 63, at 250.

79. *Intercity Bus Service in Small Communities: Senate Comm. on Commerce, Science and Transportation*, 95th Cong., 2d Sess. 17 (1978).

80. Webb, *Legislative and Regulatory History of Entry Controls on Motor Carriers of Passengers*, 8 TRANSP. L.J. 91, 105 (1976).

81. *Id.*

82. *See* Kahn, *The Bus Regulatory Reform Act of 1982 and Federal Preemption of Intrastate Regulation of the Intercity Bus Industry: Where Has It Come From? Where Will It Lead?*, 14 TRANSP. L.J. 179 (1986). Where a state has either denied a discontinuance request or failed to act within 120 days, the bus company may seek reversal by the Interstate Commerce Commission. For existing operating authority, the ICC must approve the discontinuance unless it finds that it would be inconsistent with the public interest, and that continuing the service will not constitute an unreasonable burden on interstate commerce. The ICC must also give great weight to the extent to which the carrier's combined interstate and intrastate operations generate revenues less than the variable costs of providing service on the route. 49 U.S.C. sec. 10935. It must also consider the National Transportation Policy, whether the carrier has received a subsidy offer, and whether the service is the last bus service in the area and, if so, whether reasonable transportation alternatives exist. *Id.* However, the fact that a community would be left without bus service is not, in and of itself, sufficient grounds for denying the discontinuance

request. *See* Katzman, *The Bus Regulatory Reform Act of 1982: What It Does and How It Works*, 52 TRANSP. PRAC. J. 221, 238–43 (1985).

The ICC was also granted appellate review over state ratemaking determinations by the 1982 Bus Act. On appeal, the ICC may reverse a state denial of a rate increase if it finds that the intrastate rate discriminates unreasonably against, or imposes an unreasonable burden on, interstate commerce. There is a rebuttable presumption that the intrastate rate is unreasonable if it is lower than either the comparable interstate rate or the variable costs of providing the service. 49 U.S.C. sec. 11501(e)(2).

83. *See* Kahn, *supra* note 82.

84. *Department of Transportation and Related Agencies Appropriations for Fiscal Year 1985: Hearings before a Subcomm. of the Senate Comm. on Appropriations*, 98th Cong., 2d Sess. 476–77 (1985) [hereinafter cited as *Appropriations Hearings*].

85. Missouri, Kansas and Oklahoma Coach Lines—Oklahoma Corp. Comm'n, No. MC-C–36364 (ICC served Feb. 29, 1984).

86. *Household Goods Transportation and Bus Regulatory Reform Oversight: Hearings before the Subcomm. on Surface Transportation of the Senate Comm. on Commerce, Science and Technology*, 99th Cong., 1st Sess. 145 (statement of John D. Mladinov) [hereinafter cited as *Bus Oversight*]. A prominent Washington, D.C. attorney expressed similar concerns: "In practice, the ICC is utilizing an interpretation of the BRRA which leads to the granting of relief to any carrier which comes before it, provided there is at least a tenuous link with interstate commerce." Kahn, *supra* note 82, at 198–99.

87. *Bus Oversight*, *supra* note 86, at 2 (testimony of Sen. Larry Pressler).

88. Shane, *Opinion from the Executive Office*, TRAVEL-HOLIDAY (Mar. 1984) at 61.

89. *Now That the Brakes Are Off the Bus Industry*, U.S. NEWS & WORLD REP. (Apr. 18, 1983) at 87.

90. *Id.* Blyskal, *Leave the Driving to Adam Smith*, FORBES (Aug. 1, 1983) at 100.

91. *Oversight of the Household Goods Transportation Act of 1980 and the Bus Regulatory Reform Act of 1982: Hearings before the Subcomm. on Surface Transportation of the Senate Comm. on Commerce, Science and Transportation*, 98th Cong., 2d Sess. 25 (1984) (statement of David N. Gibson).

92. Letter from ICC Chairman Heather Gradison to Senator Larry Pressler (Sept. 8, 1986).

93. The ICC found in January 1984, that of 1,294 points destined to lose bus service, 1,045 had no alternative service. *Appropriations Hearings*, *supra* note 84, at 479 (testimony of Sen. Mark Andrews).

94. Dempsey, *Deregulation Stranding Residents of the Lone Prairie*, ROCKY MOUNTAIN NEWS, Sept. 14, 1986, at 73 [herinafter cited as *Deregulation Stranding Residents*].

95. Robbins, *Dependent on Buses, Midwestern Towns Fight Cuts In Service*, NEW YORK TIMES, Oct. 14, 1986, at A14.

96. ILLINOIS COMMERCE COMMISSION, ILLINOIS BUS SERVICE SINCE THE BUS ACT: A DIMINISHING INTERCITY NETWORK (1984).

97. *Id.*

98. Thoms, *Unleashing the Greyhounds—The Bus Regulatory Reform Act of 1982*, 6 CAMPBELL L. REV. 76, 94 (1984). *See also* F. THAYER, REBUILDING AMERICA: THE CASE FOR ECONOMIC REGULATION 97–98 (1984).

99. E. HOOVER, THE LOCATION OF ECONOMIC ACTIVITY 255 (1948).

100. "Transportation has been a fundamental element in the growth of civilization and industrial development, and has had a profound effect on collective economic growth." Dempsey, *supra* note 9, at 335. Even Adam Smith recognized that the breadth of the market depends upon the price and availability of transportation. A. SMITH, THE WEALTH OF NATIONS I: 19–22 (1925).

101. Addus, *supra* note 67, at 551–52.

102. *See* Dempsey, *supra* note 42, at 311.

103. *See* Dempsey, *The Interstate Commerce Commission, supra* note 2, at 48.

104. *See* Waring, *Motor Carrier Regulation—By State or by Market?*, 51 ICC PRAC. J. 240, 242 (1984).

105. Ott, *supra* note 54, at 35.

106. Deregulators used the theory of contestable markets to rebut allegations that carriers enjoying a monopoly or oligopoly presence in a market would earn supracompetitive profits there. In theory, another carrier should enter in such circumstances and restore the competitive equilibrium. Yet, the empirical data suggests that the theory has not proven true in the post-deregulation environment. Moore, *supra* note 65.

107. Lewis, *The US Farm Crisis: Measuring the Ripple Effect*, CERES (Mar.-Apr. 1986) at 41.

108. "A blight that is economical rather than botanical is transforming small towns in the Midwest into rural ghettos—pockets of poverty, unemployment and despair." *See* Davidson, *The Rise of the Rural Ghetto*, THE NATION (June 14, 1986) at 820.

109. In contrast, airline departures in the United States under deregulation often bear little relationship to published schedules. *See* e.g., Thomas, *Texas Air's Rapid Growth Spurs Surge in Complaints about Service*, WALL ST. J., Feb. 26, 1987, at 29.

110. Although section 419 and Amtrak subsidies have been addressed herein, the broader question of state taxpayer subsidies is beyond the scope of this book. But note that those that do exist in many areas of transportation (i.e., for Amtrak, urban mass transit, the U.S. Postal Service, and the section 419 small community air services program) have come under heavy political assault by a federal government struggling in the 1980s with $200 billion deficits per year. Some states do provide Amtrak subsidies. *See* Nice, *The States and Amtrak*, 40 TRANSP. Q. 559 (1986); and P. DEMPSEY & W. THOMS, *supra* note 12, at 286–88. But most rural states are suffering stiff budget deficits of their own these days, and are least able to afford transportation subsidies. Moreover, although statutory subsidy provisions exist, not only for Amtrak but also for rail abandondment and bus discontinuance proposals, they have, in some instances, proven administratively unworkable. *See* Michel, *Casenote: Chicago and North Western Transportation Company v. United States*, 13 TRANSP. L.J. 245 (1984), and Mills, *The Lake Geneva Line: A Case History*, 52 TRANSP. PRAC. J. 51 (1984).

111. Dempsey, *Transportation Deregulation: On a Collision Course?*, 13

TRANSP. L.J. 329, 356–59, 381–82 (1984). Dempsey, *Deregulation's Toll Is Rising,* DENVER POST, Sept. 4, 1986, at 5B.

112. *See* W. THOMS, YOU CAN'T GET THERE FROM HERE—INTER-MODAL PASSENGER TRANSPORTATION IN NORTH DAKOTA (Oct. 1978). O. NASH, YOU CAN'T GET THERE FROM HERE (1958).

10

STATE REGULATION

FEDERAL PREEMPTION

Between 1976 and 1982, Congress was active not only in deregulating interstate tansportation but also in preempting state jurisdiction over transportation within their borders. For example, Congress preempted intrastate regulation of the airline industry with promulgation of the Airline Deregulation Act of 1978. Similarly, intrastate rail regulation must meet standards established by the Interstate Commerce Commission[1] under the provisions of the Staggers Rail Act of 1980.[2] In the Bus Regulatory Reform Act of 1982,[3] Congress provided that state denials of bus abandonments and rate increases may be appealed to the ICC[4] (where they are almost always reversed).[5]

Of the major pieces of legislation deregulating the various modes of transportation, only the Motor Carrier Act of 1980 left unmolested the states' jurisdiction over intrastate commerce[6] (although the ICC has recently assaulted the states' sovereignty with an ambitious definition of interstate transportation, on appeal in the U.S. Supreme Court as of the date of this writing).[7]

INTRASTATE DEREGULATION

Since promulgation of the federal Motor Carrier Act of 1980, only five states have chosen to follow the lead of the Interstate Commerce Commission by deregulating their motor carrier industries: Florida (1980), Arizona (1981), Maine (1982), Wisconsin (1983), and Alaska (1984). Note that enthusiasm for transportation deregulation began to wane at both the state and federal levels in the mid–1980s, as deregulation turned out not to be as beneficial to the public as promised by its proponents.

Florida was the first state to deregulate its intrastate motor carrier industry in the contemporary era, but not because of a strong, grass-roots political movement. Instead, the two houses of the state legislature simply failed at the last minute to agree on the language of a bill to extend the life of the existing regulatory framework. Under the Florida sunset legislation applicable to all state governmental agencies, such regulation automatically terminated at a certain date in the absence of a new statute affirmatively extending its life. In the year preceding deregulation, the Florida Public Service Commission (PSC) received only 34 complaints regarding household goods transportation; but in the first month alone following deregulation, 44 such complaints were filed.[8] Similarly, in Arizona, deregulation has resulted in more consumer complaints in the areas of household goods, taxicab, and ambulance services.[9]

In Indiana, a bill was passed in 1984 to sunset the jurisdiction of the state public utilities commission (PUC) over motor carriers, to be effective in 1986. However, subsequent state legislation, supported by a group comprised principally of small businesses, repealed the bill's sunset prior to its effective date. Thus, Indiana came quite close to deregulation, but reversed course at the eleventh hour, leaving the PUC's jurisdiction unmolested.

In Wisconsin, Joe Sweda, an early deregulation proponent and commissioner of the state Office of Commissioner of Transportation, now laments the impact of the bill he supported: "Deregulation has not been the success that many had anticipated. Most rural areas have suffered under this law. The truck service and especially the bus service to these areas has been drastically reduced. My office has received numerous complaints from rural shippers concerning the sporadic service, late shipments and the general unavailability of many Wisconsin truckers."[10] Sweda also pointed out that small shippers are disadvantged vis-à-vis larger shippers because rates are no longer published. Hence, larger shippers are able to secretly negotiate preferential rates with carriers, while small shipppers are helpless to defend themselves against rate discrimination. Loss and damage claims have escalated and carrier safety has deteriorated since Wisconsin decided to deregulate intrastate transportation.[11]

Unfortunately, deregulation has eliminated the monitoring functions which state agencies traditionally performed. Hence, there is precious little empirical evidence with which to evaluate intrastate deregulation.[12]

One notable exception is our nation's most populous state, California. In 1980, the California Public Utilities Commission partially deregulated its controls over motor carrier ratemaking. Beginning in 1984, the California PUC conducted a two-year study of the impact of intrastate deregulation and reached conclusions similar to those of Wisconsin commissioner Sweda. Some 23 days of testimony was heard by an administrative law judge, and two days of en banc hearings were held before the full commission. Producing nearly 4,000 pages of transcript and 2,000 pages of exhibits, California's study is the most comprehensive and detailed evaluation of the impact of intrastate deregulation to date.

The study revealed that widespread discriminatory and preferential rate cutting created a situation in which the industry's infrastructure became ovraged; for-hire carriers were no longer able to maintain vehicle replacement programs or acquire new equipment; adequate financing was no longer available to motor carriers; safety deteriorated, leading to increased numbers of deaths and injuries from highway truck-related accidents; there was a serious reduction in the number of independent owner-operators; and to offset the prevailing rate cutting, drivers operated excessive hours, maintained multiple log books, overloaded vehicles, drove at excessive speeds, and reduced expenditures for equipment maintenance.[13] As we have seen, these are exactly the consequences of federal interstate transportation deregulation.

The California PUC issued a decision on April 16, 1986, in which it concluded that additional deregulation would not be in the public interest. It made the following findings:

It is the intention to provide a regulatory system which promotes the financial health of the industry, equity, competitive opportunity and public safety. . . . Although competition is not and never will be perfect, . . . one of the major objectives of the regulatory policy is to prevent competitive forces in the industry from becoming destructive. . . . It is not our purpose to encourage carriers to offset losses through inadequate wages, poor vehicle maintenance or market instability. Further, if enough carriers engaged in sustaining underpricing, the industry as a whole would suffer, jeopardizing the provision of adequate, reliable service . . . . We also agree with the staff's assessment that under the prevailing circumstances, total deregulation of the state's motor carrier industry is not appropriate.[14]

The California commission concluded that rate deregulation was having a serious adverse impact upon the motor carrier industry and the public it serves. It therefore decreed a mandatory 10% rate increase and adopted a program designed to eliminate preferential and discriminatory rates.[15]

More recently, the Ohio Public Utilities Commission launched an investigation as to whether stricter rate controls should be imposed.[16] The PUC's Director of Transportation said, "We are concerned that the economic problems [of the industry] may potentially affect the service available in Ohio and the safety of the highways."[17] The investigation will be conducted in two stages, the second of which will address issues such as limited and discriminatory price discounting and below-cost pricing.[18]

Finally, the West Virginia Public Service Commission, after six years of partial motor carrier deregulation, found that the result was service deterioration and higher prices for its small towns and rural communities. In 1987, West Virginia decided to return to traditional economic regulation.[19]

IN WHICH DIRECTION SHOULD THE STATES GO?

Why Not Intrastate Deregulation?

A number of state legislators and public utilities commissions have been confronted with various motor carrier deregulation proposals in recent years. Most such proposals, particularly those in Texas and California, have been supported and generously financed by coalitions of very large shippers. Any analysis of the contemporary political, legal, and economic environment would be incomplete without a review of the principal costs of intrastate deregulation, and a suggestion as to what regulatory structure will accomplish desirable public objectives.

As we have seen, deregulation, while it benefits very large shippers (those with monopsony power), creates an anemic motor carrier industry, lots of bankruptcies, an aging and poorly maintained rolling stock of tractors and trailers, overworked and underpaid drivers, a growing number of highway injuries and fatalities, a high turnover rate among firms, and an oligopoly among large carriers.

A deregulated environment is not an environment of perfect competition. Distortions are created because of the size and power of both shippers and carriers. The monopsony power of large shippers enables them to unilaterally dictate price discounts below established rates. By selectively tendering or withholding their vast volumes of freight, they can extort extremely low rates from carriers. For unsophisticated carriers, this sometimes results in below-cost pricing, hastening their demise. For others, made desperate for freight by trucking industry overcapacity, it means marginal cost pricing.

But the fixed costs have to be picked up somewhere. Rather than having a fair allocation of the fixed cost burden placed on large shippers, the pricing structure which emerges is highly discriminatory. The monopsony power of large shippers unleashed by deregulation has created a pricing scheme which benefits large shippers and penalizes small shippers. Effectively, this means that large shippers enjoy marginal cost (or too often, below marginal cost) pricing, while small shippers pay a higher freight bill to cover the carriers' fixed costs. Pricing also becomes higher for shippers in small towns and rural communities. Consumers who purchase from these suppliers are disadvantaged.

Pricing discrimination is prohibited in the sale of goods by the Robinson-Patman Act. But for the sale of important infrastructure services, such as transportation, it is only economic regulation that protects the public against the pernicious effects of pricing discrimination.

What are those deleterious effects? Large shippers enjoy superior access to the broader market for the sale of the goods they produce. It gives them a pricing advantage vis-à-vis their smaller competitors, and creates another layer of economies of scale. Small businesses, which create most of America's jobs, suffer higher transport prices. And small towns and rural communities also pay the price of discrimination, exacerbating their contemporary economic plight of an outmigration of investment, jobs, and population.

But not only does unleashed monopsony power have a deleterious effect upon other users of the system, it has a devastating impact upon the motor carrier industry itself. Destructive competition exists where even efficient and well-managed carriers fail to cover their fixed costs over a long period of time and drop into bankruptcy. The interstate trucking industry is plagued with unlimited entry, overcapacity, a number of unsophisticated competitors with an inadequate understanding of costs, and a large number of carriers without the ability to counterbalance the enormous monopsony power of the larger shippers, which unilaterally dictate ridiculously low rates. All of this has caused the industry to suffer thousands of bankruptcies, even after the recession of the early 1980s abated and fuel prices peaked and fell, and caused the public to suffer thousands of highway accidents.

The trucking industry is one which is inherently vulnerable to overcapacity, for it sells a service which is, in essence, an instantly perishable commodity. When a truck leaves the loading dock, an empty space is lost forever. Unsold space cannot be shelved and sold another day, as could say, clock radios. Imagine a grocer whose store was filled with goods which had the spoilage properties of unrefrigerated cream cheese. Whatever couldn't be sold quickly would have to be discarded, for unsold inventory could not be warehoused. Grocers would have fire sales every afternoon to recover a portion of their investment. That's a pretty fair picture of the trucking industry in a regime of unlimited entry, overcapacity, and resultant destructive competition—plenty of bankruptcy, even among efficient and well-managed carriers.

The result is an undesirable one—even many efficient carriers go bankrupt. The vicissitudes of the national market cycle are such that during periods of slack demand, many efficient firms without deep pockets fall into bankruptcy, for they are more subject to the problems of overcapacity than industries which can warehouse unsold product. Many large carriers, with deeper pockets, are able to endure the downward slope of the market cycle even though they are less efficient. As the social Darwinist experiment with federal interstate deregulation reveals, the very big get to be bigger still, and their smaller rivals drop into bankruptcy. Unfortunately, size, rather than efficiency, too often determines which firms survive.

The empirical evidence of the federal experiment in interstate deregulation reveals market structure attributes which appear to favor carriers of size. Despite the predictions of proponents of deregulation, there are significant economic barriers to entry and economies of scale in the less-than-truckload (LTL) industry arising as a result of the high capital costs of regional terminals and distribution networks. In fact, since federal deregulation, the number of major LTL carriers has dwindled as the industry has suffered an epidemic of bankruptcies, and no major new carrier has successfully entered the market.

The economic barriers to entry and economies of scale are such that the interstate oligopoly which deregulation has unleashed may be here to stay. Only prudently administered economic regulation can ensure the survival of small and medium-size trucking companies, whose presence stimulates a healthy competitive environment, one in which the industry is productive and innovative. The concentration resulting from deregulation is anathema to the public's interest in the benefits of a healthy competitive environment.

Not only are distortions created by shippers with monopsony power, they are created by the market power of very large carriers as well. A carrier with a deep pocket, wanting to sacrifice short-term gain to achieve larger market share and ultimate long-term benefit, can certainly underprice its rivals in a manner to drive them from the market. Predatory pricing can be arrested with responsible rate regulation, which prohibits a carrier from offering rates below its marginal costs, or below an average industry-wide marginal cost standard which incorporates requirements that carriers be efficient and well-managed.

Rate of return regulation prohibits the extraction of monopoly rents which a firm with market power could otherwise reap. Not only does responsible rate regulation deter firms from exploiting their monopoly markets, it also dissuades them from targeting smaller competitors for extinction via predatory pricing.

Some suggest that antitrust remedies are sufficient to deter predatory practices. They are not. Antitrust litigation is exceedingly time and resource consumptive. Even if a party can endure the years of expensive litigation, and prevail on a difficult evidentiary path, antitrust remedies only provide compensation in the form of money damages to those who have suffered from anticompetitive practices. They do not restore a competitor once lost from the market. Hence, the public's interest in a healthy competitive environment goes unsatisfied.

Healthy competition exists when entry is reasonably limited, rates are set at reasonable levels, and carriers compete fairly for business. Only very large shippers benefit when carriers are slammed against the wall. Destructive competition can be avoided by responsible regulation of motor carrier entry, rates, and business practices.

The economic health of motor carriers is extremely important if they are to provide the safe, adequate, and dependable service needed by the public. Allowing unlimited entry, which floods the market with capacity, and allowing large shippers with monopsony power to dictate excessively low rates, makes it difficult for carriers to devote necessary resources to discretionary equipment maintenance. The public suffers in terms of a higher level of truck-related highway accidents and fatalities.

Also, unlimited competition thins the ranks of the smaller trucking firms, whose presence provides a catalyst for productivity and innovation for the larger firms. Thus, responsible regulation can ensure the existence of a healthy competitive environment for both the motor carrier industry and the public it serves.

Viable, healthy, and adequate transportation services at reasonable prices constitute an essential foundation for economic growth. Simply put, without transportation, commerce does not flow. And if commerce does not flow, that greater market for the production, purchase, and sale of goods abruptly grinds to a halt. Similarly, distortions in transportation pricing or service distort that greater market. Such distortions have a deleterious impact upon the economy.

The infrastructure of transportation services facilitated by responsible economic regulation is a framework wherein all users (no matter how small or remote) enjoy nondiscriminatory access at reasonable prices to the broader market for the sale of goods. Fair access to the gateway of commerce is required by all users if we are all to enjoy a piece of the American pie. Small shippers and small towns should have the same opportunities to participate in the cornucopia of American industrial enterprise that our nation's largest corporations enjoy solely by virtue of their market power.

Equitable access to that gateway is the infrastructure which regulation protects and facilitates. Traditionally, economic regulation has satisfied this objective well, while also ensuring that the nation enjoyed a high level of dependable service adequately adapted to the evolving, contemporary needs of commerce.

Before deregulation, Americans could boast that they had the world's finest system of transportation. After deregulation, the best you could say is that it serves the nation's largest shippers well. The industry is anemic, bankruptcies are robust, safety has disintegrated, service has deteriorated and pricing is highly discriminatory.

What Form Should Regulation Take?

The optimum form of regulation which serves the broader societal needs of all consumers, including those purchasing from small producers, those living in small towns and rural communities, those who drive on the highways, and those who do not own stock in America's largest corporations is as follows:

In a nutshell, *entry* should be regulated to ensure that the market is not flooded with so much capacity that efficiency is jeopardized. The *enforcement* power to suspend or revoke licenses should be exercised where, for example, a carrier fails to fulfill its common carrier obligations, discriminates in pricing, or fails to fulfill its safety obligations. *Rates* should be filed in tariffs with the PUC before they become effective. They should be "just and reasonable" and nondiscriminatory betwen persons or places. A zone of reasonableness should be established within which pricing would be determined by the level of competition among carriers. The pricing structure should be sufficient to allow well-managed and efficient carriers an opportunity to earn a reasonable return on investment, so that they can provide adequate service throughout their operating territories, and properly maintain their equipment. At the upward end of the zone, monopoly pricing should be prohibited, while at the lower end of the zone, predatory pricing should be forbidden. *Mergers, acquisitions,* and other *corporate practices* should be scrutinized to ensure that antitrust violations do not occur. However, antitrust immunity should be conferred to allow carriers to enter into agreements which enhance efficiency, encourage information flows, and facilitate the ratemaking principles discussed above.[20]

Let us take a closer look at the benefits of a responsibly and prudently administered regulatory structure. Responsible economic regulation of any infrastructure industry, be it electric utilities, telecommunications, or transportation, allows efficient and well-managed companies an opportunity to earn a reasonable return on investment. Usually, such regulation includes a "zone of reasonableness" within which the level of competition sets the rate charged, usually at a price approaching marginal costs. At the upward end of the zone, regulation prohibits consumers from being exploited by monopoly pricing; at the lower end of the zone, smaller competitors are shielded from the effects of predatory pricing. This keeps the market flush with competitors and ensures that healthy competition is the driving force behind pricing, a result which benefits consumers. As we have seen at the federal level, deregulation brings about industry concentration, predatory pricing, and discrimination.

The public utilities commissions encourage efficiency among all regulated industries—electric and gas utilities, telecommunications, and transportation—by engaging in ratemaking methodology that allows only those costs prudently incurred to be passed through to consumers in the form of higher rates, thereby allowing only well-managed and efficient firms to earn a reasonable return on investment. Imprudently incurred costs should be disallowed. Inefficient carriers should not be allowed to earn competitive rates of return on investment.

Usually, progressive public utilities commissions that regulate entry award an applicant a certificate of public convenience and necessity if it can demonstrate that it proposes a new service not presently available in the market. Say a shipper needs special packaging, or unusual equipment, and cannot get it from the existing complement of carriers which serve it. Many PUCs authorize the new entry on grounds that the innovative service accomplishes the desirable objective of facilitating service choice.

Once the entrant receives its license, the ratemaking protections shield it from the predatory behavior of its larger rivals. They also ensure it a reasonable return on investment so long as its operations are efficient and well-managed. Thus, prudently administered economic regulation can stimulate service choices and thereby benefit both the motor carrier industry and the shipping public it serves.

Prudently administered regulation can also encourage efficiency by avoiding the overcapacity problems created by unlimited entry. Flooding the market with empty trailers merely drives prices down to noncompensatory levels, causing economic injury to even well-managed motor carriers, while adding nothing in the way of efficiency or productivity to the market.

Moreover, by prohibiting predatory pricing and allowing efficient carriers to earn a reasonable return on investment, responsibly administered regulation keeps the market flush with small transportation competitors. Their presence continues to serve as a stimulant for cost minimization and efficiency among their larger rivals. The federal experience with interstate deregulation reveals that thousands of small carriers have been wiped out by the destructive competition which has been unleashed. Many of the strong survive under deregulation; many of the small and weak do not.

Responsible economic regulation enables small businesses, which create most of the nation's jobs, to enjoy the same nondiscriminatory access to the broader market for the sale of goods that larger shippers enjoy. As the federal experience with interstate trucking deregulation reveals, the discrimination unleashed by deregulation jeopardizes the economic health of small shippers, making it more difficult for them to survive and provide the job-creating momentum.

A prudently administered regulatory scheme also enables small towns and rural communities to enjoy adequate and nondiscriminatory access to the market. Without it, their ability to attract investment and employment would be jeopardized.

Economic regulation also creates a common carrier obligation that licensed carriers provide adequate and nondiscriminatory rates and services throughout their territories. The threat of the various sanctions available, including certificate suspension and revocation, provides a significant impetus to abide by these common carrier responsibilities.

Another dimension of quality and availability is, of course, the stability of the firms which provide an essential service like transportation. Turnovers caused by seemingly endless rounds of bankruptcies do shippers little good and cause some real harm. Take a typical scenario that occurs too often these days; the trucking company to which a shipper yesterday entrusted its goods has fallen into bankruptcy; its goods disappear or get caught up in litigation in a legal squabble among the carrier's creditors. Or take another common scenario: a shipper's goods are strewn across an expressway because the carrier didn't have the money to repair worn brakes. Endless bankruptcies and crashes hardly enhance the quality and availability of service, yet they are a common occurrence under deregulation.

Allowing efficient and well-managed carriers an opportunity to earn a reasonable return on investment enables them to provide adequate service throughout their service territories, to pay labor a fair wage, and to properly maintain their equipment. Inadequate returns on investment lead to overworked drivers, shoddy maintenance, and inevitably, increased numbers of truck-related accidents and fatalities.

Deregulation enables large shippers with monopsony power to extort extremely low rates from trucking companies. Cutting trucking rates to the bone, while enabling the stockholders of a few large corporations to enjoy healthy profits, causes society to pay more in terms of health care costs arising as a result of truck-related accidents, which by the way, are increasing in number. Of course, insurance will cover some of these costs, if the trucking company carries insurance; but many unlawful operators do not. Nevertheless, however well money can ease the pain of injury, it often fails to restore health, and never restores life.

The regulation of minimum rates, which ensures that efficient carriers have a fair opportunity to earn a reasonable return on investment, will help improve safety. So will prohibitions against discriminatory pricing, which thwart the ability of large shippers with monopsony power to cut rates to the bone.

Entry regulation would also have a positive effect upon the states' ability to regulate safety. Not only should a carrier demonstrate that its proposed operations are "consistent with the public convenience and necessity" in that it satisfies a public need for new service, the applicant should also prove that it is "fit, willing, and able" to properly and safely perform the proposed operations, and abide by the PUC's rules and regulations. Fitness includes, but is not limited to, having the financial resources to purchase and maintain safe equipment and hire a suitable staff of maintenance employees.

Fitness should also be an ongoing requirement, whereby a licensed carrier which fails to satisfy minimum standards of safety should have its operating certificate revoked or suspended. For example, if a carrier is found to operate unsafely, improperly maintain its equipment, not carry adequate insurance, or push drivers beyond federal safety standards, license suspension or revocation should be considered an appropriate sanction. No carrier should be allowed to operate without a license. Hence, the threat of license suspension or revocation is a powerful tool to stimulate compliance.

The federal experience with interstate deregulation reveals that there is a direct correlation between a carrier's financial health and its ability to devote essential resources to upgrading and maintaining its equipment, as well as the pressure placed on drivers to stay behind the wheel for excessive periods of time. And there appears to be a correlation between deregulation and aging and poorly maintained equipment, exhausted drivers, and truck-related highway fatalities. Remember, occupants of passenger automobiles involved in truck-related accidents are 40 times more likely to lose their lives than are the occupants of the heavy truck. All of this suggests that responsible regulation of rates is essential to avoid a deterioration in highway safety and needless loss of life.

The principal benefits of responsible economic regulation of the motor carrier industry are that efficient and well-managed carriers are allowed to earn a reasonable return on investment sufficient to allow them to provide safe, adequate, and dependable service throughout their operating territories, at rates that are both just and reasonable and nondiscriminatory. As the federal experiment with interstate deregulation amply demonstrates, deregulation leads to inadequate returns on investment, a seemingly endless series of bankruptcies (even of efficient, but small carriers), deteriorating safety, poor service, highly discriminatory rates, and a heavily concentrated industry.

NOTES

1. *See* Texas v. United States, 730 F.2d 339 (5th Cir. 1984), *cert. denied*, 105 S.Ct. 267 (1984).

2. *See* Railroad Comm'n v. ICC, 765 F.2d 221 (D.C. Cir. 1985).

3. *See* Thoms, *Unleashing the Greyhounds—The Bus Regulatory Reform Act of 1982*, 6 CAMPBELL L. REV. 86, 96–7 (1984).

4. Texas v. United States, 761 F.2d 211 (5th Cir. 1985).

5. For an excellent review of federal preemption of intrastate jurisdiction over transportation, *see Symposium: Intrastate Regulation*, 14 TRANSP. L. J. 179–247 (1986).

6. *See* 49 U.S.C. sec. 10521(b).

7. *See* Mann, *Back Door Deregulation of Intrastate Transportation Accelerates*, 37 YOUR LETTER OF THE LAW 33 (1987). Such cases pending as the date of this writing include State of Texas v. United States (5th. Cir. No. 87–4725), E & B v. Mattox (W.D. Tex. No. A–86-CA–446), Middlewest Motor Freight Bureau v. Interstate Commerce Commission (8th Cir. No. 87–2043), Steere Tank Lines v. Interstate Commerce Commission (8th Cir. No. 88–4001), and California Trucking Association, Inc. v. Interstate Commerce Commission (9th Cir. No. 87–7439).

8. Dempsey, *Transportation Deregulation—On a Collision Course?*, 13 TRANSP. L.J. 329 (1984).

9. *Id.* at 362.

10. Letter from Joseph Sweda to Representative James Moody (Oct. 15, 1985), reprinted in 31 YOUR LETTER OF THE LAW 33 (Mar. 1986), and made part of the Oversight Hearings on the Motor Carrier Act of 1980 held by the Subcommittee of the Public Works and Transportation Committee of the U.S. House of Representatives (Nov. 5, 1985).

11. *Id.*

12. "[A]t the state level, the total deregulation of trucking, in Florida for example, means that no reliable data on Florida intrastate trucking is available." N. GLASKOWSKY, EFFECTS OF DEREGULATION ON MOTOR CARRIERS (1986).

13. Baker, *1986 Update of Regulation of Motor Carriers by Individual States*, 33 YOUR LETTER OF THE LAW 28, 30–31 (Aug. 1986).

14. Baker, *Does the Public Benefit from Deregulation?*, 34 YOUR LETTER OF THE LAW 23, 28 (Nov. 1986).

15. *Id.* at 31.

16. *Ohio Eyes Re-Regulation of Truck Ratemaking and Procedures in New Probe*, TRAFFIC WORLD (Nov. 10, 1986) at 58.

17. *Ohio Commission Studying Economic Controls on Trucking*, MOTOR FREIGHT CONTROLLER (Dec. 1986) at 6.

18. *Id.*

19. Public Service Commission of West Virginia M.C. Case Nos 20376 and 20377, Middle Atlantic Conference, In the Matter of Investigation and Suspension of Tariffs (Mar. 6, 1987).

20. *See Symposium: Collective Ratemaking and Consensual Decisionmaking*, 32 AM. U. L. REV. 279–613 (1983).

11

FEDERAL REGULATION

After a decade of deregulation, two things are clear. First, many of the essential presumptions advanced by free-market economists regarding the inherently competitive nature of the transportation industry (e.g., the likelihood of new competitive entry emerging because of low barriers to entry and few economies of scale) were simply specious. The excessive optimism of how competitive the market would be stemmed from hostility to government regulation and euphoria over textbook economics.

After five years of deregulation, with airlines going "belly up" in bankruptcy, Alfred Kahn noted that "there's a lot of turmoil, but that's what we intended."[1] He then acknowledged that "the turmoil is more intense and lasting longer than most of us anticipated."[2] He was also willing to concede that new entrants would probably never account "for more than 5% of the total travel."[3]

By 1988, Kahn was even more conciliatory about the problems that had emerged under deregulation and the inability of pro-deregulation economists to have predicted them. He insisted that the Department of Transportation was largely to blame for these ills by, for example, approving every merger submitted to it and not expanding airport capacity sufficiently. Nonetheless, Kahn noted that "there have of course been severe problems and reasons for concern even from the public's standpoint: most prominently sharply increased congestion and delays, increased concentration at hubs, monopolistic exploitation of a minority of consumers, and possibly a narrowing of the margin of safety."[4] Subsequently, in response to a question as to whether the margin of safety had narrowed under deregulation, he conceded, "no one can deny that, under the pressure of competition, we may be walking on a thinner margin."[5] No doubt, the thinner margin was caused by the economic anemia that deregulation unleashed. Kahn conceded that "there is no denying that the profit record of the industry since 1978 has been dismal, that deregulation bears substantial responsibility, and that the proponents of deregulation did not anticipate such financial distress—either so intense or so long-continued."[6] He acknowledged that the low fares consumers had enjoyed were a short-term phenomenon, saying, "I have little doubt that . . . the disappearance of most of the price-cutting new entrants and the marked reconcentration of the industry—will produce higher fares."[7] As to pricing and entry, Kahn sounded apologetic: "We didn't dream of the way airlines could manipulate fares with such great sophistication. . . . We were a little naive about what 'freedom of entry' meant in the airline business."[8] Naive indeed. What a pity that the intellectual foundation upon which deregulation was predicated turned out to have been ill-conceived.

Second, as a consequence of this erroneous reasoning, the predictions which rested upon these presumptions have not been sustained by the empirical evidence. Textbook economics produces one result under deregulation—near perfect competition. But the world in which we live has produced quite another—an anemic industry of megacarriers providing poor service and highly discriminatory pricing. Of course, the anemic nature of the industry is being supplanted by the emerging oligopoly and monopoly opportunities, which enable carriers to exert market power. Raising prices and cutting service will improve the health of the industry, while consumers forego those deep discounts of which deregulation's proponents have been so proud.

Factors other than deregulation have been widely cited to rationalize the ills of the industry. In the early 1980s, as Braniff and Continental flew into bankruptcy, deregulation's proponents blamed the enormous economic losses sustained by the industry on the national economic recession and high fuel prices. The upstart carriers like Air Florida, World Airways, Freddie Laker's Skytrain, and Donald Burr's People Express were advanced as proof that the industry was still highly competitive.

As the years passed, the recession abated, and fuel prices fell, and the upstart airlines went "belly up" or were absorbed by the megacarriers, the rationalizations wore thin. Industry profitability during the first decade of deregulation was the worst in the history of domestic aviation.

Kahn blames the "complaisant" DOT antitrust policy (approving every merger submitted to it) for the high level of concentration which now exists in the industry. True, national levels of concentration have been advanced by the huge mergers permitted by an irresponsible DOT. But as we saw in Chapter 4, only three hub monopolies owe their existence to mergers. The rest are simply the result of open entry and exit, which are the very heart of deregulation. Deregulation, not the recession, nor high fuel prices, nor even antitrust abdication, must shoulder much of the blame for the fact that this important industry serves neither its needs nor those of the public well.

Much of the blame for such undesirable social and economic consequences must, of course, be placed on the shoulders of the governmental officials who implemented deregulation. Both Presidents Carter and Reagan appointed free-market economists and deregulation ideologues to the transportation agencies—the Civil Aeronautics Board, the Interstate Commerce Commission, and the Department of Transportation. As a consequence, these became highly political institutions, taking their marching orders from a decidedly ideological White House. In true free-market zealotry, those who led the CAB, ICC, and DOT during the past decade embraced deregulation as an end in itself. "Destroy the regulatory agency and unleash the market," became the goal. And so the CAB was "sunset" on December 31, 1984, the ICC was stripped of its staff, and Pandora's box was opened.

But deregulation should have been the means, not the end; entry and pricing, if gradually, carefully, and responsibly liberalized, could have produced a more competitive environment than that which has emerged. Deregulation should have been the means to an end of achieving enhanced competition with as few social disruptions as possible. Had a more responsible and practical approach been employed, the turmoil would have been much less onerous.

But zealotry demands immediacy, and there was little of the gradual transition to a more competitive environment that was mandated by the deregulation legislation. Indeed, precious little attention was paid to the statutes which Congress passed to implement deregulation at the CAB under Marvin Cohen, or the ICC under Darius Gaskins. Economists tend to see truth clearly, and view legislation as a nuisance if it conflicts with their vision of nirvana. Unfortunately, Congress has been incapable or unwilling to exert its constitutional power to regulate interstate and foreign commerce and rein the agencies in.

Despite vigorous pleas that the CAB constrain excessive entry and predatory pricing, the agency consistently refused to do either. It instead insisted that "in healthy competition, producers who are inefficient or make bad decisions may fail, but efficient and well-managed producers can operate profitably.... [Bankruptcies] may serve a useful purpose ... by eliminating the inefficient or imprudent operator."[9] In response to the economic demise of the industry, former CAB chairman Alfred Kahn responded, "it's destructive and it's cruel, but that's the way the market functions."[10] The Reagan administration took much the same approach as its Democratic predecessors, embracing economic Darwinism. Murray Weidenbaum, Reagan's chairman of the Council of Economic Advisors, said that "the success of individual companies is not a concern to the marketplace—there is no assurance that any particular company is going to survive."[11]

The Interstate Commerce Commission adopted much the same approach, issuing operating authority to thousands upon thousands of applicants who demonstrated little more than the ability to fill out an application form. In a landmark decision, the ICC concluded that "competition which forces an existing carrier out of business" may be desirable, for "it is preferable to replace an inefficient operator with a more efficient one and promote the introduction of innovative services or prices."[12] Survival of the fittest seems to be at the very heart of the Darwinist economics embraced by deregulation advocates. The manifest tragedy of deregulation is that many efficient carriers with shallow pockets have perished, for they found themselves unable to withstand a flood of capacity, the vicissitudes of the downward cycle of the market and the predatory pricing of their larger competitors.[13]

In 1987, the Interstate Commerce Commission celebrated its centennial anniversary. During most of its history the commission was widely regarded as among the most competent and highly respected of American legal institutions. President Grover Cleveland signed into law the Act to Regulate Commerce on February 4, 1887, and appointed the distinguished Michigan Jurist, Thomas Cooley, the commission's first chairman. During the ensuing years, presidents chose commissioners to the Interstate Commerce Commission almost as carefully as they chose justices to the Supreme Court, emphasizing their competence, integrity, and ability to apply the law as promulgated by Congress with skill and reason, weighing and balancing the competing equities.[14]

At the 50th anniversary of the ICC, the activities of the agency were complimented for their "vigor, spirit, and statesmenlike administration."[15] The ICC was praised for its "unswerving fidelity . . . to administer the laws entrusted to it for administration."[16] As an independent regulatory agency, autonomous from the executive branch of government, it was recognized as "the creature of Congress, its representative, responsible to no one else."[17] Its independence made possible a prudent protection of the public interest: "Without desire to aggrandize itself, but actuated by what it believed to be in the public interest, free from partisanship or politics and resisting pressure from whatever source, it does its work."[18]

By the time the commission had reached its 75th anniversary, it was described in still more positive terms. Supreme Court Justice Felix Frankfurter remarked:

In the first place, The Commission illustrates, throughout its life, unblemished character . . . character meaning a fastidious regard for responsibility, a complete divorcement between public and private interest, and all other concomitants of a true and worthy conception of public duty. Alas, that cannot be said of all public bodies, but it can be said that this Commission throughout its seventy-five years has had a career of unblemished character.

Secondly, I would say we are here to celebrate as striking a manifestation of competence in government as any I know of in the three branches of government. With all respect for each of those three branches . . . my deep conviction is that . . . this Commission has as high a record of competence as any . . . of the other three branches of government . . . .

Thirdly, it is a necessary condition, before a Commission can effectively act, that it be independent. I do not mean independence because the statute says it shall be independent, but because Commissioners actively assert independence when the occasion calls for independence....

It has maintained not merely formal independence, but actual independence of word and deed, and has been a laboratory demonstration of how economic problems may be worked out by trial and error. Finally, by virtue of all these considerations, the Commission has been a pacemaker, a model for the subsequent commissions which, in turn, have been created in response to economic and social demands in their fields of activity.[19]

Yet contemporary observations about the Commission suggest that it has since lost that abundance of character, competence, and independence recognized by Justice Frankfurter. Recent statements about the agency suggest that it is today viewed with contempt by those both within and without it. The executive director of the Independent Owner-Operator Association, delivering testimony before the Senate Commerce Committee, described the ICC with less than enthusiastic respect:

[T]he Interstate Commerce Commission's implementation of the act . . . [is, in] one word, miserable. The ICC has not followed the intent of the act and has failed to be a responsible regulator.

During approximately the past year, the Commission has been slapped in the face by four mandamus orders from the United States Courts of Appeals, and in one case a contempt request was filed. Only then did the Commission act in accordance with the court mandate. Enforcement has been scandalous by its absence.[20]

Although the Interstate Commerce Commission was statutorily constituted as an 11-member body (to be appointed by the president with the advice and consent of the Senate, nor more than six of whom shall be members of the same political party), by the mid–1970s our presidents were filing no more than seven seats. The large size of the commission had traditionally contributed to its conservatism; change had rarely been radical. But by appointing individuals dedicated to radical change, and by keeping the commission's membership small, the White House was successful in dynamically shifting the internal policy of the body to one enthusiastically dedicated to deregulation in a relatively brief period of time.

Further, under Reorganization Plan No. 1 of 1969, presidents beginning with Richard Nixon were given the authority to designate who among the commissioners shall be chairperson.[21] This sharply increased White House influence over the agency and its chief officer, undermining the ICC's traditional autonomy from the executive branch and its perception as an arm of Congress.

Beginning in the Carter administration, individuals who were fervently dedicated to deregulation were appointed to fill vacant seats on the Interstate Commerce Commission.[22] Although the Ford appointees (e.g., Chairman

A. Daniel O'Neal and Commissioner Betty Jo Christian) had moved moderately in the direction of liberalized entry and ratemaking, their efforts paled in comparison to the vigorous deregulatory efforts of the economists appointed by Jimmy Carter (i.e., Chairman Darius Gaskins and Commissioners Marcus Alexis and Tad Trantum). And despite campaign promises that he would only appoint qualified and experienced individuals to the regulatory agencies, President Reagan followed this unfortunate tradition with the appointment of deregulation ideologues of his own (e.g., Heather Gradison, Frederic Andre, and Malcolm M. B. Sterrett). Although the White House had previously been criticized for the quality of its ICC appointments (owing, in part, to the dominance of political patronage in the appointment process), never before had there been such a concerted attempt by the executive branch to give this quasi-judicial agency a philosophical mission via the appointment process.[23]

Beginning in the late 1970s, the ICC moved firmly toward deregulation, despite the fact that the existing statutes were far more conservative than would realistically permit unlimited entry and ratemaking; by 1979, it was granting 98% of the motor carrier operating-authority applications filed.[24] Numerous quasi-judicial decisions and rulemakings were also concluded during this period that opened the floodgates of entry and deregulated ratemaking.[25]

One court recognized the commission's actions for what they were—*de facto* deregulation despite the absence of statutory authority:

In instances admitting of any doubt, the ICC resolved them in favor of the applicant, contrary to the burden of proof then upon [the applicant]. With the basis of its conclusions not clearly indicated, the reviewing court must be left with the suspicion that the decision was made for a reason not stated in the record: solely for the purpose of increasing competition in the area in disregard of other policies articulated by Congress.[26]

The Court's suspicion was a correct one. By the late 1970s, the ICC was issuing operating authority to virtually all applicants who sought it and abdicating its responsibility to engage in meaningful rate regulation. During this period, the ICC largely ignored the objections of protestants that such actions were causing them economic injury. In reversing the agency's decisions, several courts were particularly critical of the commission's approach: "We cannot say that petitioner's questions are so frivolous or so lacking in substance as to permit the commission to treat them in a perfunctory manner."[27] They found themselves forced to remind the ICC that "[t]he very fact that Congress has seen fit to enter into ... comprehensive regulation ... contravenes the notion that national policy unqualifiedly favors competition."[28]

As almost every U.S. Circuit Court of Appeals in the nation has recognized, Congress did not write a blank check to the ICC to bring about a radical transformation in the economic environment of the motor carrier industry. It instead adopted in the Motor Carrier Act of 1980 a *moderate* approach of entry and ratemaking liberalization, attempting to provide the Commission with "explicit direction for regulation of the motor carrier industry and well-defined perimeters within which it may act."

The ICC's rejection of an administrative approach based on careful statutory construction and deference to congressional intent in favor of one resting largely on the shoulders of laissez-faire ideology necessarily establishes an environment where many public interest policies promulgated into law by Congress fall by the wayside, for only governmental regulation can protect those values which do not find a high priority in the marketplace. In its revision of the National Transportation Policy, Congress emphasized that both competition and efficiency were to be encouraged, recognizing that there may be instances where unbridled competition would lead to wasteful fuel consumption. The ICC has nevertheless recognized the promotion of competition as the only salient purpose of the legislation.

The Interstate Commerce Commission has by no means slowed its lemming-like rush into the seas of deregulation, despite the absence of statutory authority, despite strongly worded congressional admonitions to remain within the jurisdictional boundaries established by Congress, and despite a plethora of judicial reversals in almost every U.S. Circuit Court of Appeals in the nation.

Any student of law and history must note with chagrin the disintegration of a venerable legal institution whose mission and purpose, so carefully defined by Congress in legislation passed earlier this decade, has been so twisted and distorted in so short a period of time by individuals who blissfully dance to their own tune.[29] The Interstate Commerce Commission no longer represents a government of law. It is instead government by people who hold values beyond those promulgated into law. It was James Madison in the *Federalist Papers* who reminded us that government must learn not only to govern the people; government must also learn to govern itself.[30]

Undoubtedly, congressional power had eroded in recent years,[31] while executive authority has prospered.[32] But independent regulatory agencies such as the ICC were established outside the realm of the executive branch to keep them relatively free from partisan political influence.

The commission has lost the autonomy from the executive branch which traditionally shielded its decisionmaking from the political winds that blow down Pennsylvania Avenue. The U.S. Supreme Court characterized the purposes of Congress in creating regulatory agencies such as the ICC in *Humphrey's Executor v. United States.*[33] In that decision, the Court emphasized the necessary independence of such bodies:

[It was Congress' intention to create] a body of experts who shall gain experience by length of service—a body which shall be independent of executive authority, except in its selection, and free to exercise its judgment without the leave or hindrance of any other official in any department of the government.

Such a body cannot in any proper sense be characterized as an arm or an eye of the Executive. Its duties are performed without executive leave and . . . must be free from executive control.[34]

The kamikaze mission of those who currently hold seats on the Interstate Commerce Commission portends its destruction unless the judiciary is ultimately successful in wearing down the agency's obstinance, presidents begin to appoint people other than deregulatory zealots to fill vacant seats on the commission, or Congress is able to successfully reassert its traditional role as guardian, protector, and defender of the child to which it gave birth in 1887.

Section eight of article I of the Constitution delegates to Congress the power to regulate interstate and foreign commerce. Subject to certain restrictions, Congress can, in turn, redelegate that power in a manner that either enhances or diminishes presidential influence. There are at least four models for such delegation: delegation directly to the president;[35] delegation to an executive branch agency (e.g., the DOT);[36] delegation to an independent regulatory commission subject to presidential review;[37] and delegation to an independent regulatory commision (e.g., the ICC) without presidential review.[38]

At the former end of the spectrum, Congress clearly intends for the president to have a considerable role in developing and implementing national policy. Thus, with the 1985 transfer of airline regulatory jurisdiction from the CAB, an independent regulatory agency, to the DOT, an executive branch agency, decisionmaking has more clearly reflected the White House pro-industry bias and its disdain for meaningful antitrust enforcement.

At the latter end of the spectrum, however, Congress vests authority in an independent regulatory agency, such as the ICC, in order to shield decisionmaking from direct presidential influence, particularly in those areas where the Constitution delegates authority to Congress. Such delegation is a manifestation of the Framers' view that a separation of powers was needed.[39] Congress chose the approach most likely to minimize presidential influence by making the ICC an arm of the legislature independent of the executive branch.[40] As Professor Bernard Schwartz has noted:

The President has absolute removal power over the executive departments; this ensures that the policies administered by them are not in conflict with his views. The position of the ICC-type commission is different. It is outside the executive departments, and is independent of the President. Though its members are appointed by the President, they hold office for a fixed term and are not legally accountable to him. . . . The resulting lack of accountability to the White House enables the [ICC-type] commissions to make their own decisions, which may be subject to judicial review, but are not subject to legal control by the President. Their independent position is sharply different from that of the executive departments, which are under plenary presidential control.[41]

Nevertheless, the ICC has lost the autonomy from the executive branch that traditionally shielded its decisionmaking from the political winds that blow down Pennsylvania Avenue. The dominant political force that has influenced ICC policy in the contemporary era has been the White House.[42] In recent years, Congress has been divided and hence unable to reassert its dominance over the ICC.

It was the intention of former CAB chairman Alfred Kahn to so "scramble the eggs" (by deregulating comprehensively and expeditiously through the vehicle of administrative fiat) that no one would ever be able to put them back into their shells again. It is no secret that if an agency decides to perform its functions irresponsibly, those members of the public who have traditionally benefited from regulation will ultimately view deregulation as a lesser vice than irresponsible regulation, and themselves call for the death of the beast which has devoured the benefit of the regulatory burden. This, unfortunately, is the point at which many of the nation's carriers now find themselves.

The deregulation zealots appointed by Presidents Carter and Reagan to the Interstate Commerce Commission may have mortally wounded that Grand Old Lady at 12th and Constitution Avenue. With wrecking balls of steel they attacked her very foundation, determined to crush her into rubble and sow the ground with salt so that nothing would ever grow there again. At that 75th birthday party for the ICC mentioned earlier, Justice Frankfurter, perhaps prophetically, addressed the possibility that the agency might one day end, not with a bang, but with a whimper:

It is a very wise man who said that institutions do not die, they commit suicide. And you can commit suicide by just ceasing to have life. I hope, and I have the highest confidence, that the Interstate Commerce Commission will remember the other part of the phrase of Ecclesiasticus, "Let us now praise famous men, and our fathers that begat us" and continue to live in the spirit of the men who preceded them. Continue to live in their spirits with reference to your problems and seventy-five years from now there will be an even more appreciative audience and nation grateful to the Commission for its achievement.[43]

Can the ICC still be characterized as Justice Frankfurter described it, as a bastion of unblemished integrity, competence, and independence? As Frankfurter said, institutions do not die, they commit suicide. The CAB committed suicide by strongly supporting the Airline Deregulation Act of 1978, which scheduled the agency's self-destruction in 1985.

The time has come to contemplate rolling back deregulation, reestablishing the appropriate role of government in leveling the playing field and protecting those economic and social interests which do not find a high priority in a regime of laissez faire. Even Alfred Kahn has, on occasion, conceded that government needs to do more, saying that the problems that have emerged "urgently cry out for at least some government remedies."[44] He has called for more stringent antitrust and safety regulation. He has acknowledged a need for regulation of landing fees, more consumer protection, and some control over the power of the monopoly railroads. He has even acknowledged that it may be time to impose price ceilings in monopoly airline markets.[45]

Others have also called for more regulation. Washington attorney Robert Reed Gray noted that "there has to be some reregulation to make the industry more tolerable for the people of this country."[46] Washington Post columnist Hobart Rowen put it this way:

The public is entitled to more attention to air safety; to the vigorous use of antitrust laws to break up airline monopolies; to an improvement in the quality of service; to the creation of an air travelers' lobby; and (as Kahn now suggests) to assurance that the roster of experienced air traffic controllers will be brought up to snuff.

If Congress does these things, it doesn't have to use the name "reregulation." A rose by any other name . . . [47]

To suggest reform of deregulation is not to say that we need to return to the tight-fisted regulatory regime of the early 1970s, for that also ignored important public interest values. Nor could we, even if we wanted to. The structural changes have been so profound that we cannot restore what was lost when Pandora's box was opened. But we do need a more prudent balance between strict governmental regulation and laissez faire, one that enhances healthy competition while achieving desirable social benefits.

Congress has already acknowledged the need for reform. The 100th Congress tried to slap on a few band aids by proposing an air travelers' "bill of rights." The bill would have required airlines to publish statistics summarizing their delays, number of passengers bumped, lost bags, and other consumer complaints. This spurred the lethargic DOT to promulgate regulations providing for monthly disclosure of consumer information and announce the potential sanction of modest penalties for flights cancelled for reasons other than mechanical problems or weather. The Essential Air Services subsidies for small towns have been extended. But much more needs to be done. Here is a laundry list of suggestions:

Consumer Protection. The condoned practice of deliberate overbooking should be abolished. It is highly unfair for the airline to sell a consumer a nonrefundable ticket when the "confirmed reservation" given the passenger turns out not to be confirmed at all. Airlines deliberately sell more tickets than they have seats, and the "confirmed reservation" can be yanked away at will, leaving the consumer stranded. If the airlines are concerned about passengers booking more reservations than they use, let them insist that passengers guarantee their reservations with a credit card, as do hotels. Only if the reservation is guaranteed should the ticket be nonrefundable.

Penalties for market-inspired flight cancellations should be increased, and made mandatory. Carrier liability for missed connections resulting from flight delays should be imposed. Seat width and distances between them should be designated so that an average-sized person can enjoy a comfortable flight on a long trip without having his or her knees jammed up against the seat in front.

Pricing. Free-market economists predicted that pricing under deregulation would reflect carrier costs. But rates instead tend to reflect the level of competition in a given market rather than marginal costs. More competition tends to bring rates down to costs; but with the industry becoming highly concentrated and with many markets unable to support more than one or two carriers, prices are ascending. Government regulation should be imposed to prohibit the extraction of monopoly or oligopoly rents. It ought to be possible to devise an industry-wide mileage-based formula as a benchmark by which to assess reasonableness of rates, bringing those down which cannot be sustained by a cost justification. Of course, shorter trips have higher per mile costs than longer ones, so the formula would have to reflect that.

The range of rates ought to include not only a ceiling, but also a floor to prohibit predatory pricing. Pricing below marginal costs to drive out a competitor should be circumscribed. Within this "zone of reasonableness" between the aforementioned ceiling and floor, competition should establish the rate charged.

Pricing discrimination between markets and classes of customers also ought to be reined in a bit. The Robinson-Patman Act prohibits pricing discrimination in the sale of *goods*. In 1914, when the legislation was enacted, there was little perceived need for a prohibition against pricing discrimination in the sale of services, for then the service sector was a relatively small sector of the American economy and pricing discrimination in the infrastructure industries was prohibited by the regulatory agencies.

But things are quite different today. The regulatory agencies that were established to prohibit discrimination no longer do. And today we have an economy dominated by the service sector. It is time to consider either amending the Robinson-Patman Act to prohibit discrimination in the sale of services or to reestablish the regulatory mechanism for its prohibition.

Finally, something needs to be done about the unconstrained power of the monopoly railroads to extort excessively high rates from captive shippers. The Staggers Rail Act of 1980 constricted the ICC's jurisdiction over rail rates to situations in which a railroad enjoyed "market dominance" over the traffic in question. The ICC, in its zeal to deregulate even more, gave "market dominance" a terribly generous definition, saying that it did not exist where there was intermodal, intramodal, geographic, or product competition. It does seem that the last two criteria take the concept a bit far, and should be legislatively repealed. Further, the ICC needs some additional legislative guidance as to the definition of rate reasonableness and the need to constrain pricing discrimination between shippers.

Antitrust. Related to Robinson-Patman and other pricing questions are the myriad of antitrust issues that have arisen under deregulation. The legislation governing mergers and acquisitions should be amended so as to make them more difficult for competing carriers to consummate. Statutory criteria for mergers should be tightened to emphasize antitrust concerns. Since 1978 there have been 51 airline mergers.[48] In three and a half years, the Department of Transportation approved each and every one of the 21 mergers that were submitted to it.[49] Perhaps carrier divestiture would be appropriate.

For airlines, divestiture of computer reservations systems should also be considered, for opportunities for anticompetitive conduct by their owners are, quite simply, excessively abundant. United and American together control 77% of the CRS market.

Legislation might also be promulgated to force carriers to sell infrastructure at hub airports to new entrants at fair market prices. Perhaps eminent domain condemnation and resale to new entrants would be appropriate, at least where a single airline controls more than 50% of the gates at an airport.

The dominance of incumbents is facilitated not only by their stranglehold over the "fortress hubs," but also by the consumer loyalty generated by the free mileage awarded under frequent flyer programs. Perhaps a tax should be levied so as to discourage their use.

Some break on the stranglehold of the monopoly railroads should also be considered, perhaps including a forced lease of trackage rights for competing railroads. If rates are to remain *de facto* deregulated, then additional carrier competition over competitor's trackage is needed to discipline the industry. Rights-of-way across rail lines to build coal slurry pipelines should fall into this category of physical plant, which is subject to the power of the regulatory agency to order transferred, at a fair market price, of course.

Small Community Access. If we are to abandon any notion of entry regulation and cross-subsidization at the federal level, then government subsidies for small community access should be expanded to include bus transport. Buses provide the essential link for the poor and elderly to the essential services of large cities.

If the pragmatic political realities of budget deficits preclude sufficient subsidies for air and bus service, then entry and exit regulation should be reconsidered. Establishing a service territory for which a carrier is responsible for providing reasonably priced and adequate service can be the mechanism for assuring adequate service to small towns and rural communities.

Safety. In order to deal with the problems of safety that have arisen under deregulation, several things need to be done. As to airlines, the air traffic control system needs to be refurbished. The Federal Aviation Administration needs to restaff the traffic control system to the pre-PATCO strike levels of 1981. FAA equipment needs to be updated and upgraded.

Congress should devote sufficient resources to building new airports and expanding existing ones. Today, America needs 8–12 new major airports. Yet only one is on the drawing board—for Denver. Local opposition (the not-in-my-back-yard, or NIMBY syndrome) to noise, congestion, and pollution exists to throw a monkey wrench into airport expansion and development. Perhaps it is time to consider federal legislation preempting local opposition to regional airport construction.

Congestion at hub airports can be reduced by regulating landings and takeoffs, perhaps by imposing peak-period landing fees. This will flatten out the demand curve and reduce congestion. Landing fees should also reflect the opportunity costs of delay, which would suggest that a higher landing fee should be imposed upon small aircraft, and a smaller fee imposed upon larger aircraft, thereby favoring the larger number of human users of finite resources. Hence, landing fees should be predicated upon both the need to reduce congestion (and the safety problems created thereby) and the full costs to society of delays.

Enhanced safety also requires that more attention be paid to the economic health of firms, for economic anemia mandates deferred maintenance. Hence, the regulation of carrier fitness in licensing should be taken more seriously by the U.S. Department of Transportation and the Interstate Commerce Commission. The Federal Aviation Administration should keep a keener eye on aircraft and pilot qualifications. If that proves inadequate to increase the margin of safety over the long term, then more comprehensive regulation that enhances the economic health of the industry may be required.

During the Reagan administration, the DOT and FAA were saddled with strong ideological mandates in favor of laissez faire, an emphasis that emasculated the agencies from meaningful and responsible fulfillment of their statutory obligations. If the DOT and FAA cannot be divorced from the highly ideological tilt of the White House, then these regulatory functions should be taken out of the executive branch and vested in an independent agency.

As to motor carriers, enhanced enforcement is needed and will help. But with the aid of citizen band radios, the worst trucks will tenaciously avoid inspections. Nevertheless, the net of vehicular inspections should be spread more widely. And mandatory drug testing of drivers is an idea whose time has come.

While an aircraft crash will dissuade prospective passengers from flying an unsafe airline (remember the Air Florida tail sticking out of the icy Potomac River?), the same market sanctions do not exist in trucking. Of course, a shipper who loses a shipment in a truck accident will likely avoid the carrier that caused it, but the impact is usually limited to the aggrieved shipper. Hence, government must take a more vigorous role in protecting safety. Particularly here, since bus and truck accidents kill more people annually than airline disasters.

A strong enforcement role is required for motor carriers, one that allows efficient and well-managed carriers to earn a reasonable return on investment and holds the Damocles sword of license revocation over the heads of firms should they endanger the lives of those with whom they share our highways.

An additional mechanism for disciplining shippers with monopsony power, which cuts rates to the bone, is to force the internalization of the adverse safety consequences of nonremunerative rates by holding them liable in tort for the injuries resulting from their unilateral pricing decrees. If a shipper knows (or reasonably should know) that the rate is insufficient to allow the trucking firms with which it does business to replace or properly maintain its equipment, then the shipper should bear the consequences of highway fatalities caused by its greed. A shipper with a private fleet of trucks hauling its own commodities could not skirt liability for the torts created by shoddy maintenance. Neither should a shipper which utilizes a common carrier under the circumstances described herein. Of course, for reasons expressed in Chapter 7, judicial relief is inferior to regulation as a mechanism for dealing with the safety problem. But it may force shippers to internalize some of the costs upon society that they are now externalizing.

A New Federal Transportation Commission. Much of what is wrong with deregulation is the fault of the agencies that have implemented it and the zeal with which they embraced laissez faire ideology. The statutes which ordained deregulation—particularly the Motor Carrier Act of 1980 and the Staggers Rail Act of 1980—were reasonably balanced legislative agendas for moderate entry and pricing liberalization. Yet their interpretation by the regulatory agencies (i.e., the CAB, ICC, and DOT) has bordered on the irresponsible. Much of that is attributable to White House dominance and its strong ideological agenda.

We should have expected White House domination of the DOT, for it is, after all, an executive branch agency. Hence, we were asking for trouble when the remaining regulatory responsibilities of the CAB were transferred upon its "sunset" on December 31, 1984, to the DOT.

What has come as a surprise is that the nation's first independent regulatory agency, the ICC, has come under the thumb of the White House. Its establishment as an agency outside the executive branch was designed to avoid precisely that. The 1969 decision to give the president the power to designate who shall be chairperson was a poor one. Independent regulatory agencies should elect their own officers. And the commission's membership should not be so small as to give any one president the power to radically change the agency's ideological composition in too short a period of time. Radical change should be avoided.

Much of the criticism of the regulatory agencies stems from the notion that after the initial euphoria of public interest protection wears off in the first decade or two of its existence, they tend to favor the interests of the industry they regulate. After all, the industry is the one constituency regularly before the agency, year after year, pleading its case and looking to the agency for relief. Other groups may come and go. The regulated industry is also the best financed of the constituencies which will appear before the agency.

There is also the problem of the "revolving door," whereby former commissioners are recruited by the industry to serve as executive officers. This is as true under regulation as under deregulation. For example, Alfred Kahn, Mike Levine, and Phil Bakes of the deregulationist CAB subsequently joined the Texas Air empire. And the ICC chairman most dedicated to deregulation, Darius Gaskins, ended up as chief executive officer of the Burlington Northern railroad. So the "revolving door" swings as well under deregulation as it did under regulation.

In the final analysis, there are important regulatory functions to be performed by government and we have to create a mechanism to perform them without undue political and economic bias. In order to avoid the problem of "capture," all of the regulatory functions over transportation (i.e., those formerly held by the CAB and now the DOT, those held by the ICC and the Federal Maritime Commission, and the pipeline jurisdiction of the Federal Energy Regulatory Commission) should be swept into a new Federal Transportation Commission, an independent federal agency outside the executive branch. An agency with jurisdiction over airlines, bus companies, pipelines, railroads, and domestic and international water carriers would be difficult to capture by any single firm or mode.

To enhance its independence, the new Federal Transportation Commission should be comprised of at least seven members appointed by the president, with the advice and consent of the Senate, to serve staggered, six-year terms. They should be selected from a list of qualified, competent, hard-working, neutral, and unbiased candidates prepared by a blue-ribbon panel of industry and consumer members appointed by the House, Senate, and White House. By calling upon an independent body to recommend potential candidates for nomination, we can reduce the propensity of some presidents to fill commissions with political cronies. Remember that the Ralph Nader study, *Interstate Commerce Omission*, described the ICC as an elephant's graveyard for political hacks.

Potential commissioners should be selected on the basis of their competence, skill, and neutrality on the issues they will confront. They must have a deep and abiding respect for the law and the supremacy of the legislative branch in defining the perimeters within which they shall administer the regulatory function. It is not just the substantive law that defines an agency's jurisdictional limits to which there must be fidelity, but also the procedural and evidentiary requirements of due process, for the agency will inevitably be quasi-judicial in nature. It must be filled with individuals who possess judicial temperament.

It is a fact of life that legislation must be drawn broadly, not only because statutes cannot be drafted with perfect precision (because of both problems of politics and the limitations of the English language), but also because some flexibility is desirable to enable regulatory agencies to confront new challenges as they arise. Nevertheless, Congress should make more of an effort to tighten the proposed agency's discretion and identify more precisely its jurisdictional perimeters. Congressional committees should perform more rigorous oversight hearings more often, raking appointed officials over the coals when they stray beyond congressional intent. The judiciary should also take a "hard look" at the orders and rules emanating from regulatory agencies and strike more down on grounds that they are *ultra vires*.

But more importantly, no commissioner should be so wedded to an ideology that he or she loses sight of the law or principles of justice and equity. In the final analysis, it is the quality and integrity of the men and women appointed to serve the public interest as commissioners, cabinet secretaries, and in other capacites who make the critical difference in whether the public interest is actually served.

Joseph Eastman, among the most talented and dedicated public servants ever to serve in the independent regulatory agencies, said it best:

With the country as big and complex as it is, administrative tribunals like the Interstate Commerce Commission are necessities. Probably we shall have more rather than less. To be successful, they must be masters of their own souls, and known to be such. It is the duty of the President to determine their personnel through the power of appointment, and it is the duty of Congress to determine by statute the policies which they are to administer; but in the administration of those policies these tribunals must not be under the domination or influence of either the President or Congress or of anything else than their own independent judgment of facts and the law. They must also be in position and ready to give free and untrammeled advice to both the President and Congress at any time upon request. Political domination will ruin such a tribunal.... The statutes which the tribunal administers should be well, simply, and carefully framed, but the personnel which does the administering is more important than the wording of the statute. Good men can produce better results with a poor law than poor men can produce with a good law. ... The important qualifications [of a Commissioner] are ability to grasp and comprehend facts quickly, and to consider them in their relation to the law logically and with an open mind. Zealots, evangelists, and crusaders have their value *before* an administrative tribunal, but not *on* it.[50]

In order to avoid political bias, no more than a simple majority of members should be members of a single political party. In order to alleviate the

ta
gmt ye=hae_aiain>Federal Regulation 245

likelihood of White House domination, regulatory agencies should be free to elect their own executive officers. In order to avoid pro-industry bias, strict restrictions should be placed on the ability of agency members to go to work for the regulated industry when they leave office.

Improved process will vastly improve the regulatory function. In fact, had we had a neutral and responsible regulatory agency without a strong ideological agenda implementing deregulation during the past decade, it is quite likely that this book would never have been written, for the empirical results of deregulation would have been less harmful.

NOTES

1. *CAB's Ex-Chairman, Alfred Kahn, Looks at Airline Industry He Helped to Deregulate*, WALL ST. J., Oct. 4, 1983, at 35.
2. *Id.*
3. *Id.*
4. Kahn, *Airline Deregulation—A Mixed Bag, But a Clear Success Nevertheless*, 16 TRANSP. L.J. 229, 251 (1988).
5. *Interview with Alfred Kahn*, USA TODAY, Oct. 5, 1988, at 13A.
6. Kahn, supra note 4, at 248 [citations omitted].
7. *Id.* at 236.
8. Kuttner, *Why Air Fares Aren't Falling*, WASHINGTON POST, Sept. 18, 1988, at C7.
9. Oakland Service Case, CAB Order 78–4–121 (1978), at 25.
10. Some have criticized this philosophy:

The world's finest air transportation system is in a state of utter chaos. This does not speak as badly for Prof. Kahn as it does for the gullible clowns in Washington who heeded his ridiculous suggestions. The consumer has only begun to reap the "rewards" of deregulation.

Letter from Len Morgan to the Editor, WALL ST. J. (Oct. 12, 1983).
11. Rowan, *Airline Deregulation Comes Back to Haunt*, WASH. POST., Mar. 14, 1982, at G1.

[E]conomists preach that bankruptcies are *good* in a free market, beause they eliminate the inefficient operators. This textbook theory overlooks the total cost of bankruptcies. Taxpayers eventually bear much of the cost through the loss of taxes paid by the bankrupt, the cost of unemployment and welfare benefits paid to discharged employees, etc. The public also pays in the form of higher interest rates necessitated by the losses suffered by the banks. Creditors lose and pass along their losses to consumers in the form of higher prices on their goods and services.

These considerations fail to account for the more important cost of bankruptcies—the human pain and suffering experienced by the officials, employees, and stockholders of bankrupt companies. How long will the public condone an economic theory which encourages and fosters such tragedies?

W. Augello, The Deregulation Disaster 9–10 (unpublished monograph, 1982).
12. La Bar's Extension—Mountaintop Insulation, 132 M.C.C. 263, 272 (1980).
13. Letter from Joseph F. Queenan to Paul Stephen Dempsey (Apr. 25, 1983).
14. Aitchison, *The Evolution of the Interstate Commerce Act: 1887–1937*, 5

GEO. WASH. L. REV. 289 (1937). *See* Harris, *Appendix 1*, 31 GEO. WASH. L. REV. 309 (1962).

15. *Id.* at 321.

16. Esch, *The Interstate Commerce Commission and Congress—Its Influence on Legislation*, 5 GEO. WASH. L. REV. 462, 463 (1937).

17. *Id.*

18. *Id.* at 502.

19. Dempsey, *Transportation Deregulation—On a Collision Course?*, 13 TRANSP. L.J. 159 (1984). *See also* Harris, *Introduction*, 31 GEO. WASH. L. REV. 1 (1962).

20. *Statement of Marshall Siegal, Executive Director, Independent Owner-Operator Association before the U.S. Senate Committee on Commerce, Science and Transportation (September 21, 1983). See Congress and Unclear Oversight of ICC,* TRAFFIC WORLD, Oct. 17, 1983, at 1.

21. 83 Stat. 859 (1969).

22. As one prominent Washington, D.C. attorney observed:

The Commission became highly politicized during the Carter Administration, particularly after the appointment of several commissioners by President Carter. My opinion is that this was a regrettable happening and one which ought to be reversed.... As an independent regulatory agency, the ICC can be said to no longer exist....

The ICC is charged under the Interstate Commerce Act, as amended by both the Motor Carrier Act of 1980 and the Staggers Rail Act, with enforcing laws relating to transportation that are under its jurisdiction. Notwithstanding, its enforcement efforts have been feeble or nonexistent for the past several years. Many carriers are operating unlawfully and totally without required operating authority. Many carriers are charging rates other than the rates published and on file with the ICC even when they have authority. Yet the Commission does nothing.... Under the Motor Carrier Act of 1980, it has been said by some that the Commission's functions may be viewed as analogous to a three-legged stool. One leg represents entry and exit, the second represents rate regulation, and the third represents enforcement. If you cut all three legs from underneath the stool, you no longer have a viable stool. If the Commission itself cuts it own three legs off, then you no longer have a viable Commission, and one must question an expenditure of public funds to continue to support such an organization.

The better result would obtain if the Commission would wake up and start doing those things which its members were appointed to do under the law. The law says regulate entry; the Commission does not in an effective manner. The law says says regulate rates; the Commission does not even look at tariff filings any more. The law puts upon the Commission the obligation of enforcing compliance; the Commission essentially does nothing. While hardly anyone would want to return to the regulatory scheme of five or ten years ago, the current situation is an impossible one....

It is respectfully suggested that the former course of action is the only prudent and responsible one for the ICC to take and that the Commission should awake from its somnolence, depart from the direction set by political ideologues along which it presently travels, and get on with the business of responsibly regulating the motor carrier industry.

Lawyer Blames Political Ideologues for Commission's Regulatory Failures, TRAFFIC WORLD, May 24, 1982, at 34–35.

In 1977, the Senate Committee on Government Operations concluded that "for much of the past fifteen years, neither the White House nor the Senate has demonstrated a sustained commitment to high quality regulatory appointments." Study of Federal Regulation, Pursuant to S. Res. 71, Comm. on Gov't Op., 95th Con., 1st Sess. xxxi (1977).

The Interstate Commerce Commission . . . was, formerly, widely considered the most eminent and effective of all the federal agencies. Past Commissioners, such as Joseph Eastman, Clyde Aitchison, Howard Freas, Rupert Murphy, and others, were experienced, dedicated, and revered regulators, who created, molded and developed our renowned national transportation system. But with the enactment of the Presidential Reform Act of 1969, the Chairman, and the Commission itself, fell under the control of the President and his staff and became a political animal. This condition has been aggravated by the predetermined regulatory philosophies of the latest appointees to the Commission and their headlong rush to deregulate transportation. And if this means that they must disregard the governing laws, courts, Congress, or anyone else to do so, so be it.

D. Baker, Deregulation: Where We Were; Where We Are; Where We're Going (unpublished address before the Western Traffic Conference, Monterey, Calif.), at 100.

23. By the early 1970s, the role of political patronage in the appointment process had begun to come under serious criticism:

Although the appointment process ostensibly works to provide a Commission that will serve as the expert arm of Congress in the area of surface transportation, a greater interest for both the President and Congress is served by the chance to pay off political debts and provide jobs for political supporters. Therefore, two important qualifications for a Commissioner are his political connections and his political party.

R. FELLMETH, THE INTERSTATE COMMERCE OMMISSION 1 (1970).

24. Dempsey, *Congressional Intent and Agency Discretion—Never the Twain Shall Meet: The Motor Carrier Act of 1980*, 58 CHI. KENT. L. REV. 1 17 (1981).

25. *Id.* at 14–21; Freeman & Gerson, *Motor Carrier Operating Rights Proceedings—How Do I Lose Thee?*, 11 TRANSP. L.J. 13 (1979).

26. Argo-Collier Truck Lines Corp. v. United States, 611 F.2d 149, 155 (6th Cir. 1979).

27. Humboldt Express, Inc. v. ICC, 567 F.2d 1134, 1137 (D.C. Cir. 1977).

28. Trans-American Van Service, Inc. v. United States, 421 F. Supp. 308, 323 (N.D. Tex. 1976).

29. Kretsinger, Jr., *The Motor Carrier Act of 1980: Report and Analysis*, 50 UMKC L. REV. 21 (1981). "When Congress passed the Motor Carrier Act of 1980, it reduced but did not eliminate regulation of the trucking industry." Flexner, *The Effects of Deregulation in the Motor Carrier Industry*, ANTITRUST BULLETIN 185 (Spring 1983). "The legislation's early administrators greatly exaggerated the Act's deregulatory aspects and operated to liberalize its provisions far in excess of its Congressional mandate." Kretsinger, *id.* at 47. Another commentator echoed these thoughts:

The Interstate Commerce Commission and Department of Transportation, in concert, are prostituting the true intent of the Motor Carrier Act of 1980. . . . [T]he Congress is abdicating its responsibility when it allows the Executive Branch to usurp its Constitutional authority in this area.

DOT and ICC Are Held "Prostituting" Intent of Congress in Trucking Act, TRAFFIC WORLD, Sept. 5, 1983, at 13.

30. J. MADISON, FEDERALIST PAPERS NO. 15. As Justice Frankfurter noted:

The accretion of dangerous power does not come in a day. It does come, however slowly, from the degenerative force of unchecked disregard of the restrictions that fence in even the most disinterested assertion of authority.

Youngstown Sheet and Tube Co. v. Sawyer, 343 U.S. 579, 593 (1952).

31. *See* e.g., Immigration and Naturalization Service v. Chadha, 103 S.Ct. 2764 (1983).

32. *See* Verkuil, *Jawboning Administrative Agencies: Ex Parte Contacts by the White House*, 80 COLUM. L. REV. 943 (1980).

33. 295 U.S. 602 (1933).

34. *Id. See Preserving Independent Agencies' Authority*, TRAFFIC WORLD, Apr. 5, 1982, at 1.

35. *See* e.g., J. W. Hampton, Jr. & Co. v. United States, 276 U.S. 394 (1928) (upholding delegation to president of power to set certain customs duties under the Tariff Act of 1922).

36. *See* e.g., United States v. Grimaud, 220 U.S. 506 (1911) (upholding delegation of regulation-making authority to the Secretary of Agriculture); Buttfield v. Stranahan, 192 U.S. 470 (1904) (upholding delegation to Secretary of Treasury of power to set standards for imported tea). Executive branch agencies "are headed by single persons ultimately responsible to one person, the President." B. SCHWARTZ, ADMINISTRATIVE LAW 13 (1976).

37. This power of presidential approval or veto of independent regulatory action has largely been utilized in areas of foreign trade or commerce, such as international route licensing by the Civil Aeronautics Board or international economic retaliation for foreign anticompetitive practices by the International Trade Commission. *See* e.g., Dempsey, *Foreign Trade and Economic Injury—A Survey of U.S. Relief Mechanisms*, in V. NANDA (ed.), TRANSNATIONAL BUSINESS TRANSACTIONS, ch. 12, p. 1 (1981); Dempsey, *The International Rate and Route Revolution in North Atlantic Passenger Transportation*, 17 COLUM. J. TRANSNAT'L L. 393, 434–38 (1978).

38. *See* B. SCHWARTZ, *supra* note 36, at 13–18; *see also* Verkuil, *supra* note 32, at 943, 964–65.

39. *See* INS v. Chadha, 462 U.S. 919, 946 (1983); Verkuil, *supra* note 32, at 950.

40. Professor Freedman has explained the rationale for vesting legislative authority in the "headless" fourth branch of government as follows:

Closely related to New Deal views on the importance of agency expertise was the New Deal belief that the integrity of the administrative process would be protected by its independence from the executive and legislative branches of government. The theme that independence from the political process enhances the quality of administrative performance had been sounded by political scientists well before the New Deal, and those who rationalized the New Deal's reliance upon the administrative process gave particular stress to the "desire to have the fashioning of industrial policy removed to a degree from political influence."

Consequently, the grant to members of independent regulatory agencies of a substantial measure of protection against removal by the branch became one of the principal means of implementing the desire to free the administrative process from political constraints. The administrative process was further insulated from the President by legislation providing fixed terms of office for agency members which extended beyond the term of the appointing President and which limited the proportion of agency members who could belong to the same political party.

Freedman, *Crisis and Legitimacy in the Administrtive Process*, 27 STAN. L. REV. 1041, 1060–61 (1975) (footnotes omitted). "The current quasi-legislative, quasi-executive, quasi-judicial structure of the agencies gives them a powerful defense against overt political intervention." Cutler & Johnson, *Regulation and the Political Process*, 84 YALE L.J. 1395, 1401 (1975). But *see id.* at 1410–11 (arguing that presidential intervention in the regulatory process should be encouraged, rather than discouraged); *accord* Verkuil, *supra* note 32, at 958. "By their nature and organization, independent agencies have long resisted policy control by the President." *Id.* at 947.

41. B. SCHWARTZ, *supra* note 36, at 15–16. The Supreme Court similarly summarized the purposes of Congress in creating regulatory agencies such as the ICC in Humphrey's Executor v. United States, emphasizing the necessary independence of such bodies:

[It was Congress' intention] to create a body of experts who shall gain experience by length of service—a body which shall be independent of executive authority, *except in its selection*, and free to exercise its judgment without the leave or hindrance of any other official or any department of the government. . . . Such a body cannot in any proper sense be characterized as an arm or an eye of the executive. Its duties are performed without executive leave and . . . must be free from executive control.

295 U.S. 602, 625–28 (1933); *see also Preserving Independent Agencies' Authority*, TRAFFIC WORLD, Apr. 5, 1982, at 1 (discussing amendment to the Regulatory Reform Act of 1982 that would limit presidential influence on regulatory agencies).

42. One commentator has summarized many of the criticisms of the contemporary ICC as follows:

Comments from industry sources—carriers and shippers—on the quality of the current members of the Commission range from "inept" to "political hacks." Seldom, it would seem, has the Commission been held in such low regard. . . . Is the ICC, an independent regulatory agency that is supposed to be an arm of Congress, no longer listening to Congress; has it become a political body that listens to the Administration that sits in the White House?

Byrne, *ICC Chairman Taylor Again Displays Depth of Rift between Commissioners*, TRAFFIC WORLD, Apr. 16, 1984, at 46–47. Dean Verkuil has noted that "[h]ighly charged White House intervention poses a danger of frustrating the will of Congress as expressed in legislation establishing an agency and defining its mission." Verkuil, *supra* note 32, at 949–50.

43. F. FRANKFURTER, OF LAW AND LIFE AND OTHER THINGS THAT MATTER, 245 (1965).

44. *Air Travel Altered by Deregulation*, DENVER POST, Oct. 31, 1988, at 9C.

45. *Ex-Official Suggests Lid on Air Fares*, ROCKY MOUNTAIN NEWS, Nov. 5, 1987, at 100.

46. Knox, *Policy Shift Silent Factor in Crash?*, ROCKY MOUNTAIN NEWS, Oct. 4, 1988, at 2B.

47. Rowen, *Airline Deregulation at 10: Did the Theory Fail*, WASHINGTON POST, Oct. 16, 1988, at H1, H10.

48. Carroll, *Higher Fares, Better Service Are Forecast*, USA TODAY, Oct. 24, 1988, at 2B.

49. Knox, *supra* note 45.

50. Eastman, *Twelve Point Primer*, 16 TRANSP. L.J. 175–77 (1987).

12

SUMMARY AND CONCLUSIONS

Federal deregulation of transportation began a decade ago. As a consequence, things today are radically different in the air, over the rails, and on the highways. Trends toward concentration, pricing and service discrimination, and deterioration in service and safety are now readily apparent.

Airlines were the first to be deregulated, with the promulgation of the Airline Deregulation Act of 1978. The industry rapidly became an oligopoly, with an unprecedented wave of mergers, consolidations, and bankruptcies. Today, the top eight airlines dominate more than 94% of the domestic passenger market.

Billions of dollars in aviation trust funds lay idle as air traffic control towers are still staffed below pre-PATCO strike levels. That, coupled with the industry's unrealistic scheduling, funneling of aircraft into "hub-and-choke" bottlenecks, and filling of cockpits with near-adolescent pilots, have significantly narrowed the margin of safety and sent the number of near misses skyrocketing.

Airline service has gone to hell in the 1980s. We are herded aboard aerial slums, served cardboard food, overbooked, bumped, and misconnected. Our luggage is routed through the Twilight Zone, never again to be seen during our natural lives.

Business and small town travelers routinely pay several hundred dollars more than the vacation travelers seated next to them. The market gives us a choice, of course. We can either spend an arm and a leg or sleep in a strange city on a Saturday night.

The bus industry was deregulated with the enactment of the Bus Regulatory Reform Act of 1982. Since then, it has evolved from a duopoly into a monopoly, as Greyhound and Trailways merged. Deregulation has allowed them to abandon several thousand small towns and raise rates to those they still choose to serve. In much of rural America, the bus no longer stops on Main Street.

Railroads were deregulated with the Staggers Rail Act of 1980. This industry has also become highly concentrated during the last decade. Today, seven megacarriers handle 86% of the industry's freight and earn 93% of its profits. Under deregulation, they have been free to use their monopoly power to extort whatever the market will bear. Exorbitant rates for the movement of coal have been passed on to consumers in the form of billions of dollars in higher electric rates.

Since 1980, railroads have abandoned service to more than 1,200 small towns. Service curtailments by airlines, bus companies, and railroads make it increasingly difficult for small towns to attract new investment, or indeed, to dissuade existing businesses from leaving.

The trucking industry was largely deregulated with the promulgation of the Motor Carrier Act of 1980. It is also becoming an oligopoly, as the top 10 motor carriers move 60% of general freight and reap 90% of its profits. Every year since 1983, more than 1,000 trucking companies have plunged into the abyss of bankruptcy.

Since most of the industry is suffering from economic anemia, many carriers don't have the money to repair or replace aged and defective equipment. Many are pushing their drivers and equipment beyond the limit. As a consequence, truck-related fatalities have soared to more than 4,000 annually in recent years. Too often these days, we are sharing our highways with trucks and drivers in no shape to be on the road.

Under deregulation, large businesses enjoy a decided advantage as they flex their monopsony muscles to dictate pricing discounts. Meanwhile, small shippers must pay the higher, published rates. With the exception of a few winners (notably the Fortune 500 corporations), deregulation has been, at best, an inconvenience, and at worst, a disaster. Small shippers and small communities now pay more for poorer service. The short-term benefits larger shippers enjoy have been taken out of the hides of employees and investors of thousands of bankrupt corporations whose carcasses now litter the market.

The surviving companies have merged into ever larger megacarriers. Such concentrations of wealth and power would have been challenged by government during any other period of American history. Paradoxically, while the nation was initially euphoric over deregulation, experience has made the American public increasingly dissatisfied with it. Nonetheless, our federal government stubbornly adheres to its blind faith in the curative powers of Adam Smith.

Any analysis of the costs and benefits of deregulation must take into account these factors: the market for transportation services is not perfectly competitive; economies of scale and scope do exist; economic barriers to new entry in several of the modes are significant; oligopolies and monopolies have resulted; and the theory of contestable markets has not been sustained by the empirical evidence.

Moreover, inequality of bargaining power is reflected in the overwhelming monopsony power exerted by large shippers against trucking companies. The Fortune 500 wield tremendous bargaining leverage by conferring or withholding freight, and unilaterally dictate prices lower than the published rates. Such discrimination gives large shippers a decided and unfair advantage over smaller rivals in the larger market for the sale of goods. Common carriers are the gatekeepers of that larger market. If a small enterprise cannot gain access to that market at a fair price, it cannot compete. If a small town cannot obtain adequate transportation service at a reasonable rate, it cannot hope to enjoy economic growth. Regulation can ameliorate that inequality of bargaining power by prohibiting pricing and service discrimination.

Only regulation can promote public interest values which do not find a high priority in a regime of laissez faire. It can foster economic growth in rural areas by requiring nondiscriminatory access to infrastructure services. Fairly priced transportation services help facilitate access to the broader American economic pie by a larger number and more diverse group of participants. Both opportunities for wealth and pluralism are thereby enhanced. Regulation can also facilitate safety by ensuring that efficient and well-managed carriers are allowed to earn a reasonable return on investment.[1]

Congress partially or wholly preempted intrastate regulation of air, rail, and bus transport. However, it left intrastate regulation of motor carriers to the states. Although a few states embraced deregulation in the early 1980s, enthusiasm with the movement has waned as the American public has had more experience with it. Today, the overwhelming majority of states continue to regulate trucking companies. As a consequence, the deleterious social impact of deregulation has not been as severe for trucking as for the other, more comprehensively deregulated, transport modes.

Economic regulation, responsibly and prudently administered, can foster the following social and economic policies:

Avoidance of Problems of Imperfect Competition. Regulation can avoid problems of concentrations of wealth and power—the monopsony power of large shippers and the oligopoly or monopoly power of large carriers. Market power enables a firm to maximize its profits by raising prices and/ or lowering service. The transfer of wealth from consumers to producers is regressive in character, and therefore, undesirable.

Equality of Access. Regulation can ensure that all users of infrastructure services, large and small, enjoy equality of access to the market for the sale of their products. Prohibitions against rate discrimination allow small shippers the same opportunity to compete that large shippers have. In a sense, this stimulates competition in the market for the sale of goods. Moreover, giving small businesses the same chance to compete may indirectly facilitate employment, for small businesses create most of America's jobs.

Economic Growth. Regulation can enhance the social policy of encouraging a geographic distribution of economic growth. Thus, under regulation, small towns and rural communities enjoy adequate service at a fair price, in spite of the fact that less competition for such traffic exists than in larger markets. Adequate and reasonably priced infrastructure services are essential for economic growth.

Productivity. Regulation can prevent overcapacity in the transportation industry and thereby improve carrier productivity and economic health. Under regulation, efficient and well-managed carriers can earn a reasonable return on investment. This enhances service dependability and gives carriers the resources necessary to maintain and replace aged and worn equipment.

Safety. As noted above, by enhancing productivity, regulation can allow efficient and well-managed carriers to earn a reasonable profit, and thereby allow them the means to repair or replace equipment. Decent returns can also remove the incentive for drivers to sit behind the wheel for excessive lengths of time. The prospect of certificate revocation encourages voluntary industry compliance with established safety standards.

Adam Smith recognized that the width and breadth of the market is defined by the price and availability of transportation services.[2] Economist Armen Alchian notes that the competitive vitality of the market for the sale of goods is directly stimulated by transportation access thereto.[3] He observes that a nation's wealth is enhanced by the value of its cooperative resources, including transportation: "A richer country with lots of capital equipment and stable, market-facilitating institutions is a more efficient place for a given amount of labor."[4] What is true for a nation must also be true for any of its geograhic regions. Government can stimulate a geographic disbursement of economic growth and competitive alternatives for consumers by insisting that all regions (small towns and rural communities included) enjoy adequate, nondiscriminatory, and reasonably priced transportation. It is upon that foundation that commerce is built.

In order to have a healthy economy, all businesses and communities, large and small, must have nondiscriminatory access to the infrastructure industries or they cannot successfully compete. If small shippers cannot get their goods to market at a reasonable rate, they simply will not survive. If a rural community does not enjoy adequate transportation service at a fair price, it will be isolated from the mainsteam of commerce and wither on the vine.

Transportation's importance to the nation's economy is reflected in the role it plays in facilitating the nation's commerce, communications, and national defense.[5] As noted by Professor Addus, "transportation plays a vital role in economic growth.... Transportation and economic development are mutually interdependent—transportation improvement stimulates economic growth, and advances in economic development increase the demand for transportation."[6]

These features distinguish transportation from most other industries and explain why the provision of such services is regulated in the public interest, and has been since an early point in Anglo-American history. In its seminal decision in *Munn v. Illinois*,[7] the U.S. Supreme Court noted that beginning with the early common law of England, common carriers have been deemed to be "affected with a public interest" for they "stand in the very 'gateway of commerce,' and, take a toll from all who pass."[8]

Transportation firms are the gatekeepers to the larger market for the sale of goods. This gives them the leverage to facilitate or impede commerce, and makes their rate and service offerings critically important to all who require access to the market for the sale of their products. As Professor Martin Farris has observed, "in order to flourish, it is necessary to have a reliable and financially sound motor transportation system. Transportation is the 'life-blood' of the economy—the veins and arteries through which commerce flows."[9]

Economic regulation protects public interest values that might not find a high priority in the marketplace. It treats common carriers (e.g., airline, bus, trucking, railroad, and telephone companies) as industries imbued with a unique responsibility to satisfy the needs of the public for universal service at just and reasonable rates. Small and large communities and shippers are required by government to be served reasonably well and at a nondiscriminatory price.[10]

By no means does this suggest that even the most omniscient regulatory commission can make all the decisions concerning levels of production and pricing. We leave that to individual, privately owned firms, with regulatory bodies identifying the broad perimeters within which the firms may lawfully operate. While the invisible hands of the marketplace make most of the decisions regarding the level of service and price to be provided by privately owned companies competing for customers, the public utilities commissions in the vast majority of states regulate, in general terms, motor carrier entry, rates, and levels of service in order to protect the public interest. As Dabney Waring has observed:

Government has responsibilities, principal among which is maintaining the infrastructure of essential services necessary for the commerce and amenities of a civilized nation. Certainly the government would be a poor manager of the motor carrier industry or of any business. But it is the metes and bounds, parameters, if you will, of performance. It is requiring that carriers fulfill their common carrier obligation; of seeing that service is not abandoned when there is not a viable alternative; of monitoring service offerings to see that capacity is not so far in excess of demand that gross waste results; of opening entry selectively to assure adequate numbers of carriers; of preventing any semblance of predatory pricing; of forbidding exploitation of market dominance situations be they in the area of geography, commodity, size of a shipment, or whatever.[11]

Regulation imposes upon common carriers both a burden and a benefit. The burden is the obligation to provide an adequate level of service to all geographic areas within their operating licenses, at reasonable prices. In return for providing just and reasonable nondiscriminatory rates to small shippers and small communities, the regulated enterprise enjoys the benefit of a franchise of operating authority which shields it from predatory practices by its larger competitors.[12]

There are undoubtedly winners and losers in any war waged as passionately as this one, to deregulate a major American industry.[13] Any change in public policy as profound as deregulation inevitably produces serious social and economic dislocations. As we have seen, the winners of federal interstate deregulation are the Fortune 500—the largest carriers and largest shippers—which bask in the sun of deregulation. The losers are small businesses and small towns and rural communities, which have been left out in the cold.

Who would win if motor carriage were further deregulated? Again, large shippers would win. It is they who reap the bounty of discriminatory pricing in the deregulated interstate freight market, forcing their smaller rivals to bear the fixed-cost burden of common carriers. Hence, additional deregulation would benefit the relatively modest number of large shippers at the expense of the far more numerous small shippers.

Large interstate trucking companies would also win, for they have the economic muscle to drive out smaller rivals. As noted above, oligopolies have become the norm in all other deregulated modes of transportation.

Small businesses and small towns and rural communities would lose, paying a higher price for the same or poorer service. The existing regulatory system protects small businesses and small towns from the economic burden of pricing and service discrimination. This is a major feature of economic regulation that is well worth preserving.

Drivers of automobiles would lose, for the heavy trucks with which they share the highways would become increasingly unsafe, as maintenance was deferred and the costs of safety externalized. America's citizens deserve to share their interstate highways with safe trucks and truck drivers, and not be subjected to the risk of injury or death posed by unregulated truckers. Preserving the existence and vitality of efficient small and medium-sized trucking companies will not only allow them to maintain a healthy competitive presence in the economic environment but will also allow them to put safe vehicles and safe drivers on the highways.

Our federal experiment with deregulation should teach us that transportation is not a purely competitive industry, and that the theoretical benefits of pure competition have not emerged. To the extent that some pricing competition has occurred (albeit at the expense of a sharp decline in service and safety), these benefits have been unevenly distributed in favor of large shippers and some large communities. Moreover, such benefits may be a short-term phenomenon, for they are seriously jeopardized by an unprecedented level of industry concentration as the dust kicked up by deregulation begins to settle. The empirical results of deregulation also demonstrate that much is lost when the government declines to promote the public's interest in achieving broader societal benefits, such as protecting market access for small shippers and small communities, and enhancing safety.

Prudently administered economic regulation can not only accomplish important public policy goals of correcting imperfections in the market, such as those resulting from economies of scale and scope, barriers to entry, market power, inequality of bargaining power, insufficiency of information, and externalities—it can also advance important social objectives which do not find a high priority in a regime of laissez faire. The primordial imperative of economics man is the accumulation of wealth, and this may conflict with society's desire to accomplish other important objectives, such as stimulating economic growth in rural communities and small towns or enhancing safety.

Private ownership of the means of production inspires the efficient and economical allocation of scarce resources. These are important public benefits, and ought to be encouraged under enlightened regulation. But government oversight of some managerial decisions can protect other public interest values, beyond allocative efficiency. Administrative agencies with regulatory power can balance the public interest against market imperatives, assure that the economies and efficiencies of private ownership are tapped for the public good, avoid the problems of imperfect competition, and foster public interest values that do not find a high priority in an environment of laissez faire.

Neither governmental control nor unregulated competition are perfect environments. The real choice is between imperfect regulation and imperfect competition. But if applied with a gentle touch, economic regulation ought to be able to yield the best of both worlds—the economies and efficiencies of private ownership and the accomplishment of social and economic policies in the highest public interest.

NOTES

1. The following are the broader impacts of transportation deregulation:

Carrier productivity gains predicted to result from deregulation have not materialized. Perfect competition does not exist in the industry. Economies of scale and scope and economic barriers to entry do exist. Unprecedented bankruptcies and mergers have radically increased concentration to the point that the transport modes have become oligopolies and monopolies.

Under deregulation, pricing discrimination in favor of large shippers and against small shippers and small communities is widespread. Many large shippers hold monopsony power to dictate pricing discounts. Increasingly, small shippers are forced to bear the fixed costs of operation.

In most transport modes, deregulation has brought about a decline in levels of service. For small towns and rural communities, prices have increased and service has declined sharply under deregulation, making it more difficult to sustain economic growth and employment. In trucking, this impact has been tempered by the fact that the overwhelming number of states continue to regulate intrastate service levels, and prohibit pricing discrimination.

As deregulation continues to jeopardize the economc health of carriers, many firms lack the resources to upgrade or repair aged and defective equipment. Many drivers are pushed beyond reasonable limits. As a result, truck-related accidents and fatalities have soared.

2. A. SMITH, AN INQUIRY INTO THE NATURE AND CAUSES OF THE WEALTH OF NATIONS 19–23 (1985 ed.).

3. A. ALCHIAN & W. ALLEN, EXCHANGE AND PRODUCTION 275 (3rd ed. 1983).

4. Id. at 173.

5. P. DEMPSEY, LAW & FOREIGN POLICY IN INTERNATIONAL AVIATION 1 (1987).

6. Addus, Subsidizing Air Service to Small Communities, 39 TRANSP. Q. 537, 551–52 (1985).

7. 94 U.S. (4 Otto) 113 (1877).

8. Id.

9. Oversight of the Motor Carrier Act of 1980: Hearings before the Subcomm. on Surface Transportation of the Senate Comm. on Commerce, Science and Transportation, 99th Cong., 1st sess. 270 (statement of Prof. Martin T. Farris).

10. See Dempsey, The Interstate Commerce Commission—Disintegration of an American Legal Institution, 34 AM. U. L. REV. 1, 48 (1984).

11. Waring, Motor Carrier Regulation—By State or by Market?, 51 ICC PRAC. J. 240, 242 (1984).

12. Dempsey, Deregulation Stranding Residents of the Lone Prairie, ROCKY MOUNTAIN NEWS, Sept. 14, 1986, at 73.

13. See R. LEONE, WHO PROFITS—WINNERS, LOSERS AND GOVERNMENT REGULATION (1986).

SELECTED BIBLIOGRAPHY

Addus, Abdussalam A. "Subsidizing Air Service to Small Communities." *Transportation Quarterly* 39 (1985): 537–49.

Ahmed, Samir. "Air Transportation to Small Communities: Passenger Characteristics and Perceptions of Service Attributes." *Transportation Quarterly* 38 (1984): 15–21.

Areeda, Phillip. "Antitrust Laws and Public Utility Regulation." *Bell Journal of Economics and Management Science* 3 (Spring 1972): 42–57.

Areeda, Phillip and Donald F. Turner. "Predatory Pricing and Related Prices under Section 2 of the Sherman Act." *Harvard Law Review* 88 (1975): 697–733.

Augello, William J. "The Deregulation Disaster." *Eleventh International Air Forum*, 28 September 1982.

Bailey, Elizabeth E. *Economic Theory of Regulatory Constraint.* Lexington, Mass.: Lexington Books, 1973.

Bailey, Elizabeth E. and John Panzar. "The Contestability of Airline Markets During the Transition to Deregulation." *Law and Contemporary Problems* 44 (1981): 125.

Bailey, Elizabeth E., David R. Graham, and Daniel P. Kaplan. *Deregulating the Airlines.* Cambridge, Mass.: MIT Press, 1985.

Baker, Daniel W. and Raymond A. Greene, Jr. Commercial Zones and Terminal Areas: History, Development, Expansion, Deregulation, *Transportation Law Journal* 10:171.

Baker, David H. Section 214 of the Staggers Rail Act: Is It Working as Congress Intended?, *Transportation Law Journal* 14:205.

Basedow, Jurgen. Common Carriers—Continuity and Disintegration in United States Transportation Law—Part One, *Transportation Law Journal* 13:1.

———. Common Carriers—Continuity and Disintegration in United States Transportation Law—Part Two, *Transportation Law Journal* 13:159.

Baumol, William J. "Some Subtle Issues in Railroad Regulation." *International Journal of Transport Economics* 10 (April/August 1983): 341–55.

———. "Use of Antitrust to Subvert Competition." *Journal of Law and Economics* 28 (May 1985): 247–65.

Beilock, Richard. "Is Regulation Needed for Value of Service Pricing?" *Rand Journal of Economics* 16 (Spring 1985): 93–102.

Beilock, Richard and James Freeman. "Deregulated Motor Carrier Service to Small Communities." *Transportation Journal* (Summer 1984): 71–82.

Berger, Robert G. The Constitutionality of State Approval Requirements for the Acquisition or Transfer of Control of a Common Carrier or Public Utility, *Transportation Law Journal* 14:227.

Berger, Robert G. and Stephanie J. Mitchell. Predatory Pricing in the Airline Industry: A Case Study—The Policies and Practices of the CAB, *Transportation Law Journal* 13:287.

Bober, Gerald M. Elimination of Gateways in Section 5(2) and 21(b) Proceedings, *Transportation Law Journal* 9:257.

Boberg, Kevin B. and Dennis M. Gawlik. The Evolution and Implications of the Market Dominance Concept in Railroad Ratemaking, *Transportation Law Journal* 13:259.

Bock, Edwin A. *Government Regulation of Business.* Englewood Cliffs, N.J.: Prentice-Hall, 1962, 1963, 1965.

Bohlander, George W. and Martin T. Farris. "Collective Bargaining in Trucking—The Effects of Deregulation." *Logistics and Transportation Review* 20, no. 3 (1984): 223–38.

Booth, Dean. Chartered Flights and Scheduled Airlines, *Transportation Law Journal* 4:127.

Borchert, John. "American Metropolitan Evolution." *Geographical Review* 57 (1967): 301–32.

Bowersox, Donald J., Calabro, Pat J., and Wagenheim, George D. *Introduction to Transportation.* New York: Macmillan, 1981.

Boyd, Alan S., Stanford G. Ross, and Richard L. Teberg. New Dimensions in Transportation Law, *Transportation Law Journal* 1:1.

Boyer, Kenneth D. "How Similar Are Motor Carriers and Rail Rate Structures? The Value of Service Component." *Transportation Research Forum Proceedings* 19, no. 1 (1978): 523–31.

———. "Equalizing Discrimination and Cartel Pricing in Transport Rate Regulation." *Journal of Political Economy* 89 (April 1981): 270–86.

Braeutigam, Ronald R. and Roger G. Noll. "The Regulation of Surface Freight Transportation: The Welfare Effects Revisited." *Review of Economics and Statistics* 66 (February 1984): 80–87.

Breen, Denis A. "Antitrust and Price Competition in the Trucking Industry." *Antitrust Bulletin* 28 (Spring 1983): 201–25.

Brenner, Melvin A. "Airline Deregulation—A Case Study in Public Policy Failure." *Transportation Law Journal* 16 (1988): 179–227.

Brenner, Melvin A., James O. Leet, and Elihu Schott. *Airline Deregulation.* Westport, Conn.: Eno Foundation for Transportation, 1985.

Brodley, Joseph F. "Joint Ventures and Antitrust Policy." *Harvard Law Review* 95 (May 1982): 1521–88.

Brooks, Robert J. Recent Decisions of the Interstate Commerce Commission, *Transportation Law Journal* 9:9.

Brown, David and Kenneth Deavers. *Rural Economic Development in the 1980's.* Washington, D.C.: U.S. Department of Agriculture, 1987.

Brown, Terence A. "Freight Brokers and General Commodity Trucking." *Transportation Journal* (Winter 1984): 4–14.

Bruning, Edward and Edward A. Morash. "Deregulation and the Cost of Equity Capital." *Transportation Journal* (Winter 1983): 72–81.

Bruning, Edward and Larry Oberdick. "Market Structure and Economic Performance in the Commuter Airline Industry." *Transportation Journal* 21 (1982): 76.

Bruning, Edward and Peter M. Lynagh. "Carrier Evaluation in Physical Distribution Management." *Journal of Business Logistics* 5, no. 2 (1984): 30–47.

Burghardt, Steve and Michael Fabricant. *Working under the Safety Net: Policy and Practice with the New American Poor.* Newberry Park, Calif.: Sage Human Services Guide 47, Sage Publications, 1987.

CAB, "Report of the CAB Special Staff on Regulatory Reform." 1975.

Carlton, D., W. Landes, and R. Posner. "Benefits and Costs of Airline Mergers: A Case Study." *Bell Journal of Economics* 11 (1980): 65.

Caves, Douglas W., Laurits R. Christensen, and Michael W. Tretheway. "Airline Productivity under Deregulation." *Regulation* (November/December 1982): 25.

———. "Productivity Performance of U.S. Trunk and Local Service Airlines in the Era of Deregulation." *Economic Inquiry* (July 1983): 312.

Caves, Richard. *Air Transport and Its Regulators: An Industry Study.* Cambridge, Mass.: Harvard University Press, 1962.

Cavinato, Joseph L. "Pricing Strategies for Private Trucking." *Journal of Business Logistics* 3, no. 2 (1982): 72–84.

Cherington, Paul W. and David M. Schwartz. The Common Ownership Issue from Political Ideology to a Practical Consideration of Practices and Goals for Public Service, *Transportation Law Journal* 2:1.

Chow, Garland and Richard D. Gritta. "Motor Carrier Bankruptcy: An Industry Assessment of Financial Condition." *Transportation Research Forum Proceedings* 26, no. 1 (1985): 434–40.

Chow, Garland and Richard D. Gritta. Motor Carrier Bankruptcy in an Uncertain Environment, *Transportation Law Journal* 14:39.

Christian, Betty Jo. From Litigator to Commissioner—Some Thoughts on Judicial Review, *Transportation Law Journal* 9:1.

Civil Aeronautics Board. *Competition and the Airlines: An Evaluation of Deregulation.* Washington, D.C.: 1982.

———. *Implementation of the Provisions of the Airline Deregulation Act of 1978.* Civil Aeronautics Board Report to the Congress. January 31, 1984.

———. "A Staff Study: Report on Airline Service, Fares, Traffic, Load Factors, and Market Shares." Service Status as of June 1, 1984, Issue No. 31. Washington, D.C.: 1984.

Conzen, Michael P. "A Transport Interpretation of the Growth of Urban Regions: An American Example." *Journal of Historical Geography* 1 (1975): 361–82.

Cook, Cheryl A. and Charles N. Marshall. Issues of Cost Recovery in the Debate over Competitive Access, *Transportation Law Journal* 15:9.

Cox, Ernest G. One Third Century of Motor Carrier Safety Regulation, *Transportation Law Journal* 2:173.

Crew, E. C. and Lester M. Bridgeman. "Do Antitrust Laws Provide a Feasible

Alternative to Regulation?" *ICC Practitioners Journal* 47 (September/October 1980): 673–97.

Davis, Grant M. "Transportation Regulation: Another Dimension." *ICC Practitioners Journal* 42 (January/February 1975): 164–74.

———. *Transportation Regulation: A Pragmatic Assessment.* Danville, Ill.: Interstate, 1976.

———. "The Collective Ratemaking Issue: Circa 1984." *Transportation Practitioners Journal* 52 (Fall 1984): 60–68.

Davis, Grant M. and John E. Dillard, Jr. "Collective Ratemaking—Does It Have a Future in the Motor Carrier Industry?" *ICC Practitioners Journal* 49 (September/October 1982): 1112–29.

Davis, Grant M. and Linda J. Combs. "Some Observations Regarding Value of Service Pricing in Transportation." *Transportation Journal* 14 (Spring 1975): 49–58.

Dempsey, Paul S. Transportation Deregulation—On a Collision Course?, *Transportation Law Journal* 13:329.

———. "The Contemporary Evolution of Intermodal and International Transport Regulation under the Interstate Commerce Act: Land, Sea, and Air Coordination of Foreign Commerce Movements." *Vanderbilt Journal of Transnational Law* 10 (Fall 1977), 505.

———. "Entry Control under the Interstate Commerce Act: A Comparative Analysis of the Statutory Criteria Governing Entry in Transportation." *Wake Forest Law Review* 13 (Winter 1977), 729.

———. Turbulence in the "Open Skies." The Deregulation of International Air Transport, *Transportation Law Journal* 15:305.

———. "The International Rate and Route Revolution in North Atlantic Passenger Transportation." *Columbia Journal of Transnational Law* 17, no. 3 (1978).

———. "The Rise and Fall of the Civil Aeronautics Board—Opening Wide the Floodgates of Entry." *Transportation Law Journal* 11 (1979): 91, 123–27.

———. "Congressional Intent and Agency Discretion—Never the Twain Shall Meet: The Motor Carrier Act of 1980." *Chicago Kent Law Review* 58, no. 1 (1981).

———. "Rate Regulation and Antitrust Immunity in Transportation: The Genesis and Evolution of This Endangered Species." *American University Law Review* 32 (1983): 335, 345–49.

———. "The Interstate Commerce Commission—Disintegration of an American Legal Institution." *American University Law Review* 34 (Fall 1984), 1.

———. "The Dark Side of Deregulation: Its Impact on Small Communities." *Administrative Law Review* 39 (1987): 445–65.

———. "The Role of the International Civil Aviation Organization on Deregulation, Discrimination, and Dispute Resolution." *Journal of Air Law and Commerce* 52 (1987).

———. "Aerial Dogfights over Europe: The Liberalization of EEC Air Transport." *Journal of Air Law and Commerce* 53 (1988).

———. *Law and Foreign Policy in International Aviation.* New York, NY: Transnational Publishers, 1987.

Dempsey, Paul S. and William E. Thoms. *Law and Economic Regulation in Transportation.* Westport, Conn.: Quorum Books, 1986.

De Vany, Arthur. "The Effect of Price and Entry Regulation on Airline Output, Capacity, and Efficiency." *Bell Journal of Economics* 5 (1975): 327.

————. "Product Quality, Uncertainty, and Regulation: The Trucking Industry." *American Economic Review* 67 (September 1977): 583–94.

De Vany, A. S. and T. R. Saving. "Competition and Value of Service Pricing in the Trucking Industry: Reply." *American Economic Review* 70 (March 1980): 181–85.

Dewey, Donald. "Welfare and Collusion: Reply." *American Economic Review* 72 (March 1982): 267–81.

Dively, Dwight. "Applications of Regulatory Theory to the Trucking Industry." *Research in Law and Economics* 6 (1984): 211–26.

Douglas, George and James Miller, III. "The CAB's Domestic Passenger Fare Investigation." *Bell Journal of Economics* 5 (1974): 205.

————. *Economic Regulation of Domestic Air Transport*. Washington, D.C.: Brookings Institution, 1974.

Dupre, Steven C. A Thinking Person's Guide to Entry/Exit Deregulation in the Airline Industry, *Transportation Law Journal* 9:273.

Eads, George. *The Local Service Airline Experiment*. Washington, D.C.: Brookings Institution, 1972.

Eckhardt, Robert C. The Western Coal Traffic League Case: Condoning ICC Eschewal of Rail Monopoly Ratemaking, *Transportation Law Journal* 13:307.

Ellison, Anthony. "The Structural Change of the Airline Industry Following Deregulation." *Transportation Journal* 21 (1982): 58–69.

Enis, Charles and Edward A. Morash. "The Economic Losses from the Devaluation of Motor Carrier Operating Rights." *ICC Practitioners' Journal* 50 (July-August 1983): 542–55.

————. Market Protection, Deregulation, and the Question of Industry Losses, *Transportation Law Journal* 15:89.

Erenberg, Michael and Bruce M. Kasson. Railroad—Motor Carrier Intermodal Ownership, *Transportation Law Journal* 12:75.

Fair, Marvin L. and John Guandolo. *Transportation Regulation*. Dubuque, Iowa: Wm. C. Brown Co., 1979.

Farris, M. T. "Discrimination in Transportation and Antitrust Laws." *ICC Practitioners Journal* 46 (May/June 1979): 509–25.

Felton, John Richard. "The Impact of Rate Regulation upon ICC-Regulated Truck Back Hauls." *Journal of Transport Economics and Policy* 15 (September 1981): 253–67.

Ferrar, Tery A. Route Assignments and the C.A.B., *Transportation Law Journal* 5:215.

Folse, Parker C. "Antitrust and Regulated Industries: A Critique and Proposal for Reform of the Implied Immunity Doctrine." *Texas Law Review* 57 (May 1979): 751–828.

Freeman, James and Richard Beilock. "State Regulatory Responses to Federal Motor Carrier Reregulation." *University of Florida Law Review* 25 (Winter 1983).

Freeman, James. The Ties that Bind: Railroads, Coal, Utilities, the ICC, and the Public Interest, *Transportation Law Journal* 14:1.

Freeman, James W. and Robert W. Gerson. Motor Carrier Operating Rights Proceedings—How Do I Lose Thee?, *Transportation Law Journal* 11:13.

Frew, James R. "The Existence of Monopoly Profits in the Motor Carrier Industry." *Journal of Law and Economics* 24 (October 1981): 289–315.

Friedlaender, Ann F. *The Dilemma of Freight Transport Regulation.* Washington, D.C.: Brookings Institution, 1969.

Friedlaender, Ann F. and Richard Spady. *Freight Transport Regulation: Equity, Efficiency and Competition in the Rail and Trucking Industries.* Cambridge, Mass.: MIT Press, 1981.

Friedman, Jesse J. "Collective Ratemaking by Motor Common Carriers: Economic and Public Policy Considerations." *Transportation Law Journal* 9 (October 1978): 33–53.

———. "What's Wrong with the Case against Collective Ratemaking: Rejoinder to James C. Miller III." *Transportation Law Journal* 11 (December 1980): 301–22.

Gardiner, Paul S. "Rate Bureau Functions without Antitrust Immunity: A Suggested Strategy for Motor Freight Carriers." *ICC Practitioners Journal* 46 (July/August 1979): 651–68.

Gaskins, Darius W. and James M. Voytko. "Managing the Transition to Deregulation." *Law and Contemporary Problems* 44 (Winter 1981): 9–32.

Gawlik, Dennis M. and Kevin B. Boberg. The Evolution and Implications of the Market Dominance Concept in Railroad Ratemaking, *Transportation Law Journal* 13:259.

Glaskowsky, Nicholas A. *Effects of Deregulation on Motor Carriers.* Westport, Conn.: Eno Foundation, 1986.

Goetz, Andrew R. "The Effect of Airline Deregulation on Air Service to Small and Medium-Sized Communities: Case Studies in Northeastern Ohio." Ph.D. Dissertation, Ohio State University, 1987.

Goetz, Andrew R. and Paul S. Dempsey. "Airline Deregulation: Ten Years After." Working paper, 1989.

Goodman, Leonard S. Getting Started: Organization, Procedure and Initial Business of the ICC in 1887, *Transportation Law Journal* 16:7.

Graham, David and Daniel Kaplan. "Airline Deregulation is Working." *Regulation* (May/June 1982): 26.

Gritta, Richard D. Profitability and Risk in Air Transport: A Case for Deregulation, *Transportation Law Journal* 7:197.

Gritta, Richard D. and Garland Chow. Motor Carrier Bankruptcy in an Uncertain Environment, *Transportation Law Journal* 14:39.

Guandolo, John. Intermodal Acquisition under the Interstate Commerce Act, *Transportation Law Journal* 2:11.

———. *Transportation Law.* Dubuque, Iowa: Wm. C. Brown Co., 1965, 1973.

Hardaway, Robert. "Transportation Deregulation (1978–1984): Turning the Tide." *Transportation Law Journal* (1985): 101.

Hardman, James C. *The FLSA and Motor Carrier Operations.* Chicago: Pilgrim Enterprises, 1974.

Harmatuck, Donald J. "Effect of Economic Conditions on Motor Carrier Tonnage and Regulation." *Transportation Journal* 24 (Winter 1984): 31–39.

Harper, Donald V. "Consequences of Reform of Federal Economic Regulation of the Motor Trucking Industry." *Transportation Journal* 21 (Summer 1982): 35–58.

———. Entry Control and the Federal Motor Carrier Act of 1980, *Transportation Law Journal* 12:51.

————. "The Marketing Revolution in the Motor Trucking Industry," *Journal of Business Logistics* 4, no. 1 (1983): 35–50.

Havens, Arnold I. and David A. Heymsfeld. "Small Community Air Service under the Airline Deregulation Act of 1978." *Journal of Air Law and Commerce* 46 (1981): 641–86.

Hoover, Harwood, Jr. "Pricing Behavior of Deregulated Motor Carriers." *Transportation Journal* 25 (Winter 1985): 55–61.

Illinois Commerce Commission. *Illinois Bus Service since the Bus Act: A Diminishing Intercity Network*, Springfield: 1984.

Interstate Commerce Commission. Missouri, Kansas, and Oklahoma Coach Lines— Oklahoma Corporation Commission, No. MCC–36364, February 29, 1984.

Jacobs, Leslie W. "Regulated Motor Carriers and the Antitrust Laws." *Cornell Law Review* 58 (November 1972): 90–135.

Janis, Russell A. A Law and Economics Study of Rail Freight Regulation: Traditional Standards, Ramsey Prices, and a Case of Neither, *Transportation Law Journal* 15:31.

Jaskiewicz, Leonard A. and Edward J. Kiley. *Free Wheeling? A Reference for Economic Deregulation of the Motor Carrier Industry*. Alexandria, Va.: Interstate Carriers Conference, 1987.

Jemiolo, Jerzy and Clinton V. Oster, Jr. "Regional Changes in Airline Service since Deregulation." *Transportation Quarterly* 41 (1987): 569–86.

Johnson, James C. "Going, Going, Gone!—The ICC's Regulation of Trucking Mergers." *ICC Practitioners' Journal* 51, no. 4 (1984).

Jordan, William. *Airline Regulation in America: Effects and Imperfections*. Baltimore: Johns Hopkins University Press, 1970.

Kahn, Alfred. "The Airline Industry: Is It Time to Regulate?" William A. Patterson Transportation Lecture, National Economic Research Associates, Inc. (April 28, 1982).

————. *The Economics of Regulation: Principles and Institutions*. Boston: MIT Press, 1971.

Kahn, Fritz. "Abolition of the Trucking Exemption: Pros and Cons." *ICC Practitioners Journal* 47 (January/February 1980): 154–61.

Kahn, Jeremy. "The Bus Regulatory Reform Act of 1982 and Federal Preemption of Intrastate Regulation of the Intercity Bus Industry: Where Has It Come From? Where Will It Lead?" *Transportation Law Journal* 14 (1986): 179.

Kalish, Steven J. "Antitrust Considerations for Shippers in a Changing Environment." *Transportation Practitioners Journal* 52 (Winter 1985): 185–97.

Kasson, Bruce M. and Michael Erenberg. Railroad—Motor Carrier Ownership, *Transportation Law Journal* 12:75.

Keeler, Theodore E. "Airline Regulation and Market Performance." *Bell Journal of Economics* 3 (1972): 399–424.

Kenworthy, William E. "Antitrust Considerations in Motor Carrier Ratemaking: Rate Bureau Operations and Alternatives." *Transportation Law Journal* 11 (1979): 65–89.

Keyes, Lucile. *Federal Control of Entry and Exit into Air Transportation*. Cambridge, Mass.: Harvard University Press, 1951.

Kihl, Mary. "The Impacts of Deregulation on Passenger Transportation in Small Towns." *Transportation Quarterly* 42 (1988): 243–68.

Kim, Moshe. "The Beneficiaries of Trucking Regulation, Revisited." *Journal of Law and Economics* 27 (April 1984): 227–41.

Levin, Richard C. "Railroad Rates, Profitability, and Welfare under Deregulation." *Bell Journal of Economics and Management Science* 12 (Spring 1981): 1–26.

———. "Railroad Regulation, Deregulation, and Workable Competition." *American Economic Review* 71 (May 1981): 394–98.

Levine, Michael. "Is Regulation Necessary: California Air Transportation and National Regulatory Policy." *Yale Law Journal* 75 (1965): 1416–47.

———. "Revisionism Revisited? Airline Deregulation and the Public Interest." *Law and Contemporary Problems*, 44 (1981): 179.

———. "Airline Competition in Deregulated Markets: Theory, Firm Strategy, and Public Policy." *Yale Journal on Regulation* 4 (1987): 393–494.

Levitan, Sar and Isaac Shapiro. *Working But Poor: America's Contradiction*. Baltimore: Johns Hopkins University Press, 1987.

Littleton, Arthur R. Judicial Review of I.C.C. Orders under the Hobbs Act: A Procedural Study, *Transportation Law Journal* 7:189.

Lowenfeld, Andreas. *Aviation Law*. New York: Matthew Bender, 1972.

Mabley, Robert E. and Walter D. Strack. "Deregulation—A Green Light for Trucking Efficiency." *Regulation* (July/August 1982): 36–56.

MacAvoy, Paul and John Snow, eds. *Regulation of Passenger Fares and Competition among the Airlines*. 1977.

Maraffa, Thomas A. and Don Kiel. "Air Service to Cities Abandoned by Piedmont Aviation since Deregulation." *Southeastern Geographer* 25 (1985): 16–29.

McFarland, Robert E. Work in Progress—The Latest Solution to the Small Shipment Problem, *Transportation Law Journal* 10:201.

Meyer, James S. "Section 419 of the Airline Deregulation Act: What Has Been the Effect on Air Service to Small Communities?" *Journal of Air Law and Commerce* 47 (1981): 151–85.

———. *Deregulation and the Future of Intercity Passenger Travel*. Cambridge, Mass.: MIT Press, 1987.

Meyer, John R. and Clinton V. Oster, Jr., eds. *Airline Deregulation: The Early Experience*. Boston: Auburn House, 1981.

———. *Deregulation and the New Airline Entrepreneurs*. Cambridge, Mass.: MIT Press, 1984.

Meyer, John R. and William B. Tye. "The Regulatory Transition." *American Economic Review* 75 (May 1985): 50.

Miller, James C., III. An Economic Analysis of Airline Fare Deregulation: The Civil Aeronautics Board's Proposal, *Transportation Law Journal* 10:15.

———. Collective Ratemaking Reconsidered: A Rebuttal, *Transportation Law Journal* 11:291.

Molloy, James F., Jr. *The U.S. Commuter Airline Industry*. Lexington, Mass.: Lexington Books, 1985.

Moore, Thomas Gale. "The Beneficiaries of Trucking Regulation." *Journal of Law and Economics* 21 (October 1978): 327–43.

———. "Keep on Deregulating Trucking." *Wall Street Journal* (July 12, 1985).

———. "U.S. Airline Deregulation: Its Effects on Passengers, Capital, and Labor." *Journal of Law and Economics* 29 (April 1986): 1–28.

Morash, Edward A. Entry Controls on Regulated Households Goods Carriers: The Question of Benefits, *Transportation Law Journal* 13:227.

Morash, Edward A. and Charles R. Enis. "Motor Carriers Mergers, Mobility Barriers, and Regulatory Reform." *Transportation Journal* (Fall 1985): 38–50.

Morrison, Steven A. and Clifford Winston. *The Economic Effects of Airline Deregulation.* Washington, D.C.: Brookings Institution, 1986.

Muller, E. K. "Regional Urbanization and the Selective Growth of Towns in North American Regions." *Journal of Historical Geography* 3 (1977): 21–39.

National Academy of Sciences. *Motor Carrier Economic Regulation.* Washington, D.C.: NAS, 1982.

Nelson, James C. "The Emerging Effects of Deregulation of Surface Freight Transport in the United States." *International Journal of Transport Economics* 10 (April/August 1983): 219–36.

Noll, Roger O. *Reforming Regulation.* Washington, D.C.: Brookings Institution, 1971.

Noll, Roger O. and Bruce M. Owen. *The Political Economy of Deregulation: Interest Groups in the Regulatory Process.* Washington, D.C.: American Enterprise Institute for Public Policy Research, 1983.

Nupp, Byron. National Transportation Policy in the United States—An Analysis of the Concept, *Transportation Law Journal* 2:143.

O'Hare, William P. "The Rise of Poverty in Rural America." In *Population Trends and Public Policy.* Washington, D.C.: Population Reference Bureau, 1988.

Olson, C. and J. Trapani. "Who Has Benefited from Regulation of the Airline Industry?" *Journal of Law and Economics* 24 (1981): 75.

O'Neal, A. Daniel. Price Competition and the Role of Rate Bureaus in the Motor Carrier Industry, *Transportation Law Journal* 10: 309.

Oster, Clinton V., Jr. "Deregulation and Commuter Airline Safety." *Journal of Air Law and Commerce* 49 (1984): 315–16.

Oster, Clinton, V., Jr. and C. Kurt Zorn. "Airline Deregulation, Commuter Safety, and Regional Air Transportation." *Growth and Change* 14 (1983): 3, 7–8.

Owen, Wilfred. *Distance and Development: Transport and Communications in India.* Washington, D.C.: Brookings Institution, 1968.

Pearce, Jack. Common Ownership of Transport Modes—Some Antitrust Political Perspectives, *Transportation Law Journal* 2:83.

Peterson, Rodney. "An Economic Analysis of Statutory Changes in Rail Carrier Entry and Exit." *Transportation Law Journal* 13 (1984): 189, 210–13.

Popper, Andrew F. Collective Ratemaking; A Case Analysis of the Eastern Central Region and an Hypothesis for Analyzing Competitive Structure, *Transportation Law Journal* 10:365.

———. "The Antitrust System: An Impediment to the Development of Negotiation Models." *American University Law Review* 32 (Winter 1983): 283–334.

Pustay, Michael W. "Regulatory Reform of Motor Freight Carriage in the United States." *International Journal of Transport Economics* 10 (April/August 1983): 259–80.

———. "Reform of Entry into Motor Carrier Markets: Was the Motor Carrier Act of 1980 Necessary?" *Transportation Journal* (Fall 1985): 11–24.

Rakowski, James. "Motor Carrier Size and Profitability." *Transportation Journal* 16 (Summer 1977): 36–45.

Rose, Jonathan C. Surface Transportation and the Antitrust Laws: Let's Give Competition a Chance, *Transportation Law Journal* 8:1.

Rose, Nancy L. "The Incidence of Regulatory Rents in the Motor Carrier Industry." *Rand Journal of Economics* 16 (Autumn 1985): 299–318.

Schack, Edward J. and Bruce M. Kasson. Recent Decisions of the Interstate Commerce Commission, *Transportation Law Journal* 10:1.

Sims, Joe. Inedible Tallow, the Maximum Charges Rule, and Other Fables; Motor Carrier Regulations by the ICC, *Transportation Law Journal* 10:55.

Sloss, James. "Regulation of Motor Freight Transportation: A Quantitative Evaluation of Policy." *Bell Journal of Economics and Management Science* 1 (Autumn 1970): 327–59.

Spychalski, John C. "Antitrust Standards and Railway Freight Pricing: New Round in an Old Debate." *American Economic Review* 71 (May 1981): 104–09.

Stafford, George M. The Interstate Commerce Commission and The Consumer, *Transportation Law Journal* 4:1.

———. Maintaining Essential Services: Railroads in Bankruptcy—S. 2494, *Transportation Law Journal* 4:115.

Straszheim, Mahlon R. The Scheduling and Route Impacts of Increased Fare Flexibility, *Transportation Law Journal* 10:269.

Sugrue, Paul K., Manfred H. Ledford, and Nicholas A. Glaskowsky. "Operating Economies of Scale in the U.S. Long-Haul Common Carrier, Motor Freight Industry." *Transportation Journal* (Fall 1982): 27–41.

Sutherlund, David A. and Robert A. Peavy. The Incidental-To-Air Exemption: Conflict and Confusion, *Transporation Law Journal* 1:87.

Sweeney, Daniel J., Charles J. McCarthy, Steven J. Kalish, and John M. Cutler, Jr. *Transportation Deregulation: What's Deregulated and What Isn't*. Washington, D.C.: National Association of Small Shippers Traffic Council (NASSTRAC), 1986.

Taneja, Nawal K. *The International Airline Industry: Trends, Issues, and Challenges*. Lexington, Mass.: Lexington Books, 1988.

Thayer, Frederic. *Air Transport Policy and National Security*. Chapel Hill: University of North Carolina Press, 1965.

Thoms, William E. Amtrak Revisited, *Transportation Law Journal* 5:141.

———. Clear Track for Deregulation—American Railroads, 1970–1980, *Transportation Law Journal* 12:183.

———. Rollin' On ... to a Free Market: Motor Carrier Regulation 1935–1980, *Transportation Law Journal* 13:43.

———. *Reprieve for the Iron Horse: The AMTRAK Experiment—Its Predecessors and Prospects*. Baton Rouge, La.: Claitor's, 1973.

Tierney, Paul J. The Evolution of Regulatory Policies for Transport Coordination, *Transportation Law Journal* 1:19.

Tolchin, Susan and Martin Tolchin. *Dismantling America: The Rush to Deregulate*. Boston: Houghton Mifflin, 1983.

Tye, William B. "Scenarios of the Motor Carrier Industry without Collective Rate-making." *Transportation Practitioners Journal* 52 (Summer 1985): 493–511.

————. "On the Application of the 'Williamsonian Welfare Tradeoff' to Rail Mergers." *Logistics and Transportation Review* 21 (September 1985): 239–48.

————. *Encouraging Cooperation among Competitors: The Case of Motor Carrier Deregulation and Collective Ratemaking*. Westport, Conn.: Greenwood, 1987.

U.S. Congress. "Department of Transportation and Related Agencies Appropriations for Fiscal Year 1985: Hearings before a Subcommittee of the Senate Committee on Appropriations." 98th Congress, 2d Session, 1985.

U.S. Congress. "The Economic Impact of Federal Airline Transportation Policies on East Tennessee: Hearings before the Senate Committee on the Budget." 99th Congress, 1st Session, 1985.

U.S. Congress. "Household Goods Transportation and Bus Regulatory Reform Oversight: Hearings before the Subcommittee on Surface Transportation of the Senate Committee on Commerce, Science and Technology." 99th Congress, 1st Session, 1985.

U.S. General Accounting Office. "Deregulation: Increased Competition is Making Airlines More Efficient and Responsive to Consumers." Washington, D.C.: GAO, 1985.

U.S. General Accounting Office. "Effects of Regulatory Reform on Unemployment in the Trucking Industry." Gathersville, Md.: GAO, 1982.

Webb, Charles A. Legislative and Regulatory History of Entry Controls on Motor Carriers of Passengers, *Transportation Law Journal* 8:91.

Wheatcroft, Stephen and Geoffrey Lipman. *Air Transport in a Competitive Market*. London: Economist Intelligence Unit, 1986.

Williams, Ernest W., Jr. *The Future of American Transportation*. Englewood Cliffs, N.J.: Prentice-Hall, 1971.

Williamson, Kenneth C., Marc G. Singer, and David J. Blomberg. "Impact of Regulatory Reform on U.S. For-Hire Freight Transportation: Carriers, Perspective." *Transportation Journal* (Summer 1985): 28–51.

Wilner, Frank. "Creating a Linkage between Rate and Costs: A Survival Tactic for Small Carriers under Deregulation." *ICC Practitioners Journal* 48 (November/December 1980): 65–81.

INDEX

nomic effects of, 36–39; and pricing discrimination, 43–44; and safety, 115–25; and service deterioration, 44–45; and small communities, 105–12; three stages of, 36–39
Destructive competition and airline service, 110–11
Detroit, Toledo & Ironton R. Co. Control, 153–54
Dingell, John, 160
Dole, Elizabeth, 147
Drew, Daniel, 9

Eastman, Joseph, 17, 244
Economic growth, transportation as fundamental to, 5
Economic regulation and transportation, 196–98
Efficiency: allocative, 75–76; and perfect competition, 75–76; public policy objectives of, 76–79
Eisenhower, Dwight, 19
Employer Retirement Security Act (ERISA), 79
Erie Canal, 6
Erie Railroad, 8–9
Esch-Cummins Act. *See* Transportation Act of 1920 (Esch-Cummins Act)

"Failing company" doctrine, 139–40
Fanara, Professor, 121
Farris, Morton, 79
Federal-Aid Road Act of 1916, 15
Federal Aviation Act of 1958: and airline mergers, 134; and service to small communities, 202
Federal Aviation Administration (FAA): and safety after deregulation, 31; public pressure on concerning air safety, 118–19
Federal Express, 20
Federal Highway Act of 1921, 15
Federal Motor Carrier Safety Assistance Program, 122–23
Friedlaender, A., 48
Fisk, Jim, 8–9
Florida, deregulation of motor carriers in, 217–18

Florida East Coast Railway v. United States, 152
4-R Act of 1976, 19, 151
Frankfurter, Felix, 161, 232–33, 237
Fuel consumption, and environmental concerns under deregulation, 34–36
Fulton, Robert, 11

Gaskins, Darius, 22, 31, 231
Gibbons v. Ogden, 11
Glaskowsky, Nicholas, 84, 121, 123
Glickman, Dan, 145
Goldschmidt, Neil, 28
Gorell, Edgar, 198
Gould, Jay, 9
Government regulation, and public policy, 76–79
Gradison, Heather, 161, 234
Granger movement, and railroad reform, 9–12
Grant, Ulysses, 12
Gray, Reed, 238

Harrison, Benjamin, 13
Harper, Donald, 98
Highways, federal support for, 6–7
Highway system, national development of, 15
Hill, James, 9
Hille, Stanley, 80
Hillie, Dean, 98
Household Goods Transportation Act of 1980, 22
Huff, David, 98
Humphrey's Executor v. United States, 235

ICC. *See* Interstate Commerce Commission
Indiana, deregulation of motor carriers in, 218
International Brotherhood of Teamsters v. United States (Teamsters II), 156
International Brotherhood of Teamsters v. ICC (Teamsters I), 155
Interstate Commerce Act, 31, 153–56, 161

About the Author

PAUL STEPHEN DEMPSEY is Professor of Law and Director of the Transportation Law Program at the University of Denver College of Law. He is the Faculty Editor of the Transportation Lawyers Association. The author of nearly thirty law review articles, he has written two related books: *Law and Economic Regulation in Transportation* (Quorum Books, 1986) and *Law and Foreign Policy in International Aviation*. Dempsey formerly served as an attorney with the Interstate Commerce Commission and Civil Aeronautics Board. He is a member of the Bars of Colorado, Georgia, and the District of Columbia.